es
WORKER PARTICIPATION IN EUROPE

WORKER PARTICIPATION IN EUROPE

J.R. CARBY-HALL

CROOM HELM LONDON
ROWMAN AND LITTLEFIELD TOTOWA N.J.

© 1977 J.R. Carby-Hall
Croom Helm Ltd., 2–10 St John's Road, London SW11

British Library Cataloguing in Publication Data

Carby-Hall, Joseph Roger
   Worker participation in Europe.
   1. Employee's representation in management –
   Europe
   1. Title
   658.31'52'094   HD5660.E9

   ISBN 0-85664-337-8

First published in the United States 1977 by
Rowman and Littlefield
81 Adams Drive,
Totowa, New Jersey

Library of Congress Cataloging in Publication Data

Carby-Hall, Joseph Roger.
   Worker participation in Europe.

   Includes bibliographical references and index.
   1. Works councils – European Economic Community
countries. 2. Employees' representation in management –
European Economic Community countries. I. Title.
Law   344'.4'0189   77–4863
ISBN 0-87471-992-5

Printed in Great Britain by Biddles Ltd, Guildford, Surrey

CONTENTS

Preface 11

1. Perspectives 14

2. Representative Establishment Councils 35

3. Employee Representation 163

Appendices 253

Index 263

PREFACE

Two aspects of worker participation in France, Belgium, Luxembourg and Britain have been chosen for the purposes of this comparative study. The comparative study is the primary aim of this book. This is based on research carried out during the years October 1968 to January 1975. The two institutions examined in this book are representative establishment councils and employee representatives. Before treating these two aspects it is considered necessary that they be put in perspective, hence the first chapter entitled 'Perspectives' which attempts an overview of the field covered by employee participation in each of the countries under examination. Here will be found the meaning of employee participation, its development, opinions expressed by different bodies in each of the countries and what is currently being done on a European basis.

The work then narrows itself down to an examination of the two chosen topics. The chapter on representative establishment councils (chapter 2) treats the collective representation of employees, while that on employee representatives (chapter 3), broadly speaking, treats individual representation.

The pattern adopted throughout in making this comparative study is to examine, and where possible to analyse, the relevant statutes and common law of the different countries, and expose the legal and other problems which have arisen in each of these. Examination is also attempted particularly in chapters 2 and 3 on how these laws are applied in practice and what opinions have been expressed by the persons most directly concerned. This necessitates a substantial intrusion into the industrial relations field in all countries examined which is considered essential to a fuller understanding of the background and to a better appreciation of both the existing laws as well as of the proposals to be made for law reform in Britain. These proposals for law reform form only a secondary aim. They are intended as an academic exercise and for possible discussion.

It would be naïve to suggest that the proposals made in this book for such reform would not meet with a great deal of opposition from various quarters, since it could be argued that these two institutions, namely representative establishment councils and employee representatives, work reasonably well in Britain, and that anyway there is no desire, especially on the part of trade unions, some politicians and various bodies and individuals, to extend especially consultation or even employee representation any further. This is certainly one view, which is strongly held and illustrated within the pages of this work. Despite this strong view there is another view which is that one (but not the only) of the objective ways which will possibly help improve the present climate of industrial relations in Britain is to have some code on both consultative bodies and employee representation which would generalise these institutions throughout industry and thus help create a spirit of collaboration. These would of course be in addition (i.e. the middle layer) to the proposals on worker directors made in the Bullock Report (January 1977).

The contribution which would be made by these institutions in improving industrial relations would lie in the fact that there would be at the heart of the enterprise a standard platform throughout industry and commerce upon which, in the case of representative establishment councils, consultation would take place and where information would be given, thus airing employer/employee views in areas where strained relations occur or in areas where problems arise. Another aspect of this contribution is that it would give employees the opportunity to run and manage certain welfare and other matters proposed. This would give them, apart from a sense of belonging, a responsibility in the running of the various schemes. As will be seen, this is already happening in some establishments in Britain where unionisation is strong; why not therefore generalise it throughout to establishments employing more than a certain number of persons? Two further advantages will be reaped by such generalisation in that firstly there will already exist a firm base upon which to build in the event of the proposed European company statute being passed, and secondly that all companies of a certain size will achieve a minimum standard of participation. The submissions made on employee representatives lie mainly in establishing a uniform pattern which as will be shown does not exist in Britain. Uniform procedures would contribute towards greater general awareness in the representative's functions, and in the tidying up of the whole structure of this important institution, which as will be seen varies considerably.

It would be impossible to mention the names of the numerous individuals, companies, employers' associations, trade unions, embassies, government departments, libraries and other bodies who have helped make this research possible. Without them it would have been difficult to carry it out. I am particularly indebted to Professor Sir Otto Kahn-Freund who initially gave me invaluable guidance and advice as to what course to pursue in this research, to Professor Roger Blanpain for his advice on Belgian materials, to Mr Schuster and Judge Pescator for sparing their time to discuss with me various aspects of Luxembourg law, to Messrs Coleman, Roberts and Peel who discussed with me the European Community's attitude on worker participation, to Mr J. Piron of the Fédération des Entreprises Belges and his colleagues who, apart from discussing various legal problems which have arisen, have put me in touch with employers, trade unions and government officials, and finally to all the authors of books, articles and reports in the countries examined without whose materials I would have been at a loss.

The views and opinions expressed in this work are purely my own, and none of the above persons or bodies is in any way responsible for these. Nor are they of course responsible for any imperfections which may be found. The law is stated as on 1 February 1975, but in the case of Britain it has been possible in certain instances only to deal with some of the provisions of the Employment Protection Act 1975.

1 October 1976   J.R.C-H.
                                                Faculty of Law
                                             University of Hull

1 PERSPECTIVES

Before making an examination of (a) representative establishment councils[1] and (b) employee representatives, both of which form part of worker participation, it is important to survey worker participation in broad terms so as to put (a) and (b) above within their context. This chapter is therefore concerned with participation in its broadest term.

An extensive debate is taking place at the European[2] level (which in turn has provoked debate at national level) on the laws applicable to companies in the member states. An important aspect of this debate is the decision-making structure of companies and the role to be played by employees within that structure. The question might well be asked as to why it is necessary to have common legislation on *inter alia*[3] employee participation. This research shows that the answer is twofold. The one relates to *expediency* emanating out of the European, economic idea, the other out of the *emancipation* of the modern employee. The first answer therefore lies in the varying company structures within the Community. Fundamental differences exist for example between French, Belgian, Luxembourg and British company law on such matters as the rights of employees and shareholders, the power of directors, the structure within the company etc. These differences form a barrier for both the company itself and its customers. Investment and trading with a company which is incorporated under a foreign law constitutes an obstacle, the main one being substantially higher costs than need be. Another obstacle is the lack of common legal standards. This is so in cases where the branch of a parent company incorporated in another member state does not necessarily offer its customers the same guarantees as a company incorporated in the state, and in cases where a company can only with difficulty take advantage of markets in other community states.[4] A statute for European companies would overcome the problems mentioned briefly above, and commercial and industrial activity would achieve its full meaning by developing across national boundaries. The second answer lies in the emancipation of the employee. The modern employee wishes to have a say in the establishment in which he works,[5] although it is also the case that only a minority of employees are in practice active in putting forward the views of their colleagues.[6] An explanation for this phenomenon has been found to lie maily in the fact that employees are a great deal more

14

educated and more aware than they have been. This education and awareness emanates from the mass media (rather than from school, further or higher education). Recent legislation giving the employee what is tantamount to a property right in his employment[7] contributes to giving him a sense of belonging[8] to the establishment. Another reason why there is an ever-increasing number of employees seeking participation rights is the great number of recent mergers and takeovers in companies, which create a growth in size with the result of depersonalising the individual employee in both his entity and his value. A desire for participation helps towards combating this depersonalisation. A further reason is found in publicity. In Britain the Labour Government in its manifesto did talk of industrial democracy as the third stage in its industrial relations programme, and the Bullock Committee of Inquiry on Industrial Democracy 1975—6 is currently examining this aspect.[9] The European Commission has produced a 'green paper' as a discussion document on employee participation,[10] and possible solutions are suggested as a basis for discussion on a European level. In France the comités d'Entreprise have been required by law in certain enterprises since the end of the Second World War, similarly in Belgium the Conseils d'Etablissement have existed since 1948[11] and in Luxembourg the comités mixtes were first required by a law passed in May 1974. From a historical aspect a number of converging influences were discernible in the occupied countries, e.g. France and Belgium. In these countries one of the reforms examined by the respective Conseil National de la Résistance was the participation of workers in the running, with the employers, of the establishment. During the Occupation and without legislative intervention the employees formed themselves into 'comités du personnel' and undertook to run the enterprise in cases where management was arrested by reason of being collaborators.[12] In Britain Mr E. Bevin introduced in 1940 mixed committees. These committees operated during the period of the war and contributed greatly towards improving productivity in establishments. In the United States President Roosevelt encouraged voluntary mixed committees in establishments. These spread throughout the country and played an important role in firms producing war equipment. In Germany works councils were required by law as from 4 February 1920. These had important functions as they not only provided opinions on technical matters but also had access to reports and other documents concerned with the running of the enterprise. The council members selected the delegates to the administrative council. A law in 1934 replaced the works councils with the 'councils of confidence', dependent on the then political party-socialism. The Works Constitutions Law of 1972 regulates the rights of employee participation in Germany and a works council (Betriebsrat) must be set up in every private industrial establishment employing five or more employees.[13] All this international publicity creates awareness and causes additional pressure for the seeking of worker participation.

Work of a repetitive nature is found to be another important reason why employee participation is sought. Employees, especially in the motor car and agricultural manufacturing industries, feel that repetitive work impoverishes the quality of their working life. Worker participation will help towards improving their working life. One final reason was found to be the newly acquired freedom and leisure which the employee experiences and which generates within him a need of involvement and creativity in his work.[14]

Two further questions should then be asked. The first one is why have any legislation on employee participation?[15] The second, what does participation comprise? Having answered these two preliminary questions, which will give the breadth of the meaning of participation, it will then be necessary to analyse two aspects of employee participation, namely 'works councils' and the equivalent in the other countries under examination, where the employees are represented collectively, and the shop steward and his near-equivalent in the other countries where individual representation takes place. Furthermore, (a) the laws of each of the countries under examination will, where appropriate, be examined and analysed; (b) the problems which have arisen in each will be exposed; (c) a comparison will, where appropriate, take place between both the laws and the problems; (d) an examination will be made based on how the laws are applied in practice and what opinions have been ascertained by the persons most directly involved, (e) submissions will then be made for reform in Britain. (d) above will require this writer to go into the realm of industrial relations. This, it is considered, is essential to a fuller understanding and to a better appreciation of the legal background, both in terms of already existing statute and case law, as well as in terms of the proposals made for law reform in the 'employee representation' field and the 'representative establishment council' field. Thus, this research will be restricted within its terms of reference. Then through a process of the convergent and divergent elements in each of the laws of the countries examined, it is proposed to reach some conclusions and make objective proposals. The European Communities' proposed draft legislation on European works councils will also be considered where appropriate.

Why have any legislation on employee participation? A number of British companies already provide participation rights for their employees in the shape of works councils and other representative institutions,[16] and in France, Belgium and Luxembourg worker participation is taking place to a larger or smaller extent.[17] The practice is therefore recognised and accepted in the countries examined, and in Britain existing arrangements for negotiation and consultation, though varied, are in some cases highly developed. It is submitted that the reason why legislation is required is to enable all companies to have a reasonable minimum standard on participation. Whether this legislation should be compulsory or not will be discussed later. The point which must be made is that some form of 'norm' (whether a statue or a code of practice)[18] which will develop worker participation in line with the other European countries, is required in Britain. The reasons for that have already been considered above.[19] This research shows that there is an increasing desire on the part of employees to take part in the decision-making process and thus to be assured that their reasonable views are considered at all levels. Furthermore, the pressure for some 'norm' in Britian is even greater now, especially since the matter is currently being considered by the Commission of the European Communities.[20]

These developments and current ideas which have been gathering momentum both in Britain and the Common Market countries indicate that it is time for the reform of certain social institutions to take place. It is clear from this research that there now exists an increasing recognition of democratisation, in that employees who are substantially affected by decisions made by their establishments want to be involved in the influencing and the making of those decisions.[21] The interest of the employee in the functioning of the establishment can be as substantial as that of the shareholders, in that employees spend a great part of their working lives in, and devote considerable thought to, the establishment for which they work. For the great majority of employees their employment is their only source of income. The policy of the establishment therefore affects them as much, if not more, than shareholders and customers, not only in their immediate and longer term economic prospects, but also in their terms and conditions of employment, health, safety, welfare and job satisfaction.

Then of course there is the industrial relations problem. It is not suggested that this formula will be the *deus ex machina* which will once and for all times solve the industrial relations problems within the establishment, but there is little doubt that such problems will be more readily solved. Employee participation provides the framework for the finding of effective solutions and the avoidance of serious confrontation by ensuring a reasonable degree of understanding and some level of acceptance.

Looking at the problem in a European dimension, and in order to ensure a harmonisation of the European economic idea discussed above,[22] employee participation must not be so divergent in the different member states as to create a barrier in the development of this economic idea. Too great a divergence in the laws which concern employees from a decision-making structure aspect constitutes a denial of the idea of a community as far as employees are concerned. Thus if one aspect of the European Community, namely for employees, is to become a reality, then the laws governing employees cannot be allowed to remain at variance. Some sort of harmonisation is therefore necessary in the law which will ensure that the employee, in whichever country he might be employed, enjoys parity with employees in another country. It therefore follows that the laws of the member states on employee participation should develop within a Community legal framework. Consequently it becomes apparent that no action should be taken at national level which does not take account of the European economic idea. This does not mean instance changes in national laws, but it does mean that any developments, whether current or future, made in one member state *must take into account the structures and policies of other member states.* It is towards this aim that this research is directed.

Having given reasons as to why some form of 'norm' is required on employee participation both in Britain as elsewhere, the next question to be answered is, what forms does actual participation take? Employee participation has a number of facets. These facets are not constant and within them there exist great variations. There also exist variations between the systems of each of the countries examined. There exists therefore a complex system within a complex system which calls for examination.

Employee participation may take the form of *share and profit participation* schemes. In France there is a legal requirement for companies over a certain size to have such a scheme,[23] and participation by employees in the capital and profits of the company may be found in isolated cases in the countries examined.[24] These however are the exception rather than the rule and employees in all countries examined do not have decision-making powers in the enterprise. All they have are saving schemes, incentive schemes and bonus schemes resulting from collective agreements, management initiative and, in the case of France, legislation.[25]

Employee *participation in the establishment's decision-making body* is another form of participation. In the countries examined only France and Luxembourg have legislation stating that employee representatives must be appointed on the establishment's decision-making bodies. These representatives might either be appointed by the employees or at least be approved by them. Britain and Belgium have no such legislation. In France, legislation provides that in all 'sociétés anonymes' with fifty or more employees, members of the 'comité d'entreprise' must attend in a consultative capacity all meetings of the 'conseil d'administration' or the 'conseil de surveillance'.[26] The Sudreau commission was appointed in 1975 in order to examine company reform. Its recommendations, apart from 'co-surveillance' (joint supervision) by employee representatives on the 'conseil d'administration' or 'conseil de surveillance' have been overtaken by events. The commission proposed that 'co-surveillance' should be approached through a period of experimentation and be initially, during an experimental period, optional for all establishments. Whether the optional element should subsist for large establishments (those consisting of over one or two thousand employees) after the period of experimentation (five years) received no degree of unanimity. Employee representatives would have full voting rights on these councils, and they would occupy one-third of the seats, thus allowing autonomy of decision of the executive to remain unaltered. The French government did not feel inclined to accept the Sudreau recommendations mainly because of substantial opposition to these.[27] In Luxembourg, employee participation in the decision-making bodies of the establishment is taking place,[28] but it will be noted that though the legal responsibility of the employee representative is identical to that of the other members of the 'conseil d'administration', there is no parity of representation on the council.[29]

In Belgium, like in Britain, there exists no legislation on employee participation in decision-making bodies. Apart from a few exceptions,[30] in Britain there exists no employee participation in the private sector. There does exist, however, in both these countries employee representation in the public sector. In Belgium, for example, it was found that the 'Cie. de Transport intercommunal de Bruxelles' has employee representatives on its 'conseil d'administration'[31] whereas in Britain nationalised industries since 1946 provide for members with trade union experience to sit on the board. This does not mean that there is employee representation in the fullest sense, because most — the British Steel Corporation excepted — of the regulations of nationalised industries provide that no one who has an interest in the establishment should be on the board since he would prejudice the exercise of its functions. In practice, only retired trade unionists are on the board, e.g. the late Lord Feather, Frank Cousins etc. The exception lies in the British Steel Corporation where as a result of an agreement with the TUC Steel Committee, worker directors who are also active trade unionists may sit on the BSC divisional boards. In both Belgium and Britain moves are currently being made towards employee participation in the decision-making bodies of the establishment, but the opinions and ideas in each of these countries are different, and this writer furthermore finds a conflict of ideas between organisations or political parties within the debates in each of these. In Britain, the Labour Party Manifesto[32] indicated that new legislation would be enacted for a radical extension of industrial democracy in both the public and the private sectors. In order to achieve this, company law would be changed and the legislation governing both nationalised industries and public services would be amended.[33]

The TUC General Council formulated a policy on participation in decision-making bodies and proposed that where more than 200 employees are employed in an establishment there should be a two-tier structure. One half of the supervisory board members would be appointed through trade union machinery. There would be supremacy of this board over both management and shareholders on major decisions. Any decisions on the structure of the enterprise and appointments to the board of management would have to be consented to by the employee representatives who would be directly responsible to trade union members in the firm rather than to the company or shareholders.[34] It will be noted that nowhere in the provisions will be found anything, should a deadlock occur. It will be recalled that at the TUC Congress a resolution to adopt the report of the General Council was passed, *but* another resolution was also adopted. It rejected the obligatory imposition of worker directors on supervisory boards and stressed more the importance of the collective bargaining machinery and the giving of statutory backing to the right to negotiate on important issues.[35] Consultation has no place in TUC policy. It seems to this writer that the policies adopted by these two bodies are inconsistent and therefore a rift is evident in the ideas to bring about this kind of industrial democracy. Furthermore, from interviews held with union officials this writer gathers that this development of a two-tier system is not supported generally in the movement. They do not feel that a unionist can possibly join a board of directors and at the same time remain committed entirely to the trade union movement.[36]

An almost identical policy was proposed by the sub-committee on industrial policy of the Labour Party.[37] It suggested a two-tier system to be adopted by the largest companies. The supervisory board would have half its membership appointed through the trade union machinery. Employee directors would owe allegiance to the enterprise but at the same time they would also consider the interests of their constituency. The final say on important changes in the company would rest with the supervisory board. A jointly co-opted or alternating chairman would have a casting vote where deadlock occurs.

The Liberal Party's policy is for employee participation.[38] It proposes to have a single board of directors elected by employees and shareholders in equal proportions in establishments where between fifty and 200 persons are employed. Where over 200 are employed a supervisory board must be instituted which would supervise the management board.

The Conservative Party is not in favour of legislation on employee directors though it is in favour of experimentation.[39] Consultation on works council level is favoured by the Conservative Party. In this writer's opinion this of course is sound policy since there exists no compulsion but the freedom of experiment should it be desired. Support for this view has been expressed by numerous persons and bodies.

The CBI is opposed to worker directors but considers an option should exist under present company law.[40] Similarly, apart from some exceptions, consultation rather than representation on the board is also a preference stated by most industrialists.[41] A British Institute of Management working party was opposed to legislation being imposed providing for employee directors, it preferred experimentation with different forms of employee participation.[42] Again the Engineering Employers' Federation considers that the concept of worker participation is *unacceptable* because it is *premature*.[43] Opposition has also come from the Stock Exchange[44] and from the City Company Law Committee.[45] Opposition on the compulsory two-tier board system (a distinct issue to the employee director issue) was also found as a result of an interview with the Institute of Directors and the CBI. Both organisations consider that the two-tier board system is contrary to what has been established in Britain over numerous years and contrary to the idea of collective board responsibility. They are not opposed however to the introduction of non-executive employee directors who would present the shop-floor point of view.

It is therefore clear that during the past three years in Britain the debate has raged — the left demanding legislation on employee participation, yet they are divided as to how to achieve it, the right considering that compulsory legislation is dangerous and that experimentation should be encouraged. In this writer's view, it is premature to enact compulsory legislation at this stage; this for three reasons. Firstly, because there exists no unanimity as to how it should operate. Secondly, the imposition of mandatory rules on persons unwilling to operate them (see opposition to the system briefly mentioned above) will not make the system work satisfactorily. Thirdly it is invidious to compel persons to submit when there exists no unanimity even amongst the protagonists and when there exists so much opposition to the scheme. Clearly, this cannot be a democratic process, and furthermore freedom of choice would completely disappear.

Similar differences of opinion exist within the Belgian debate on employee participation on the establishment's decision-making body. The Confédération des Syndicats Chrétiens wishes to introduce a 'conseil des travailleurs' (in replacement of the conseil d'entreprise). The employee councils would represent employees exclusively and would have greater powers, in particular the power of veto on layoffs, works rules, redundancies etc.[46] In order to further this proposal this union wishes to see company law reformed in such a way as to allow a substantial voice in the financial policy of large companies.[47] What is meant by 'substantial voice' is not defined in the official document but this writer understands that this aspect is at the time of writing being discussed. It is therefore clear that sights have been set towards a particular aim, but that its method of implementation is as yet uncertain.

The Fédération Générale du Travail de Belgique on the other hand has opposing views. It considers that works councils should become 'control bodies' as well as 'consultative bodies'.[48] Participation in the decision-making bodies of the enterprise is opposed by this union mainly because it fears that unions will become capitalistic in notion, to which the union is fundamentally opposed.

The employers' federation,[49] though it is prepared to consider the problem, is opposed to employee participation in the private sector *simpliciter*. The persons with whom this writer had the opportunity to discuss the problem felt that to allow employee participation would result in loss of freedom in the formulation of company policy and in its administration.

It is considered that there exists a serious diversion of views in Belgium, not only *within* each of the main organisations, but also *between* each of them. There is therefore, clearly no sound basis, it is submitted, for any legislation on employee participation to take place in Belgium. The three conclusions reached in the case of Britain are equally applicable to Belgium. An analysis of the overall employers' views in Belgium and Britain shows that a strong similarity exists, but Britain tends to differ in that a number of employers' bodies favour experimentation.[50] The fear expressed in both these countries is that employee participation in the decision-making bodies will affect adversely from a financial point of view privately owned firms, since participation would bring with it powers to veto unilaterally the implementation of important economic policies. Furthermore, employee participation would be used as a lever to weaken employers' bargaining power with organised labour. The other fear common in both these countries is that this system will give organised labour even greater powers which could be the decisive blow in the power struggle. As for trade unions' views in Britain and Belgium, all that may be said is that there is a strong desire for participation, common in both countries, but the two countries differ as to the approach to be adopted. The two-tier system seems to be the overall favourite in Britain,[51] whereas in Belgium unions are sceptical of employee directors since they would be absorbed within the capitalist society to which they are opposed.[52] The two-tier system would substitute class collaboration, whereas it is class struggle that the unions want in Belgium.[53] This fear has been expressed in Britain,[54] and certain echoes of this have also been found as a result of interviews in Belgium, that union independence as bargaining units would be jeopardised. This school of thought does not seem to go as far as to demand 'worker control', but it does stress the need that the unions' bargaining powers and their freedom to pursue the interests of their members be maintained. Cannon[55] expressed himself thus: 'It is not the duty of trade unionists to participate. Their duty is to protect and advance the interests of their members. Frequently this will necessitate the utmost co-operation with management. At other times it will require them to say unequivocally that a certain course of action is not in the interests of their members.'

From what has been said, this research shows that the concept of employee participation is not constant — in that different persons mean different things by this term, and different persons have varying aims and fears.[56] These variations do not only occur within each of the countries examined, but are general to all these countries. What the unions seem to want is firstly not to have any *responsibility* for the decisions made within the enterprise, secondly not to take any part in the *management* of private companies, thirdly to be fully *informed* and *consulted* over a great number of matters which consequently, and that is the fourth point, enables them to *bargain* over all these matters.

Despite the differing opinions, dissensions, doubts and suspicions on employee participation in the decision-making bodies, expressed in some member countries (in this instance Belgium and Britain), it is a fact that this aspect can hardly be ignored. Moreover a number of member countries make provision for this kind of participation (in the case of this study, France and Luxembourg).[57] The European Commission therefore considers that it would be failing in its duty if it does not ensure that the laws of the member states provide for certain safeguards and obligations. It is with this in mind that the draft fifth directive on company law[58] and the proposed European company statute[59] were drafted.

It will be recalled that within the title of 'Perspectives'[60] the question that is being answered is 'what forms does employee participation take and what conclusions may be drawn from these forms?[61] Some of the forms which 'employee participation' covers have been considered and conclusions given. Each of these forms are discussed in order *only* to indicate the scope and breadth of what employee participation comprises and to help orientate the reader on this complicated and broad topic. The discussion of these forms also serves as a backcloth towards a better understanding of the main theme of this research, namely the works council as a representative institution – providing information, consultation, approval etc. – and the shop stewards etc. in the countries under examination. Deeper research into the other forms of participation, namely share and profit participation schemes, and participation in the establishment's decision-making bodies which includes employee directors and the two (or three) tier structure of companies, lies beyond the terms of reference set out in this research and takes one within the realm of company law. What has already been said has a further function, namely it helps accentuate what has been found to be the case in this research, that the ideological perspectives by the exponents of employee participation lie in their belief for a better industrial society. The opponents of employee participation likewise have ideological beliefs of an opposite nature. One school of thought in Britain is for 'worker control'; this school of thought believes that Britain will move towards a socialist organisation of society based on the existing social order by 'the establishment of working-class centres of authority within the hostile framework of capitalist society'.[62] 'Worker control', according to this school of thought, means the superintendence of one human being over another.[63] It seems obvious to this writer that what this school of thought is trying to achieve is to change society from one capitalist order to another. In other words, the shoe will be on the other foot.

The 'perspective' serves to illustrate one fundamental issue. Share and profit participation and employee participation in the establishment's decision-making body considered above, are only two forms amongst others (to be discussed below) of participation in the economic and social policies of the establishment. These forms are *in addition* to the collective bargaining structure through the negotiation and conclusion of collective agreements and action through employees' representative institutions, as, for example, shop stewards and works councils. It follows therefore that the school of thought which states that worker directors would accentuate class collaboration (whereas it is class struggle which is the function of the unions) through the institution of worker directors, must as a consequence believe that the institutions of collective bargaining will come to an end, or be considerably reduced. This cannot be the case in reality since these two institutions are separate and distinct. Worker directors will perform their work and collective bargaining will play its role; worker directors complement the possibilities of intervention. Furthermore, worker directors add a dimension otherwise lacking in that an opportunity is given for allowing the effective exercise of decision-making on the part of the establishment on a *continuing basis* and for consultation on every important economic and social event.

The other forms of participation are collective participation through the representative institutions, such as works councils and their equivalents, where information and approval may be given and where consultation may take place, and individual representation through shop stewards and their equivalents. These are the kernel of this research. It is thus proposed to critically examine, analyse and compare all aspects of the works council as a representative institution in each of the countries concerned. The draft proposals made by the European Commission on European Works Councils will also be considered. Individual representation will be treated in the same way, i.e. critically examined, analysed and compared. The divergent and convergent aspects of the existing laws and proposed European regulations, where applicable, will be analysed and consequential submissions based on this analysis will be made in relation to Britain. The reason for making these submissions is that this writer believes that (a) Britain will have to align itself with the rest of the continent (where legislation does exist on employee representatives and representative institutions) and (b) they will, from a British point of view, help towards the harmonisation of the proposed European legislation.

Notes

1. This term embraces a wide range and type of works council in Britain from small plant and local establishment level to central works councils in large companies. The term also embraces such bodies as the comites d'entreprise in France, the conseils d'entreprise in Belgium, and the comités mixtes in Luxembourg.
2. See e.g. the submission of the Commission to the Council on 30 June 1970 on the statute of the European company (Supplement to EC Bulletin No. 8 – 1970); that in October 1972 (Supplement to the EC Bulletin No. 10 – 1972) on co-ordination of laws on the structure of the public limited liability company (or the société anonyme in France and Luxembourg, or the naamloze vennootschap in Belgium) known as the fifth directive; that on 4 January 1973, clause 2113 of the EC Bulletin No. 1 – 1973 on the amended proposal for a third directive on the co-ordination of safeguards concerning mergers between public limited liability companies (or their equivalents in the member states); the 'Statute for European companies – Amended proposal for a regulation', Supplement to the EC Bulletin No. 4 – 1975; and the 'draft convention on international mergers of public limited liability companies' which at the time of writing is being considered by a working party under Professor B. Goldman.
3. The proposed legislation common to the European Community member states is the Statute of the European Companies; it is within this, hence the term 'inter alia', that the proposed legislation on the role of employees in relation to the decision-making structure will operate (see Title V.S.I., arts. 100–29 on the European Works Council; S.2, arts. 130–6 on Group Works Councils; S.3, Employee representation on supervisory boards, arts. 137–45 of the amended proposal of the Statute for European companies, Bulletin EC Supplement No. 4 – 1975).
4. Normally a company incorporated in one member state is not able to merge with a company incorporated in another member state. It therefore cannot expand its market beyond the national frontier in the same way and with the same ease as it can within its own country. Nor may a company transfer from one member state to another without going through complicated procedures, e.g. virtual dissolution and starting from scratch again.
5. Of the sample of 150 examined in each of the countries an overwhelming majority of employees stated that they felt entitled to have a say in establishment matters. The sample was taken from both the private and public sector as follows: in Britain the proportion was 87 per cent; in France 94 per cent; in Belgium 93 per cent, and in Luxembourg 85 per cent.
6. An investigation took place in order to examine the proportion of activists in the establishment. Again both the public and private sector were investigated. It is found that it is only a minority who are active in actual participation. In Britain, of the sample examined only 8 per cent were active; in France 7 per cent; in Belgium 6 per cent, and in Luxembourg 4 per cent.
7. Particularly in Britain by the unfair dismissal provisions of the former Industrial Relations Act 1971 and now the Trade Union and Labour Relations Act 1974 and the Employment Protection Act 1975. See Carby-Hall (ed.), *Studies in Labour Law*, study entitled 'Three termination aspects

of modern employment', particularly p. 205 et seq.
8. This tendency has been found throughout the countries under examination. The sense of belonging manifests itself in the following percentages: in Britain 73 per cent; in France 81 per cent; in Belgium 83 per cent and in Luxembourg 89 per cent of 150 employees interviewed in each of the countries.
9. The terms of reference are:
  'Accepting the need for a radical extension of industrial democracy in the control of companies by means of representation on boards of directors and accepting the essential role of trade union organisation in this process, to consider how such an extension can best be achieved, taking into account in particular the proposals of the Trades Union Congress report on industrial democracy as well as experience in Britain, the EEC and other countries. Having regard to the interests of the national economy, employees, investors and consumers, to analyse the implications of such representation for the efficient management of companies and company law.'
  Since going to press, the Bullock Committee has reported in January 1977.
10. See Bulletin of the EC Suplement No. 8 – 1975 entilted 'Employee participation and company structure in the European Community'. See also note 2 above for other documents.
11. A detailed examination of each of these laws will take place below.
12. This in fact did happen in Berliet, the motor manufacturers in Lyons.
13. These are but some of the publicity and historical factors influencing participation rights. Others are the Yugoslav works councils, see Jiri Koloja, 'Workers' Councils – the Yugoslav experience', bodies such as the BIM on participation (see Incomes Data Services Study, Workers' Participation, August 1975, p. 6); TUC proposals for workers on the boards (see TUC Industrial Democracy 1974, particularly p. 39); CBI on participation (see Incomes Data Services Study, Workers' Participation, August 1975), Employee Participation – CBI's contribution to the debate (October 1974), The provision of information to employees – Guidelines for action (June 1975). The statutory provisions on disclosure of information also play an important role in influencing worker participation. See e.g. the Employment Protection Act 1975 ss. 17–20; the Health and Safety at Work etc. Act 1974 s.2(3) and 28(8) (a) (b); the Industry Act 1975 s.30(1)–(4) and s.31(1). Other documents on disclosure, such as the TUC's 'Good Industrial Relations – A Guide for negotiators' 1971, pp. 17–18, also have considerable influence.
14. These reasons are the sum total of answers given in a questionnaire sent to a sample of 150 employees in both the private and public sectors in each of Britain, France, Belgium and Luxembourg. The relevant question asked in the respective language was 'Why is it that you seek participation in the establishment in which you work?'
15. Britain has no legislation on any aspect of employee participation, except of course the insignificant collective agreement provisions in the Trade Union and Labour Relations Act 1974, the provisions on disclosure of information for collective bargaining purposes under the Employment Protection Act 1975 and the safety representatives and safety committees required under the Health and Safety Act 1974. The information requirements under the Health and Safety at Work Act 1974 and the disclosure requirements to the Minister under the Industry Act 1975 are of lesser importance in the collective bargaining field. No *legislation* will be found in Britain on for example share and profit participation or on employee participation in decision-making bodies; nor does any legislation exist on works councils, joint negotiating bodies etc., or on shop stewards. In Belgium, collective agreements are legally

binding on all employers represented on the 'commissions paritaires' and their employees. 'Conseils d'entreprise' have been required in private sector enterprises and have been regulated by law since 1948. Since 1975 an enterprise is obliged to have a council even though it employs on average only fifty employees provided the council was in existence when the last election of members was held. A health and safety committee has been required by law since 1952 in all establishments employing more than fifty employees. Though no enactments exist in the private sector for employee representation on the boards of companies in the private sector, in the public sector employee representation is often required. For example, the Minister of Transport nominates three railway employees on the twenty one member council of administration for the railways. No laws on share and profit participation exist in Belgium. In France, collective agreements are under the 1950 law (as amended in 1971) legally enforceable. This applies to the 'convention collective ordinaire', or 'susceptible d'extension', as well as to the 'accords d'établissement ou de salaires'. The office of 'délégué du personnel' is regulated by a law in 1946 (as subsequently amended); the 'comité d'entreprise' is regulated by an ordinance of 1945 (as subsequently amended). In 1968 a law was passed regulating the office of 'délégué syndical'. Under ordinance 45–280 of 1945 'sociétés anonymes' employing fifty or more employees must have on its 'conseil d'administration' (board) or 'conseil de surveillance' (supervisory council) *two* delegates appointed by the 'comité d'entreprise' in a consultative capacity. Since 1972 where there are at least twenty five supervisory and technical staff in an establishment these constitute a special college and the number of representatives is increased to four — one representing the 'maîtrise', one the supervisory and technical staff and two the remainder of the employees. In the nationalised industries, one-third of the seats of 'conseil d'administration' is occupied by employee representatives. These have the same rights and obligations as other council members. Legislation also exists in France on share and profit participation under ordinance 59–126 (amended in 1973 by 73–1197). Implementation of this optional system of allowing employees to participate in the profits of a company, or in 'operations d'auto-financement' (operations of a self-financing nature) is achieved through collective agreement either with the most representative trade unions in the establishment or with the 'comité d'entreprise'. J. Chazal in a paper entitled 'La participation des travailleurs aux décisions dans l'entreprise en France' and delivered to the ILO symposium on 'Workers' Participation in decisions within Undertakings' (August 1974), pp. 11–12, pointed out that 232 establishments had concluded such collective agreements and 135,000 employees were covered. Ordinance 67–693 of 1967 instituted a new obligatory form of participation in companies employing *more than one hundred* employees. Stringent rules exist on the special reserve for participation. Employees' rights in the reserve and methods of its administration are determined through collective agreements. Under the 1967 Ordinance, 8,971 collective agreements (81 per cent concluded by conseils d'entreprise) had been concluded by March 1974, benefiting 4 million employees in 10,051 companies (see Chazal, op. cit., p. 15). Fifteen per cent of the companies had less than 100 employees. This shows that even companies with less than 100 employees took advantage of this law which is *not* compulsory on them. Ets. Renault, and the national banking and insurance establishments (public sector) have share distribution schemes. Share participation was further promoted in the private sector (companies with shares quoted on the stock exchange or those admitted to the market without a quotation where transactions are sufficiently frequent or of importance) (see law 73–1197 of 27

Perspectives 29

December 1973 and supplementary decree 74–319 of 23 April 1974). In Luxembourg, collective agreements were first put on a legislative basis in 1965. A legal obligation exists to observe its terms during its validity. Collective agreements must have a minimum of six months' duration. There also exists an extension process. Legislation on 'délégué du personnel' has existed since the end of the *First* World War. In 1962 legislation provided for a 'délégation ouvrière' (delegation representing manual workers) where an establishment (whether in the private or public sector) employs at least fifteen manual workers. The 1962 law also provides for a 'délégation d'employés' (white-collar workers) where twelve or more such employees are employed in the enterprise. 'Comités mixtes' were put on a legislative basis by a law in May 1974. These operate in the private sector (where 150 or more employees are employed in an establishment) and consist of an equal number of representatives from both sides of industry. The 1974 law also provides for representation of employees in 'sociétés anonymes' (public limited liability companies) employing 1,000 or more employees (by means of a 'conseil d'administration' on which one-third of the members represent employees), or where an enterprise is state financed to a minimum of 25 per cent, or where a state concession is given in the establishment's principal activities. In the two latter instances the 'conseil d'administration' must have an employee representative for every 100 employees, but there must be a minimum of three employee representatives and these cannot constitute more than one-third of the 'conseil'. No share and profit participation laws exist in Luxembourg.
16. e.g. organisations such as the Scott Bader Commonwealth, Landsman's (Co-ownership) Ltd, Kalamazoo Ltd and the John Lewis Partnership are examples giving the employees the benefits of the ownership of shares as regards both profits and control. (See Gordon Brown, 'Participation in Industry', 1972.)
17. See note 15 above which deals with the legislation in the respective countries. Consider also the results achieved by this legislation, discussed in the same note.
18. In the continental countries examined, this 'norm' appears in the form of legislation. See note 15 above.
19. See p. 14 ante on (a) expediency emanating from the European economic idea, and (b) the emancipation of the modern employee.
20. Bulletin of the EC Supplement 8/75.
21. See pp. 14 et seq ante.
22. See pp. 14 et seq ante.
23. See note 15 above for brief details.
24. See note 16 above for brief details.
25. The concept of profit sharing or share distribution is not a new one. In Britain for example the Ministry of Labour reports on co-partnership of 1912, 1920 and 1956 clearly show that such schemes have been tried in the past and that even with government backing their success has been disappointing.

T. Haddon in his 'Company Law and Capitalism' shows that most of the schemes started were abandoned for either apathy on the part of employees, little or no profits, or disillusionment. (See particularly pp. 423–7.) In Belgium and Luxembourg it is found that no such schemes exist, whereas in France share and profit participation legislation exists and a great number of establishments have put the scheme into practice (see note 15 above for details).
26. Note 15 above gives a more detailed, though brief exposé of the French

situation.
27. The French Journal Officiel of 5 August 1975 stated that bearing in mind that the majority of employer and employee organisations clearly rejected the representation of employees, even as a minority, in decision-making process of 'conseils d'administration' or 'conseils de surveillance', the Economic and Social Council was not convinced that such reform could be imposed through legislation. Legislation should therefore confine itself to imposing structures and procedures on information and consultation and to provide legislation for those bodies who possess powers of negotiation.
28. See note 15 for greater detail.
29. It will be recalled that the conseil d'état and the chambre des députés of the state of Luxembourg amended the draft law which originally provided to the contrary.
30. E.g. the Scott Bader Commonwealth and a few other such enterprises in Britain. See Note 16.
31. See also note 15 above in connection with the Belgian railways.
32. September 1974, p. 13.
33. The first two phases in this government's industrial relations policy have already taken place through the Trade Union and Labour Relations Act 1974 and the Employment Protection Act 1975. Neither of these introduces to any significant degree (except for disclosure of information and safety representatives and committees), the concept of industrial democracy. No doubt an Industrial Democracy Bill will be introduced in 1977 as a result of the report of the Bullock Committee (which has since August 1975 been considering how best to achieve representation on boards of directors, taking into account the union organisation in Britain). The Government is currently enquiring into the decision-making role of employees in the nationalised industries. This writer believes that it may well be that such a Bill will take a long time to materialise. See also 'In Place of Strife' (1969) (of historical interest now). Para. 47 of the White Paper provided for disclosure and para. 48 supported the experimentation in worker participation including representation at board level. See also the Code of Practice, instituted under the Industrial Relations Act 1971 containing advice which encourages greater participation (paras. 25, 44, 49, 92, 93 and 94) and the Draft Code prepared by the ACAS to become operative early in 1977.
34. The full text of these proposals reads as follows:

'(i) The present boards of companies should be divided into supervisory boards and management boards. One half of the supervisory board should be appointed by the workpeople through trade union machinery, normally at company or combine level. (This in turn will encourage the development of company and combine-level joint-union organisation.) This will apply in the first instance to all companies with more than 2,000 workers. The Minister should have power in this legislation by order to extend its application at a later stage to enterprises employing over 200 workers.

(ii) The supervisory board would be the supreme body of the company and while it would take into account the interests and views expressed at the AGMs of shareholders it would not be bound by them. The supervisory board would be responsible for determining company objectives, the policies necessary for their achievement, and for monitoring and reporting progress to workpeople as well as the shareholders and, through returns to the Registrar of Companies, to the wider public. It would consider all major management decisions concerning expansion or contraction of company activities, organisation, investment, employment, training and manufacturing, and relations with other commercial bodies, in the light of agreed financial and other criteria and legal responsibilities. In the coming period, a particular responsibility in larger companies would be the formulation of planning agreements and discussion of them with the government. The management board would be appointed by the supervisory board and would be responsible to it for the day-to-day running of the company, according to the objectives and policies laid down.

(iii) This change should be reflected by a statutory obligation on companies to have regard to the interests of its workpeople as well as its shareholders.

(iv) Workers' representatives should not be obliged to relinquish union office; they should be appointed for two years and subject to recall and re-election on the basis of their total record. They would be subjected to extraordinary recall during this period only in exceptional circumstances, which would need to be provided for in the election procedures. Election procedures would be devised by the unions represented at the enterprise, either individually or jointly, in consultation with the TUC.

(v) Provisions about board-level representation should only apply where there is trade union recognition . . . ' *Industrial Democracy*, TUC publication July 1974, p. 39.

35. 'The first prerequisite of any widespread improvement of industrial democracy is the extension of bona fide trade union organisation, and the right to bargain collectively in all sectors and in all enterprises in the economy.' Professor John Wood puts it aptly when he says, 'The theme of this document is progress through the strengthening of collective bargaining . . . ' Whenever the term 'worker participation' is used by the TUC it must be taken to mean 'trade unionist participation'. The anticipated difficulties derived from the TUC attitude are spelt out clearly. 'Progress is tied to trade union recognition; the areas where this is most lacking are those where participation is most needed'. (See 'Worker Participation in Britain', *Financial Times*, p. 13.)
36. Cf. the similar feelings officially expressed by the Fédération Générale du Travail en Belgique, p. 12 post.
37. 'The Community and the Company.' Report of a Working Group of the Labour Party Industrial Policy Sub-Committee 1974, pp. 12–17.
38. Liberal Party Manifesto – February 1974 and that of September 1974 entitled 'What the Liberals stand for', *The Economist*, 29 September 1974.
39. 'A lack of harmony over participation', *Financial Times*, 26 November 1973.
40. See CBI on 'The responsibility of the British public company', pp. 20 and 22. See also CBI's 'Contribution to the debate', October 1974, and 'The provision of information to employees – Guidelines for Action', June 1975, in Incomes Data Services study on workers' participation, August 1975. The CBI defines participation as involving the following processes:
    Communication – a two-way flow of ideas and information.
    Consultation – involvement of employees in the discussion of proposals, ensuring that their views are taken into account in making a decision, which as far as possible should be agreed, but on which management retains final authority.
    Collective bargaining – a voluntary process of negotiation, leading normally or eventually to an agreed decision which both or all parties implement.

The CBI stress that the processes which are developed will depend very much on individual company circumstances and that harmonisation should not be enforced for its own sake. The report discusses the type of information which can be communicated and discussed and the institutions and procedures necessary for a participative system, and gives a checklist for those planning action.

The Confédération reiterates its opposition to mandatory two-tier boards and urges managements 'to take the desire for more employee participation seriously and to consider how best they might take action to suit their own circumstances'.

The CBI have also produced a Guide on the Provision of Information which provides a checklist on the kind of information which should be given, under two main headings: information about the company as a whole, and information relevant to employment. The report also discusses communication in general: written and verbal communication and training for communication. Summaries are given of legislation which affects information provision: the Companies Acts, Contracts of Employment Act, Health and Safety at Work Act and the Finance Act, as well as proposed legislation.

41. See *The Times*, 15 July 1973, 'Top executives back shop-floor directors', where a report as a result of a study of industrialists on employee participation is discussed.
42. 'Employee Participation: a management view.' BIM, April 1975 — Incomes Data Services study on workers' participation, August 1975.

Definitions of Participation

Collective bargaining is essentially concerned with negotiations about wages and working conditions. *Participation* is a broader concept based on the community of interest between employer and employee in furthering the long-term prospects of the enterprise and those working within it, rather than the separation of interests which is generally associated with collective bargaining. If industrial relations in Britain were fully satisfactory, there would be less need to examine participation. Since this is not the case it is right that we should consider ways of improving relationships by working more constructively with trade unions and by giving employees greater scope to take part in decisions.

In considering participation we have viewed it as a practice in which employees take part in management decisions. Such decisions vary considerably in scope, ranging from the determination of the overall policies of an enterprise to the day-to-day operations which have a direct impact on employees at their place of work.

Information

They state that there can be no effective participation without a good information policy. 'An effective information system should ensure that:
   Managers receive relevant information in advance of other employees
      (or their representatives) for whom they are responsible;
   Managers are kept informed about all other important developments
      within the enterprise in a systematic way; and
   Employees are given relevant information at the same time as shareholders
      but before the general public.'

Confidentiality

Some disclosure may harm the company's interests — e.g. new product launching; some future plans where there are competitors; share-sensitive information, and closure plans — 'before management is ready to say how they would propose to deal with the problems arising from the closure'. BIM recommend the drawing up of a code of participation practice and that 'confidentiality contracts could be made between union officials and management'.

43. Policy Paper — Employee Participation, November 1974. See also *Financial*

Times, 11 July 1973, 'Worker-director proposal premature'.
44. 'Company Law Reform – The Stock Exchange's View', 1973.
45. First report of City Company Law Committee, February 1975. 'Employee Participation.'
46. See 'Du conseil d'entreprise au conseil des travailleurs', a Confédération des Syndicats Chrétiens publication, March 1974.
47. 'Du conseil d'entreprise au conseil des travailleurs', op. cit., pp. 3 and 4.
48. See J. Gayetot (secretary of the FGTB) in 'La participation des travailleurs aux décisions dans l'entreprise en Belgique'. ILO Symposium on Workers' Participation, August 1974. 'Control bodies' means that any company proposals must be submitted to the works council which would be enabled to reject them and substitute for them proposals of their own.
49. Fédération des Entreprises Belges.
50. See p. 21 above.
51. See p. 20 above.
52. See pp. 22 and 23 above.
53. From an ideological point of view see K. Coates (ed.), *Can the Workers run Industry?* (Sphere Books, London, 1968), who echoes the same feelings (p. 232) on the German system. '... the workers' leaders are in this way incorporated into a structure which remains no less hostile than ever to the interests of the work force as a whole.'
54. By the TUC Congress – see p. 20 above.
55. President of the ETU in *Daily Telegraph*, 5 May 1967.
56. Cf. K.F. Walker in 'Workers' Participation in Management – problems, practice and prospects', International Institute of Labour Studies, Geneva, who holds the same view. He says (p. 2), 'The debate on its desirability and effects has been confused by the fact that the parties often have different concepts of workers' participation in management as well as different goals and fears concerning it.'
57. Others are Denmark under the Danish Companies Act No. 370 of 13 June 1973, for joint stock companies (Lov om aktieselskaber), or No. 371 of the same date for private establishments (Lov om anpartsselskaber); Germany under a law of 1957, Mitbestimmungsgesetz, an amended law of 1956, Mitbestimmungserganzungsgesetz, and one of 1952, Betriebsverfassungsgesetz; and Holland under a law of 1971 for public companies – Wet op de structuur van naamloze en besloten vennootschappen.
58. See *inter alia* Incomes Data Services study on workers participation, August 1975, stating that its aim is to co-ordinate and harmonise the company laws of EEC member states and it applies to all public limited liability companies with more than 500 employees. Such companies would be required to set up a two-tier management board, with separate membership on each board. The supervisory board would appoint (and dismiss) members of the management board.

For election or nomination of employee representatives to the supervisory board, member states would have a choice between the German system (one-third employee representatives) or the Dutch system. Supervisory board consent would be necessary for decisions on partial or total closure of a company; significant organisational changes; restriction or extension of the company's activities; arrangements for long-term co-operation or termination) with other companies. In companies with less than 500 employees the supervisory board would be appointed by the general shareholders' meeting. See also Proposal for a Fifth Directive on the Structure of Sociétés Anonymes, Bulletin of the EC Supplement 10/72.
59. See proposed statute for European companies, Bulletin of the EC Supplement

4/75 and Incomes Data Services study on workers' participation, August 1975, p. 5, stating that the first Commission proposal was presented to the Council in 1970 and after the incorporation of significant amendments recommended by the European Parliament was approved by the Commission in April 1975 and is now before the Council. Its adoption is *optional* for companies which operate in two or more member states. The European company statute is not intended to replace domestic laws but to provide facilities for companies to overcome present legal and practical difficulties. The European Company or Societas Europaea (SE) would have a two-tier management structure and a European works council.

The supervisory board would consist of one-third of shareholders' representatives, one-third of employee representatives and one-third of members co-opted by these two groups who must be independent of both groups. Candidates for co-option would be proposed by the general meeting, the management board and the works council. Employees would decide by a simple majority whether they want representatives on the supervisory board. Trade unions would have the statutory right to submit a list of candidates for the election of employee representatives. Elections to the European works council would involve all employees of the SE on the principle of proportional representation, irrespective of whether or not they were trade union members.

Participation in the European Works Council would extend to all matters not dealt with in collective bargaining and the rights of information, consultation and co-determination would be much in line with those of the German Works Council. The SE could reach collective agreements with trade unions represented in the different companies, which would then be binding throughout the Community for all employees who were members of a trade union involved in such negotiations.

60. See p. 14 ante.
61. See pp. 18 et seq ante.
62. See p. 112 of W. Kendall, 'Workers' control and the theory of socialism' in Coates and Williams (eds.), *How and Why Industry must be Democratised*, Institute of Workers' Control, 1969.
63. See Coates (ed.), *Can the Workers run Industry?*, 1968, p. 232. He says, 'It implies a dual relationship, in which one human party *constrains* another' (stress added). Similarly, G. Lyon-Caen in 'La participation par le contrôle', pp. 293–331, in G. Spitaels (ed.), *Crisis in the Industrial Relations of Europe*, College of Europe – Bruges, 1972, talks of 'contestation'.

2 REPRESENTATIVE ESTABLISHMENT COUNCILS

Section i. Origins and formation

Apart from the institution of the délégué du personnel, to be discussed in the third part, French law provides for two other forms of representative institutions which can and often do co-exist in an establishment, namely, the 'comité d'entreprise' and the 'délégué syndical'. This latter is officially provided for since loi du 27 décembre 1968, though 'délégués syndicaux' have, of course, existed before that date on a non-legislative basis. Though this research tells that the number of 'délégués syndicaux' has increased substantially and that their operations have also expanded, the institution lies outside the limits laid down by this research, and cannot consequently be discussed. It must be stressed, however, that their influence is increasing considerably and that it may well be that in the future their functions will be considered as important as those of the 'délégué du personnel'[1] and that 'comités d'entreprise' could eventually be entirely controlled[2] by them.

The institution of the 'comité d'entreprise' has existed in France since 1945.[3] The 1945 ordinance provided for 'comités d'entreprise' to be formed only in industrial and commercial concerns employing more than fifty workers, but the Act of 1946 extended the field to the professions, to societies, to trade unions and to associations of whatever nature they be,[4] and recently to agriculture.[5] Thus the institution applies to the private sector where more than fifty workers are employed; the public sector being excluded.[6]

The question that is asked is whether or not the Act of 1946 governs the public sector industries with a commercial or industrial bias, or whether the public sector is catered for under its appropriate legislation. This question has been generated as a result of the 1945 ordinance.[7] This provided that in the public-sector industries having a commercial and industrial bias, 'comités d'entreprise' would be instituted. The Act of 1946 however repealed art. 1 of the 1945 ordinance. Does therefore the present legislation on 'comités d'entreprise' become operative as of right in the public sector or has the repeal by the 1946 Act meant that the public sector is prohibited from instituting such comités originally authorised by the 1945 legislation? It appears that the conseil d'état,[8] and Brèthe de la Gressaye[9] and other authors[10] consider that the 'législation du droit commun' (common law) applies to the public sector with industrial or commercial bias. Others however[11] and even the Minister of Labour[12] consider that the repeal of art. 1 of the ordinance of 1945 does not invest the government with power to extend to public services the common law rules relating to comités d'entreprise. The present writer supports this latter opinion since, in France, like in Britain, when previous legislation is expressly repealed by subsequent legislation, the institutions created under that former legislation can no longer remain constituted.[13]

Despite what has been said, it is however found that 'comités d'entreprise' do in fact exist *in practice* in the public sector. This research also indicates that these 'comités' do not perform the entirety of the functions of the 'comités d'entreprise' in the private sector.[14] Finally it is found that the establishment of these 'comités d'entreprise' rests, not on the Act of 1946, but on collective agreement.[15]

In the public sector the welfare duties of the 'comité' are exercised at *national* level by the Caisse Centrale des Activités Sociales,[16] and at *entreprise* level by the Caisse d'Action Sociale[17] and the 'comités d'hygiène et de sécurité'.[18]

'Comités mixtes de production' are also to be found in the public sector, but their field of operation is restricted to matters of a technical nature[19] and can in no way be compared with the broad functions of the 'comités d'entreprise'. As for the economic and financial spheres employee representatives in the public sector normally occupy one-third of the seats of the 'conseils d'administration' and they have the same voting rights as the other members.[20]

In Belgium 'conseils d'entreprise' have in the private sector been required by law since 1948.[21] These must be set up where over 150 permanent employees are employed, but by a decree in 1975 an establishment must have a 'conseil' where fifty or more permanent employees are employed, provided that a 'conseil d'entreprise' was in existence when the last election of members for such a 'conseil' was held.[22] The two other representative institutions are the 'comités de sécurité et d'hygiène' and the 'délégations syndicales du personnel'. The former institution will be looked at later; the latter[23] is outside the terms of this research and cannot therefore be discussed. Until recently[24] it was not all enterprises which had, under Belgian law, to have a 'conseil d'entreprise', it was only those which have a technical unit of production (unité technique d'exploitation). This must now be analysed. The question which must be asked is this. Did the law of 1948 apply only to commercial and industrial establishments, or did it apply to any establishments employing 150 employees, even if their object was devoid of any production or of any economic gain? It is submitted that by adopting the literal rule of interpretation of statutes, the term 'unité technique d'exploitation' comprised only establishments with an economic gain, and that therefore an establishment with over 150 employees which was non profit-making, such as a trade union, a professional association, a benevolent society etc., was not legally compelled to have a 'conseil d'entreprise'. This deduction is made by this writer from the following factors. As will be seen later, one of the functions of the 'conseil d'entreprise' is to receive economic and financial information on the enterprise itself, and information on the total cost of production. Furthermore, the legislation on the 'conseils d'entreprise' constitutes part of the overall law on the economic organisation of the country. For these two reasons it is submitted that the intention of the legislature must have been that an economic bias be attributable to the enterprise. This opinion is reinforced by an interpretation given by the Ministry of Labour on 28 February 1950.[25]

Further analysis must take place on the term 'unité technique d'exploitation'. It has been said (during the Parliamentary debates) that the enterprise described as a 'unité technique d'exploitation' characterised itself by a certain amount of autonomy. According to Mr Harmel (in the Chambre des Représentants) this autonomy manifested itself in two ways: economic autonomy and social autonomy. Economic autonomy means a relative independence of direction of the division or branch within the enterprise. The limits of this independence can only be ascertained by the facts in each individual case. Social autonomy presupposed a splitting up of groups of employees which comes about as a result of the different distribution or commercial locations (branches) of the enterprise or units of production (factories) of the enterprise. According to Mr van Zeeland[26] the dominant factor was the social autonomy one. With respect, this cannot be accepted by this writer. It is considered that both factors were equally important: economic autonomy because without it there can be no 'conseil d'entreprise' and social autonomy, which implies within it economic autonomy, because of the necessity of creating 'conseils d'entreprise' in different branches or factories each of which had economic autonomy. This argument has further support when one examines the raisons d'être of the 'conseils d'entreprise' themselves. The 'conseil' delegates must primarily receive information on matters of a social nature as well as on matters relating to the establishment in which they work (financial information, production, profits etc.). A number of judgements perused seem to support this writer's views.[27] It does however seem from an examination of the cases decided by the commissions paritaires[28] or conseils professionnels[29] that they were more ready to constitute 'conseils d'entreprise' where branches or factories were great distances apart from the head office of the enterprise.[30] It is noticeable here that 'social autonomy' predominated. Though this be the case, this writer has not found one single case where economic autonomy has not featured as an equally important factor.[31] The term 'unité technique d'exploitation' is now no longer a requirement and 'conseils d'entreprise' may be constituted in all establishments, e.g. schools, hospitals etc.

The problems which have arisen in Belgium in the private sector are therefore different from those which have arisen in France. In the public sector the problems that have arisen in France have not occurred in Belgium, mainly because a separate law regulates representation in the public sector in Belgium. The public sector in Belgium is based on the royal decree of 20 June 1955 which provides for three different types of representative bodies, namely the General Trade Union Council for Advice,[32] the Trade Union Council for Advice,[33] and committees of personnel.[34] The function of the last of these is to *advise* on personnel matters, on health safety and embellishment of the establishment, and on the organisation of services and conditions of work. Unions have been dissatisfied with the advisory function of the committees or councils imposed by the 1955 law, and have asked for negotiation rights. The national collective agreement of 29 July 1969 provides that there should in the public sector be a shift from advice and consultation to negotiation on wages and terms and conditions of employment.

A comparatively new development took place in the private sector in Luxembourg[35] in that for the first time 'comités mixtes' have come into existence.[36] As is the case in Belgium, these 'comités' must be constituted where 150 or more employees are employed in all private-sector enterprises. Unlike Belgium however there is no minimum figure of fifty where such committees existed before the election of committee members. The 'comités mixtes' vary in size from between six and sixteen members depending on the number of employees. Again there is a difference from Belgium since in the case of the latter no specified numbers are given except that the employer's representatives must not exceed those of the workers'. In the public sector no great debate has ensued.

In Britain, unlike France, Belgium and Luxembourg, there exists no legislation covering works councils, nor do collective agreements examined generally deal with the institution of works councils, though it has been found that a few companies do operate a works council or an equivalent system.[37] Some works councils have been found to exist without there being a collective agreement in existence. These are non-unionised bodies (though there may be trade union members in them);[38] the unions therefore do not participate. No uniformity may be attributed to them since they are established according to the desires of the interested parties. Accordingly, a great variety is found in Britain.[39]

From the above study, certain conclusions may be drawn. Firstly, in each of the countries under examination there seem to be problems and inconsistencies in the laws governing works councils (or similar bodies). In Britain no laws exist, but inconsistencies are numerous. In France, for example, the laws of 1945 and 1946 created an inconsistency in the public sector/private sector field. It is found that in the public sector there exist 'comités d'entreprise' based on collective agreements, when in fact there should not strictly be any so based, again in the public (as well as in the private) sector the functions of these comités vary considerably. In Belgium we have seen that the 'unité technique d'exploitation' had caused considerable problems, which in turn had obscured the limits as to when a 'conseil d'entreprise' should or should not be instituted in an establishment. In Luxembourg, the system being too new it is not possible to assess with any degree of objectivity any problems, suffice to say that of all the major employers interviewed there was a large measure of approval. In Britain the system is chaotic. There exists no statutory requirement on works councils, most industries do not have such bodies or similar ones, and of those firms which have instituted these councils each has a different system from the other,[40] and changes from one system to another are quite frequent.[41] Therefore there is no uniformity.

In the second instance, there exists no uniformity and little similarity between the systems of the countries under examination. It may be said that the advisory and consultation element exists in the works councils of all these countries, but apart from these, the criteria for their formation is different,[42] their names are different[43] and the problems experienced are different.[44] Some have had laws governing this institution for some time, others recently, and one of the countries does not have any statutory requirements on this aspect;[45] there is also a variance in the degree of influence of these bodies.[46]

Thirdly, it is found that the response to these bodies by unions and employers varies in the different countries under examination. In Belgium each of the main trade unions interviewed[47] had different opinions. The FGTB wants reforms based on the November 1973 decree (providing for more information to be given to the 'conseils d'entreprise'[48]).

This union also wishes to see an element of control in addition to the 'conseils' ' consultative role.[49] The CSC wishes to have employee exclusivity on the 'conseils' in addition to powers of veto on certain policy matters, mass redundancies, work rules and company closures.[50] The CGSLB has similar ideas. The employers' body interviewed expressed the view that the concept of the 'conseils d'entreprise' is working satisfactorily, that the union demands would encroach on management prerogatives, but that they had no objection to divulging the information required by law. From interviews carried out in Luxembourg both unions and employers approve of the 1974 law instituting 'comités mixtes'. It is still too early to judge the effect of the law. In France the demands of the Confédération Générale du Travail (CGT) are not as great as those of the Belgian unions, all they want is a total right of information on the economic position of the company, and if it is multinational, on the whole group.[51] The Confédération Française Démocratique du Travail (CFDT) holds similar views. The employers are, however, sceptical of works councils, and seem opposed to the *part* of the Surdeau Commission report[52] which provides for the strengthening of consultation, and the appointment of personnel representatives in multi-nationals which would deal with the real holder of power. Finally in Britain, there is great divergence of opinion. The TUC and the Labour Government are committed to the idea of industrial democracy,[53] though 'Wilson's recipe for contented workers'[54] did at one time favour elected works committees in factories where more than 100 employees are employed. Of a sample of twenty union officials interviewed, eighteen of them asked for industrial democracy. The Conservative Party wishes to see the extension of consultation[55] to medium and large size companies on dismissal procedures, redundancies, profit sharing schemes and share ownership schemes. The CBI, while it does not reject the works council concept, does not wish to see it put on a statutory basis, it prefers to see it as a voluntary body solely for purposes of consultation.[56] The private members' 'Works Council Bill' introduced by five Liberals[57] portrays the Liberal Party idea: to have compulsory elected works councils in all large companies. The members of these councils would be elected from the employees of the company who might be trade union members but who would represent *all* employees, and not only trade union members. These councils would have negotiation and consultation powers as well as limited powers of co-decision.[58]

These conclusions show the convergent and divergent elements which arise in the formation of this institution, not only within the laws of the individual state itself but also between the laws (where they exist) of the states themselves. The convergent and divergent element also manifests itself in the ideologies, philosophies, policies and opinions of governments, opposition parties, employer and union organisations, and individual employers and unions.

It is a fact that Britain is the only country in the European Community (with the exception of Ireland which is currently making progress in this direction[59]) which does not have an enactment[60] or requirement in a collective agreement[61] on the formation of works councils. Though it may be said that works councils have failed to achieve their purpose of helping to foster employee influence and of providing benefits to companies,[62] in recent years works councils have had a rebirth in Europe, not only through employer initiative, but more through tougher legislation and revised collective agreements. It is this writer's opinion that the institution of the works council is not given the attention it deserves in the worker participation debate. It is submitted that the works council is a powerful mechanism in the exchange of ideas between management and labour and exercises a more important influence on the operations of the establishment than a system of board representation does. The Business International European Research Report[63] puts it very aptly, 'It is ironic that, after some twenty five years of experience with works councils, their potentials should only recently have been recognised. In any case, it is likely that they will be acquiring increasing importance in the future.'

It seems imperative therefore that procedures whereby employees are given rights to be consulted and informed about management decisions on all matters which concern them[64] should be extended to all significant firms in Britain. These procedures should be entirely consultative with no rights within them of co-determination, negotiation and collective bargaining. All other aspects of industrial democracy should be allowed to develop at their own pace outside these procedures. These procedures are best carried out by the 'works council', despite the objections which have been raised[65] in the past. What this writer is concerned with exclusively is the 'works council' and though the other forms of participation[66] should exist and be encouraged to develop, these are beyond the bounds of this book and therefore cannot be considered.

Most compelling reasons exist why works councils should be encouraged to develop in Britain. In the first instance, if the other aspects (i.e. other than works councils) of employee participation are to be allowed to develop, the interrelationship between the different forms of such participation (including works councils) will become of importance. The institution of works councils will therefore pave the way and contribute significantly towards this development. The German experience clearly illustrates this. Research[67] carried out in that country showed that there is a significant relationship between employee participation on the supervisory board on the one side and the amount of co-operation between management and the works council on the other. 'The scope of the latter appeared to be related to the efficiency of the former.' From this may be deduced that there is more management inducement to give information to the works council representatives when management knows that the non-giving of the relevant information would be criticised or taken up by the members of the supervisory board who are either appointed or approved by the company employees. This would by analogy probably be true of Britain or any other country, although there is as yet no similar structure (i.e. supervisory boards) in Britain. This is a further argument for the setting up of works councils. They will provide the basis of the worker participation edifice which will eventually and inevitably come about. Secondly, it is found that the giving of information and general consultation is practised in Britain in many sectors by employers, even though they have not hitherto[68] been required to do so. It is thought that the setting up of work councils will facilitate the statutory requirement on disclosure of relevant information, and will be either a confirmatory or an additional source of information for the trade unions and joint negotiating committees. Thirdly, the statutory requirements which exist at present[69] do not establish the form of participation required by a works council, which is primarily concerned with the representation of interests and views of the employees within the establishment; in other words, matters which are of direct concern to the employees themselves. Works councils whose functions are to co-ordinate employee representation in connection with matters which affect employees collectively are therefore essential at plant level. Fourthly, works councils should be required on ethical grounds. Large companies employing a vast number of employees should have certain duties towards them. It seems ethical that employees should have a legal right to information and to consultation in all matters which affect them, and in all social matters. Fifthly, and assuming that in the foreseeable future employee participation at board level (as a result of the Bullock report) does take place (as in France or Germany), the effectiveness of such participation largely depends on the setting up of effective representative bodies which will portray employee opinion within the establishment. Sixthly, it is found that works councils in Britain exist where unionisation is weak, and that as the industry gets more organised negotiation takes the place of consultation. This need not be the case however. In the countries under consideration (and others, e.g. Germany) this situation has not arisen, consultation and information taking place along with negotiation by two *different* bodies. Why is it that this cannot be so in Britain? Furthermore, works councils do exist in practice in *some* British establishments, and in these it is found that they play an important part in influencing the decision-making process of the establishments. Since this is the case, why not extend this institution to the larger establishments so that the benefits of influencing the decision making may be reaped more generally? In the seventh instance, the function of a two-way communication system can only be effectively achieved through the aid of a works council. Negotiating bodies are not the proper channel of communication. It cannot be denied that effective decision making on the part of management cannot be implemented without there being a two-way flow of information. Decisions which affect the employees cannot be properly considered or smoothly implemented without this two-way flow — namely shop-floor opinions, concerns and ideas to management and management's problems and ideas to the shop-floor.[70] Furthermore, it is at shop-floor level that industrial relations take place and that the attitudes of management and employees are formed and determined. Both the TUC[71] and the CBI[72] recognise from their respective points of view this two-way communication system. The emphasis here is the attempt at a solution of common problems, collaboration and integration, as opposed to collective bargaining.[73] In the eighth instance, the creation of a works council should, *with properly constituted terms*, avoid the entrenchment and rigidity of certain ideas and their fertilisation and consequent crystallisation, which, this writer has found, have grown between employers and unions. Of the sample of 130 private-sector firms examined in Britain it was found that those which did not have works councils[74] feared that with formal works councils in existence management's prerogative to manage would be diminished, and that there would be a consequent abdication of its responsibilities. The great majority of unions of the sample examined felt that works councils operated against the idea of trade unionism, that works councils would involve them in a certain amount of responsibility for managerial policy, which in turn would detract from their collective bargaining functions. These arguments clearly show suspicion as well as weakness on the part of employers, and both suspicion and unco-operativeness on the part of unions. A properly instituted works council (i.e. with precise terms of reference) should, provided *the will* is present on both sides, generate a new spirit which should in turn overcome the suspicions and fears expressed above. It must be accepted that opposing views exist in industry, and that in the words of Alan Fox,[75] 'By the very nature of its function, management must sometimes act against the interests of work people . . . '; nevertheless and it is for this very reason, works councils have an important function in lubricating the *distinct and separate* collective bargaining machinery. The term 'lubrication of the collective bargaining machinery' is very important because this writer has found that one of the major criticisms, on both sides of industry, was that works councils are limited in the topics which may be discussed, and that therefore they are ineffective. This of course need not be so, for as well as discussing welfare matters[76] or areas of common interest[77] which are not always[78] the subject of collective bargaining, matters which *are* subject to collective bargaining[79] and which involve the firm's employees can also be aired and discussed, before (or concurrently) they are collectively bargained for in a separate and distinct negotiating committee. Two further advantages may be attributed to works councils vis-à-vis negotiating machinery. Where two or more unions are involved in negotiation it is advantageous to have a joint consultative committee with representatives from each, which would enable the parties to discuss each other's point of view and exchange ideas prior to negotiation taking place. One further advantage of consultative machinery is that matters which are of a borderline nature to collective bargaining may be dealt with as a preliminary. Thus there will exist 'lubrication', in that employees', trade unions' etc. views and opinions will be sounded in the light of management's problems etc. expressed at the works council meeting, i.e. a wider exchange of views and of information. The negotiating machinery will then perform after having been better informed and therefore having already been lubricated.[80] All this, it is submitted, demands a change of attitude on the part of both management and unions. It is possible, however, with the will to co-operate for the climate to be changed. The Donovan Report did stress that the conduct of industrial relations was best achieved by collective bargaining, and that effective collective bargaining stemmed from unions which are strong and which are recognised by the employer.[81] This is of course true, but in collective bargaining entrenched and rigid attitudes invariably prevail with either party pushing forward his view and often being unwilling to understand the other person's view. 'Power politics' therefore prevail in collective bargaining. The works council members should have a different aim in mind, namely that of attempting to understand the other person's point of view. Consultation should through de-entrenchment and understanding lubricate the collective bargaining machinery. In the ninth instance, a great number of matters arise within an establishment which have nothing to do with negotiation;[82] a forum therefore is necessary for their discussion. A works council would be the most suitable place to discuss these matters. In the tenth instance, and from a psychological point of view, there can be little doubt that employees who are given the opportunity to contribute in the decision-making process take a greater pride in their work and the motivation to co-operate in the implementation of these decisions is stronger. Finally, the European Community in its statute for the European company proposes to provide a works council for the European company as well as a group works council.[83] It would be both unwise and retrograde if Britain did not have some basis upon which to build in this sphere. The other European countries examined (and most others, in particular the works council system in the Netherlands) have such bodies, and therefore a basis upon which to build when the European works council comes about.

For these eleven compelling reasons it is considered that works councils should be instituted in Britain. Joint consultation will then effectively *supplement* and *support* collective bargaining by making this latter more effective, and not, as is currently thought in some quarters, by replacing it.

As stated above (p. 25) submissions will in consequence be attempted so as to lay down a possible basis for the implementation of a works council system in Britain. In order to ensure that the proposed British system is not alien to the already existing systems in the countries examined (though there already exists a considerable divergent element, both between and within these countries' laws or practices (see pp. 39–41)), what is considered best in these systems should where possible be adopted, and in the light of the difficulties which have already arisen in these countries lessons must be learned from these and avoided. It is important therefore that the convergent element existing between these countries be considered in the discussion of these submissions. It is pointed out however that the proposed system must also take into account, and where possible preserve, present British practices on works councils. Finally the proposed European works council must also be considered.

Within these terms of reference submissions must now be attempted on the first aspect, namely formation. It is considered that the only effective way for a universal formation of a works council in Britain is through legislation.[83a] Legislation should provide for all companies employing fifty or more employees to institute a works council. Though the numbers vary from country to country,[84] there is a convergence in their laws in that a fixed number exists. Bearing in mind the existing practices in Britain, this would not involve any hardship on already constituted works councils. The suggested figure of fifty permanent[85] employees accords with the proposed statute for European companies.[86] What kind of companies are to have works councils? We have already seen that problems have arisen in France in connection with public sector enterprises[87] and in Belgium with 'unité technique d'exploitation'.[88] Bearing in mind current practice in Britain in the nationalised industries where a requirement for joint consultation exists under the relevant nationalisation Act, and also bearing in mind the problems that arose in France, and the fact that France, Belgium and Luxembourg all have separate legislation for nationalised industries (convergent element), it is thought that the proposed legislation should not, at the moment at least, extend to the nationalised industries. It should therefore be limited to the private sector. This would not in any way contravene the proposals made for the statute for the European companies since under this latter, works councils are only to be established in the private sector — Societas Europea — having two establishments in different member states.[86] Would, as was the case in Belgium, only private sector commercial enterprises be included, or would all private sector enterprises (whether commercial or not), as in the case of France,[89] be covered? It is submitted that *all* enterprises should be covered, thus avoiding the serious problems which had arisen in Belgium.[90] This submission would again not be contrary to the statute for the European companies.[91] It will be recalled that three conclusions[92] were reached after an examination of the various countries' laws had taken place. The first conclusion was to the effect that inconsistencies existed in the domestic laws on works councils themselves. The submission that legislation be introduced in Britain will certainly not solve this problem, but as far as Britain is concerned, it will alleviate it, in that a set pattern, now non-existent, will be laid down. The second conclusion reached was that there was no uniformity and little similarity between the systems of the countries examined. The introduction of legislation in Britain will not create uniformity with the other countries examined but it will bring similarity in that substantial legislation will exist as it does in the other European countries. Thirdly, the divergence of opinion by different bodies in the various countries, as well as in Britain, will not be solved by legislation, but as far as Britain is concerned legislation will provide a basis for further discussion and, if need be, reform. When the provisions on the European works council come into operation, they should provide a partial solution to these three conclusions, certainly in the case of the European company. There will be uniformity *between* the member countries and *within* these in the case of the European company. Its influence might be extended to other establishments. More important however is that when the European works council provisions of the statute for the European companies become operative, a basis will already exist in Britain for any adaptation which will have to be made to meet the requirements for the European company.

It is submitted that the figure of fifty employees, above which it will be compulsory to have a works council, should not create a barrier below which no works council should be instituted. Any establishment wishing to institute a works council but which has less than fifty employees should be enabled to on a voluntary basis.[93] Furthermore, in prescribed cases the Secretary of State should be empowered to institute such a body in either a particular enterprise or a category of enterprise where less than fifty employees are employed.[94] Agricultural establishments should also be included if they are caught within the numerical limits, or if the Minister so prescribes.[95] Throught these submissions, a certain amount of convergence with the countries under examination will take place.

Section ii. Membership and structure

In France, the members of the comité d'entreprise consist of the employer or his representative who chairs the meetings and the delegates elected by the employees;[96] varying from three to eleven, depending upon the size of the establishment.[97] An equal number of acting members are also elected, and they take part in meetings in a consultative capacity only.[98] The statutory numbers may be increased by collective agreement between the employer and the most representative trade union. Each trade union is entitled to send a representative, from among the employees of the establishment (who must fulfil the eligibility conditions (see below)) to the meetings of the comité, but in a *consultative* (non-voting) capacity only.[99] There exists an obligation on the trade union to inform the employer by registered letter of the name of the trade unionist selected.[100] A feature which is considered of importance in the convergent element (to be discussed during submissions for proposals in Britain) is the fact that though the comité d'entreprise is a body whose basis is orientated on the establishment's employer-employee relationship, the law as early as 1945 recognised the role and power of the trade unions. It is found that the role may have appeared limited at one time in that unions had, according to the Minister of Labour, no right to representation in the comité central d'entreprise.[101] The courts, however, held otherwise.[102] The law originally had not provided for representation of all the different categories of employees. It only provided for two colleges, one consisting of manual workers, home workers and clerical grades, and the other of engineers, foremen and senior foremen (i.e. supervisory staff). The most representative trade unions establish the list for each of the colleges.[103] The number of seats varies according to the size of the enterprise. It is thought that the reason why only two colleges were provided for originally, was to avoid the dispersion of employees and thus avoid the weakening of employee power vis-à-vis the employer. Both the distribution of seats and the classification of the employees within each of the colleges must be agreed upon between the employer and the most representative trade unions within the establishment. Where the parties cannot agree the directeur départemental du travail must, upon reference, decide on these matters.[104]

Prior to the possibility (since 1966 and 1972) of establishing a third electoral college, it is found that there was a desire for such increase when both parties agreed. An argument put forward by these protagonists, but which cannot be accepted by this writer, was based on art. 23 of loi du 16 Avril 1946.[105] A strict interpretation of article 23 clearly shows that it does not (a) aim at increasing the number of colleges and (b) mention the election of members of the comité. All this article talked about was that the comité's *powers and functions* only could be settled by collective agreement or custom.[106]

Since 1966[107] the number and composition of electoral colleges may be modified by collective agreement, or by agreement between the employer and all representative trade unions. The inspecteur du travail must be given a copy of the agreement. The present situation is, however, different from what it was from 1966 to 1972. During that period a third electoral college could have been instituted for technical and managerial staff in establishments consisting of more than 500 employees, where twenty five or more technical and managerial staff were employed and these represented at least 5 per cent of the total number of employees at the time when the comité was being constituted.[108] Since 1972[109] it is possible to institute a college for the 'cadres' (technical and managerial staff) where twenty five or more staff of this kind is employed.

The representation of personnel in the conseil d'entreprise in Belgium is divided into two colleges. The manual workers and the clerical workers each have a number of seats corresponding to the numerical importance of these two categories.[110] It seems as though this law had been badly drafted as it did not provide for the number of seats available in each of the two electoral colleges to be decided before the election took place. The older employees[111] described to this writer the problems which occurred.[112] Criticisms of a different nature have also been expressed.[113] A subsequent statutory instrument amended the law by providing that the number of seats in each electoral college is to be decided *before* the election takes place.[114] The employer may appoint one or more persons to assist him.[115] There is no legal requirement that there should be equality between management and employee numbers, but the management members cannot exceed those of the employees.[116] Interviews held with a sample of sixty Belgian employees who are on the conseil d'entreprise in different firms in the private sector, and interviews held with management, revealed two weaknesses in this aspect of the law. Firstly, there is discontent in that the employer's nominees are often changed during the course of the year; this means that any continuity is often broken. There exists no legal requirement as to length of service on the conseils d'entreprise for the management representatives. The sample of management interviewed answered this problem by stating that when a specialised problem appears on the agenda then a specialist is appointed to tackle it. This is found not to be entirely the case.[117] It is submitted that an employer ought to select his colleagues from the start by anticipating the kinds of problems which could arise during such meetings, and furthermore act more responsibly in the selection of persons who would be genuinely interested in the work of the conseil. There is of course nothing to stop the employer from inviting a specialist to attend a meeting. Another way of remedying this problem is for legislation to provide the same period of service for management as it does for employees. This sort of problem has not arisen in France; the reasons, it is submitted, are firstly that there is not such a large number[118] of employer representation on the comités d'entreprise as there is in theory on the Belgian conseils d'entreprise, and secondly, in France the management serves for the same period of time as the employee representatives. Secondly, the Belgian law is silent as to whether or not the employer must nominate his colleagues on the conseil from members of management. It appears that the law does not compel him to do so, and it was found in practice that though numerous employers nominate their colleagues from management,[119] some select them from among the employees who had appeared on the electoral roll but who had not been elected. Management may also select technical or supervisory staff. This is an aspect that has not been found in any of the other countries under examination. The most representative trade unions have the exclusive right to nominate lists of candidates in both the clerical workers' college and the manual workers' college.

Two electoral colleges only existed until 1963 but since then a third has been added. Where there are twenty-five or more manual workers of over twenty-one years of age and twenty-five or more clerical workers of over twenty-one, each of these will have a spearate electoral college. The elections for each are separate and distinct. Should there be twenty-five of either manual workers or clerical workers, there will then be one electoral college for both. Each member of the electorate receives two electoral forms, one for each of the groups.[120] Foremen and technical staff are not represented, but if they are nominated by management to serve on their side they are unable to defend their own interests. This is an odd phenomenon, that firstly the supervisory and technical staff should not have a separate college, and that if they are nominated by management they have to support the management and cannot defend the interest of the electoral college to which they belong (namely that of employees). It happens occasionally that technical or supervisory staff chair, or are invited to, the meeting in their capacity as experts in their field. In these circumstances they have no vote. Since 1963 a third electoral college has been added for young workers (both manual and clerical workers) between the ages of sixteen and twenty-one, if twenty-five such workers are employed.[121] It is evident that the Belgian system is totally different from the French one.

It has already been pointed out that the numbers representing management in Belgium cannot exceed[122] those representing manual workers and/or clerical workers. On this latter side there is a minimum of three and a maximum of twenty[123] delegates with an equal number of acting delegates.[124] The number of representatives, and the representation in the various categories for all establishments or for a particular industry, are determined by ministerial regulation.[125] As regards the third electoral college, the system is different. There is no one delegate for from twenty-five to 200 young workers, and two for over 200. It is odd that fixed numbers exist for the third college, whereas there are none for the other two. Furthermore, the system of numbers differs completely from that under French law.

It is too early for problems to have arisen in the comités mixtes in Luxembourg since the law bringing them into being has only at the time of writing become operative. An assessment cannot therefore be made. Comités mixtes in the private sector are, unlike France and Belgium, composed *equally* of employer and employee representatives. Depending on the number of employees (and similar to the Belgian, but different to the French system), the size of each comité varies from six to sixteen members. It must be noted that the trade unions *in theory* do not participate in the nomination of the employee candidates (as happens in France and Belgium). These are elected by secret ballot according to the rules of proportional representation from among the employees themselves.

The British situation is highly complex in that there exists no legislation on works councils, and the comparatively few works councils which exist are based in the private sector on agreement or custom[126] (and in the public sector on the Nationalisation Act).[127] Each of the works councils examined is tailored to meet the requirements of the particular industry or plant. Consequently, a great variety exists[128] and generalisations on membership and structure become difficult and could, if made, be inaccurate. It may therefore be said that compared to the countries' laws under examination (as well as the other European countries), Britain lags considerably behind in this area. Despite this, it has been possible to find common features (under the 'membership' head) within some of the works council structures examined.

It has been found (apart from a few exceptions[129]) that there exists in many British unionised forms examined, multi-union representation, not only within one company but also within a department or departments of that company.[130] This was not found to be the general practice in the other countries' unionised establishments examined. On the other hand, a number of companies have works councils which are not union based, and therefore, although there may be members on these councils who belong to a union, the union has no official influence in them.[131] This latter situation is akin to France and Belgium where works councils are in theory non-union based (except for the fact that the unions initially nominate the candidates for the election).

The management-employee representative ratio varies from one company to another. This is of course inevitable since such factors as the electoral college, the union(s) representation, the size of the department etc. must be considered. This is also true of the other countries' works councils examined. It is found that in multi-unionised companies there is a tendency for a higher ratio on the employee representative side, because of each of the unions having to be represented by one or more persons. It is therefore impossible to give an accurate management-employee ratio. Roughly, in multi-unionised establishments the proportions are three-quarters employee representatives to one-quarter management representation. In non-unionised establishments, the proportions are about one-third management and two-thirds employee representatives — and on rare occasions an equal number may be found on both sides.[132] This feature is also found in Belgium where management representation is fluid. One common feature found in all countries examined is that no management representatives outnumber employee representatives.

As in France, Belgium and Luxembourg, so it is in Britain, that the employer or his representative chairs the works council meetings. Who is the employer? A common feature found is that the personnel director chairs these meetings. The reasons given in all countries examined was that he is the only person who is qualified to do so since his department is mainly concerned with industrial relations and works councils are concerned with this aspect. Another argument has been advanced by some firms interviewed, to the effect that subsequent to consultation most often negotiation takes place. The personnel department in many firms conducts these negotiations, therefore it is right that it should also be concerned with consultation. This was found in all the countries examined. In other firms it was found that the departmental manager chairs the meeting, and where there is a hierarchy of councils, then the council is chaired by the appropriate senior manager right up to the general manager (as was found in British Steel Corporation, Rotherham works). Again this is found to be a feature in France, Belgium and Luxembourg. In some instances, it was found in Britain that the chair rotates between management and employee representatives,[133] and in others the chairman is elected from among the whole of the membership of the works council.[134] Neither of these two aspects were found in the countries under examination, and in no country is a chairman a member of the employee side.[135]

Although in practice the employee representatives are elected from particular units (usually departments), there exist no fixed electoral colleges in Britain. In one instance — namely Unilever (Blackfriars group of buildings) — it was found that there exist *departmental units* on the one hand and *grade units* on the other. There are thus grade committees consisting of five members from each of service and clerical employees, and assistant, middle and senior management (twenty-five members in all). On the other hand there are departmental councils with up to ten members, and a committee of departmental councils with one to three representatives from each of the seventeen departmental councils. Both the grade committee and committee of departmental councils are represented (five members from each) in the Blackfriars consultative council. This is an interesting feature combining two different conceptional units. Instances have also been found, namely in Cadbury Schweppes Confectionery Group, where no election takes place and where members of works councils are nominated by the trade union on both the works council and the six divisional consultative committees.

As far as Britain is concerned, the main conclusion which may be drawn is the divergence which occurs in both membership and structure amongst the comparatively few consultative bodies which exist. Membership and structure vary considerably so that within the system it is found that both unionised and non-unionised structures exist; that there is a one- to three-tier system; that representative numbers vary from one firm to another; that there is a variety on such matters as employee representative-employer representative ratios, who chairs the meetings, the number of representatives, and whether they must be recognised union members, single, multi- or non-union representation, and so on. It is noticeable therefore that there is a great divergent element within this country. As between Britain and the other countries, the divergent element is stressed even further when one compares the orderly system (at least in theory) which exists in the other countries under examination. Furthermore, in the other countries the consultative bodies are not, in theory, dominated by trade unions. In addition there is in Britain no compulsion to constitute consultative bodies, whereas there is in the other countries. This perhaps is the fundamental divergent element.

Despite this double divergent element, some convergence may be attributed both to the system as it exists in Britain, and to the systems as between Britain and the other countries. The convergent element in Britain is noticeable in the fact that of the consultative councils which exist, a number are unionised (whereas there also exist many which are not); the majority of these bodies have a greater employee ratio (despite the few exceptions); that it is normally the employer who chairs the meetings (again with a few exceptions); and that the general practice is that employee representatives are elected from units, usually departments.

The convergent element between Britain and the other European countries under examination lies mainly in the fact that the non-union-based councils in Britain may be compared to the system in the other countries; that the variation in employee representation within councils which exists in Britain is similar to the Belgian situation; that the employer in Britain normally chairs the meetings, which is always the case in these countries; and that the election is the normal channel of providing employee representatives in Britain. This is so in the other countries.

Having considered the divergent and the convergent elements under the membership and structure heading in Britain and in France, Belgium and Luxembourg, it is necessary to consider these and make recommendations on possible legislation to bring Britain in line with these other countries. In this context, the relevant proposed provisions of the European works council must also be considered.

Because of the great element of divergence which exists within the British system on both membership and structure, it is submitted that those companies which already have consultative bodies set up at the time of the passing of that legislation be allowed to keep their established membership and structure.[136] Any legislation should therefore apply to all consultative structures constituted *after* the passing of the Act, or to any existing structures which are subsequently modified. Furthermore, it would be wrong to impose a statute of such rigidity as to disallow variations in membership and structure. Companies should be allowed some flexibility in order that their particular circumstances and arrangements be met. It is therefore recommended that legislation should provide a framework within which management and labour may work.

Our system of industrial relations being different from those of the other European countries, it is felt that unlike what happens in these countries *in theory*, trade unions in this country should continue to be represented on the works councils where there exists such a wish.[137] It was said previously that negotiating machinery should exist in parallel with consultative machinery;[138] this latter therefore should exist in order to *supplement* (and not supplant) collective bargaining. Professor John Wood put it very aptly when he said,[139] 'A classic difficulty is the question of whether participation should amalgamate consultation and negotiation. It is, of course, impossible to keep the two functions rigidly separate, but there is a strong feeling that they should be dealt with in different ways. The trade union view, based as it is on the central feature of collective bargaining, has to be taken into account. The decision whether to aim for the maximum separation of the two functions can only be made with regard to individual circumstances.

Where there are no trade unions, for example, a mixture of functions in the same body seems logical. But where unions operate, great care must be taken to ensure that conflict is not created by giving the participative bodies important functions, involving negotiation. Otherwise these institutions may fall into disfavour.'

There are five advantages to this proposed system. Firstly, the expertise and experience which exists in union representatives will enhance the consultative aspect. Secondly, by having union representation there will be a direct link with the negotiation machinery in that the issues will have already been discussed and the problems which have arisen in consultation would be fully understood and appreciated. Thirdly, the accusations of remoteness which have often been attributed to consultative bodies will be partially dissipated since there will be a single channel of communication (though the two should be kept separate) with the same union representatives taking part in consultation and subsequent negotiation. Fourthly, as has already been pointed out, there often exists in Britain multi-union representation not only within the establishment but also within the individual departments. This, it is found, often causes friction within each of the unions because *inter alia* of the inevitable and different policies, rules, structures etc. of each. From a negotiating point of view it is more convenient for the employer to negotiate, not as is the usual practice, with each union separately, but with all the unions as a joint body. It is thought that a consultative body will not be the *deus ex machina* which will solve this problem, but it could pave the way towards this by creating a better understanding between the different unions through exchanges made by the different union representative members and management in the consultative body deliberations. There should of course be no compulsion that consultative bodies should have trade union representation. Such proposal would allow for consultation to take place outside the unions if the parties so wish. The present sample establishments examined above, which do not have union representation, would therefore continue to operate as at present. Finally, a consultative committee is more informal and can meet at regular and frequent intervals. Such a committee (separate from the negotiating committee) would allow greater discussion and expression of opinion and be used as a safety valve for complaints and problems which could develop to unmanageable proportions in a negotiating committee. It also allows opinions to be aired and points of view to be expressed, and an opportunity for the more active to organise social functions etc. and thus get additional fulfilment. All this cannot be achieved at negotiation meetings. Thus the consultative body should be competent to discuss any topics except those considered to be reserved for the negotiation committee.

All legislation need provide for is that there should compulsorily be works councils in all establishments of over fifty employees and that the parties should consist of the employer and/or his representative(s) and delegates elected from trade union members, though there should be an outlet on union membership if the firm is not unionised or if the parties do not wish official union representation. The effect of such legislation would be firstly to institute in all companies of over fifty employees which do not have works councils, such a body; secondly, to lay a general framework for these companies; thirdly, not to upset already existing arrangements, and fourthly, give freedom to each company as to how it should set up this consultative system, i.e. equal employer-employee representation, union representation, or not, number of such committees to be set up within the establishment, hierarchy of such committees, who should chair meetings and so on. Obviously, this will not be in line with the more specific and wide-ranging legislation which exists in the other countries under examination, but the systems, methods, laws and institutions of one country cannot, and should not, be transplanted *in toto* to another. It will however help Britain converge towards what is occurring in Europe and smooth the path towards meeting the relevant requirements of the draft proposals of the European works council.[140]

As far as the electoral college is concerned this again must be determined at plant or company level and all that legislation need say is that 'constituencies' or 'electoral colleges' must be formed. This would allow freedom to have the 'grade' type of constituencies which exist in Unilever (Blackfriars) or the 'departmental' type of constituencies which are the more common in Britain. There would then be a convergence with European practice examined above, with its different electoral colleges. Finally the ratio of representatives to constituents should be provided for by legislation,[141] as is already the practice in the European countries. This again will pave the way when and if the legislation on the European works council comes into being.[142] Having examined the practices in Britain and the other countries under examination, and compared them to the ratio adopted by the statute for European companies (see note 142)), it is felt that the latter ratio is extremely low. The views of employees cannot be properly determined with such a low ratio. A more realistic one would be between three representatives for 50 to 100 to twelve representatives for over 10,500 employees.[143] The 'deputy representative' has not been found to exist in Britain. It is submitted that there should be an equal number of deputies elected at the same time as actual representatives. It has often been found in Britain, as well as in Belgium, France and Luxembourg, that representatives were unable to attend meetings because of death, holiday, sickness, days off, etc. It is the practice in all the countries examined (and it is a proposal for the European works council) that 'suppléants' be also elected. Their uses have been invaluable in replacing the actual representative; it is therefore recommended that a similar system be instituted in Britain.

The above advances submissions for legislation on the membership and structure of a British system of works councils. These submissions must however be considered in the light of the problems which have been found in the other countries under examination. In establishing electoral colleges it is always important to bear in mind not to have too many, otherwise there will be a dispersion of employees and a consequent weakening of employee power.[144] Upon the establishment of a third electoral college in France (namely 'cadres') a number of persons interviewed expressed the wish that such legislation were not passed as it changed the balance of ideas within the second college (namely supervisory staff). The distribution of seats and the classification of employees within each of the units must therefore be carefully agreed between employers and unions/employees. Any disagreement on this matter should (as in the case of France[145]) be capable of being referred to the ACAS.

It was stated earlier that works councils in Britain should have either trade unionists as employee representatives, or non-trade unionists. In this latter case, and where union representation exists in the company, it would be advisable to involve the trade union(s) concerned in the setting up of the works council. So that, as is the case in France and Belgium, the unions could propose nominations for elections and even be allocated a seat in the works council, as happens in France. Furthermore, where there exists a two- or three-tier system of works councils, legislation should provide that where the works councils' representatives are non-unionists, trade unions should be represented at all levels, thus avoiding the difficulties created in France.[146]

In France, Belgium and Luxembourg the electoral colleges are divided strictly according to status, i.e. supervisory staff, manual staff, management, persons between sixteen and twenty-one etc.[147] This formula has not been adopted by the writer in his submissions for works councils in Britain. The reason is that a natural unit such as a department is sometimes broken up by the continental structure and a number of employees of varying grades and status interviewed in the countries examined expressed their grave concern over this aspect. Britain must therefore avoid falling into this difficulty, and will probably do so naturally because the trend as shown above is not according to status or grade (apart from a few exceptions such as Unilever Blackfriars) but according to department or other unit.[148]

The problem which arose in Belgium over the number of seats in each electoral college[149] should be avoided by a simple provision that the number should be decided *before* the election takes place.

Employer representatives on the works council should remain for the whole period of the works council's life, thus preventing the situation which arose in Belgium.[150] Furthermore the system which exists in Belgium of having a fixed number of representatives for the third electoral college (young workers) and no fixed number for the other two colleges[151] is confusing and illogical. This is the reason why one system only has been suggested[152] for Britain.

Section iii. Elections

The election process to the relevant countries' consultative organs are both lengthy and complex. It is proposed to critically examine and analyse each of these, point out the problems which have arisen, compare them and examine the divergent and convergent aspects. These will be used as a basis for making appropriate suggestions for legislation in Britain.

In order to qualify as an elector in France, employees of either sex must (a) be over sixteen,[153] (b) have worked in the establishment for at least six months,[154] must not have been convicted under arts. 5 and 6 of the Electoral Code,[155] or for 'indignité nationale'.[156] The elector must be an employee of the establishment and not one employed by the 'comité d'entreprise' or other such body within the establishment.[157] It is found that difficulties have arisen in relation to the requirements of the period of service within the establishment. Do certain lapses in employment within the six-month period break the chain of continuity? It appears that a layoff from work does not break the continuity of employment.[158] If an enterprise consists of numerous branches,[159] the electors' names on the electoral list will only be those in the branch.[160]

Conditions of eligibility as an employee representative on the 'comité d'entreprise' are somewhat stricter. Close relatives of the employer are excluded. The candidate must be over twenty-one years of age. The French nationality requirement has been done away with since 1972.[153] He must be able to read and write and must have worked in the establishment for one year without interruption.[161] The term 'without interruption' must not be taken strictly, so that authorised absences,[162] a period of illness,[163] or a suspension of the contract of employment over the wrongful dismissal of a comité member[164] is permissible.

In Belgium, the conditions for membership of the electorate[165] are somewhat different. The employee must not be a member of the board of directors; he no longer has to have Belgian nationality or possess a working permit for two years (cf. France); have attained the age of sixteen and have since worked in the establishment for a minimum of three months. Furthermore, he must have been employed for the minimum of a year in the type of work in which the establishment is concerned. Because it has not been possible to find legal cases on the two last requirements, and because this could have litigious consequences, enquiries were made as to the exact meaning of this phrase. It appears that the three-month requirement in the establishment must be continuous,[166] whereas the one-year requirement in the type of work (branche d'activité) carried out by the establishment need not apparently be continuous.

Eligibility as a representative on the conseils d'entreprise[167] again differs from the French situation. Candidates must not be members of a board of directors, they must be over twenty-five years of age, employed in the enterprise for a minimum of six months and for three years in the same type of work being carried out by the enterprise, and must not be deprived of their civic rights. The situation in Luxembourg is similar in both respects to the Belgian one and therefore need not be elaborated. Collective agreements examined, and practice in all three countries, do not depart substantially from the legal requirements.

In Britain, there being no statute, recourse had to be made to collective agreements and practice. An examination of these clearly indicates that in terms of eligibility to vote and eligibility to be a member of a works council there is little consistency and the formulation of any kind of general rule is impossible. One company examined[168] told this writer that there were no qualifications except that both electors and candidates for election had to be in the appropriate *'constituency'* and have worked with the company for *three months*. In another[169] the employee representatives (involved both in consultation and negotiation) in the departmental committee, area councils and works councils are elected through the appropriate trade union machinery and are *trade unionists*. No other qualifications are needed. This same feature has been observed in other establishments.[170] Another variety exists where the only requirement is that employee representatives be *elected* on the council. There do not exist any qualifications either to be on the roll of electors or to be a prospective candidate.[171] In another company it was observed that before he could be eligible for election a member on the departmental council had normally to have a minimum of two years' service with the company, but a waiver to this rule is sometimes made.[172] A summary of the present British system shows that in most cases elections are held, in others members are appointed. Sometimes elections take place through the trade union machinery, in others elections take place from among the employees. Qualifications as an elector or as a potential candidate other than either being a union member or a member of a 'constituency' (such as a department or grade) hardly exist. Room for considerable improvement exists; it is therefore submitted that legislation should regulate this aspect in a more comprehensive manner. The qualifications as an elector should be twofold. Firstly an age qualification, secondly a service qualification. It is submitted that the age qualification be sixteen on the day of the election. This is like the provisions which exist in France. It has the advantage of giving an opportunity to apprentices to take part and have a say in the election of their representatives. This also accords with the European works council proposals.[173] The service qualification should be continuous employment[174] in the company (in whichever branch) for three months. This is sufficient time to enable an employee to get to know his colleagues (including the candidate standing for election). Nationality requirements are outmoded and therefore should not exist.[175] Nor should there be a bar to a vote where a person has been convicted of a crime.

In order to qualify as a potential candidate, the requirements should be more stringent. As to minimum age, it is submitted that it be twenty-one as is the case in France. It is considered that sufficient maturity exists at that age. Nationality or previous convictions[176] again should not feature, but a minimum of six months' employment must be a prerequisite.[177] This enables the candidate to familiarise himself with the establishment in which he works.

The conditions which relate to elections of the comité d'entreprise member in France are identical to those of the délégué du personnel.[178] These are based on a secret ballot through a system of proportional representation, and the system of nomination by lists of candidates, whereby the most representative trade unions put forward candidates' names in the first instance. A number of difficulties in connection with the conditions of election have however been found. Firstly, there exists a stringent requirement that voting must be by secret ballot. Non-observance of this requirement makes the election null. An absence in the isolation of voting booths, the presence of the employer at the polls, and other such irregularities which falsify the result of the election also render the election void.[179] It is thought however that an inconsequential error will not nullify the election. Secondly, there is no compulsion to constitute up to three colleges and therefore hold elections in each of these. The election held in only one college, where it is agreed that the other colleges will not be constituted, will not be null merely because there are no elections in the other colleges.[180] Thirdly, trade unions are not bound to insert on their list, during the first cycle of the election, a member of the other electoral colleges (namely supervisory staff and/or cadres). Their not doing so does not nullify the election.[181]

Any dispute relating to the irregularity of elections or to persons allowed to vote come within the jurisdiction of the 'juge de paix' of the 'canton'. It follows therefore that it is the judge who is empowered to pronounce *inter alia* upon the 'representative element' of the trade union and not the 'inspecteur divisionnaire du travail'.[182] The court held that there exists no legislation that gives the 'inspecteur' competence to deal with election disputes and that only the judge is qualified to do so with a right of appeal to the 'cour de cassation'. The role of the 'inspecteur du travail' is thus limited to giving advice and expressing opinions.

Recourse to the courts is only available to the person who has some patrimonial interest in the election; so that a person will not be qualified to contest an election if for example he does not belong to the particular college.[183] The initial statutes had laid no period of limitation within which contested electoral matters had to be brought,[184] but a statute[185] now provides for a period of limitation of fifteen days from the date of the election if its regularity is contested, or a three-day limitation period from the date of publication of the electoral list when the dispute relates to the electorate.

This litigation in electoral matters must be distinguished from the administrative disputes procedure, such as the distribution of personnel in the colleges or the number of seats. The courts are incompetent on these latter matters and only the 'inspecteur du travail' may pronounce on these since they are of an administrative nature.[186] On the other hand, the court may intervene if the 'inspecteur' does not deal with matters which are within his competence. So that if an employer disagrees with a trade union on the distribution of seats, and if the dispute had not been submitted to the inspector who is the only person qualified to deal with it, the court will declare the election null and void.[187]

The form the election for the conseils d'entreprise takes in Belgium is most complicated. Every aspect of the election process[188] is provided for by statute[189] in minute detail. The most representative trade unions have the *exclusive* right to nominate lists of candidates to be elected by secret ballot and who will represent the employees in the appropriate electoral college. Since the details of the manner and form of the election process will be of use later in this research it is proposed to outline these in a note.[190]

An appeal may be made by any interested party(ies) within eight days of the posting of the election result. The appeal will normally be based on any irregularities in the election process. The 'conseil de prud'hommes' or the 'juge de paix' hear the appeal. Extensive powers are given to these courts, including the examination of witnesses, election and other documents etc. The decision must be given within sixty days. A further appeal exists to the 'conseil de prud'hommes d'appel' or to the 'tribunal de première instance' which must also give their decision within sixty days. If the election is declared null and void by the courts a new election will be held within two months.

The above illustrates the very complicated laws on elections to the 'conseil d'entreprise' which exist in Belgium. In comparison with France, the laws are perhaps more detailed and the organisation more complicated; a convergence element is however visible between these two systems as well as that of Luxembourg, in that these countries deal in detail — albeit stressing different points and experiencing different problems — with the whole election process for membership of their respective consultative organisations. Britain, it is found, does not offer anywhere near such sophistication with regard to the election of members to works councils, firstly because there exists no standard legal procedure and secondly because each of the establishments interviewed or examined conducts elections according to its respective rules. It may therefore be said that the system of elections to works councils in Britain is both informal and unsophisticated.[191] Nor are there collective procedures which relate to election disputes and election appeals. Those which exist come within the ordinary appeals or grievance procedures laid down by the trade union rules or company rules respectively. The conclusion as far as Britain is concerned is clear, that in both these respects, i.e. election procedures and election disputes and appeals, the divergent gap in comparison to the existing continental systems is wide; in addition the divergent element as regards the practices which exist within this country is also great. It is considered that the only way in which a convergence may come about, both within Britain and without, is for a standard procedure to be set up by legislation. Proposals are therefore made below, as to what this legislation should contain. These proposals are based on the systems of the countries under consideration bearing in mind the problems which have arisen, and at the same time taking into account the proposals of the European Communities on the statute for European companies. It is however considered that this legislation should have an exemption clause for establishments which already have satisfactory election procedures and arrangements, thus enabling them to continue with their system until it comes to an end when the statutory procedures will thereafter have to apply.

It is considered that, in line with the other countries examined, representatives' works councils be elected by *secret* ballot. Interviews held by this writer showed that a number of cases in Britain, employees were concerned at the practice of voting by a show of hands. This, they felt, allowed for pressure groups to 'bully' employees into voting for a particular individual. Upon similar enquiries made in the other countries examined, no one made a similar complaint. Such a provision would therefore remedy this situation.[192] Furthermore, votes must be cast on ballot paper and any such papers which are soiled will be void.

This writer believes it essential for reasons already given that, though there be two different bodies for two different functions, i.e. consultation and negotiation, the same persons, or at least most of them, should be on both these bodies. He also believes that trade unions should take part in works councils. In order to achieve this, legislation should provide that lists of candidates should be submitted by trade unions represented in the establishment.[193] Where trade unions are not represented then the employees entitled to vote should prepare the list,[194] which should be signed by one-tenth of the employees entitled to vote. To avoid the difficulty which previously arose in Belgium, it is considered that the number of candidates on either the trade union or employee lists, whichever is appropriate, should not exceed twice the number of seats available. This would mean that the number of seats will have to be determined in advance. An equal number of 'deputies' should also be elected from a separate list. The simple majority rule should operate.[195]

In order to conduct and organise the election an electoral committee should be set up, as exists in Belgium, and in Britain in Unilever (Blackfriars) and in some unions. Unlike Belgium however where there exist rigid rules as to procedure,[196] and unlike the proposals for the

European works council,[197] the electoral committee should provide for its own procedures. This method has the advantage of enabling the electoral committee to take into account any particular circumstances in the establishment, which a statute cannot do. The electoral committee should be set up by the appropriate union(s), but where an establishment is not unionised then the employer should have this responsibility. Where an employer or union refuses to set up such a committee and the statutory minimum number of employees exist to qualify for a works council, then the aggrieved party — whether the employer, the appropriate union(s) or employees — should have a right to have his grievance heard. The Central Arbitration Committee of the ACAS would be the best body to deal with this problem (and not an industrial tribunal).[198] No specified number of members on the electoral committee need be provided for,[199] since it is considered that discretion should be given to the body concerned — whether union or employer. A president,[200] a secretary, assessors and any other officials should be appointed, as is the case in Belgium, on each electoral committee.

The electoral committee should agree with the management when the election should be held. This should be during working hours. The employer will have to provide a room for the occasion. Absent employees should be allowed a postal vote. These arrangements should be made by the electoral committee. Other arrangements such as the drawing up and displaying of the list of electors and the hearing of complaints on these, must also be made by the committee. Any disputes on such complaints should be referred to the ACAS and dealt with promptly. The ACAS decision should be final in order to save time. If required, an extension should be given where either the union(s), employer or employees ask for one. The electoral committee should have the further task of publishing its composition, of deciding the address to which electoral correspondence should be sent, the place and times where the list of voters will be displayed, the number of vacancies on the works council and the closing date for submission of candidates' names. A copy of the legislation providing for the election process should be displayed at all times during the election period.[201] On the election day the electoral committee should appoint one of its members to attend the poll and to make sure that no irregularities occur. The counting of votes, the allocation of seats and the notification to the union(s) and to the employer, employees and successful candidates should be the function of the electoral committee.[202] When the election has taken place a report should be made by the electoral committee recording the results of the election, and the allocation of seats. A copy should be handed to the employer, the newly-constituted works council and the trade union or employees as the case may be. Ballot papers should be kept in a sealed box for a month in case the election is contested.

A procedure should also exist where the election is contested, because of infringement of the election rules. A period of limitation of one month should be placed, firstly so that the matter may be dealt with speedily and secondly, because the matter would still be fresh in the minds of all concerned. Such appeal should be referred to the appropriate industrial tribunal (and not to the ACAS), since it is a legal matter rather than a matter which requires conciliation or arbitration.[203] If the election is declared null and void another one should be arranged within three months.

The responsibility of planning as to how long before the election date various events have to happen, as for example the submission of names of candidates, contested matters, closing date of submission, posting of notices, announcing the election date etc., should remain with the electoral committee. From interviews carried out with past members of the 'bureaux électoraux' in Belgium, it is found that the inflexible statutory provisions provided for in that country[204] at times create serious timing difficulties. In the other countries under examination such rigidity does not occur, though it is noted that certain time limitations are placed by the proposed statute for European companies.[205] Such limitations, admirable as they appear in theory, are likely to create problems in practice; hence the submission that there should not be any in Britain.

The members of the 'comité d'entreprise' in France[206] hold office for two years and in Belgium for four. A right of re-election however exists.[207] A member of the comité d'entreprise may be removed from office in the same circumstances and under the same conditions as those in which the délégué du personnel may be removed.[208] The acting member (délégué suppléant) in both France and Belgium replaces him; but in France where he is not available then the member of the same electoral college who obtained the greatest number of votes will replace the acting member.[209] An interesting feature is that in Belgium where the members or acting members reach below the minimum number and there are no further acting members to fill the vacancies, these latter do not, as is the case in France, go to the person who had the most votes; instead, a new conseil d'entreprise will be constituted.[210] Another difference found in Belgium is that the acting member does not replace the actual member when this latter is prevented from attending a meeting; the actual member is only replaced when any one or more of the situations in note 208 exist.[211] One month before the member's office expires, it is the duty of the employer to notify the competent trade unions to produce a list of proposed candidates to fill the post on the new comité d'entreprise. Elections must take place during the fortnight following the invitation.[212] Should there be a failure to institute a new comité d'entreprise in France the fact must be reported by either the employer or the trade union and sent to the 'inspecteur du travail'.[213] In Belgium however on the expiry of the term of the 'conseil d'entreprise' this body ceases to be validly constituted. It is up to the conseil d'entreprise itself to fix the election date when nearing its completion period.

So as to enable the members (membres titulaires only) of the French comité to carry out their functions, a maximum of twenty hours a month is allowed them. This time is remunerated as though it were time worked. The same time off is given to acting members when they are performing the functions of the member, but their time cannot be deducted from that allowed to the actual member.[214]

In Britain, this writer's investigations indicate a variety in the period of tenure of representatives of works councils. In most it is two years,[215] but in some, representatives are elected for two years, half standing for election each year so as to ensure continuity.[216] In others it was found that there is no fixed period.[217] A right to re-election has been found to exist in every case. This writer's investigations indicate that acting representatives do not exist. No rules have been found giving any special protection against dismissal or discrimination for works councils' representatives, and although time off on full wages during working hours to take part in works council meetings and other activities has been found invariably to be the norm, no specified maximum as is the case in France exists. The general impression which is left is that the system, where it exists, varies from establishment to establishment and is very haphazard. It is therefore submitted that more specific rules are required in these respects so that a standardisation might take place. Legislation should therefore provide for works council members to be elected for a period of *three* years with a right to subsequent re-election.[218] It is considered that two years, as has been found to be the general practice in Britain, and as is the case in France, is too short a period to get the members used to the system. A majority of the sample examined in Britain (64 per cent) considered that the two-year period was too short. The same examination in France produce a larger

Representative Establishment Councils 67

percentage (70 per cent). A similar examination in Belgium showed that 84 per cent thought that four years was about right. No attempt was made in Luxembourg because the system being new, opinions would not necessarily be based on past experience and could therefore be inaccurate.

Nothing in writing has been found in Britain which lays down the circumstances under which a member of a works council may be removed, but interviews carried out indicate that in practice suspension or dismissal (with or without notice), illness, resignation of the member from either the works council or the company, promotion of the member thus ceasing to represent the class of employees, in some cases resignation from the union,[219] all terminate his mandate. Death and termination of the term of office without re-election to the new works council obviously terminate the member's mandate. Since all these exist in practice, it is thought that legislation should lay down these customary rules, as is the case in the other countries under examination.[220] There existing no deputy representative in the sample examined, any representative who vacated his post was found in practice not to be replaced.[221] It would in these circumstances be simpler, as was recommended above, to have a deputy who would immediately replace him, rather than have the seat vacant or have to hold an election for that seat.[222] Where the deputy representative is also unable to carry out his functions, it is submitted that the Belgian system (see above) is the better one since it has been found in practice that it works well. The French system of selecting the person with the greatest number of votes has on occasions proved difficult to apply.

The employer should have the duty to notify the trade union (or employees) some time before the expiration of the works council term of office so as to allow it to organise elections for a new one. It was found in France that one month (see above) is too short, and difficulties have arisen in practice in organising elections. It is therefore considered that the employer should notify the trade union(s) etc. *two* months before. An alternative, which seems to work well in Belgium, is to put the onus on the works council itself to organise its dissolution, and notify the trade union(s) or employees. Legislative proposals consisting of either of these alternatives should therefore be made.

The abrupt termination of a works council without a new one being constituted may sometimes cause problems. Such problems have arisen in Belgium where upon the expiry of the 'conseil d'entreprise' the body is no longer validly constituted. It is submitted that in cases where elections for the new works council have for some good reason not been held, the representatives on the former works council continue in office until the election has been held.[223]

A maximum monthly time allowance should be given to the works council member in order that he be enabled to carry out his duties. The French experience indicates that twenty hours a month is ample. Of the sample interviewed in France 83 per cent were satisfied with this time allotted by legislation and only 21 per cent of the 83 per cent used all the time that was allowed. When asked whether twenty hours a month would be an acceptable figure in Britain, 91 per cent of the sample stated that it would. It is therefore submitted that legislation provide for a maximum of twenty hours a month to enable the works council member to carry out his functions. This should also be given to the deputy member but should, unlike France (see above), be cumulative.[224]

The procedure on dismissal of members of the 'comité d'entreprise'[225] is more stringent than that of ordinary employees and is identical to that of the 'délégués du personnel' already discussed,[226] but for a few observations which must be made.

When the 'comité d'entreprise' is called upon to decide on the dismissal of one of its members,[227] the decision is made after the member has been given the chance of a hearing, and after a secret ballot has been held.[228] Where the 'comité' does not agree to the dismissal, this cannot take place until after the 'inspecteur du travail' has agreed to it. Before doing so he must carry out an enquiry into the matter. During the course of this enquiry the member may if he wishes be assisted by a representative of his union.[229] A written report of the proceedings which took place at the 'comité d'entreprise' must be given to the inspector within forty-eight hours. The inspector must, after completing his enquiries (see above), give his decision within fifteen days.[230] Where however there is a suspension of the member, then he must decide the issue within eight days. These periods can only be extended if the enquiry justifies it and notice is given to the parties by the inspector.[231] The Minister of Labour is empowered to nullify or modify the inspector's decision within four months, upon request of either the employer or the member or upon his own initiative.[232] This writer's investigations show that this provision does not find favour with either the majority of employers or the majority of employees. On the employer's side, the main complaint has been that the procedure is too long and that this ties the employer's hands. On the employee side, again the procedure is criticised as being too long thus leaving the employee in the 'limbo' of uncertainty and preventing him in some cases from obtaining other employment. In cases where the dismissal is of a collective nature, the inspector (or the Minister) must examine whether the measure taken by the employer meets with the collective agreement or other terms.[233] In case of 'faute grave' the employer may immediately suspend the member until the decision of the 'comité' or of the inspector is reached but the interested party is reinstated if dismissal is refused by either the 'comité', the inspector or the Minister of Labour.[234]

Special protection is afforded to a member who has served the 'comité' for two years or over as well as to the candidates whose names appeared on the electoral list (first cycle) submitted by the trade unions. In the former case dismissal can only take place after six months from the time when his period of office terminated,[235] and in the latter case three months from the time either of posting by registered letter to the employer the list of candidates, or from the time the lists were handed over or acknowledged.[236]

It is found that the decision of the 'comité d'entreprise' to dismiss need not be unanimous, a simple majority is all that is required. Case law supports these findings.[237] No exceptions have been found in the sample of 'comités' interviewed, but some persons thought that the rule of unanimity should apply. It is considered that a simple majority in favour of dismissal does not put the matter beyond doubt, and that therefore the member is not as secure as he might otherwise be. Unanimity on the other hand could give unreasonable security. It has been found in practice however that sometimes a minority of the 'comité' disagrees with the employer's proposal to dismiss, and at one such meeting attended by this writer threats were made to the employer by such a minority to report the event to the inspecteur du travail. Clearly, the minority was not entitled to do so in these circumstances.

Employers interviewed in France do not seem clear at what stage the dismissal should be reported to the comité. This admittedly is a small minority. Some have told this writer that they dismiss the employee first and then inform the 'comité' for purposes of ratification. Although this practice does occur, it is contrary to the intention of Parliament, and the Cour de Cassation so held.[238] It is however quite in order, as is found frequently to be the practice in the more urgent cases, for the 'comité' to 'unofficially' accept the suspension with subsequent ratification.[239]

It is clear therefore that in France the employer cannot dismiss (whether instantly or with due notice) an employee who is a member of the 'comité d'entreprise'. All he can do is to suspend (in case of fundamental breach[240]) and await the decision of the 'comité' or 'inspecteur'.[241] The suspension being provisional the employee's contract of employment is not terminated.[242] Suspension operates only as far as the contract of employment[243] is concerned, the employee therefore remains eligible to be a 'comité' member and his right to vote in 'comité' decisions is not taken away from him.[244] Some employers interviewed expressed concern over this matter in cases where very serious misconduct had occurred, and considered that suspension should operate throughout the employee's function in the establishment. The majority of employee opinion is that the present law should be kept intact.

The procedure in Belgium is found to be different from that of France, though one of the reasons for dismissal is similar — namely 'faute lourde' (serious misconduct). The other is 'raisons d'ordre économique ou technique' (economic or technical reasons).[245]

As far as serious misconduct is concerned the employer may dismiss an employee who is a member of a 'conseil d'entreprise', but unlike the French system the employee is not, it is submitted, safeguarded. All he may do is to bring a common law action for wrongful dismissal. No reference is made to the 'conseil d'entreprise' etc. as is the case in France.[246] It is therefore found that this protection is there only in name. An interesting feature which exists in Belgium alone is that the trade union which has put his name forward may itself be sued by the member if the union in alleging gross misconduct against it unilaterally dismisses him from his membership of the 'conseil'. Before a member of the 'conseil' be validly removed from his union, and therefore from the 'conseil', the court must find that gross miscondut (vis-à-vis the union) such as to justify expulsion from the union, has occurred. The union itself, even though not a legal persona, may sue its member in such circumstances.

The other reasons which may justify dismissal are economic or technical reasons. Stringent provisions exist before the employer may dismiss a member of the 'conseil' for such reasons; these being that previous agreement for dismissals in these circumstances must have been reached by the 'commission paritaire nationale'; alternatively, that this 'commission' had previously approved the general *criteria* applicable to this type of dismissal.[247] The law is singularly silent as to what amounts to 'economic and technical reasons' which would justify the 'comission paritaire' to affirm the occurrence of such event. Investigations were therefore carried out in order to find out how this provision is operated in practice. This research shows that the 'commission paritaire' is not concerned with the actual dismissals, but with whether or not there exist 'raisons d'ordre économique ou technique'. If the 'commission paritaire' decides that these exist, then dismissals can take place; if not, dismissals of 'conseil' members cannot do so.[248] The decision of the 'commission paritaire' must be unanimous. Let us suppose that the 'commission paritaire' is not unanimous and that therefore it cannot approve or disapprove mass dismissal for economic or technical reasons. Does this mean that the employer cannot dismiss a member of a 'conseil' for these reasons? It appears that he still can do so. According to a senate debate[249] it appears that it is the intention of Parliament that the dismissal may still take place and that the member of the 'conseil' who has been dismissed may complain to the 'conseil de prud'hommes' claiming its unfairness. The employer will then have to put forward his case that dismissal took place for 'raisons d'ordre économique et technique'. Thus despite the fact that the 'commission paritaire' was unable to reach a unanimous decision the dismissal may still be justified if the 'conseil de prud'hommes' so finds.[250]

A considerable difference in procedure has been found between France and Belgium; this difference may be epitomised as follows. Whereas in France the dismissal procedure starts from within the establishment and extends outside it,[251] in Belgium the procedure is found to be entirely outside the establishment[252] and the 'conseil d'entreprise' has officially no involvement with the dismissal.

A considerable difference also exists between the two countries as far as the period of protection from dismissal is concerned.[253] The French provisions have already been examined. In Belgium, unlike France, protection starts from fifteeen days before the announcement of the election date and continues for the full period of membership, nemely four years.[254] It does not extend beyond that period as it does in France. Nor is there any qualifying period in Beligum as there is in France.[255] This writer's submission for the differences lies in what he previously referred to as procedure starting from within and that resting on outside bodies. In France, the member of the 'comité d'entreprise' does not need protection while he is serving, since he already has such protection in that he cannot be dismissed without the consent of the 'comité' itself or failing that, of the 'inspecteur' or of the minister. The protection he needs is when he leaves the 'comité' after the period of two years. There are of course flaws in that a person who has served for under two years, because the 'comité' had to be disbanded because for example of a reduction of employees to below the legal minimum, is not protected. In Belgium, on the other hand, the member of the 'conseil d'entreprise' needs protection because the dismissal not resting with the 'conseil', and there being no other internal procedure, the law has to provide a safeguard. Again flaws may exist in that a 'conseil' member who has completed his four years' service is not protected for a period thereafter.

Candidates who are not elected in Belgium are protected for two years. It will be recalled that non-elected candidates in France receive protection for only three months.[256] Case law in Belgium makes a distinction between a candidate whose name appeared on the final list, and a candidate whose name appeared on the list but was struck off before the definitive list was posted. It is only those candidates whose names appear on the definitive list who are given the statutory protection.[257] The divergent gap as far as safeguards of employee representatives are concerned is therefore considerable between these two countries.

It is submitted that one weakness exists in both these countries in that no provision has been found in the law which safeguards conduct by the employer falling short of dismissal. Nothing has been found in the respective laws which states that discrimination will not take place and therefore guaranteeing that the representatives' remuneration (including bonuses, allowances and other monetary benefits) and promotion chances will not be affected as a result of their activities.

Special legislation connected solely with the protection of members on works councils in Britain does not exist and therefore such members have to rely on the dismissal provisions or actions falling short of dismissal which apply to all employees.[258] An examination of rules of a sample of existing works councils do not provide any special procedure in connection with the dismissal of members. Of the number of employees and members of works councils interviewed, there is unanimity that any dismissal rests in practice with the general statute on dismissal or on common law. This writer is of the opinion that special legislation in connection with the dismissal or discrimination of members on works councils should exist, not so much because the dismissal of such a member could not come within the already substantial provisions which exist, but because of the special nature of a member's activities and therefore the requirement of special protection in relation to these activities.[259] It is also important that there be an element of convergence (at least in that some statutory provision exists on this aspect) with the other European countries. Consequently it is considered that legislation provides that a member and substitute member of a works council should not be dismissed from his employment during his period of office and two years thereafter, unless misconduct (gross or otherwise) or redundancy has occurred. In both these cases the works council should first be consulted. Gross misconduct should, as is the case in France, entitle the employer to suspend the employee and such suspension should also deprive him (unlike France) of his works council activities. Where the works council agrees to the dismissal, then this can take place.[260] It will of course be open at any time to the dismissed or suspended member to bring an action in the industrial tribunal for unfair dismissal if he so wishes. In the case of ordinary misconduct, again the works council should approve the dismissal before the requisite notice is given.[261] Legislation should also make it clear, thus avoiding the flaw found under French law,[262] that the works council should be informed and the procedure gone through *before* the member is dismissed, though there should be a provision allowing the employer before suspension to informally consult the works council with subsequent ratification. In the case of dismissal for redundancy, this must have the prior consent of the trade union(s)[263] and will be a function of the negotiating committees (as is the case under Belgian law, and as is the practice in France). The rule of unanimity of negotiating committees as exists in Belgium has its drawbacks,[264] it is therefore not recommended for Britain. The reaching of an agreement that redundancy occurs is all that should be necessary, and that is the normal practice. The advantage of the proposed system is that, like France, the dismissal procedure starts from within the works council. Furthermore, the period of protection suggested, namely during the member's mandate and two years thereafter, seems realistic.

Protection should also be extended to those candidates who were not elected; such protection lasting from the date of their nomination to three months after the date the election was held.[265] Such provision would avoid the flaws in the law which exist in both Belgium and France and which have been suggested by this writer.[266] Legislation should also make it clear that the persons to be protected should be those whose name appeared on the *definitive* list of candidates.[267]

The situation where a trade union dismisses its member who also happens to be a member of a works council must be considered. The solution to this problem should be similar to what has been found to be the case in Belgium.[268] The expulsion of a trade union member should be based on the union rules. If the member is dissatisfied with the purported expulsion the courts should pronounce whether or not the member has been wrongfully expelled. Until the appeal has been heard the member should remain on the works council. If the court finds against the union member then he could rightfully be dismissed from the works council.

The aim of such legislation would be to make employers, works councils etc. more aware of their responsibilities and by introducing additional obstacles it would consequently make dismissal of members of works councils more difficult, and therefore different from the dismissal of ordinary employees.

In France, if the dismissal procedure of a 'comité' member is not followed such dismissal is null and void[269] and therefore reinstatement must take place,[270] otherwise the employer is liable to pay damages.[271] Furthermore, the dismissal being null, the contract of employment continues and there is an obligation on the employer to pay wages as from the date of dismissal,[272] and also since the dismissal is void the employer will lose his right in law to dismiss his employee for the 'faute grave' which he committeed and which would justify dismissal.[273] This solution, it is submitted, is hard on the employer since non-observance of procedure on his part makes him lose his right to dismiss his employee for serious misconduct. Of the employers interviewed most seem aware of the procedure and of the consequences should the procedure not be followed, but within that sample a substantial number have expressed dissatisfaction with this aspect of the law. It has also been found in practice[274] that many employers prefer not to reinstate and pay damages in order to get rid of troublesome employees.[275]

At times the wrongful dismissal of a 'comité' member has been assimilated by the courts[276] to a criminal offence. This is based firstly on the fact that a fine[277] may be imposed on the employer for such wrongful dismissal and secondly on the wording of an article in the statute based on intentional obstruction[278] of the work of the 'comité' by the employer. It is submitted that the wrongful dismissal of the 'comité' member by the employer does not necessarily amount to 'intentional *obstruction* of the work of the "comité" ', and that this article should be interpreted literally to mean what it says. If it is found that the dismissal had intentionally taken place to disrupt the functioning of the 'comité' then of course there should be liability under this article but normally[279] this is not the case. A danger therefore exists in that a court might go too far and interpret this article as meaning that wrongful dismissal equals intentional obstruction of the 'comité's' work.[280] Where intention to disrupt occurs, the onus of proof is on the employer to rebut this presumption. Acquiescence by the 'comité' at the time of dismissal is not necessarily proof that no bad motives existed.[281] An action against the 'comité' which acquiesced to the dismissal, albeit wrongful, cannot be brought by the dismissed member. This writer's investigations seem to suggest however that the comité might be liable in tort if negligence can be proved.

Similar sanctions exist under Belgian law. Where the employer wrongfully dismisses a member of a 'conseil d'entreprise' within the period of protection (see above) he must be reinstated.[282] Before this can be done the dismissed 'conseil' member or his union must apply to the employer by registered letter[283] within thirty days of the date of receipt of notice of dismissal,[284] the date of instant dismissal, or the date when candidates' names for the election of membership to the 'conseil' has been posted. As is the case in France, the employer must refund the reinstated member his wages from the date of wrongful dismissal. Should the employer refuse to reinstate within thirty days of the application, and the court finds the dismissal wrongful, the employer has to pay (without prejudice to damages for breach of contract or customary breach) two years' wages where the member has been employed in the establishment for under ten years, three years' wages for between ten and twenty years and four years' wages for over twenty years' service. These rules on compensation also apply to constructive dismissal as well as to dismissals allegedly for serious misconduct which have been found by the court not to be justified.[285] No case law has been found in Belgium to the effect that if the procedure for dismissal of a member of a 'conseil' has not been followed the employer is estopped from alleging 'motif grave'.[286] It is submitted however that since the procedure for dismissal in Belgium is based from without[287] the procedure is not of such great importance as it is in France.

As is the case in France, criminal sanctions also exist where obstruction relating to the legal provisions of 'conseils' by the employer has occurred,[288] but no case has to this writer's knowledge come before the courts which has construed dismissal of a 'conseil' member as an obstruction.[289]

In Britain the dismissal of members of a works council comes within the law of dismissal for all employees[290] and no special rules exist. Constitutions of works councils examined do not provide for any special safeguards. It is significant that the statute for European companies does not provide for dismissal in this respect. The reasons given in interviews varied with the appropriate body in the European Commission that this should be left to the law of the respective countries and that anyway criminal sanctions were not in this respect appropriate. When one examines the laws of the other countries under consideration in relation to members of 'comités' or 'conseils' with the British law of dismissal, no additional protection is given to these members. In other words the British law applicable to all dismissals is as effective in terms of compensation etc. as the laws applicable to members of 'comités' or 'conseils' of the other countries under examination.[291] It is therefore submitted that, as is the case in France, so it should be in Britain that if the dismissal procedure of the works council member or a non-elected candidate (as recommended above) has not been followed, the dismissal whether constructive or otherwise upon demand of the trade union be annulled[292] and reinstatement take place. If the employer refuses to reinstate he will be liable for the additional award over and above the compensatory and basic awards[293] under the present laws. As a deterrent to the employer, some unions with whom this writer conferred suggested that a fixed scale should exist (as it does in Belgium), whereby in addition to the normal compensation under the 1974 and 1975 Acts the employer should pay the longer-standing employee the sum fixed on that scale. The employer is already under heavy burdens and therefore this suggestion cannot be recommended. Furthermore it will contribute little towards the achievement of the aim desired, namely deterrence. Unlike France however, the employer's right to subsequently dismiss for gross misconduct should not be removed merely because he has not followed the procedure. The dissatisfaction found in France amongst employers has already been stated,[294] and there is no reason why British employers should not be as resentful if this practice were allowed to occur in Britain. Though fines and/or imprisonment should not normally be provided for, a carefully worded section in the legislation should, it is submitted, provide for such criminal penalties only when it can be proved[295] that the employer *intentionally* obstructed the work of the works council. A prosecution therefore under this section would rarely apply to the dismissal of a works council member.[296] It was earlier submitted that before dismissal of a works council member takes place, the works council must be consulted.[297] If the dismissal is subsequently found to be wrongful or unfair the works council as a body should not be liable. All it would have done would have been to homologate the employer's action. In the unlikely event of gross negligence by such a body, then that liability should be pertinent.[298]

Representative Establishment Councils 77

Section iv. Frequency of meetings

A legal requirement exists to the effect that a French 'comité d'entreprise' must be convened by the employer at least once a month. An additional meeting or meetings may also be held where the majority of the 'comité' so request. The agenda is prepared by the chairman (the employer) and secretary and distributed to all members three days before the meeting. In cases where the 'comité' is to meet at the request of the majority of members a note of the special matters for discussion must be attached to the agenda. Decisions are normally[299] taken by majority vote. The employer who refuses or otherwise fails to summon a meeting may be compelled by the 'inspecteur du travail' to convene and preside over a meeting if one-half of the members so request.[300] Minutes of all matters discussed are taken and the secretary must communicate these to the employer and to all 'comité' members.[301] The employer must normally[302] disclose by the following meeting of the 'comité' the decision he has taken upon matters submitted to him. Such decision is recorded. Sometimes the 'comité' may make proposals on matters which have been detailed to a 'comité d'organisation'.[303] If these are rejected by the employer the 'comité' may if it wishes, appeal to the 'Inspecteur général de la production industrielle', who must consult the 'conseil consultatif paritaire'. When this latter body examines matters of this nature a representative of the Ministry of Labour must attend in a consultative capacity.[304] The 'comité' may notify the 'directeur départemental du travail et de la main d'œuvre' of any matters it wishes. The 'inspecteur du travail' may request to be informed of any of the proceedings of the 'comité d'entreprise'.[305] The actual deliberations of the 'comité' have on occasions come before the courts. Are members of the 'comité' privileged and do they have freedom of expression during meetings? The courts have held that a distinction must be drawn between matters which are relevant to the functions of the 'comité' and those which are not. In the former there is qualified privilege, in the latter there is not.[306] A legal requirement is imposed on the employer to provide premises, furnishings and staff for the meetings of the 'comité'.[307]

Although a great deal of what has been said on the frequency of meetings in France also applies to Belgium, there exist marked differences between the laws and practices of these two countries. In Belgium there is a legal requirement for the chairman (employer) of the conseil or at the request of half of the members to convene a meeting at least once a month.[308] It is found in practice that as a general rule the larger the establishment the greater the frequency of meetings, the smaller the establishment the fewer the meetings.[309] There exists a specific provision in Belgian law, unlike French law, which states that meetings held *outside* working hours are remunerated as time worked.[310] Unlike France where a decision is taken by majority vote, in Belgium it must be unanimous.[311] Enquiries have been made as to whether the solution presented problems in practice. It appears that the rule of unanimity works will in Belgium[312] in cases where the constitution of the 'conseil' provide for this kind of decision.[313] There is in Belgium (unlike France) a legal requirement for the existence of a constitution for each 'conseil'. It is the duty of the 'commissions paritaires'[314] to draft such a constitution for all the 'conseils' under their jurisdiction or for a part of them. At least the ten matters prescribed by law[315] must feature in such a constitution but adaptations within each of these are allowed so as to suit the individual 'conseil'.[316] The law, though it imposes a constitution, does therefore give the 'conseil' a certain amount of freedom, but if no initiative is taken by the 'conseil' to adopt the constitution then this latter will operate as prescribed by the law.

Of the sample of constitutions examined it was found that the legal requirements are very seldom departed from so that the length of notice to be given by a 'conseil' member for discussion at the following meeting varies from twenty-four hours to three days before the agenda is sent out; the notice to convene the following meeting is sent out from three to five days prior to that meeting being held; in all cases agendas for the coming meeting provide for all matters to be discussed; a provision is normally found to the effect that the chairman is the managing director or equivalent who may be replaced by his second in command; the secretary is often proposed and nominated by the 'conseil' members; a copy of the minutes is normally given to each member (as opposed to deputy member), and copies are displayed on notice boards for all employees to consult; changes in the constitution normally take place after the 'commission paritaire' has been consulted. Such additional matters as the remuneration of the secretary to the 'conseil', or the remuneration of its members when engaged in work for the 'conseil' outside working hours (meetings excepted since these are covered by law), or again the provision of premises for unofficial meetings held only by the employee or manual workers' representatives, and finally the possibility of inviting experts or outsiders to advise the 'conseil', have been found in constitutions of various 'conseils d'entreprise'.[317] As is the case in France, premises and the necessary materials necessary to hold meetings of the 'conseil' are the employer's responsibility.[318]

Britain generally lags well behind its other European neighbours in connection with meetings of the works councils, written constitutions and related matters; but it is found that despite there being no legislation *some* establishments have regular meetings and efficient and reliable procedures.[319] This however is the exception rather than the rule in Britain. It is therefore submitted that legislation should lay down principles with regard to meetings of works councils and related matters. This would guide those firms which do not have an effective system to improve, and those which have no system, to institute one. In the first instance it is important that a constitution be formulated. This could be done by a special working party of the first works council, or by the works council itself, and not by outside bodies.[320] It is suggested that a constitution similar to that which exists in Belgium, having proved itself to be both successful and comprehensive in that country, should be adopted for Britain.[321] Legislation should however provide that each of the ten matters referred to should be adaptable to take into account the contingencies of the particular establishment. Secondly, certain basic provisions should be spelt out. The basic provisions are considered to be as follows: (a) a works council must meet at least once monthly,[322] and more frequently when half the members so request. Of the sample examined in this country, 83 per cent felt that such intervals were reasonable. An examination carried in the other countries subject to this research, again showed a high proportion for a monthly (or when required, more frequent) meeting (76 per cent in France, 89 per cent in Belgium). The majorities are significant in Belgium and France since such requirements exist in law and therefore these countries can speak with a certain amount of experience behind them. (b) the formal rules of running a meeting must be observed — i.e. an agenda to be prepared and circulated a few days before the meeting, minutes should be kept, a record must be kept of all proceedings, apologies for absence, signing of minutes by the chairman as a correct record, matters arising from the previous minutes, matters for discussion, chairman's business, any other business etc. A majority of works councils' members interviewed felt that a formal meeting was desirable and that better results were achieved in that way. This is also the opinion in the other countries examined. (c) a progress report on matters requested by the meeting must be made at regular intervals — six-monthly seems the most favoured period. (d) all decisions of works councils should be by majority vote rather than by unanimous decision. It was felt by the majority of members interviewed that 'unanimity' has two disadvantages, firstly it is time consuming and secondly decisions cannot be taken so readily.[323] (e) a system must exist for the dissemination of information, both to members of the works council as well as to all employees. For members the obvious way is a copy of the minutes, but for employees the question is problematic. Of the sample interviewed in Britain the majority favour a résumé of the proceedings to be displayed on notice boards. The minority wished to see all employees receive a copy of the minutes. The majority felt that the minutes may be too detailed.[324] (f) all works council meetings held outside working hours should be remunerated as time worked.

A statutory provision to enable members unable to attend the meeting to have their opinion heard through another member does not exist in the statutes of any of the countries examined. This writer has attended a few meetings where this practice occurred. The general opinion of the sample interviewed thought this a good practice since a person unable to attend a meeting should nevertheless have his opinion voiced. Legislation should therefore provide for such contingency.[325]

Sanctions against the employer such as exist in France and Belgium for not convening a monthly meeting should not be imposed. Two reasons are given for this. First, Britain does not have a social inspectorate as exists in the other countries, and to institute one, apart from the expense, would go against the industrial relations practice in this country. Second, sanctions should be based on pressure being applied indirectly by the trade unions or employees.

No works council in Britain has, to this writer's knowledge, been faced with an action for defamation. Nevertheless, with the growth of the works council system, as submitted, this is a distinct possibility for the future. Legislation should therefore provide that discussions in works council meetings should have qualified privilege.[326]

Section v. Role and functions

The role and functions of the representative institutions are the 'solar plexus' of their existence. It is found therefore that legislation in Belgium, France and Luxembourg makes detailed provisions on these matters. Though it is generally agreed in industry[327] that the role and functions of the works councils in Britain are also their 'solar plexus', these are in no way regulated or provided for by any legislation. Where works councils exist it is found that their role and functions are tailored according to the development which has taken place within the industry.[328]

Since the role and functions of these representative bodies are their 'solar plexus' a critical study of each of these in Belgium, France and Britain will follow. Consequent submissions will be made as a result of this analysis. Such study will not take place in the case of Luxembourg; the law on 'comités mixtes' being so recent has not allowed this writer to seek informed opinion.

It is found in Belgium and France that a distinction may be drawn in the functions of the 'conseils d'entreprise' and 'comités d'entreprise' respectively between (a) consultative and advisory powers and powers to receive certain information and (b) limited powers of decision making and supervision. The convergent element is therefore apparent in these countries. This distinction has not been found to exist in as clear-cut a way in Britain. In certain establishments it is found that limited powers of decision exist in the works council, alongside its consultative etc. powers but the latter, as will be seen, is the predominant feature, and the two functions are not distinct enough and vary from establishment to establishment. The divergent element is implicit between Britain and the other countries in this reference. In the countries under examination (Britain included) the functions of the respective 'committees' are predominantly consultative, advisory etc., except for the administration or supervision of the social welfare programmes (Britain generally excepted) within the establishment where limited powers of decision exist.

It is first proposed to examine, analyse and compare the various 'committees' ' powers of decision or supervision (i.e. management) in social matters, and then examine, analyse and compare their consultative etc. functions and the topics relevant to these. Submission will then be made within each of these two groups.

A distinction must initially be drawn between 'services sociaux' and 'œuvres sociales' in France. The two are distinguished by the fact that the former services are mandatory where a certain number of employees are employed, whereas the latter services are not. Each of these will be analysed and compared with the identical expressions which have been found to exist in Belgium.

In France it is found that the 'comité d'entreprise' should play an active part in both the organisation and functioning of the 'services sociaux',[329] the formation of which is compulsory in estabishments employing 250 permanent employees or more. The 'comité' also plays an active part in the organisation and functioning of the 'services médicaux'.[330] In establishments where 'services sociaux' are required, an 'assistant' or 'assistante social diplômée' must be appointed in order to devote at least three half-days a week for each group of 250 employees. The 'services sociaux' in an establishment or a group of establishments are run by a 'conseiller-chef' or 'conseillère-chef du travail'. Such a person must within a year of appointment obtain a certificate[331] issued by the Minister of Labour. The 'conseillère-chef du travail' is appointed by the employer with the assent of the 'comité d'entreprise' or failing agreement, by the 'inspecteur du travail'.[332] Special protection against dismissal of both these persons is provided for by law.[333] The functions[334] exercised at the place of work by the 'conseillère' are (a) to look after the employee's welfare and to facilitate adaptation in his work; (b) to study in particular the problems which arise from the employment of women workers, mentally deficient workers and young persons; (c) to co-ordinate and promote decisions on social matters reached by the employer and the 'comité d'entreprise', and to exercise for this latter the functions of technical councillor on social matters; (d) to unite with the social services all action of an educational nature undertaken by the 'comité d'entreprise'. The final function (e) is eventually to promote and extend the social services, outside the place of work to employees' families, upon matters which are related to the industry.[335] In order to achieve their task the 'conseillers' collaborate with the medical services of the establishment, they suggest to the employer and to the 'comité d'entreprise' improvements in conditions of labour, in the welfare of workers and in the functioning of the 'œuvres sociales'. They also keep themselves in constant liaison with the bodies within the establishment which are concerned with retirement, social security, medical services and other services of a public nature, in order to facilitate the exercise of the employees' social legislation rights and to guide and direct them to the competent authority.[336] In fact the functions of the 'conseillère' are those of a Florence Nightingale clad in social trappings. Interviews carried out with a sample of 'conseillères' indicated that in practice only some [337] of the functions mentioned above are performed since not all exist in a particular establishment or group of establishments. Furthermore, it is found that a number of establishments which should have 'conseillères' do not in fact have any. Of those that do,[338] it appears from interviews carried out with members of 'comités', employees and workers that as a general rule (i.e. 83 per cent of the sample) they are not effective. It is therefore considered that the 'services sociaux' are often confused with 'œuvres sociales', and this writer would suggest that there is no need for both. This would avoid the confusion which these two expressions bring about, and also avoid some duplication which has been found to exist between the items within each of these expressions.[339]

It may be for these very reasons that Belgian law talks of 'œuvres sociales'. Indeed it was found in the parliamentary debates of Belgium that the term 'services sociaux' appeared in the draft bill, but a suggestion was made and accepted, to the effect that 'services sociaux' be replaced by 'œuvres sociales'.[340] The 'conseils d'entreprise' in Belgium therefore have, unlike France, nothing to do with the 'services sociaux'.[341]

Seeing the little success achieved and the disadvantages of the 'services sociaux' in France, it is not thought that such a system would enhance the industrial relations system of Britain and therefore no recommendation can, and no submissions need, be made in this respect.[342]

The decision-making role of the 'committees' in the 'œuvres sociales'[343] is apparent in all countries under examination, except for Britain where, although it has been found to exist, it varies from establishment to establishment.

Social welfare programmes, i.e. 'œuvres sociales'[344] in a French enterprise are *managed*[345] or *supervised*[346] by the 'comité d'entreprise'[347] which has legal personality.[348] The terms 'manage' and 'supervise' call for closer attention. These, it is submitted, form a trilogy, which this writer divides into ensuring, controlling and participating in the management of the 'comité'. The 'comité d'entreprise' *ensures the management* of the 'œuvres sociales'[349] but it *controls the management*[350] of certain specified welfare matters. These are social insurance or mutual assistance schemes within the establishment, housing and the provision of other premises for workers, apprenticeship schools and training centres.[351] The way in which that control is exercised is by means of two members of the 'comité d'entreprise', preferably chosen from among the beneficiaries of these institutions, who attend the meetings of the 'conseils d'administration' etc. of these institutions, and who report back to the 'comité d'entreprise' both the proceedings as well as the decisions of such 'conseils d'administration' etc.[352] Before the 'conseil d'administration' is enabled to reach a decision on any of the matters above, the opinion of the 'comité' must be sought. The 'comités' have a right of veto if they are opposed to the implementation of the 'conseil d'administration's' etc. decision.[353]

It was stated above that the 'comité *ensures the management* of the 'œuvres sociales'. Management of the training schools or apprenticeship centres are however excluded.[354] The management of the 'œuvres sociales' irrespective of how they are financed is carried out by the 'comité' itself, through a special sub-committee, an individual member or through organisations constituted by the 'comité'. These individuals, organisations or sub-committees must act *intra vires* the authority given to them by the 'comité' and are directly responsible to it.[355]

'Management' and 'supervision' (see above) includes *participation* by the 'comité' in the running of benevolent societies[356] and 'sociétés co-operatives de consommation', which qualify as 'œuvres sociales' if they function for the sole advantage of employees, retired employees or their respective families living in the same house.[357] 'Comité' participation takes place, in that half the members of the 'conseil d'administration' must be representatives of the 'comité d'entreprise', though they need not be members of this latter body but be chosen from the members who are beneficiaries of these institutions.[358] These have the same voting rights etc. as the other members.[359]

Within this trilogy of management powers, i.e. ensuring, controlling, participating of the 'comité', an investigation was made to examine which were the most frequently exercised 'œuvres sociales' in French enterprises. This is considered to be important for two reasons, firstly in order to compare practice in that country with the theoretical possibilities, i.e. the provision of the law, thus examining how effective the law is in practice, and secondly in order to examine the popularity of each of the 'œuvres sociales'. From the sample examined[360] the results are as follows:

1.	Canteens, refreshments at work,[361] restrooms and cloakrooms, works' medical services[362]	30
2.	Clubs, gardening, tools, etc.	28
	Helping new employee adapt himself to his new environment[363]	28
	Apprenticeship schemes[364]	26
3.	Sport[365]	26
	Colonies de vacances	26
4.	Training and retraining centres[366]	
	Libraries[367] and cultural activities	23
5.	Retirement pension schemes (additional to state pensions)[368]	18
6.	Private social security schemes — industrial injuries, unemployability, death[368]	17
7.	Capital investment schemes[368]	
	Private medical schemes[368]	
	Family protection schemes[368]	5
8.	Housing[369]	7

9. Nurseries for children of working mothers   3
10. Others (smoking booths, social councillors etc.)   1

It was pointed out that the French 'comité d'entreprise' has power of management and supervision over 'œuvres sociales'.[370] Though the emphasis is different these powers are also given to the Belgian 'conseil d'entreprise', but the powers of management extend over a wider field than is the case in France, because they not only cover the field of 'œuvres sociales' but also the management of certain other matters.[371] The supervisory powers also extend over a wider field.[372] These powers are given to them by both statute[373] and national collective agreement.[374]

Since the most important function of the 'conseils' is considered to be the 'œuvres sociales' it is proposed to examine the Belgian laws which relate to these, before dealing with the other matters. The term 'œuvres sociales' has already been analysed and the confusion which, it is submitted, arises in France but which has been avoided in Belgium has been mentioned.[375] The 'œuvres sociales' in Belgium are not defined in as great a detail by statute[376] as in France, nor are there any provisions which state how these should be managed.[377] The trilogy[378] which exists in France does not therefore exist in Belgium. Though statute defines the general norms of the 'œuvres sociales',[379] the 'accord national' is more specific[380] and enumerates exhaustively the consistency of these 'œuvres'. These are mutual assistance schemes, private pensions schemes,[381] saving schemes, works canteens, loans and other payments made by the establishment for the purpose of house purchase, and cultural and recreational activities.[382] It is important to note that this exhaustive enumeration of 'œuvres sociales' is subject to the general criteria already mentioned,[383] namely a nature of permanence, financed by the establishment, reserved for the employees or their families, and which are not provided for by either a statute, a contract of employment or a collective agreement.

An important distinction exists between France and Belgium in the legal interpretation of the term 'management of œuvres sociales'. In France it will be recalled that the 'comité d'entreprise' possesses legal personality,[384] the Belgian 'conseil' on the other hand is not a legal persona. The result is that though it is enabled to 'manage', it cannot 'execute' its decisions, and can only do so through the enterprise (being a legal persona) to which it belongs. The 'conseil' is therefore not as legally independent as its counterpart the 'comité'. Again, in the economic field it is found, unlike the 'comité' in France, that its powers are limited to suggesting what sums should be put at the disposal of the 'œuvres sociales', and to the supervision of these. The 'conseil' cannot decide upon the means of financing the 'œuvres sociales'. The 'conseil's' powers are also curtailed in another important field in that it is only the employer who can decide which 'œuvres sociales' are to be instituted and which are to be abolished. The 'conseil' has powers of management of these 'œuvres' only when they are in existence. These restrictions indicate that the 'conseil' is not as omnipotent as the 'comité'. It was therefore necessary to examine whether these restrictions were acceptable to the members of the 'conseil' or whether they felt that changes should be made in order to give them more powers.

It is interesting to find that a majority of the sample (78 per cent) accepted the fact that the 'conseil' did not possess legal personality, and did not feel that this was in any way a drawback. Within that percentage (i.e. 78 per cent) it was found that 59 per cent felt that there was an added advantage in that it was the employer who had the headache of executing the management decisions of the 'conseil'. This majority therefore felt that no change is required on this aspect. The remaining 22 per cent felt that it would be advantageous for the 'conseils' to possess legal personality for various reasons, e.g. greater independence. These same questions asked by this writer to a sample in France showed again that the majority (86 per cent) of the members were pleased with the 'comité' having corporate personality, the advantage being total independence from the employer's clutches. It is submitted that the contentment on this aspect in both these countries shows that the system in each works well; it also shows that each system has its advantages which are acceptable to the members.

Less happy however is the employer's power to decide upon the means of financing the 'œuvres sociales'. Interviews carried out with members showed that a large majority (89 per cent) disliked the present system and preferred to have a certain sum allotted, per capita for example, to the 'conseil', though all agreed that the employer was usually sympathetic to suggestions made by the 'conseil'. A minority considered that the allocation of a certain sum could affect the economic development of the enterprise; this minority also considered that the present system was flexible in that it allowed the employer to allot sums according to profits made by the enterprise. In France, the system of financing the 'œuvres sociales' is different. The employer has a statutory duty to pay the 'comité' a certain sum.[385] Interviews carried out there showed that 92 per cent of the sample of 'comité' members were satisfied with the system, but all felt that the statutory amounts were not high enough. It is submitted that disadvantages and advantages exist in both systems. The Belgian system allows for greater flexibility, but is disadvantageous in that it is left to the employer's discretion as to what sums will be paid – the mean employer will pay less than the generous one. The French system is more rigid (a disadvantage) but it has the advantage of not being dependent upon the employer's generosity or otherwise.

On the practice that only the employer may initiate or abolish 'œuvres sociales', there seems to be discontent. Ninety-three per cent of the sample stated that the 'conseil' should have autonomy in this matter, but it also agreed that the majority of employers took account of the wishes of the 'conseil' in both the initiating and abolishing process. The remainder felt that the employer should have the prerogative because he is the person best suited to know which 'œuvres' he can and which he cannot initiate, and that anyway this point was academic since employers generally took notice of the 'conseil's' wishes. In France, the employer cannot interfere and therefore the question does not arise. The 'comité' is omnipotent irrespective of the employer financing its 'œuvres sociales'.[386]

Although the powers of management of the Belgian 'conseil' are not considered as complete as those of the French 'comité', because of the restraints placed upon it,[387] it may nevertheless be said that, within these limits, the Belgian 'conseil' has powers to ensure the management of 'œuvres sociales'.

Like the French 'comité'[388] the Belgian 'conseil' *participates in the management* of 'œuvres sociales'[389] (though unlike the 'comité' it does not control it, i.e. there is only a duality of nature in the Belgian management of 'œuvres sociales' and not 'a trilogy' as is the case in France) in that when the management of an 'œuvre social' is delegated to an 'association sans but lucratif'[390] a liaison must be established (as is the case in France) between the 'association' and the 'conseil d'entreprise'.[391] The 'conseil d'entreprise' must, *unless it otherwise decides* (see below) appoint half the members of the 'association'; these will normally consist of the beneficiaries of the particular 'œuvre sociale'. A conflict has however been found between the interpretation of the statute[392] by the courts on the one hand and the 'accord national' of 1958 on the other. Prior to the 'accord national' of 1958 the courts held that the 'conseils d'entreprise' could not participate in the management of the 'associations sans but lucratif', firstly because the 1948 law is clear that the 'œuvre sociale' must emanate from the employer[393] and not the

'conseil' and secondly because the 'association sans but lucratif' which is set up for a particular 'œuvre social' is a legal persona distinct from the enterprise, is governed by its own 'conseil d'administration' and is subject to its own rules, and therefore the 'conseil d'entreprise' cannot substitute itself for the 'conseil d'administration' which is the sole body which manages the 'œuvre sociale' in question. Though this interpretation is still valid members of both sides of Belgian industry interviewed feel that this interpretation by the courts which excludes 'conseil' participation is contrary to the spirit of the statute. A majority on both sides of industry furthermore consider that the 'conseil' members should participate in the management of matters which concern them. The 'accord national' portrays this attitude by stating '... lorsque la gestion d'une œuvre sociale est confinée à une association sans but lucratif, une liaison sera établie entre celle-ci et le conseil d'entreprise...'[391] Though the 'conseil' cannot manage entirely on its own the 'association sans but lucratif' has a choice of either
(a) submitting to the courts' interpretation as described above,
(b) appointing members of the 'conseil' and/or beneficiaries from among the employees if the employer is adequately represented, or
(c) appointing a 'commission paritaire' from among the employer and the 'conseil' and/or employee beneficiaries.

This 'arrangement' created by the national agreement is considered to be contrary to the legal pronouncement and therefore strictly speaking it is unlawful; despite that, however, it seems to be working satisfactorily since both sides accept this situation and consequently neither side has litigated this aspect. It is suggested that the law be changed to take into account what now is current, accepted and desirable practice. It may therefore be said that the second aspect of 'conseil' management of 'œuvres sociales' exists on an extra-legal basis, and if it were not for current practice the 'conseil' would not have a dual nature of management. Thus whereas French 'participation in management'[394] (in the trilogy) derives its source from statute, Belgian 'participation' derives its source from collective agreement.

The national agreement goes further than the statute by providing that where numerous enterprises take part in the 'association sans but lucratif' for a common 'œuvre sociale' a liaison between the different 'conseils d'entreprise' and the 'association' must still take place.[395] The composition of the 'conseil d'administration' is not decided upon until all the 'conseils d'entreprise' concerned have agreed to its form. It is usually found in practice to be 'paritaire'. Where no agreement can be reached no 'association sans but lucratif' can be instituted. Regular reports must be made by the 'association' to all 'conseils d'entreprise' concerned and it must take note of any observations made by the 'conseil'.

A similar investigation to that of France, and for the same purposes,[396] was made in Belgium in connection with the duality of nature of the management of 'œuvres sociales'. The results from the sample[397] were as follows :

1.	Canteens, refreshments at work, restrooms and cloakrooms	30
2.	Sports	27
3.	Apprenticeship schemes	25
4.	Training and retraining schemes	23
5.	Clubs/of a technical nature – libraries	21
6.	Loan schemes by the establishment for the purpose of house purchase Pension schemes	18
7.	Cultural clubs (reading, drama, general studies)	17
8.	Mutual assistance schemes Savings schemes	15
9.	Others	4

In both France and Belgium it appears that works canteens etc. is the 'œuvre sociale' which keeps the respective committees most occupied. Sport and technical clubs are also high on the list. At the other extreme the various schemes (i.e. savings schemes, housing loans, pensions etc.) appear, but even though they are at the bottom of the list, this does not mean that they are not being operated. In France for example seventeen social security schemes have been found, and in Belgium fifteen mutual assistance and savings schemes, and eighteen loan schemes and pension schemes exist. Featuring low are nurseries and the provision of housing. Apprenticeship training and retraining and cultural activities come near the middle in both countries. Perhaps the main difference between the two countries lies in the various schemes being run; there seem to be less in France (i.e. capital investment, medical and family protection where in the sample only five were found) than in Belgium; otherwise there is a considerable similarity.

The fact that there is no legislation in Britain does not mean that works councils do not possess management powers (whether decision-making or powers of supervision) in certain limited fields. These powers are however only very occasionally found[398] and they are neither as developed nor as well defined[399] as they are in the other countries under examination.[400] Relatively few British establishments' works councils possess decision-making powers; it is therefore considered that this power should be generalised, developed and better defined. The convergent element is apparent in these countries, in that management powers (decision-making and/or supervisory) are vested in the various committees, but there is also a divergent element in that in France 'a trilogy'[401] has been found to exist, whereas in Belgium 'a duality of nature of management'[402] is apparent, and in Britain there exists the uncertainty and ill-defined system of management which lies mainly under the title of 'ensuring the management'.

The underdevelopment and ill-definition of management functions in British works councils leads this writer to suggest some solutions.[403] It seems however that the greatest weakness lies in the lack of generalisation in industry in the management functions aspects; perhaps these solutions will particularly help remedy this lack. The distinction drawn between (a) the consultative etc. and (b) management powers will be recalled;[404] at this stage it is only in connection with (b) that suggestions will be made.

It has been seen that in Britain comparatively few establishments' works councils have their management functions defined,[405] and that when these are defined the stages at which decision making may take place are not always clear.[406] As a first step it is suggested that legislation should clearly define the areas in which works councils should have management powers.[407] By 'management powers' is meant decision-making and/or supervisory powers. By having such legislation which defines the areas of management of works councils the ill-definition of these functions which is found to be the case in Britain (and not found to be the case in the other countries examined) should be remedied. Legislation will also help remedy the underdevelopment of management powers of the works councils and would make these more generalised. The greater the number of topics the better, but it is essential that only welfare and social matters be given for decision making or supervision to works councils. In other words areas in which the common interests of the employees and of the establishment override their divergent interests. Thus the consultative system must not trespass on the negotiation system. By having the topics defined there will be an additional advantage, namely the exclusion of any matters which are subject to negotiation.[408]

The welfare and social areas in which the management powers of works councils could best develop are, it is considered, threefold. Firstly, *social matters* which should include leisure-time activities such as clubs of various kinds, societies, sport, staff and family social functions, children's parties etc. Secondly, *welfare matters* which would deal with nurseries for working mothers, facilities at work such as rest rooms, seating arrangements, when to start and finish the day (after negotiation on working hours has taken place), smoking booths, protective clothing, clean overalls and towels, washing facilities, car parking etc. Thirdly, *welfare schemes* which should include retirement pensions schemes, social security schemes, savings schemes, loan schemes, schemes whereby employees of the company may buy the product of the company at a cheaper rate, training and retraining schemes[409] etc.

The above three areas of management show the actual functions which the works councils should perform, they do not delimit these. A more orderly division ought therefore to take place, and these ought to be divided again to show the exact limits of powers of the council in each of these functions. The 'trilogy' in France[410] has been examined and has proved a success in practice. The 'duality of nature'[411] in Belgium has also been examined and again has proved a success in practice. A comparison between the two systems shows that there is greater scope in 'the trilogy' than in 'the duality' because the management can be spread about in a more realistic manner. The French system is therefore preferred. It is for this reason that a recommendation is made that management of works councils should be divided into (i) ensuring the management, (ii) controlling the management and (iii) participating in the management.

The next problem is to decide which items of the three different areas of functions should be inserted under each of these three headings. It was felt that it would be wrong merely to take similar or the same items from French law, and transpose these in Britain. The parties most concerned had consequently to be consulted. Interviews[412] were therefore carried out with members of works councils and the majority came out in favour of the following division. Under *ensuring the management* there should be total decision making by the works council on social matters (e.g. leisure-time activities which include clubs, societies, sport, staff and family social functions, Christmas and other parties for children etc.). No one would therefore be able to interfere with the works council's decision on these matters. Because of the great number of social matters which the works council might have to decide, this body should be empowered to delegate its functions to sub-committees which would be accountable to it. In some welfare matters there should be a change of emphasis of the works council's management powers. The emphasis should be on *controlling the management* by being represented on the appropriate bodies and by having considerable say and a right of veto. Decision making is implicit in the control of the management of welfare matters but it is not total — it is shared. The reason why this must be so is that the matters which come under this heading are not necessarily matters which are totally in the hands of the works council. So for example nurseries for working mothers is a matter upon which the employer will also be involved. The same applies to facilities at work. The employer is involved in the provision of rest rooms, the starting and finishing hours, washing facilities, car parking etc. It is envisaged here that committees will be set up by the works council on the establishment for each of these matters or groups of matters and that works council representatives will play a prominent part both in numbers and in say. Finally, the majority of the sample came out in favour of the works council *participating in the management* of various welfare schemes. According to present practice such schemes as retirement schemes are run sometimes by the employer, sometimes through an insurance company and sometimes jointly. It would therefore be inadvisable to change this pattern, but it would be desirable for the works council to participate in such a scheme. The same would apply to social security schemes, savings schemes and loan schemes as well as such schemes whereby employees of the company may buy the product of the company at a cheaper rate, where obviously employer involvement is essential. Under the participation aspect of management, the works council would not have either powers of control or powers of veto, but it should have an equal say in proceedings. This writer would have preferred to have seen training and retraining schemes come into the second category[413] but because of serious resentment[414] by employers in works councils having a considerable say in the running of such schemes it is felt that their role should only be participative.

    Management in the proposed British works council system will therefore range from decision-making powers at one extreme, to supervisory powers at the other. The system as proposed has the advantage of not drastically changing the pattern which exists in some establishments, with the added advantage that such legislation will define more accurately the areas of participation which have so far been found to be ill-defined and will generalise them throughout industry. It will also be found that these proposals do not diverge greatly from the continental systems examined[415] but that the writer's proposals are more akin to the French (which is more regulated[416]) than to the Belgian system. This has been purposely done in order to better define not only the areas of participation but also their limits. It will also be noted that the 'nature of permanence' which is a criterion in Belgium is not included in the British proposals. The reason for that is that it is implicit without having to legislate on it and it has been found in Belgium that it is an artificial requirement,[417] and serves no purpose in practice.

The weaknesses found in the Belgian system[418] must be avoided in Britain. First, works councils should be enabled to 'manage' and 'execute' their decisions. For this purpose some degree of legal independence should be given to the works council. It is suggested that a limited legal personality[419] would give it the necessary independence to execute its decisions. Although this would not be akin to the French system[420] nor would it be akin to the Belgian, it would be peculiar to Britain alone and would have the effect required. A 79 per cent majority of the sample of 130 interviewed in Britain considered this a good idea. Secondly, considerable independence should be given to the works council in the economic sphere. The weaknesses of economic non-independence as existing in Belgium have been pointed out.[421] It is therefore proposed that the employer contributes towards the social and welfare schemes. It is thought that the best way is to base the contribution on a per capita employee basis rather than, as is the case in France,[422] on the previous year's contribution. Of the sample interviewed, this seems to be the preference (54 per cent) (38 per cent wanted a fixed sum rising with the cost of living and the remainder did not know). It has the advantage of increasing or decreasing the contribution according to the number of employees in any one year. Increases to take account of rising costs should be based on an agreed index. Once the contributions have been made the works council should (unlike Belgium)[421] be in complete control as to how it should dispose of its funds. Thirdly, the works council should have the sole power[423] of not only managing, but also deciding which social matters (under the 'ensuring the management' aspect of its functions) it should institute and which it should abolish. The situation would be however different in 'controlling the management' aspect. Here its powers should consist of persuasion and if need be a power of veto against the employer. The nature of the works council's function under this heading makes it essential that the employer be involved. A majority of the sample of 130 members examined agree with this proposal. The minority felt that the works council should have absolute control, while others felt indifferent. What is not realised by the minority is that the pressures which could be put by the works council members upon the employer by their powers of persuasion could be tantamount to absolute control. Finally, by being represented on the appropriate committee with an equal voice the works council members will be participating in the management of the various welfare schemes. Again, there cannot be full control over these because other organisations, e.g. insurance companies, would necessarily be involved. The institution of these schemes would, it is anticipated, stem from the works councils themselves. There would in this case be a similarity with the other countries in this reference. Of the sample examined the majority agreed with this proposal, the remaining being indifferent. One problem may well arise on matters of welfare schemes where participation takes place. Such a scheme need not normally be run by one establishment or even one enterprise, it might be more practicable to run it in conjunction with other enterprises. In these circumstances acceptance and representation should be based on common agreement, and regulations set up to allocate seats to the various works councils' members. Legislation should give freedom to works councils to organise their own procedures.[424]

It was said above[425] that the powers of management of the Belgian 'conseil d'entreprise' extend over a wider field than is the case in France, because they cover not only the field of 'œuvres sociales' but also certain other matters. It was also pointed out that the 'conseil' is not as omnipotent[426] as the 'comité' in that in 'œuvres sociales' it does not have total decision-making powers. The same may be said of the other matters which the conseil manages. These must now be analysed.

Statute provides that another of the 'conseil's' functions is to make and modify works rules.[427] From the wording of the statute it could be implied that it has complete decision-making powers in this aspect. Such implication has however been found to be erroneous in practice. Of the sample examined the 'conseils' have practically never drafted works rules. These either existed before the 'conseils' were established, or were drafted by the employer himself.[428] It is however often the case that 'conseils' (and the employer) do propose amendments to existing works rules. Before a works rule can be altered it is found that there must be unanimity between the employer and the 'conseil'. If there is no unanimous agreement no alteration to the rules may take place. In some instances it was found that the disagreement was taken before a conciliation committee appointed by the competent 'commission paritaire'.[429] Despite what the statute says it can therefore hardly be said that in practice the 'conseil' has decision-making powers in this field. In France the 'comité d'entreprise' does not even have the powers the 'conseil' has in Belgium. In practice it is consulted on any change of works rules. If the 'comité' refuses it does not have the power of the 'conseil' to disallow the alteration. The same is true of Britain. Works rules very much affect the individual employee, therefore he should have a say. Of the sample interviewed in Britain the preference was that before the works rules can be altered, the works council should consent, so that if the works council does not agree with the alteration it could veto it, thus retaining the original rules. Though the procedure would be different the result would be the same as in Belgium, and would amount to total decision making rather than consultation as is the case in France and at present in Britain. It is not considered right that works councils should themselves draft works rules, this is more suited to the employer and to collective bargaining.[430]

Another decision-making aspect of the 'conseil' under Belgian law is to organise if necessary the rotation of personnel for annual holidays.[431] This was found to be the case both in works councils in Britain and 'comités' in France. No change being necessary in Britain no recommendation is therefore made except that statute should so provide.

The final statutory decision-making function of the 'conseil' in Belgium is to take over the functions of the 'comité d'hygiène et de sécurité',[432] but only in certain circumstances.[433] Though in Belgium the 'comité d'hygiène et de sécurité' is an independent body with an independent constitution, e.g. election, rules etc., in France this body forms one of the special or standing committees of the 'comité d'entreprise', where this latter body exists. It may therefore be said that the 'comité d'entreprise' controls the management of the 'comité d'hygiène et de sécurité'. This control, it is suggested, is different from the kind discussed previously in that unlike the 'comité' being represented on the 'conseils d'administration' of the various schemes with an important say in their running,[434] the control of the 'comité d'entreprise' over the 'comité de sécurité et d'hygiène', being one of its standing committees, is more direct.[435]

In Britain it was found, prior to the coming into effect of the Health and Safety at Work etc. Act 1974, that works councils sometimes[436] exercised health and safety functions.[437] In non-prescribed establishments this will continue to occur[438] otherwise the health and safety committees[439] will take over independently of works councils. The situation in prescribed cases will be similar to the practice in Belgium where there is total independence between the 'conseil d'entreprise' and the 'comité d'hygiène et de sécurité'; in non-prescribed cases the situation would continue to be similar to the French one. Because of the already existing provisions of the Health and Safety Act any submissions on safety could not improve the situation in Britain except that it is recommended that all voluntary safety schemes (whether committees or works councils) should observe the statutory provisions.

The two remaining management powers given to the 'conseil d'entreprise' in Belgium, though they originate from statute,[440] are also considered under the national collective agreement.[441] The first, dealing with security of employment, is the power given to the 'conseil' to determine the general criteria to be followed in cases of mass dismissals, e.g. for redundancy, and mass re-engagements.[442] As is the case with most of the 'conseil's' powers these are *limited* to making rules on an equitable basis as to who should and who should not be dismissed. The powers of the 'conseil' in this respect are further *limited* by the fact that numerous 'commissions paritaires' have now fixed the criteria to be followed in an industry, the usual one found being last in first out. Where this occurs the 'conseil' must follow the agreed procedures; it consequently has little room to manoeuvre.[443] The 'conseil's' powers are *limited* because it is the employer alone who decides which part(s) of the establishment will be shut down, or which trade(s) will be made redundant. This is specifically provided for in the agreement[444] and investigations show that this operates in practice. It is after the employer's decision is made to create redundancies that the 'conseil' (with the employer's approval) has powers to establish the order of dismissal. 'Conseil' members interviewed have told this writer that the criteria are not always the principle of last in first out; humane considerations such as heavy family responsibilities, being a cripple or deformed, age, personal problems etc. are often taken into account. Employers interviewed see their role in the 'conseil' while discussions are taking place on who should be dismissed as twofold. Firstly, as protectors of the orderly running of the establishment, so that decisions made by the 'conseil' do not affect the establishment. Secondly, to see that arbitary decisions are not made. The same procedure is followed in cases of either mass or programmed re-engagement.

The power of determining the general criteria to be followed in mass dismissals given to the Belgain 'conseil' is not given to the French 'comité'. The 'comité' has to be compulsorily consulted and informed and it may express its opinions.[445] In practice, however, it is found that though the law does not invest the 'comité' with powers of execution on mass dismissals (as is the case in Belgium) nevertheless in expressing its opinions on the mass dismissals and how they should be effectuated it is doing a job similar to the Belgian 'conseil'. According to a strict interpretation of the statute, in France the employer must inform the 'comité' and seek its opinion *before* mass redundancies occur. In Belgium the legal requirement is that the employer first decides and then informs the 'conseil' asking it to determine the general criteria. It is found however that practice does not allow for such rigidity and that the 'conseil' in Belgium is often informed of impending dismissals whereas in France the 'comité' is asked to give its opinion as to how the dismissals should be effectuated. As is the case in Belgium so it is in France that the 'comité's' hands are often tied by an existing collective agreement which provides these criteria for mass dismissals.[446]

In Britain it is found that security of employment, including proposed redundancies, is often[447] a topic for consultation,[448] but it is found not to be as widespread as it is in France and Belgium. It is important for good industrial relations that this aspect be one of the topics for discussion in works councils and that therefore legislation (which will make the practice more widespread) should so provide and delimit the functions between the consultative and negotiating ones.[449] A system whereby the works council, after being informed of the redundancies, has the power to determine the general rules to be followed in mass dismissals, would enhance the industrial relations system in that it will be seen that equitable principles have been applied.[450] The proposed system is more akin to the Belgian one except that firslty, this will not be regarded in Britain as a management function but a consultative one and that secondly, it is not proposed to give the employer the two 'watchdog' functions[451] which exist in Belgium. It was found that though the Belgian employers have these functions they only exist in theory and invariably prove almost non-effective. As a matter of courtesy (and this again would enhance industrial relations) works councils should be informed and consulted, though not compulsorily as is the case in France,[452] of possible future redundancies at the time when negotiations are about to take place. At this stage the works council would only be able to express its opinion. It has been found that where this has been done, in France and in a few cases in Britain, a better industrial relations climate has prevailed in the establishment.

The second of the two remaining functions which feature both under statute[453] and in the national collective agreement in Belgium[454] concerns the language to be used in the various deliberations of the 'conseil' so as to best enhance the relationship between employer and employees.[455] Such a provision has an important significance in a country like Belgium where a deep conflict exists between Flemish and French-speaking Belgians. No similar provisions exist in France since there exists no language conflict. Similarly, as there is no such *open* conflict in Britain there is no need to suggest proposals of the kind which exist in Belgium.

Statute, it will be recalled,[456] imposes two further duties upon the Belgian 'conseil'. The first is supervision over the observance of protective industrial and social legislation.[457] How does this supervision manifest itself? Discussions carried out with 'conseil' members made it clear that the supervision is executed in a spirit of co-operation rather than one of an accusatorial nature.[458] There exists no legislation on separate supervisory powers in the French 'comité' but it was found that such matters as social and protective industrial legislation are in practice occasionally brought up. The same is true of Britain where works councils do very occasionally deal with social or protective legislation.[459] In this respect the works council could fulfil the useful function of reminding the employer not so much of the protective legislation[460] as of the welfare legislation[461] which exists and which has been found in the course of this research to be sadly neglected in numerous instances. It is therefore recommended that legislation should provide for supervisory duties of this nature to be carried out by the works council.

The second supervisory duty of the Belgian 'conseil' is that in connection with extra-legislative matters[462] (as for example internal rules and collective agreements) generally concerning the establishment. Such supervisory powers are not expressly provided for under French law but, since the 'comité' must be compulsorily consulted on matters which related to the organisation or general running of the establishment,[463] it has been found that these 'matters' sometimes originate from agreements etc. The end result is therefore that there is in practice an element of 'supervision' in the 'comité' although this term is not used. No doubt this sort of function must exist in Britain, but this writer has not come across it in the sample examined.

Both this and the previous function were the subject of discussion and a majority of the British sample, though small (52 per cent), considered that these two supervisory duties could be included in the list of functions of works councils. Any legislation on these two aspects will, it is suggested, duplicate the functions of the works council because a lot of the welfare matters will come under the aspect of 'controlling the management' already discussed. The same would apply to the second supervisory power proposed immediately above. Nevertheless what may appear as a duplication is in fact proposed as an additional safeguard, and also as an additional ground for the works council to be vigilant of existing welfare matters in legislation or collective agreement.

A critical analysis of the different aspects of management functions in the different countries, along with a comparison, was made. Also analysed were some aspects of the consultative and supervisory functions which exist, and in the case of all these, submissions were made on law reform in Britain. The various problems and difficulties which were found to exist in the other countries were examined in order that they be avoided in this country. It is now proposed to examine, analyse and where appropriate make submissions on the remaining functions. These are the receiving of information, and the expression of opinion, the examination and the power of suggestion resulting from consultation.

Belgian law provides that the 'conseil d'entreprise' must receive financial information on the state of the establishment. A productivity report (at least quarterly) and periodical reports on the trading position of the company must also be given.[464]

An analysis of this provision must be made by attempting to answer two questions. Firstly, why is it necessary that such provision *does* exist in Belgium and France, and why is it necessary that similar provisions should also exist in Britain? Secondly, what is the nature of the information which should be given in each of these countries?

In order to answer the first of these questions one should, it is submitted, look at the spirit behind these provisions. The whole is tied up with the concept underlying the functions of works councils — this being that the supply of such information is a vehicle for communication which constitutes an important means of providing a climate of reciprocal understanding and in consequence co-operation within the establishment.[465] One may even go beyond this and say that understanding and co-operation are also essential to the future economic well-being of the country, and that therefore they would contribute in creating a *psychological* climate[466] favourable to achieving such an aim. It must be remembered that it is the workers who are the motive power behind the production process, and therefore they should be kept informed if, from a human point of view, morale is to be kept high and, from an economic point of view, production is to improve.

There is a further reason why such provision does and should exist. By keeping the 'conseil' regularly informed of the financial state of the establishment, not only will the spirit of collaboration be enhanced, but it enables the 'conseil' to be in a better position to express an opinion and to make more realistic suggestions (or objections) on the conditions of work, its organisation and productivity. In other words there is, it is submitted, substantial relevance in the relationship between art. 15(b) and art. 15(a);[465] [466] the fulfilment of article 15(b) giving article 15(a) its full significance.

This relationship which it is submitted exists in Belgium between arts. 15(a) and 15(b) has its counterpart in France in that the French 'comité' must receive financial information to enable it to study the measures envisaged by the employer (and the employees' suggestions) with a view to improving productivity, and accordingly to expressing its opinion to the employer.[467] It is considered however that this provision is not as spelt out in France as it is in Belgium. A certain element of convergence is however apparent between these two countries' laws.

In Britain there exists no legislation which provides that works councils should be given such information (though there does exist legislation for such information to be given to recognised unions in negotiating committees).[468] It is found however that financial information on the company periodically given to some works councils and the relationship discussed above between financial information and a better understanding, does occasionally occur.[469] On the other hand some management on works councils who were interviewed expressed the opinion that to divulge financial information would be detrimental to the future of the company and anyway it was not the province of works councils to know the details of the company's financial affairs.[470] This argument cannot be accepted by this writer for two reasons. Firstly, because the balance sheet of a public company is anyway published and secondly, and more important, it hinders the psychological element upon the employees which has been described above. For these reasons it is therefore submitted that legislation provide, as it does in the other countries examined, that financial information on the state of the enterprise be given at least annually.[471] An overwhelming majority of works council members interviewed would wish to see such a situation being *generalised* in Britain.

Having attempted an anlysis on the meaning and impact of the financial information, an attempt must now be made at answering the second question, namely what is the information relevant to the financial aspects which should be given (for consultative purposes only) in each of these countries.

There exists a legal requirement in Belgium that the employer must provide quarterly (1) a productivity report, as well as (2) general information relating to the enterprise. Of the sample of 'conseils d'entreprise' examined, it is found that each of these reports are given *viva voce*.[472] The reason for this is that there exists more freedom for discussion and there is no permanent record made.

Productivity reports inspected related to a number of facets: (a) the work organisation in the establishment, (b) the best means of improving the organisation, (c) production of the various categories of workers, and (d) how to improve such production.[473] It was generally agreed by the sample interviewed that the giving of these reports greatly enhanced the work of the 'conseil' in giving its opinion and making suggestions on these matters.

A variety within each of these facets have been found, so that in three cases, time and motion experts were brought in to examine and suggest improvements at the request of a works council, in two others a study of the productivity potential of units of workers was made, and comparisons were made with the national average — a most complicated exercise — and in four others, with other units in the same establishment, — a much simpler exercise. It is also found that each employer has his individual way of presenting his report on these matters and a great variety has been found to exist from one 'conseil' to another.

It is found that there is a legal requirement in Belgium for the employer to give, concurrently with the productivity report, general information on production and related matters.[474] Each of these matters has been closely examined during the course of meetings attended. It is a striking feature that because the information is given orally and that therefore no written report appears, the members of the 'conseil' are not given the opportunity to analyse in depth the contents. All they can rely on, and ask questions on in order to clarify matters, is what has been said by the employer. The sample examined was asked whether they found this oral report satisfactory. Fifty-three per cent said that it was not, but the remainder considered that it was. This latter group thought that the information so given was sufficient for their purposes. At most of the meetings the employer gives his appreciation of the *state of production* within the establishment, and comments briefly on whether or not the target has been reached and compares it with the production in his last report and at the equivalent time the previous year. Another topic relates to the *total cost of production* and of *manufacture* and *sales campaigns* in the enterprise. At most meetings these are expressed in percentages, but some are given in round figures. It was also found that in some cases the details given are greater than in others; some of the more detailed examples are the cost of raw materials, the cost of running the machines, wages, heating and electricity charges. The *company order book* is another topic upon which the employer gives such information as the delay periods in meeting orders, when these will be met etc., and finally *competition* in the particular field has also been found to be a topic of information and such matters as imports of raw materials, exports, and comparisons with competitors are often discussed. Though statute does specify the matters to be given to the 'conseil' this obviously is a guide and it is found that each 'conseil' adapts the statute to suit its requirements. In France a similar situation has been found to exist and at the meetings of 'comités' more or less the same information is given by the employer. One striking difference was however found and that is that since the law[475] does not require the information to be given orally, a number of employers prepare a brief outline on some or all of the matters discussed above. Thus every quarter the employer is compelled to inform the 'comité' on any or all of the state of production, orders received, measures relating to improvement, the renewal or alteration of equipment, methods of production etc.

There exists no statutory requirement for such information to be given in Britain, but it has been found in practice that some or most of the above topics are given to works councils for their information.[476] It is however found that this is by no means universal. It is for this reason that it is considered necessary that legislation provides for a minimum of information to be given on the above topics. It is recommended firstly that any proposed legislation be as general as possible, and similar to the laws which exist in Belgium and France, thus allowing room for each establishment to adapt it to its own requirements. Secondly, as a result of interviews held in Belgium (and the dissatisfaction expressed) (see above) and in this country (as to the desirability for such legislation) there is unanimous agreement that the information should be put briefly in writing so as to allow members of the works council to study and digest the material and thus be in a better position to give their opinion.

In addition to the financial, production and general information relating to this latter, there is a further requirement for information to be given to the 'conseil' in Belgium. The employer must provide yearly a balance sheet, profit and loss account, performance of the enterprise, production costs etc., a comparison between the performance of the company with that during the two preceding years, and an explanation of changes in the enterprise.[477]

It is found that this information, like the quarterly information on production etc.[478] is given orally, and is discussed at meetings. Unlike the quarterly information however there is a legal requirement that the report be confirmed in writing.[479] A number of these reports examined indicate that they are written in strikingly simple and clear language, and are very general in form. It was found that the reason for this was to facilitate its understanding to the most simple of minds! It was also found that the majority of these reports contain percentages rather than figures between the total cost of production or manufacture and profits, though it is a common feature to find in them figures relating to overheads of the establishment. It is also found that the information given on total production and manufacturing costs, and the consequent results upon the company as a whole, is not dissimilar to the quarterly information given. In a number of cases there has been found to be a condensation of the quarterly reports, with a subsequent analysis and explanation of the variations which existed from one quarter to another.[480] The reason why the 'conseil' is given information on the comparative results of the company's performance as compared to the preceding two years, and an explanation on this, is to give an overall view of the general performance of the company.

An interesting feature existing in Belgium and in France is that the type of supporting documents to the report varies with the nature of the company, so that limited liability companies must attach to their report a full statement of the profit and loss account, the board and accountant's report; in other companies all that has to be attached to the report is what the legal requirements for such companies demand.[481] In the smaller private companies it was found that the requirement is only what is customary for the employer to provide. All these documents must be communicated to the 'conseil' fifteen days before the annual general meeting of the company in the case of limited liability companies, and in all other companies that do not have an annual general meeting, at the most six months following the end of the financial year.[482] Auditors may also be appointed to check and certify as correct the various documents and financial reports.[483] The information to be given to the 'conseil' is extensive, but despite the great number of documents inspected, it was found that they were clearly set out, well explained, and easy to follow.

A comparison with the French requirements shows that these latter are not as demanding. The 'comité' must be compulsorily informed by means of an annual general report of the activities of the establishment.[484] Of the small sample of documents examined the contents of the report talked of the establishment's turnover, the overall production results, sales figures, salaries (with percentages on rises), company investments, and future planning. There is a similar legal requirement to

Belgium in the case of limited liability companies. The 'comité' must be given the profit and loss account, the annual balance sheet and the auditors' report *before* (though there is no specified time as in Belgium) they are presented to the shareholders. The 'comité' may summon the company auditors to hear their opinion on the different documents and on the financial situation of the establishment. The 'comité's' comments must compulsorily be brought to the notice of shareholders in the annual general meeting. As is the case in Belgium the 'comité' may call upon the services of a chartered accountant paid by the establishment to check the documents.[484] There exists therefore a considerable element of convergence between the two countries, but perusal of the various documents within the small sample in each of these shows that a greater degree of sophistication and detail exists in Belgian reports etc. than it does in France, and generally speaking more information is given in Belgium.

There being no statutory requirements to provide information of this nature in Britain, of all the works councils it is found that though information is sometimes given,[485] the wealth of information which is supplied in France and Belgium with a few exceptions[486] is lacking in Britain.

A sample of members of works councils in Belgium were asked if they considered the mass of information given annually really helped them in their functions; 51 per cent considered that it did not. There was far too much material given and at times the picture became confused. The remainder thought they wanted to hold on to the legal right which has been given to them, despite the great amount of material which most of them admitted was confusing. The majority therefore felt that a simplified form giving all the relevant information would be more acceptable. The French sample exained considered that the information given was adequate for their purpose but considered the safeguards, i.e. appointment of auditors, appeals etc.,[487] though necessary, very cumbersome. The various alternatives based on the French and Belgian experience were put to a sample of works council members in Britain and the majority, though they felt that more information could be given annually, did not consider it necessary to have the detail that is given in other countries. Basically what they would wish to have is the annual report of the company giving such details as profit and loss account, production and marketing performance against competitors, future trends, investments, rationalisation projects etc.[488] All these should be put in a simplified way so that it could be transmitted to all employees. In other words, they do not want to see the detailed information which has by statute to be given to negotiators or shareholders[489] but a short, concise and simple report based on that information. It is therefore recommended that legislation in Britain so provides.

The consultative functions where the expression of opinion, the examination of certain matters and suggestions made as a result give the representative institutions in the different countries a power of *intervention* in the running of the establishment, but not a power of decision. Such power of decision in all countries examined rests, without exception, entirely with the employer. Of the sample of employees interviewed in the countries under examination, none stated that he (the employer) did not analyse and given serious consideration to the opinions, suggestions, observations and criticisms made by the representative institutions.[490] This 'serious consideration' has invariably been found to take place among the employers who examine the opinions, suggestions or criticisms of the representative institutions with some degree of objectivity and consideration from the employees' point of view. In order to check these findings, a survey was carried out by asking employee representatives in each of the countries whether they found that the employer 'seriously considered' the respective representative institutions' opinions etc. It was found that in Belgium 82 per cent of the sample thought that the employer 'seriously considered' the 'conseil's' opinions etc., 12 per cent stated that the employer considered *most* but not all opinions, and the remainder thought that the employer considered only some. In France 73 per cent thought that the employer 'seriously considered' the 'comités' opinions, 10 per cent thought that the employer considered *most* of them, and the remainder thought that the employer considered a few of these opinions only when it suited the employer. In Britain the same questions asked produced 63 per cent, 13 per cent and 24 per cent. It becomes quite clear therefore that in Britain employers do not take as much notice of works councils' opinions etc. as in the other countries. This writer would suggest that the reason for this is that whereas legislation in France and Belgium provides that consultation must take place, there exists no such legislation in Britain; therefore the employer is not as ready to 'seriously consider' opinions after consulting his works council. In other words, though he accepts the works council as a body for *inter alia* consultation purposes, there is no statutory compulsion for him to 'seriously consider' certain matters for consultation which as we shall see exist in the other countries examined. It is of course accepted that no amount of legislation will compel any employer to 'seriously consider' any matter; the psychological effect will however be there, and awareness of the matters upon which consultation must be sought will be enumerated rather than leaving these matters to circumstance. It is with this in mind that proposals for legislation on specific subjects for consultation will later be made.

First, however, it is proposed to examine what topics have been found to be matters for consultation in each of the countries under consideration.

The Belgian 'conseil' has to be consulted on a number of topics specified by statute[491] (also considered in the national collective agreement).[492] Statute implies that the 'conseil' must not only be consulted but must also show some initiative by expressing opinions and by making suggestions or objections on a given matter. The statute, however, does not, in the writer's opinion, go so far as to allow the 'conseil' to take any action on these suggestions, opinions, advice etc. upon the recalcitrant employer. In other words there is *no* way of compelling the employer to accept the 'conseil's' opinions etc. In the first group of matters[493] upon which the employer must consult, this latter is confined to the statutory requirements. *Prima facie* these may seem very limited, but enquiries carried out show that, being generic, a great number of matters may be brought under each. Consultation must take place on all matters relating to the *organisation of work*. Investigations were made to find out what kinds of topics were treated under this heading. It was found that these included such matters as the optimum use made of scrap metal, pieces of glass, tobacco leaf remnants etc., the division of work among different categories or even the same category of employees, the different shift systems and organisation within each of these, methods of production and methods to save production time, the best qualified persons to carry out certain duties such as cleaning, servicing and adjusting machinery and when that should be done etc. Consultation must also take place on all matters relating to *conditions of work*. Again, investigation showed that such matters as coffee or refreshment and lunch break times and duration, the starting and finishing times (after the total weekly amounts were agreed through collective bargaining, which is not the province of the 'conseil' or of this research), rest times and rest rooms and cloakroom facilities, were discussed at various times. Finally, in the first group, consultation on *matters relating to production* must take place. In this area it was found that such matters as company productivity and methods to improve productivity were discussed.

Enquiries were made to find out whether the employer always

consulted the 'conseil' in all three of the statutory matters. It was found that though in the majority of cases the employer did so consult the 'conseil', in other cases it was the 'conseil' itself which put forward in its agenda for the following meeting questions relating to these three matters. It may therefore be said that a high proportion of employers do not consult on these matters unless specifically asked to do so.

Statute also provides for a second group of matters upon which consultation may take place,[494] namely an *opinion* or a *report* on all points of view expressed on all economic matters upon which the 'conseil' has competence and is referred to it by either the 'conseil central de l'économie' or the relevant 'conseil professionnel'. *Prima facie* this statutory provision seems to indicate that the 'conseil' is entitled to have such consultative matters referred to it. This is not so since it was found firstly that none of the 'conseils' examined has ever had such matters referred to it, and secondly, the 'conseil' has no initiative to demand that consultation be given to it on such matters. It can only do so if it has been *invited* to express an opinion or make a report. The article of the statute, it is submitted, is quite ineffective in this particular field mainly because of its restrictive terminology.[495]

Finally, the 'conseil' has consultative powers on all matters concerning the criterion for recruitment[496] of workers.[497] This research shows that the 'conseils' concern themselves only in determining the general criteria upon which future recruitments are to take place. In no 'conseil' examined, was it found that they had any say in *who* was to be recruited. It is furthermore found that recruitments are made according to the individual qualifications of the worker concerned and that therefore the 'conseil' has little say. It is only in cases where two 'workers' have identical qualifications that the criteria laid down[498] are followed. The 'conseil' can thus examine the possibility of laying down certain rules upon the criteria to be followed on collective recruitment, and the employer invariably adopts in whole or in part the recommendation of the 'conseil',

No such *specific* provisions exist in France for consultation to take place in these three specified areas, but general provisions do exist in relation to some,[499] and it is found in France that some of these consultative powers are often enlarged by collective agreements.[500] Yet the French 'comité' has consultative powers which do not exist in the Belgian legislative provisions. Thus where a collective agreement does not provide for the period of holidays with pay, this must be done by the employer who takes into account the customary rules in the trade, after consultation with the 'comité d'entreprise'.[501] One case has been found in the course of this research giving competence to the 'comité' to deal with matters relating to salaries.[502] This is an isolated case which cannot be considered as good law; it was decided upon its particular facts. Another example is that in joint stock companies two members of the 'comité d'entreprise' must attend in a consultative capacity all meetings of the 'conseil d'administration' or 'conseil de surveillance'.[503] The 'comités' may also give their opinion on any proposed price increase, and may be consulted on the fixing of prices.[504] Another consultative function of the 'comité' relates to the general problems of apprenticeship, industrial training and retraining. Where more than 300 employees are employed the 'comité' is compelled to create a sub-committee to be responsible for the study of problems arising from training and retraining, apprenticeship, and the work of women and young persons.[505] Although this has not been found to exist as a general rule in the sample examined, in matters of social security the 'comité' appoints 'correspondants d'entreprise des caisses primaires',[506] on a consultative basis.[507] It may therefore be said that the consultative functions of the French 'comité' lie over a wider field than those of the Belgian 'conseil', though there do exist some consultative functions in Belgium which are not provided for by French legislation.[508]

Some of these consultative functions which exist in Belgium and in France have also been found in Britain.[509] These are however sparse and legislation should provide for a list of matters upon which British works councils should be consulted. It is not proposed to repeat the above matters, but the list should include each of them, apart from the appointment of works council members in local social security offices. This would cause, it is thought,[510] a hindrance in the running of such schemes. Nor should there be representation of the works council on the board of management (or supervisory boards if as a result of the Bullock Report (January 1977) these are eventually instituted in Britain). In addition, it is submitted that within the genera of conditions and organisation of work[511] the matters be more specifically enumerated, thus avoiding the situation of too great a generalisation which was found to exist particularly in Belgium. Matters which in Britain persons interviewed specifically asked to see in any legislation on consultation are job evaluation, the takeover or closure of an establishment, important organisational changes within the undertaking, alteration or curtailment in the activities of the establishment, the introduction of technical devices which are used to control worker performance or punctuality (i.e. clock-in devices), and any agreements on long-term co-operation proposed to be entered into with another firm.[512]

In France the 'comité d'entreprise' may form separate ad hoc committees to examine problems which arise,[513] and it is empowered to appoint experts from outside the members of the 'comité' but from company employees, and in an advisory capacity. Any reports and recommendations made by the *ad hoc* committees are submitted for the consideration of the 'comité d'entreprise'.[514] These experts are subject to professional secrecy on all matters relating to the process of manufacture and with regard to information of a confidential nature given by the employer.[515] Whereas the French law provides for *ad hoc* committees to examine any problems which might arise, the Belgian law provides for a subdivision of the 'conseil d'entreprise'.[516] It is found however that any subdivisions which sometimes exist do not have the power of the 'conseil d'entreprise' and those examined were created in order to study a certain problem and report back to the 'conseil', to enquire into any matters given to it by the conseil and, in one instance, minor executive powers were given to it. Although it would appear *prima facie* that the subdivision of the 'conseil d'entreprise is part of it, it is more like the French *ad hoc* committee of the 'comité', except that a subdivision of the 'conseil' invariably consists of appointed members of the 'comité' and members appointed by management. In both these countries it is found that the 'comités' or 'conseils' take very little advantage of this provision.

No legislation regulates this aspect in Britain but in practice it is found that works councils or other similar bodies have associate committees[517] which report back to the works councils. As is the case of the other countries under examination it is found in Britain that associate committees seldom exist. The convergent element is implicit. It is submitted that legislation should provide for the sub-committee possibility[518] and the appointment of experts in difficult cases.[519] Such provision would leave establishments free, as at present, to institute such bodies if they so wish. The advantage of such legislation is that it will create awareness of this possibility, as well as provide a more complete piece of legislation.

Finally the French 'comité' exercises quasi-judicial functions, by acting as a disciplinary body for its members,[520] the 'délégué du personnel',[521] the 'conseiller chef du travail'[522] and the factory doctor.[523] Of the sample examined, no case of this nature was heard by the 'comité'. Nor is this considered an important function. A parallel has not been found either in Belgium or in Britain and such a function is not considered important enough to suggest for an equivalent in Britain.

Section vi. Conclusions

It is found that the statutes on 'comités' or 'conseils' in each of the countries examined have considerably helped towards the spirit of co-operation and collaboration so essential between the employer and his employees.[524] Of this there is no doubt and both employers and employees readily admit of the success of the relevant legislation. It is indeed one of the reasons[525] why Luxembourg has recently enacted a statute creating for the first time the concept of the 'comité mixte';[526] it is also one of the reasons[527] that the European works council has been proposed. The submissions made throughout this part for similar legislation to be enacted in Britain is based on the firm belief that this spirit of collaboration, so essential to British industry, will be greatly enhanced. The time is now ripe for Britain to be thinking in these terms, despite the fact that no firm commitment has been put forward in this sphere by any of the main political parties.[528] It has been shown that some convergence exists in practice within the works council systems in Britain, and furthermore this research shows that the convergence which exists between the other countries examined, the proposed European works council and Britain is considerable. Legislation would increase and make more general the institution of the works council in Britain and would bring a rapprochement between employers and employees and consequently help ameliorate industrial relations within the establishment (see also preface). A works council would therefore have as its principal task the crystallisation of the spirit of collaboration which it is essential should exist between employer and his employees. The functions now attributable to works councils in Britain, and the submissions made in this research for reform, are based mainly on consultation with powers of decision making in certain welfare matters, thus putting no fetters firstly on the authority of the employer upon whom lies the responsibility of running the enterprise, secondly upon free collective bargaining, or thirdly on any other form of participation[529] which might come about. The works council is considered to be the pinion from which a good industrial relations system emanates, and can do a great deal more for industrial relations than any other form of participation. It is the small yet powerful cogwheel which creates good industrial relations and which engages with the larger one of participation.

Another reason why works councils should be put on a statutory basis in Britain is that a greater degree of convergence will exist between Britain and the other countries examined, and will also pave the way (as has Luxembourg legislation) towards the proposed European works council of the European company.

This research shows that there is a large measure of agreement (with possible reservations on the part of some employers in regard to the disclosure of information on financial and economic matters) on the necessity to consult, give information and give management powers in limited fields to workers. In the little-explored domain[530] of the works council there is scope for further but cautious[531] exploration, and the drawing up of legal contours to bring in, expand and generalise this institution throughout industry and commerce.

The main advantage in generalising works councils in Britain has been stated to be the development of the spirit of collaboration between employers and workers (this of course is essential as a basis for a rapprochement and the amelioration of industrial relations within the establishment which must be the intention upon which the structure of the proposed statute is drafted). There are however secondary advantages which automatically come out of the consolidation of the spirit of collaboration; these are respect for the dignity of work, the awareness of values which are at the basis of the hierarchy, a definition of rights and obligations concerning all the members of the enterprise, the safeguard of mutual esteem in the daily relationship between employer and employee, and the implication for the whole of the elected works council members and for labour generally of an undeniable social promotion. It is envisaged that the spirit in which the proposed British statutory works council will function is the key to its success and to its future influence upon industrial relations. The above optimism is based on the experience of the other countries examined, which have since the end of the Second World War had legislation on similar institutions. Legislation in these countries has been the object of progressive and dynamic application[532] and generalisation of the institutions, and this research shows that where they exist 'comités' or 'conseils' function well within the limits given to them by the respective statutes.

During the course of this research a large number of the sample in Britain have objected to legislation being enacted because, they say, of the rigidity which it would bring about. This of course is a valid argument, but it is considered to be the lesser of two evils. There is no doubt that statute is indispensable where manifestly (as has been shown in this research) one cannot rely on a sufficiently generalised voluntary institution of works councils throughout British industry. Legislation should in no way prevent existing and voluntary works councils from functioning in the way agreed (and this point was succinctly made), nor should legislation prevent voluntary agreements from being entered into so as to take into account the contingencies of the particular establishment, as for example has been seen in Belgium[533] or in France.[534] It will be recalled that the Belgian 1958 agreement, as amended, attempts to make more precise the legislative provisions on certain matters,[535] and even to correct, in some instances, the statute[536] itself. Did not the Belgian 'convention collective du 4 décembre 1970 concernant l'information et la consultation des conseils d'entreprise sur les perspectives générales de l'entreprise et les questions de l'emploi dans celle-ci' provide the basis for mandatory application by the 'arrêté du 22 janvier 1971'? Statute, in the case of works councils would, it is envisaged, provide a framework only and it will be up to the parties themselves to see what they will do with it. One cannot speculate at this stage. The British works council is envisaged as being called upon to evolve and develop its functions within the framework of the enterprise whose social and to a lesser extent economic aspects, will no doubt substantially rub on to the works council.

The proposed statutory works council, being an organ of *co-operation* and *collaboration*, will (and does) distinguish itself from the negotiating bodies whose functions are totally different. The negotiating bodies' functions are collective bargaining whereas those of the works council are the expansion of the spirit of co-operation which *excludes* collective bargaining. The two functions are totally distinct and should remain so.[537] The works council does not and cannot replace the negotiating bodies — these latter to be effective must receive their power from a healthy, vigilant, constructive and vigorous trade union. The former's powers are limited mainly to consultation and to representation of all the employees within the establishment. As was suggested above[538] there is room for both, and one complements the other.

Notes

1. Investigations carried out show that in practice (though not in theory) 'délégués du personnel' do not play as important a role as the 'délégués syndicaux'. In this writer's opinion there exist the beginnings of an apparent withering away of the institution of the 'délégué du personnel'. The increase in the 'délégués syndicaux' is apparent from the figures released by the French Ministry of Social Affairs. Firms employing 50 to 149 employees have a 23 per cent representation; 150 to 299, 50 per cent representation; 300 to 1,000, 72 per cent representation; and firms employing over 1,000, 92 per cent representation. An increase in union representation is also discernible within the industries themselves. In the chemical industry, 54 per cent representation; in the metallurgical industry, 51 per cent; in the engineering

construction industry, 48; per cent in the paper industry, 39 per cent; in the textile industry, 34 per cent; in banking, 34 per cent; in public health and commerce, 29 per cent in each; in the furniture industry, 27 per cent; in the entertainment industry, 26 per cent and in the public works, 20 per cent. (See Notes du Ministère d'Etat Chargé des Affaires Sociales, November 1972.) A survey by J.P. Bachy, F. Dupuy and D. Martin, under the direction of G. Adam, indicates that the number of 'sections syndicales' increases with the size of the company. So that companies employing from 50 to 149 employees have one or two 'sections', whereas half of those employing over 500 employees have some five 'sections'. (See 'Représentation et Négotiation dans l'Entreprise', Université de Paris-Sud, 1974, p. 53).

2. CIR Study No. 4, 'Worker participation and collective bargaining in Europe' (1974), p. 50, makes this point in relation to the private sector 'comités d'entreprise' in 1972. 'The major general confederations . . . between them controlled 54 per cent of the seats on the enterprise committee.' It must also be remembered that the role of trade unions has not been neglected, since it will be recalled that they play an important part in the election and removal of 'délégués du personnel' and members of the 'comité d'entreprise'. See also Adam, 'La représentativité syndicale dans l'entreprise', Droit Social 1972, 90.

3. By ordonnance du 22 février 1945 and loi du 16 mai 1946. Since then a number of amendments have been made, i.e. loi du 12 août 1950, 7 décembre 1951, 9 juin 1954 and 18 juin 1966. This is what Professor P. Durand calls 'la troisième phase de l'évolution', Droit du Travail vol. III. 'La représentation des travailleurs sur le plan de l'entreprise dans le droit des pays membres de la CECA', p. 205. The reason why there have been two Acts so close to each other is that the 1945 legislation (ordonnance) which instituted the 'comités d'entreprise' was made by the provisional government following advice of the Consultative Assembly. The government however did not follow the approach recommended by the assembly and the ordonnance was a watered-down version of this advice. This displeased the trade unions. When the provisional government's power to legislate through ordonnances expired, the assembly voted in a new law (that of 16 May 1946) which took into account most of the previous advice given by the assembly. What Durand calls the third phase starts at the time of the French liberation. During the war efforts were made to associate workers to the production effort through the creation of 'comités mixtes à la production'. These committees had a consultative role only and their functions were limited to problems of a technical nature. They merely studied the suggestions made by the employees in order to improve production and proposed the ones which they considered valid — the committees acted as a filter. The 'comités de gestion' were created during the French occupation in cases where the employer was arrested etc. for being a collaborator. These committees managed the enterprise. The other two phases, according to Durand, were the institution of the 'délégués ouvriers' up to 1936 and from then on to 1945 the 'comités sociaux d'établissement' created under the 'charte du travail' (loi du 4 octobre 1941) whose main function was to collaborate with management and improve the conditions of employees and their families (Durand, op. cit., pp. 203–5). It should be noted that all 'conventions collectives susceptibles d'extension' should include a clause concerning the establishment of a 'comité d'entreprise'. (loi du 11 février 1950, art. 31g (5). Code du Travail, livre 1).

4. Loi du 16 mai 1946, art. 1.
5. Agriculture was originally excluded by the 1946 Act, but it is now included

under loi du 18 juin 1966.
6. e.g. Charbonnage de France, Houillères de Bassin, RATP, Gaz et Electricité de France, ets. Renault; in banking (Banque de France, Comptoir National d'escompte, Banque Nationale pour le commerce et l'industrie, Société générale, Crédit Lyonnais); in insurance (la Séquanaise, l'Union, l'Urbaine, l'Aigle, le Phénix, le Soleil, la Nationale); in engineering (industrie aéronautique); in transport (SNCF, Air France, Compagnie générale transatlantique) etc. The reason why the 'comités d'entreprise' only apply to the private sector is that the public-sector industries have employee representatives on their 'conseils d'administration', one-third of the membership consisting of employees. Representation through a 'comité d'entreprise' would therefore be futile. This research indicates however that the organisation of the 'conseils d'entreprise' differs according to the industry since there is no one statute regulating all nationalised industries. It is found therefore (collective agreements excepted, see p. 36 ante) that the statutes instituting a particular nationalised industry sometimes do not provide for the institution of 'comités d'entreprise' because the 'conseil d'administration' has autonomy over all economic, social and technical matters. Sometimes 'comités d'entreprise' have been created by statute, but with limited powers, subject to the 'conseil d'administration'. Sometimes the 'comité d'entreprise' has been replaced by some other body with limited powers.
See also P. Durand, 'La représentation des travailleurs sur le plan de l'entreprise en droit français' in 'La représentation des travailleurs sur le plan de l'entreprise dans le droit des pays membres de la CECA', p. 210.
7. Art. 1, al. 1.
8. See the two statements made by the 'section des travaux publics' of 17 June 1947 and 19 October 1948.
9. In 'La reforme des comités d'entreprises', JCP 1946, vol. 1, p. 570.
10. Amiaud, 'Comités d'entreprise', RATP. See also the conclusions of the avocat Général Rolland, in Cour de Paris, 3 November 1955, Droit Ouvrier 1956, p. 25.
11. e.g. Durand, 'La constitution des comités d'entreprise dans les services publics de caractère industriel et commercial'. Droit Social 1954, p. 680; Rouast et Durand, 'Précis de législation industrielle', no. III; P. de Guay, 'La constitution et le fonctionnement des comités d'entreprise dans le secteur public', Revue Française du Travail, Sept/Oct. 1949, pp. 480 et seq.
12. See JO, 23 July 1947 and 30 January 1948, replies to written parliamentary questions nos. 501 and 551.
13. The Trade Union and Labour Relations Act 1974 repealed the Industrial Relations Act 1971, consequently the NIRC was abolished, the office of Registrar of Trade Unions and Employees' Associations was also abolished, the CIR was replaced by the ACAS, instituted as a statutory body by the Employment Protection legislation, and the Employment Appeal Tribunal took the place of the NIRC. Had, for example, the new legislation not provided for alternative bodies (as indeed happened on a temporary basis with the NIRC, before the EAT was instituted) it would be impossible to deduce that bodies instituted by previous legislation remained operative despite the repeal.
14. In 'Houillères' and 'Charbonnages' the powers of the 'comités' are limited in social matters to the directives of the 'conseil d'administration' and in economic matters to a report on production, and the 'comité' can only make suggestions to improve production.
15. Both Charbonnages de France and Houillères de Bassin have concluded a collective agreement with the appropriate trade unions constituting 'comités

d'entreprise'. On the other hand Gaz de France and Electricité de France have negotiated no such agreement. This writer found that the possibility of instituting 'comités d'entreprise' was discussed in these establishments but it was decided that such an institution would be of little value because the personnel is represented on the 'conseil d'administration'. In a number of other establishments in the public sector it was found that 'comités' are of little value (see e.g. note 14 above) since the employees are represented on various committees, e.g. conseils d'administration, comités consultatifs and comités de gestion, which cover all and even a greater number of the functions of the comité d'entreprise. See also the ICE of 1956, p. 867, which gives a comprehensive list of public sector enterprises which have a 'comité d'entreprise' or other similar body.

16. Art. 2 décret du 3 février 1955, JO 6 février 1955, and art. 6 arrêté du 10 octobre 1955, JO 21 octobre 1955.
17. Décret du 3 février 1955, JO 6 février 1955.
18. A detailed study of these types of committee is irrelevant for the purposes of this research.
19. i.e. such as the making of suggestions for the increase of production or its improvement. See e.g. art. 33 of the Statut National du Personnel des Industries Electriques et Gazières.
20. See e.g. loi du 21 mars 1948 where the employees of the conseil d'administration of RATP (Régie Autonome des Transports Parisiens) take part in the running of the enterprise. Eight (out of some twenty-five members on the conseil) employee representatives represent the different kinds of personnel in the establishment. These are divided as follows: three persons representing management, clerical staff and foremen, one representing the directors, and four representing the blue-collar workers.
21. Loi du 20 septembre 1948.
22. Art. 14 of loi du 20 septembre 1948 provided '... des conseils d'entreprise sont institués dans toutes les entreprises occupant d'une manière permanente au moins 50 travailleurs'.

    The 1948 legislator has therefore provided a minimum below which a conseil d'entreprise is not mandatory. By so doing a preferable solution was adopted to that which was initially envisaged, namely where the Executive would be entrusted, without any guidance, to fix the minimum number of employees. The legislator has obviously chosen 'progression' as his theme, since in 1950 only enterprises employing more than 200 employees were compelled to form 'conseils d'entreprise'. This 'progression' was to take place at different stages, thus progressively reducing the number of employees. It appears however that suddenly there was a change of policy (in 1954), because by loi du 15 mars 1954 (see Moniteur Belge of 2 April 1954) it was left to the Executive to determine the future stages, after advice had been sought from the conseil national du travail. The most representative trade unions (i.e. FGTB, CSC and CGSLB) represented on the 'conseil national du travail' asked the council to intervene and ask the Minister of Labour to decrease, by regulation, the number of workers to 150 as the minimum before a 'conseil d'entreprise' be instituted. Arrêté du 6 octobre 1958 so provided. See also loi du 17 février 1971.
23. 'Délégations syndicales du personnel' are to be found in companies employing over twenty employees. These delegations have rights of individual and collective representation of *union* members within the establishment, and are based nationally on an interprofessional collective agreement concluded in the 'conseil national du travail' in 1971. Subsequent industry-wide collective agreements based on the 1971 document were concluded and some have been ratified by royal decree. Workers are either elected or

nominated by the union members of the most representative unions within the establishment. In the private sector, these are the Fédération Générale du Travail de Belgique (with some 1,080,000 members); the Confédération des Syndicats Chrétiens (with some 970,000 members); and the Centrale Générale des Syndicats Libéraux de Belgique (with some 149,000 members). The 'délégations syndicales du personnel' must be informed of proposed changes in terms and conditions of employment and wages, and an opportunity must be given to them to make representations on such matters.

24. Loi du 23 janvier 1975 and arrêtés royaux du 24 janvier 1975.
25. 'Il est bien évident que la loi du 20 décembre 1948 ne vise que les entreprises industrielles et commerciales, c'est-à-dire celles dans lesquelles il y a recherche d'un gain matériel. En effet:

   (a) l'article 15a dispose notamment que les conseils d'entreprise donnent leur avis sur les mesures qui pourraient modifier le rendement de l'entreprise;
   (b) l'article 15b prévoit la communication périodique au conseil de documents sur les résultats d'exploitation obtenus par l'entreprise;
   (c) l'article 19 relatif aux conditions d'éligibilité fait allusion à l'occupation pendant trois ans 'dans la branche d'activité' dont relève l'entreprise.

   Les dispositions prévues aux (a) et (c) n'ont aucun sens si elles ne visent pas les entreprises industrielles et commerciales.

   (d) l'article 24 dispose notamment que les contestations résultant de l'application de la loi et de ses arrêtés d'exécution sont tranchées par la commission paritaire ou le conseil professionnel compétent. Or, les commissions paritaires sont créées pour l'industrie, le commerce et l'agriculture (arrêté-loi du 9 juin 1945, art. 1a).'
26. Minister of Economic Affairs.
27. In a Ghent conseil professionnel case (CPA Grand (0) 28 novembre 1955) it was held that when an enterprise has two commercial or industrial branches, at which in one branch tobacco is manufactured into cigars, and in the other the sales and administrative machinery is put into operation, there exist two different 'unités techniques d'exploitation'. On the other hand, the Brussels Commission Paritaire held that where different services or sections within an enterprise are geared towards the same aim (in this case paper manufacturing) on the same premises, the different sections must be considered as one entity. There would therefore only be one 'conseil d'entreprise' constituted. (CPA Bruxelles (E), 4 octobre 1955.)
28. There exist 88 commissions paritaires d'industrie in Belgium each for the different industries. Under loi du 20 septembre 1948, art. 24, as amended by loi du 18 mars 1950, loi du 15 juin 1953 and that of 15 mars 1954, the competent commission paritaire or the conseil professionel will decide the criteria for the establishment of a conseil d'entreprise. Other matters relating to 'conseils d'entreprise' are referred to the labour courts.
29. The conseils professionels, of which there are nine, perform the same function as the commissions paritaires in the trade field.
30. Monsieur Harmel, during the Parliamentary debates, seemed to hold a similar opinion. He said that where two branches of an establishment were situated far apart, then two conseils d'entreprise should be instituted. 'L'éloignement des divers centres d'activité contribue', he said, 'à constituer des milieux humains originaux. En revanche, les divers puits d'un charbonnage assez proches l'un de l'autre et bien qu'ils jouissent d'une certaine liberté, ne constitueront qu'une entité et n'auront donc qu'un conseil d'entreprise.'
31. The commercial office of a company though situated in a different place from that of the head office was held not to constitute a 'unité téchnique

Representative Establishment Councils 117

    d'exploitation' since no commercial or industrial process was taking place there. (CP Huy, 23 février 1950). This case clearly shows that economic autonomy must also feature and that social autonomy alone is not sufficient for the constitution of a 'conseil d'entreprise'. See also Conseil de Prud'hommes, Anvers, 25 April 1963, Revue de Droit Social 1963, p. 284; Tribunal du Travail, Mons, 4 mai 1971, Journal des Tribunaux du Travail 1971, p. 113; Tribunal du Travail Nivelles, 8 avril 1971, Journal des Tribunaux du Travail 1971, p. 126, where only one 'unité téchnique d'exploitation' existed. cf. Conseil de Prud'hommes, Mons, 16 mars 1967, Revue de Droit du Travail 1967, p. 219.
32. This Council meets at Prime Ministerial level. It is composed of a president and twelve members of certain status appointed by the Prime Minister, and of twelve members appointed by trade unions. This bipartite organ is the most senior of the three.
33. Each department or public service having a minimum of 100 employees has to have a trade union council for advice. The president is appointed by the relevant minister, and between eight and twenty members, according to how many employees are employed, of which half are appointed by the minister and the other half by the trade unions corresponding to the election results held every four years.
34. Committees of personnel are constituted where in a service or a group of services twenty-five employees are employed. Their composition is identical to that for the Trade Union Council for Advice.
35. By a law passed in May 1974.
36. The 1974 law was the result of the report of the Economic and Social Council of Luxembourg on mixed committees (1972).
37. In the procedure agreement between an electric motor manufacturer and unions (23 Oct. 1974), for example, section 3 provides briefly for a joint works committee. This consists of a chairman who is the industrial relations director with a casting vote, union representatives consisting of senior elected shop stewards from each of the signatory unions (not to exceed seven in total), and the personnel manager (non-voting) as the secretary. It is found that there need not be an equal number of management representatives but that management should nominate a balanced team depending on matters arising. Provision exists for sub-committees responsible to the JWC to be instituted. (See section 3(15) (a)–(f). In another procedure agreement examined (of 10 Aug. 1973), section G and sections (1)–(10) provided for joint consultation. The British Steel Corporation (Stockbridge works) had from 1965 introduced departmental committees, section councils and works councils. These bodies are of an advisory and consultative nature, and no norm is found as to how many employees there should be in the establishment before such committee or council is established, though the section council is said to consist of an absolute maximum of thirty-five members, representing each department or sub-department from both management and trade unions. The works council consists of sixteen management members (four of whom are non-voting members because of the specialist nature of their jobs) and sixteen trade union members. The trade union membership is found to be proportionate to the membership of the main trade unions, but provisions are made to have two members, one from each of the two unions with smaller membership. The British Iron and Steel and Kindred Trades Association which represents a large majority of employees agreed to limit its representation to half the trade union side of the works council. The chairman is a trade union representative elected annually by the union members of the council. Trade union influence rather than employee

influence in these committees is found to be strong. Cadbury Schweppes Foods Ltd have nine departmental committees of which seven are production committees, one trade and one for the offices. The head of each department and three members of management as well as six employee members, who are normally shop stewards, compose these committees. Also found in this firm is a works committee with no fixed composition except that management members are appointed by a management committee and employee members are nominated from the various departmental committees. Hoover Ltd, after the unions' withdrawal from consultation because of their wish to have a forty-hour week, immediately implemented a new joint consultative committee with eight employee representatives of manual workers (convenors) appointed by the shop stewards' committee. An equal number of management representatives appointed from the board of directors complete the committee. In TI Stainless Tubes Ltd, it is found that a site committee has been established consisting of five union representatives (two from the TGWU and three from the AEF) and five managers of which one is the line manager, with a chairman from the senior personnel. A works committee consisting of some twenty members from the trade union representatives of each of the departments and management has recently also been set up and it is understood at the time of writing that the site committees will be reduced to three representatives from each side. English Clays Lovering Pochin and Co Ltd have instituted productivity groups for consultation purposes. These are limited to joint consultation in improvement of production and to promote employee involvement in the establishment. These groups consist of elected employee representatives, the shop steward (ex officio) and the foreman who acts as chairman. Management attends the group meetings and is invited to discuss particular problems. It has been difficult to find out what the exact number of each of these groups is. Mullard Ltd have a central plant committee and area committees. These latter are chaired by management, and an equal number of union and management representation. The central plant committee consists of three management members (production manager, works manager and personnel manager) on the one side and on the other the senior shop steward of each of the main manual and staff unions. There is a management secretary and a joint union secretary. Gallaher, one of the main cigarette manufacturers, has three national agreements (for purposes of negotiation and consultation): one with ASTMS and APEX establishing a senior staff council; another with the Tobacco Workers' Union and APEX establishing a staff council; and a third with the TGWU and TWU establishing a council for hourly-paid workers. Similarly Dunlop also established a national joint committee (with negotiations and consultative powers) with the GMWU, the TGWU and the Rubber, Plastics and Allied Workers' Union. Tate & Lyle have separate consultative committees by agreement with the TGWU and the GMWU. All the above examples illustrate unionised consultative committees (i.e. the union(s) is represented) resulting from a collective agreement. There also exist non-unionised consultative committees, their origins therefore do not stem from the collective agreement. (See note 38 below, for example.)

38. In the Fred Olsen Line terminal joint works committees employee representatives are elected by constituencies established in the particular dock. Management appoints its members. There are five on each side. All decisions relating to the operation and future development of the terminal are taken by this committee on a unanimous basis (i.e. no voting takes place). The John Lewis Partnership is another example which has a central council consisting of some 145 persons — some 125 elected by secret ballot from the

employees and some twenty appointed by the chairman with powers to make recommendations. At local level branch councils have been instituted.

39. This variety of systems is clearly illustrated in reference 37 above, where different names are given to works councils, where their structure and composition varies, where their effectiveness varies from firm to firm etc.
40. See note 37 above.
41. In Cadbury Schweppes Ltd, for example, prior to 1968 'joint consultative schemes' operated before the present two-tier system of departmental committees and a works committee. In Hoover Ltd works committees which were union-based existed for some twenty-one years before bringing into operation the new system (in 1969–70) of a joint consultative committee. In Mullard Ltd a different structure existed prior to 1968. In TI Stainless Tubes Ltd the old site committees provided the experience upon which a more permanent committee structure may be based.
42. In France it is all private sector enterprises consisting of fifty or more employees, in Belgium until recently it was only the 'unité téchnique d'exploitation' with 150 or more employees which qualify, with a requirement that where a conseil d'entreprise existed before the election and there were only fifty employees employed there after 1975 there is a statutory requirement for such a committee to be instituted. In Luxembourg there is a requirement to form a 'comité mixte' where 150 persons are employed in an enterprise, whereas in Britain the formation of works councils is not required by statute, and where they exist they come about either through a system of trial and error or when there is a requirement for such an institution to be formed it is done through collective agreements, union pressure or expediency.
43. Conseil d'enterprise (Belgium), comités d'entreprise (France), comités mixtes (Luxembourg), works councils, information committees, consultative committees etc. (Britain).
44. In Belgium the problems with the 'unité technique d'exploitation', in France with the effectiveness of the statute which brings them about i.e. despite the law there exist numerous establishments without 'comités d'entreprise' (Industrial Democracy in Europe, 'The challenge and management responses', Business International European Research Report, p. 79, puts the number of recalcitrant firms as high as half). It is well known that in France, mainly because of the private nature of business, employers do not give the 'comité d'entreprise' the information required by statute. In the 1,600 firms in Belgium subject to the law, however, employers interviewed approve of the conseils d'entreprise because they can put their views across and receive those of their employees. In Britain the numerous reorganisations which have taken place in firms which operate works councils is clearly illustrative of problems. (See 'Some Examples of effective consultative committees', Industrial Society.)
45. Since 1948 in Belgium, 1945 in France, 1974 in Luxembourg, and no statutory requirement in Britain.
46. If one were to arrange in a continuum according to the strength of the representative institution system in the countries under examination, France and Belgium would come first, Luxembourg second and Britain cannot even be classified because there is no mandatory requirement for the institution of a works council, and where they do exist the variety is so great and terms of reference so varied that an objective assessment cannot be made.
47. i.e. the Fédération Générale du Travail de Belgique, the Conféderation des Syndicats Chrétiens, and the Centrale Générale des Syndicats Libéraux de Belgique.

48. Information must *inter alia* be given on the position of the firm vis-à-vis its competitors, on the policy for the raising of finance and the investments made by the enterprise.
49. See also J. Gayetot, 'La participation des travailleurs aux décisions dans l'entreprise en Belgique.' ILO Symposuim on Workers' Participation, August 1974.
50. See the CSC publication entitled 'Du conseil d'entreprise au conseil des travailleurs', March 1974.
51. See *Le Peuple* of 15 October 1974, 'Non à l'austérité — la CGT et la réforme de l'entreprise'.
52. Rapport du comité d'étude pour la réforme de l'entreprise, February 1975.
53. See Labour Party Manifesto, October 1974, p. 13, and 'Industrial Democracy', TUC General Council Report, July 1974, p. 29.
54. See *The Observer* of 18 March 1973, 'Wilson's new recipe for contented workers'.
55. See Conservative Party Manifesto, September 1974, p. 12.
56. 'CBI Rethink on Works Councils', *Daily Telegraph,* 13 September 1974.
57. HC Bill 131 of 9 May 1973.
58. See Liberal Party manifestos of February 1974 and September 1974.
59. The works councils which exist in Ireland have usually been established in the private sector as a result of joint management-union decision. The majority opinion in Ireland is that works councils should be instituted. The Minister of Labour in his address to the Irish Congress of Trade Unions on 14 July 1974 strongly supported the 'works council' idea, though he did not propose to legislate. The 'Draft National Agreement on the Establishment of Works Councils' prepared by a sub-committee on Worker Participation of the Employer-Labour Conference 1973, recommended that a national collective agreement be entered into to institute works councils as consultative bodies in all establishments where more than twenty-five employees are employed. Information, not of a confidential nature, should be given and elections will be trade-union based. Furthermore, in their 'Submission to the Minister of Labour on the Statute of the European Company proposed by the European Commission' (1973), the Irish Congress of Trade Unions has accepted the draft proposals with one proviso, that representatives be elected from the recognised trade union(s) within the establishment. These moves indicate that all parties concerned — government, trade unions and management — agree to the formation of works councils as an organ of consultation.
60. France, Belgium and Luxembourg have already been considered. In the Netherlands 'ondernemingsraden' (enterprise councils) were established by statute as early as 1950 and their functions extended considerably in 1971. In Germany there is a statutory requirement (the amending Works Constitution Law 1972) to set up Betriebsrat (works councils) in all private-sector establishments where five or more employees are employed.
61. In Denmark a national 'agreement on co-operation committees' concluded by the Danish Employers' Confederation and the Danish Federation of Trade Unions (1970) sets up 'co-operation committees' in all industrial and craft establishments employing fifty or more employees. In Italy, consigli di fabbrica have been set up by agreement since 1968.
62. Study sponsored by the International Confederation of Free Trade Unions in 1972 which examined *inter alia* works councils of twenty-two countries (including Britain) said that this system was inferior '... to fully developed collective bargaining, largely because it does not involve the worker to the same degree in the process of decision making'. Criticism was also made of

Representative Establishment Councils 121

the lack of sanctions which exist '... the absence of any provision for counter-measures in the event of non-compliance with the agreed procedure'. More particularly in Britain, works councils have had a chequered history. After the impetus given by the Whitley Committee reports 1917–18, joint consultation has excelled only in times of war or other crisis, but backing for this aspect of industrial democracy has had constant support. The Royal Commission on Trade Unions and Employers' Associations (Donovan Report) heard evidence supporting this aspect, from the CBI, the TUC, the Department of Employment and individual firms and unions, as well as from representatives of nationalised industries. W.E.J. McCarthy did however show, in 'The role of shop stewards in British industrial relations', Research Paper I (1966), Royal Commission on Trade Unions and Employers' Associations, that between 1955 and 1961 joint production committees in federated engineering establishments were reduced by one-third. Thus only one in ten had formal consultative bodies. Since McCarthy's research, of the sample of 130 firms in the private sector examined by this writer between the years 1970 and 1976 it was found that only thirty-one had any kind of *formal* consultative machinery. Of those that did not, management believed that *informal* consultation took place in that employees were told of future company policy and any collective grievances were considered by management.

63. 'Industrial Democracy in Europe – the challenge and management responses', p. 9.
64. e.g. detailed information on the progress of the firm, on production costs, plans for future investment, closures etc.
65. W.E.J. McCarthy in Research Paper No. 1, 'The role of shop stewards in industrial relations', found that joint consultative committees '... cannot survive the development of the effective shop-floor organisation. Either they must change their character and become essentially negotiating committees carrying out functions which are indistinguishable from the process of shop-floor bargaining, or they are boycotted by shop stewards and, as the influence of the latter grows, fall into disuse' (p. 33). See also Report of the Royal Commission on Trade Unions and Employers' Associations 1965–68, Cmnd. 3623, paras. 96–110.
66. See 'Perspectives', p. 1 et seq ante.
67. See part III, sectn. 62, of the Report of the Commission of Experts under the chairmanship of Mr Biedenkopf, commissioned by the West German government in 1968 to carry out a study of co-determination in industry. The report, entitled 'Mitbestimmung im Unternehem', was published in 1970. Deutscher Bundestag 6, Wahlperiode, Drucksache V1/334.
68. The Employment Protection Act 1975 now requires employers to disclose to trade union representatives information for purposes of collective bargaining (ss.17 et seq). Employers now have a statutory duty to inform and consult with union on mass redundancies (ss.99 et seq). Similarly the Industry Act 1975 imposes a duty of disclosure on the employer. Previously the Industrial Relations Act 1971 also provided for a duty of disclosure to unions for collective bargaining purposes (s.58). Furthermore, major employers had a duty of disclosure to their employees (s.57). The Code of Industrial Relations Practice also makes similar provision (paras. 96–8).
69. See note 68 above.
70. Fred Olsen Lines Ltd, one of the companies interviewed, believes that participation through works committees is the most efficient way to run their company. Employees' points of view and any information which they might have superimposed upon the decision-making process, is conducive to

a fairer and sounder decision to be taken. (See also note 80 post.)
71. 'To bring about greater common understanding, by giving work people a chance to know what is going on and a chance to make a contribution to the running of the enterprise in which they work.' Extract from 'Trade Unionism', TUC, 1967.
72. '(1) To enlist the co-operation of all employees in the efficient operation of the company, department or workshop, and in the implementation of management decisions;
(2) to obtain the opinions of employees in specific matters which affect their interests; and
(3) to deal jointy with matters of personal concern to employees which are not appropriate for formal negotiation.' Extract from 'Communication and Consultation', CBI, 1966.
73. Collective bargaining has the opposite aim, namely negotiation to reach a settlement acceptable to both sides, which involves conflict and compromise, rather than *collaboration* which is the key word in consultation.
74. See note 62 above.
75. See Research Paper No. 3 (1966) for Royal Commission on Trade Unions and Employers' Associations entitled 'Industrial Sociology and Industrial Relations'.
76. An examination of the constitutions of works councils reveals that their competence revolves around the time of the tea break and trolleys for snacks, facilities for changing, lunch hour, excursions, Christmas or other company parties and other functions, holiday times, retirement presents, fire drills and first aid, seating arrangements and facilities and other comfort aspects, e.g. heating, lighting, cleanliness, vending machines, tool and gardening clubs, crèches, the use of company and public buses, training methods and use of notice boards for social functions.
77. For example (a) Health and safety. In the national collective agreement (1957) of the electricity supply industry one of the functions of the joint consultative committee was '. . . to encourage measures affecting the safety, health and welfare of persons employed . . . to discuss matters of mutual interest . . . [and] efficiency in the operation of services'. The NJAC (National Joint Advisory Council) functions relate mainly to health and safety regulations, advice on these and related matters, and some research. Matters of 'mutual interest' are also discussed.
(b) Training. The electricity supply industry has a joint training committee which has powers of policy making.
78. Because even in areas of common interest, such as health and safety, collective bargaining, may feature e.g. the conflict between safety and increased productivity.
79. For example, future redundancies, matters relating to contracts of employment, wages, terms and conditions of employment.
80. An example of such organisation operating smoothly may be found in the Fred Olsen Line at Millwall docks, a 100 per cent unionised firm. All major decisions affecting the operations of the company are taken by a works committee constituted in 1967 and composed of an equal number of management and elected representatives of the 460 employees. Sub-committees are given the task of organising the work on a practical basis and of testing and buying equipment, e.g. loading equipment, fork lift trucks etc. The stress lies in mutual agreement rather than collective bargaining. The latter does however take place on such matters as wages, holidays with pay etc., but it is felt that the works committee system is more productive than the collective bargaining which predominates in the

Representative Establishment Councils   123

Port of London. Newcastle Breweries in one of their loading bays have introduced a committee consisting of all the men employed therein, and decisions on the method of work are taken by the whole group. This is on a limited scale but the arrangement is working satisfactorily. British Airways have a scheme whereby elected employees form part of joint working parties. Management members on these parties are nominated. Joint decision making takes place at every stage of the working parties' functions which are to improve efficiency and productivity. A novel approach was adopted by Tate & Lyle, where joint working parties have been set up consisting of GMWU representatives and management representatives. These parties manage the collective agreement entered into between the union and the company to the effect that savings on increased productivity would be divided at the rate of 60 per cent to employees and 40 per cent to the company.

81. It must be noted that the Donovan Commission was more concerned with collective bargaining. Worker participation was not its main concern and anyway agreement could not be reached on this and there consequently was little contribution from Donovan on this aspect.

82. Such matters as the safety policy required under the Health and Safety at Work etc. Act 1974, the alternatives offered by the Contracts of Employment Act 1972 on whether to issue individual notices of the terms and conditions of employment or whether to put these on a board, any joint problems faced by both sides of industry, e.g. strikes by suppliers of raw materials threatening production, policies on new laws passed etc. Future problems which may arise could most profitably be discussed in a works council, this will help avoid entrenched positions and create a better understanding of these problems and thus avoid or minimise future industrial action.

83. Bulletin of the European Bulletin, Supplement 4/75, entitled Statute for European Companies, article 100 et seq. The powers of these works councils will include representation of workers on all matters not subject to collective agreement or collective bargaining, the receipt of quarterly reports from management, the regular meeting with management, the requirement of council's agreement on all important matters *before* any decision is taken by management.

83a. The reasons for this are given at pp. 179–180.

84. France, fifty employees (see p. 35 ante), Belgium 150 employees, and sometimes 50 (see p. 36 ante) and Luxembourg 150 (see p. 38 ante).

85. It is thought that the term 'permanent' might be a litigious question. A definition section should provide the parameters to this term. (a) In seasonal employments, the occasional employees should not be included in the total number of employees nor should the part-time employees; (b) where there has been a reduction or increase in personnel as a result of layoffs due to a strike elsewhere, or a temporary increase to meet additional orders, then the average number for the year should be taken. This provision would be similar to a French one, except that it would have the additional advantage of being simpler, by not involving the authorities. In France where an enterprise has since 16 May 1946 had a substantial decrease in its employees to under fifty, the 'directeur départemental du travail et de la main d'œuvre', after hearing the opinion of the most representative trade union(s), may authorise the abolition of the comité d'entreprise (see loi du 12 août 1950); (c) where the number of permanent employees fall below fifty then there would be no obligation to re-elect a works council; (d) finally, the number of persons employed should be based on the number of personnel on the day when the notice announcing the election date is displayed. Unlike Belgian law but like French law (See art. 33 livre 14 Code

du Travail, loi du 26 juillet 1957 and loi no. 61–749 du 27 Juillet 1961) home workers should be included. See also the practical rules suggested by the Belgian Ministry of Labour in its circular in *Moniteur Belge*, 10 October 1958.
86. Article 100.
87. See pp. 35 et seq ante.
88. See pp. 36 et seq ante.
89. See p. 35 ante.
90. See p. 37 ante.
91. Article 101.
92. See pp. 39 and 40 ante.
93. Either by collective agreement, through custom, or through demand for such a body to be set up. cf. also French law of 16 May 1946, art. 23.
94. cf. the French art. 1, al.2 of loi du 16 mai 1946 and loi du 12 août 1950 where similar provisions exist.
95. cf. The French situation where decrees may be made by the Minister of Agriculture for the compulsory formation of a comité d'entreprise in agricultural concerns where by the nature of their activity and conditions of work there exists a similarity to industrial, commercial etc. enterprises (loi no. 66–427 du 18 juin 1966).
96. Loi 66–427 de 18 juin 1966.
97. Décret 66–697 du 21 septembre 1966 details the proportions as follows:
    from 50 to 75 employees, three members are elected;
    from 76 to 100 employees, four members;
    from 101 to 500, five members;
    from 501 to 1,000, six members;
    from 1,001 to 2,000, seven members;
    from 2,001 to 4,000, eight members;
    from 4,001 to 7,000, nine members;
    from 7,001 to 10,000, ten members;
    from 10,000, eleven members.
98. These are known as 'suppléants'.
99. Ordonnance du 22 février 1945, art. 5.
100. Décret 66–697 du 21 septembre 1966, art. 2.
101. Avis du Ministre du Travail of 12 mars 1950, JO, p. 15.
102. Cour de Colmar, 19 janvier 1956. Droit du Travail et de la sécurité sociale 1956, No. 9, p. 40.
103. Ordonnance du 22 février 1945, art. 6.
104. Ordonnance du 22 février 1945, art. 6, al. 4.
105. This article stated, 'La présente ordonnance ne fait pas obstacle aux dispositions concernant le fonctionnement ou les pouvoirs des comités d'entreprise qui resulteront d'accords collectifs ou usages'.
106. Some support for this may be found in M. Ribas' dictum on 20 January 1955 in Droit Social 1955, p. 565, to the effect that the law of 1946 did not authorise such extension by increasing the number of colleges.
107. Loi 66–427, 18 juin 1966.
108. Ordonnance du 22 février 1945, art. 6 as amended by loi 66–427 du 18 juin 1966.
109. Loi du 11 décembre 1972.
110. 'Les candidats passent dans l'ordre du nombre des voix obtenues. Les sièges sont à attribuer selon une proportion conforme à l'importance de chacune des catégories d'ouvriers et d'employés' (loi du 20 septembre 1948 as amended by loi du 28 janvier 1963, art. 20 al. 6).
111. i.e. those who recall the provision of art. 20 al. 6 of the 1948 law, and who

had to put it into practice.
112. In one instance there were too many seats in one college and too few in others; in another instance the election process was affected because it was realised that too many candidates were being elected for fewer seats.
113. See 'La représentation des travailleurs sur le plan de l'entreprise dans le droit des pays membres de la CECA', essay by Professor P. Horion, pp. 152–3.
114. Arrêté du régent 13 juillet 1949, art. 17.
115. Loi du 20 septembre 1948, art. 16(a).
116. Arrêté du régent du 13 juin 1949, art. 2. Who are management members? Foremen are not (Conseil de Prud'hommes d'Appel, Liège, 26 octobre 1963, Revue de Droit Social 1963, p. 319; Conseil de Prud'hommes, Anvers, 9 juillet 1969, Revue de Droit Social 1969, p. 413); chief clerks (Tribunal du Travail, Liège, 13 avril 1971, Journal des Tribunaux du Travail 1971, p. 125) are not, service managers do not form part of management (Tribunal du Travail Bruxelles, 13 avril 1971, Journal des Tribunaux du Travail 1971, p. 115). Departmental managers however do (Conseil de Prud'hommes, Namur, 28 juillet 1970, Revue de Droit Social 1970, p. 312; Conseil de Prud'hommes, Charleroi, 20 février 1969, Revue de Droit Social 1969, p. 232) as do branch shop managers (Tribunal du Travail, Verviers, 6 avril 1971, Journal des Tribunaux du Travail 1971, p. 118).
117. Some of the ex-management representatives on the conseil which this writer interviewed gave a variety of reasons why they have not always been able to attend the meetings – pressure of work, meetings, giving way to younger and more energetic persons and giving way to specialists, were a few of the reasons given.
118. Usually it is either the employer or his representative, i.e. only one member representing the employer.
119. See accord national du 16 juillet 1958 stating 'En ce qui concerne la détermination des personnes chargées d'un poste de direction visées à l'article 14 de la loi: . . . le chef d'entreprise désignera nominativement les personnes chargées effectivement d'un poste de direction' (article 1).
120. Loi du 20 september 1948 as amended by loi du 28 janvier 1963, art. 5. Prior to 1963, the requirement was fifty manual workers or employees.
121. Loi du 28 janvier 1963, art. 5.
122. Arrêté royal du 18 février 1971, art. 19.
123. Loi du 15 juin 1953, art. 1. Practice varies from establishment to establishment – because collective agreements may vary the numbers within the statutory minimum and maximum – but it has invariably been found throughout the sample of Belgian establishments examined that the statutory minimum number of employee representatives (i.e. three) is seldom observed. Numerous persons interviewed felt that it was better to have more representatives than the statutory minimum to allow for natural wastage, illness, absences etc . . . Because of this variation in practice it is impossible to give an accurate number of representatives in every case but an attempt below gives an average of the ratio of representatives to the total number of employees. Where there are 50 to 100 workers in an establishment it is found that there exist an average of four representatives; 101 to 500 employees, six representatives; 501 to 1,000, eight representatives; 1,001 to 2,000, ten representatives; 2,001 to 3,000, twelve representatives; 3,001 to 4,000, fourteen representatives; 4,001 to 5,500, sixteen representatives; 5,501 to 6,500, eighteen representatives; and over that number twenty representatives. There exist an equivalent number of acting representatives. Arrêté royal du 18 février 1971, art. 14, has increased the

number to a minimum of four representatives to twenty-two for over 8,000 workers.
124. These take over from the main delegate if he resigns, retires, dies or is suffering an industrial injury or disease or is sick. Prior to 1953 there was only half the number of acting delegates. It was found on numerous occasions prior to that date that the work of the conseil d'entreprise could not effectively take place because resignations from employment etc. ... so reduced the numbers as to make the conseil ineffective; alternatively that on occasions the number was reduced to less than the statutory requirement of three.
125. It has been found in practice that the way in which the proportion of representation for the two electoral colleges — namely manual and clerical workers — is worked out, is in accordance with the following formula:

If an establishment employs 2,150 manual workers and the worker representatives for that number is twelve (see note 123 above) and at the same time 150 employees are also employed, making a grand total of personnel of 2,300, then:

$$\frac{2{,}150 \text{ (manual workers)} \times 12}{2{,}300 \text{ (grand total of personnel)}} = 11.21$$

$$\frac{150 \text{ (clerical workers)} \times 12}{2{,}300 \text{ (grand total of personnel)}} = 0.78$$

The proportion of representation in this example is: eleven seats are taken by manual workers' representatives, and one seat is taken by the clerical worker representative. The fact that the clerical representation is below one makes no difference since otherwise there would be no clerical representation. Even if the figures were supposedly 11.98 to the manual workers and 0.10 to clerical workers, the latter would still have one seat. Where, on the other hand, the clerical workers have at least one seat, then the category with the greater fraction would have the additional seat. Thus if the manual workers had 8.47 seats and the clerical 4.48, then the manual workers would have eight seats and the clerical workers five. It has on occasions happened that the fraction in both categories has been equal. In these circumstances the seat will go to the category with the most personnel. So that if there is a greater number of clerical workers and the fraction is identical with the manual workers then the clerical workers will have the additional seat.
126. Cadbury Schweppes Confectionery Group have (i) *departmental committees* consisting of management and elected employee representatives, one representative from the works council and a shop steward who attends as of right; (ii) six *divisional consultative committees*, composed of management and union representatives. Employees on these committees are not elected but appointed by the unions (TGWU, USDAW mainly). The six committees cover the four production divisions, the trades, and the offices; (iii) *Bournville works council* with twelve members of management and twenty-two union representatives from each of the six divisional committees. Though all trades are represented at divisional committee level it is found that not all trades are represented on the works council. Because of the numerous and complicated activities taking place, standing committees of the works council have been set up. There are company schemes committees which concern themselves with disciplinary tribunals dealing with disciplinary matters within the establishment and with a right of appeal to the ordinary courts, and with matters not subject to negotiation with the union; the joint consultative committee deals with the works council organisation; the

Boeke Trust manages the trust set up to help workers in need and pensioners of Cadbury. Other committees deal with catering, safety and health, education and training. A proposed change is contemplated in Cadbury's in that (a) joint consultative committees at all levels will be created, for contact between employees and management; (b) group councils for contact with group boards and (c) company conferences with the main board. ('The responsibilities of the British public company', CBI 1973.) All members in (a), (b) and (c) above will be elected.

In Pilkington Brothers, fibreglass insulation division, an elaborate framework of both consultation and negotiation exists (see chart in 'Worker Participation in Britain', *Financial Times*, p. 94), because a distinction cannot be made between negotiation and consultation, according to a joint working party report on negotiating procedure in July 1970. At *site level* there is a works consultative committee of sixteen members, two of whom are elected from each of the eight groups. The committee is chaired by the works manager with a union member as vice-chairman and the personnel manager as secretary. At departmental level there are *departmental committees* for most departments (some have fallen into desuetude). Joint working parties are occasionally set up when the need arises. Representation is equal on both sides.

In Unilever (Blackfriars) there has been a change in the consultative machinery in 1973 because the old system was too cumbersome and anyway there was need to have joint consultation on a departmental basis. The core of the consultation machinery is the joint consultative manager with his secretarial staff, information and communication system and supervision of electoral procedures. He is the executive of the consultation system. There then exist two limbs, one being the grade committees based on classification of staff grade, the other being departmental councils based on the departmental members. The Blackfriars consultative council is at the top of the pyramid and both limbs are represented therein. This is a complex structure not found in other companies in Britain or in the other countries under examination. (A useful chart of this structure may be found in 'Worker Participation in Britain', *Financial Times*, p. 124.) There are seventeen *departmental councils* consisting of five to ten elected members each. An attempt is constantly made to represent every category of staff within each of the departments. The elected representatives appoint a chairman and secretary. The *committee of departmental councils* is the second in the three-tier system of consultation in the departmental staff limb, and consists of twenty-one members with one to three representatives from each of the seventeen departmental councils depending on the size of the departmental council. The chairman is elected from among the representatives. Experts or line management are sometimes called in to express an opinion, and the joint consultative manager attends by invitation to advise or assist. The departmental manager cannot be a member because he is required to attend on at least six occasions yearly as a company representative. At the top of the pyramid is the *Blackfriars consultative council* consisting of five members from the committee of departmental councils and five from the grade committees. One member is elected to be chairman from among the members and his vacancy is filled by a member of either the grade committee or the committee of departmental councils. The head office manager attends as the company representative and the joint consultation manager is secretary to the council. There are therefore thirteen persons on this council. It is interesting to note that only at the top level of the consultative machinery is management officially represented by one person. Throughout the system, representatives and their chairman come from the employee side, though management and other experts may attend on invitation, and the joint consultation manager advises when invited to do so and asks line management to settle problems which have arisen and answer questions. The *grade committee* system, as the second limb in the consultative structure, runs parallel to the *departmental council*'s structure with ultimate representation (one from each of the five grades) in the Blackfriars consultative council. This committee is based on seniority. Employees in the senior, middle and assistant management grades, clerical and service staff grades elect five members (total of twenty-five). As is the case with the departmental councils and the committee of departmental councils, the chairman is chosen from among the members and the company is not represented. The joint consultation manager attends when invited. The grade committee limb is concerned with problems relating to the particular grade, whereas the departmental staff limb is concerned with the receiving of information by the manager on all decisions which would affect their work, and a discussion between the manager and employee representatives on all matters affecting the department. Imperial Chemical Industries (Lostock works) is an example of a unionised consultative system. Each factory has *plant committees* consisting mainly of shop stewards as employee representatives. A *works committee* is the next in the hierarchy and consists only of shop stewards representing employees. Management is represented from the different levels of plant and works management and the personnel officer is the secretary. The chair is always taken by management. There also exist *staff committees* for the purpose of consultation between management and monthly staff but these committees are not union-dominated though efforts are being made by ASTMS to recruit white collar workers. ICI generally has a three-tier system. There is the *site staff committee* elected by staff, which sends representatives to division staff conference and to a central staff conference. A division standing committee at divisional level has been set up for each division and a central standing committee for the company. In the ICI Mond division there are sixteen *staff site committees*, with elected representation from either a department or persons doing the same kind of work at different places. A management member chairs the meeting. Each of these committees elects a representative to the *division staff standing committee* and two representatives to the *division staff conference*.

127. In the British Steel Corporation, Rotherham works, the joint consultative organisation is based on a three-tier system, namely (a) *departmental committees* and (b) *area or section councils*, each having its own individual sub-committees, (c) the *works council* at the top. The employee representatives on each of these are elected by the trade unions from trade union members. Management is nominated on each of these and it is interesting to note that the general manager chairs the works council meetings. The works council employee representatives are also on the other two committees (namely area or section council and appropriate departmental committee). On the works council there are thirty-nine elected representatives and eleven nominated from management.

128. The complexity and variety is well illustrated in notes 126 and 127 above.

129. At the Chirk site of Cadbury Schweppes there is only the TGWU which organises *all* production and clerical employees. The joint negotiating committee took over the functions of its predecessor, the plant committee, and deals with both consultation and negotiation. Similarly with the Guardian Royal Exchange Assurance group where an equal number of

members of management and the union meet at joint national council level and at joint local committee level.
130. Gallaher, the cigarette manufacturers, have separate agreements with the different unions, all of which cover negotiation and consultation. The hourly paid staff is represented by the TGWU and the Tobacco Workers' Union; the staff council by APEX and the TWU and the senior staff council by ASTMS and APEX. Within this national structure there exist agreements with more than a single union for consultation for the different levels of staff within each branch of the establishment. Tate & Lyle have consultative committees established at their Liverpool refinery. These result from agreements entered into with the GMWU and the TGWU. There also exists a refinery council with a purely consultative role. All members of this council are members of one of the recognised unions but there is no requirement for proportional union representation on this council.

Dunlop has entered into an agreement with the TGWU, the GMWU and the plastics and Allied Workers' Union, setting up *inter alia* consultative machinery over a wide range of issues. The electricity supply industry has an efficient and well-developed joint consultation system established by agreement with eight different unions. It has a three-tier structure: the *local advisory committees*, consisting of recognised union representatives elected by employees who need not be union members, and members of the electricity boards. Each power station or distribution district has a local committee. Local committees make recommendations to local management or to *joint advisory councils* consisting of union representatives, with each union having a specified number of representatives, elected representatives from the local committees and members appointed by the various electricity boards. Recommendations from this body are made either to the particular area board or to the *national joint advisory council for England and Wales*.
131. In the Scott Bader company the community council, which has advisory and minor decision-making powers, consists of members who are trade unionists (TGWU and ASTMS) but the unions themselves are not represented on the council. The same may be said of the various standing sub-committees dealing with welfare and social matters. This situation has also been found in the John Lewis Partnership, Pilkington and Unilever. In Esso Petroleum the consultative committee is elected from the various 'constituencies'. The only qualification for representatives of constituencies is that they should work therein and meet certain time qualifications. There is no requirement that a person should be a trade union member, nor is there any agreement with unions constituting this body. In Unilever Blackfriars joint consultative machinery is not unionised though members belong to unions.
132. In the Esso Petroleum head office staff committee, there is an equal number of employee and management representatives. This is also true of the Fred Olsen Line works committee structure. Although not quite on equal numbers, the gap in Castner-Kellner is narrow. There are sixteen elected representatives (eight from GMWU and another eight from other unions) and fourteen management representatives on their eight plant committees.
133. As for example in Mobil, or in Cadbury Schweppes, Chirk site, where the joint negotiating committee (which has a consultation role) is chaired alternately by the appropriate union representative and the factory manager.
134. In the Unilever Blackfriars consultative council the chairman is elected from the members of the council itself. His place as a member is then filled in from the appropriate lower echelons. This is true of the chairman and secretary of each of the committee of departmental councils, departmental councils and

grade committees, who are appointed by the elected members of the appropriate committee.
135. Apart from the exception in note 134 above.
136. So e.g. the novel and interesting structure of grade committees and departmental councils which exist at Unilever (Blackfriars) should continue despite any legislation.
137. Of the sample of companies having consultative bodies and examined above, a majority have union representation. Such a proposal would therefore follow common practice.
138. In some establishments already examined the two sets operate side by side. Pilkington Brothers fibreglass insulation division is an example where consultative and negotiating machinery operate at three levels, namely company level, site level and departmental level side by side. A joint working party on negotiating procedure reported that an effective distinction cannot '... be drawn between the terms negotiation and consultation...' and that negotiating bodies '... also met for communication purposes' (July 1970).
139. In 'Worker participation in Britain', Financial Times, p. 137.
140. The proposed statute for European companies allows for existing systems to continue into being (cf. this writer's suggestion, p. 54 ante). Art. 101 states 'Unless otherwise expressly provided for in this statute, organs of employee representation formed in the establishments of a European company pursuant to national laws shall continue in existence with the same functions and powers as are conferred upon them under that law'. Art. 102 refers to annex I listing the various employees' representative bodies in the European Community countries, and states that 'The Commission of the European Communities will amend this Annex on the basis of changes in the statutory or otherwise agreed provisions governing employer representatives, as soon as the member state notifies it of such changes' (art. 102(2)).

The number of fifty employees is provided as being the minimum number before a works council be set up by election by the establishment's employees (art. 103(1)) (cf. this writer's suggestion, p. 56 ante).
141. Here the French system of so many seats per electoral college depending on the number of representatives in each is preferable since it is very much simpler than the proportional method used in Belgium (see note 125 above).
142. The proposed statute for European companies provides (art. 103(2)) that one representative be elected for establishments employing 50 to 199 employees; two for 200 to 499; three for 500 to 999; four for 1,000 to 2,999; five for 3,000 to 4,999, and an additional representative for every 5,000 employees over 4,999. The same number of 'deputy representatives' should also be elected.
143. A more detailed arrangement is as follows:
    50 to 99 employees, three elected representatives.
    100 to 199 employees, four elected representatives.
    200 to 399 employees, five elected representatives.
    400 to 699 employees, six elected representatives.
    700 to 999 employees, seven elected representatives.
    1,000 to 2,499 employees, eight elected representatives.
    2,500 to 4,999 employees, nine elected representatives.
    5,000 to 6,999 employees, ten elected representatives.
    7,000 to 10,499 employees, eleven elected representatives.
    over 10,500 employees, twelve elected representatives.
144. See p. 48 ante.
145. See p. 48 ante.

146. See p. 48 and notes 101 and 102 ante.
147. This division according to 'status' exists within the composition of the 'comité d'établissement', and 'comité central d'entreprise' and the 'comités inter-entreprise' which exist in France. These are the various tiers in the works council hierarchy. Within each of these tiers 'status' operates, i.e. manual workers, clerical grades, supervisory staff, 'cadres'. Similarly in Belgium where the law (art. 17) is more vague but provides that subdivisions for each 'category of workers' may be created within the conseil d'entreprise if necessary. This article states 'Le conseil d'entreprise peut, d'après l'importance de la structure de l'enterprise, se subdiviser en sections d'entreprise dont les membres délégués du personnel appartiennent aux catégories intéressées des travailleurs et sont désignés suivant une procédure fixée par arrêté royal' (loi du 20 septembre 1948 as amended by loi du 18.8 mars 1950, loi du 5 juin 1953, and that of 15 mars 1954). The 'status' is therefore still maintainable within each of these subdivisions. Throughout the tier hierarchy system 'status' therefore operates. Thus where in France an establishment has numerous branches, each branch must have a 'comité d'établissement' with identical functions and composition to those of the comité d'entreprise. The liaison between the various branches' 'comités d'établissement' is the 'comité central d'entreprise' consisting of one or two delegates and an equal number of acting delegates (suppléants) elected from each of the 'comités d'établissement', to a maximum of twelve (ordonnance du 22 février 1945, art. 21, al. 1 et 2). Both the number of branches and the distribution of seats must be agreed upon by the employer and the most representative recognised trade union. Where there is disagreement the matter is referred to the appropriate 'directeur départmental du travail et de la main d'œuvre' who decides on both these matters. The comité central meets half yearly at the headquarters of the entreprise (loi 66–427 du 18 juin 1966, al. 1 et 2). Every recognised trade union appoints a non-voting representative to the comité central. He might be the trade union representative to the various comités d'établissements, or be one of the elected members of these comités (loi 66–427 du 18 juin 1966, al. 3). 'Comités inter-entreprise' are established only when many categories possess or intend to create common institutions (décret du 2 novembre 1945, art. 9, al. 1).
148. The intention is that each works council be representative of *all* the staff within the department, with at the same time a proper balance between the grades, status and jobs represented.
149. See p. 49 and see notes 110–114 ante.
150. See p. 49.
151. See p. 50.
152. See p. 56 and note 143 ante.
153. Until 1972 he had to be of French nationality, or if a foreigner, to have worked in France for at least five years. Those who had a card of 'résident privilégie' had a right to vote and were not subject to the five-year qualifying period (ordonnance du 30 juin 1946, art. 10, now repealed by loi du 27 juin 1972). Loi du 22 juin 1972 reduced the age from eighteen to sixteen.
154. The reasons why there is a time qualification are thought to be (a) that the employee is enabled to get acclimatised to his work, (b) that he gets to know the other employees in his electoral college, thus knowing who he is voting for, and (c) to build up a certain amount of allegience within the enterprise. An exemption to the time qualification is sometimes given by the inspecteur du travail under the powers given to him by ordonnance du 22 février 1945, art. 9. It is found that an exemption is occasionally

given where a quarter of the total number of employees do not fulfill the time qualification.
155. Décret organique du 2 février 1852.
156. Loi du 16 mai 1946, art. 7, al. 1 to 3.
157. So that where the works' canteen or a crèche etc. is run by the comité d'entreprise who employ staff to cook, serve etc., such staff does not form part of the electorate. See Cour de Cassation, Ch. Civ., Section Sociale 28, octobre 1949, Bull. IV. 975, 1048.
158. Cour de Cassation, Ch. Civ., 9 juillet 1953, Jurisclasseur Périodique (Semaine judiciaire) 1953, IV, 130. It is also suggested that by analogy suspension of the contract through illness, authorised absences or even wrongful dismissal does not break the continuity of employment (see notes 162–4 post).
159. Consequently there will be a 'comité d'établissement' in each branch.
160. Cour de Cassation, Ch. Civ., 27 décembre 1955. Informateur du chef d'entreprise 1956, p. 408.
161. Loi du 16 mai 1946, art. 8.
162. Cour de Cassation, 27 mars 1952, Droit Social 1952, p. 399.
163. Cour de Cassation, Ch. Civ., Section Soc., 21 mars 1952, Droit Social 1952, p. 397.
164. Cour de Cassation, Ch. Civ., 26 janvier 1956, Droit Social 1956, p. 285.
165. Loi du 20 septembre 1948 as amended by loi du 18 mars 1950, 15 juin 1953 and 15 mars 1954, art. 18.
166. As is the case in France, suspension of a contract of employment because of a temporary layoff, short-time, illness (Tribunal du Travail, Nivelles, 30 avril 1971, Journal des Tribunaux du Travail 1971, p. 114), military service, annual holidays etc. does not break its continuity.
167. Loi du 20 september 1948 as amended by loi du 18 mars 1950, 15 juin 1953 and 15 mars 1954, art. 19, al. 1 et 2.
168. Esso Petroleum.
169. British Steel Corporation (Rotherham works).
170. In Cadbury Schweppes, Bournville site, on the departmental committees, apart from one works council member and management representatives a shop steward sits as of right and the remaining employee places are filled through an election. On the six consultative committees and on the works council, however, there are no elections by the employees as these latter are represented and appointed by the trade unions. Similarly, in ICI weekly staff it is found that on plant committees *most* of the representatives are shop stewards, and on the works committees *all* the representatives are shop stewards. In the Mond division of the same company the works committee consists of *inter alia* ten union representatives. Six are elected from the GMWU and the TGWU and four from UCATT, EETPU and AUEW (Lostock works). At Castner-Kellner the works committee elects sixteen union representatives, eight from the GMWU and eight from among UCATT, EETPU and AUEW.
171. At the Chirk site of Cadbury Schweppes, for example, the employees are *elected* on the joint consultative committee, the group councils and the company conference. The monthly staff of ICI elect their own representatives on the site staff committee, and this committee in turn sends representatives to the division staff conference and the central staff conference. Similarly at Mond division of the same company the monthly staff representatives are *elected* from either each department or from persons in different parts of the site who are doing the same type of work. In Pilkington Brothers, fibreglass insulation division, employees *elect* two representatives on the works consultative committee from each of the categories of employees,

e.g. supervisory staff, managers, manual workers etc. up to a total of sixteen.
172. Unilever (Blackfriars) has seventeen departmental councils, based either on a department or a group of smaller ones. Each council *elects* between five and ten *employees* according to the number of employees represented. The committee of departmental councils is composed of representatives (one to three from each of the departmental councils, depending on size) from the departmental council. No elections take place; again, the grade committees of which there are five *elect* one each of their number to the Blackfriars consultative council. Similarly the committee of departmental councils elect five of their members on the BCC.
173. Proposed statute for European companies, art. 104 and annex II, art. I.
174. The term 'continuous' should be construed as it has been in France — see note 158 and p. 58 ante.
175. This also seems to be the opinion of the European Commission — see Bulletin of the European Communities, Supplement 4/75, p. 220, col. 2 (annex II 2)).
176. cf. proposed statute for European companies, annex 11, art. 2 (2).
177. Proposed statute for European companies, annex II, art. 2(1).
178. Loi du 16 mai 1946, art. 7, al. 1 à 3. See pp. 176 et seq post.
179. Cour de Cassation, Chambre Civile, Section Sociale, 26 novembre 1954, Droit Social 1955, p. 166.
180. Cour de Cassation, Chambre Civile, Section Sociale, 25 juillet 1947, Recueil Dalloz, p. 47.
181. Cour de Cassation, Chambre Civile, Section Sociale, 27 mars 1952, Bulletin 1954, IV.270.198.
182. Cour de Cassation, Chambre Civile, 26 novembre 1954, Droit Social 1955, p.164.
183. Cour de Cassation, Chambre Civile, 10 juin 1955, Informateur du chef d'entreprise 1955, p. 835.
184. Cour de Cassation (Chambre Civile, Section Sociale, 3 juin 1950, Jurisclasseur Périodique (Seminaine Judiciaire) 1950 11.5943) had held that no period within which to bring a case was therefore necessary.
185. Loi du 7 décembre 1951.
186. Cour de Cassation, Chambre Civile, Section Sociale, 8 décembre 1955, Droit Social 1956, p. 159.
187. Cour de Cassation, Chambre Civile, Section Sociale, 24 November 1955, Informateur du chef d'entreprise, 1956, p. 409.
188. e.g. the displaying of notices giving the election dates; deposit, scrutiny and closure of electoral lists for each of the colleges; method by which the electoral lists are formulated; delays in the presentation of candidates; special cases where a ballot will not take place, i.e. where lists of candidates are invalid or where the number of seats vacant are equal to the number of candidates; constitutions of electoral colleges, constitution of the 'bureau électoral'; organisation of the actual ballot, i.e. election centre(s), opening and closing hours, duties of electors, soiled ballot papers, powers of the president, witnesses, method of voting; the counting of votes, classifications, suspected dishonesty, recounts; announcement of those elected; display of notices, appeals and period of limitation within which to appeal.
189. Arrêté du régent du 13 juillet 1949 (Moniteur Belge, 25–26 juillet 1940) as amended by arrêté du régent du 11 janvier 1950 (Moniteur Belge, 12 janvier 1950), arrêté royal du 27 octobre 1951 (Moniteur Belge, 8 novembre 1951); arrêté royal du 30 mars 1954 (Moniteur Belge, 4 avril 1954); arrêté royal du 9 octobre 1954 (Moniteur Belge, 14 octobre 1954) and arrêté royal du 6 octobre 1958 (Moniteur Belge, 8 octobre 1958). SS 1–IX, arts. 1 to 32, and annex I.

190. The detail and form are peculiar to Belgium and since the proposals to be made for Britain are simpler and less formal the Belgian system is seen as peripheral. A chronological table of the election procedure is however provided below for completeness. (This writer is indebted to a number of members of the Fédération des Entreprises Belges who have helped him by the production of charts and other materials and by spending a great deal of time discussing the complicated electoral procedure.) The Circulaire Ministérielle of 16 February 1951 on the election procedure provides the source.

Date announcing the election = A.
Actual date of the election = A + 50 or 60 days = H hour.

List of candidates

(i) Final date for presentation of lists by the trade unions to the employer (the different sections/ departments of the enterprise must be represented) — A + 15 days

(ii) Display of list consisting of candidates' names (within five days of final presentation date) — A + 20 days

(iii) Any observations to be made to the employer by the electors on the list of candidates (must be made within two days of the display date) — A + 22 days

(iv) Reply to these observations made by the employer and notified to the appropriate recognised trade union (three days) — A + 25 days

(v) The list of candidates may be modified by the union if it thinks fit — A + 30 days

(vi) Closure of list of candidates eight days before the election — H hour − 8 days

Electoral lists

(i) Submission date of provisional electoral lists — A + 3 days

(ii) Any contested matters in relation to these provisional lists — these must be made within *five* days of the submission date to the conseil d'entreprise (or where no conseil exists to the employer) — A + 8 days

(iii) Reply to these contested matters by the conseil (or the employer) to be affixed on notice board — A + 11 days

(iv) Appeal (if the reply is found to be unsatisfactory) to the conseil de Prud'hommes or the competent juge de paix (within three days of unsatisfactory reply) — A + 14 days

(v) Decision of the appeal (within eight days) and notification to personnel concerned, the employer and the conseil d'entreprise. This decision is final. — A + 22 days

(vi) Closure of final electoral lists (taking into account reply (in (iii) above) and appeal (in (v) above)). Lists close six days before the election — H hour − 6 days

Representative Establishment Councils 135

All eligible electors should be summoned five days before the election date and urged by the employer to vote. There is an obligatory clause which states 'Pour assumer le caractère vraiment représentatif de la délégation qui sera élue, tous les travailleurs ont le devoir de participer au vote'. Voting is not compulsory and there exists no penalty for not doing so.

An electoral office(s) (bureau électoral) must be set up and is responsible for the administration of the ballot. This normally consists of a president, a secretary and four assessors. The president is normally nominated by the employer with trade union agreement or the délégation syndicale du personnel' (A + 20 days). The 'inspecteur social' is notified if the union disagrees with the employer's nomination. He may nominate one or take up the presidency himself. The secretary is appointed by the president and the assessors by the 'conseil d'entreprise', or if this latter is non-existent then the president nominates them; H hour – 8 days. The secretary and assessors cannot obviously qualify as candidates but they are members of the electorate. The question has often been asked as to whether there should be an electoral office for each college. The law seems so to indicate but it is found from various interviews carried out that in practice one electoral office deals with all colleges. Witnesses are nominated by the trade union(s) five days before the election takes place, H hour – 5 days. Their function is to observe all the stages during the electoral operations. Eighty per cent of trade unions interviewed stated that they normally nominated witnesses to supervise the election process. The remainder did not as they felt that supervision was adequate through the electoral office. The days after the closing of the election (at the latest) (H hour + 1 day) the president of the electoral office(s) must display the results of the election.

191. The informality and unsophistication varies from spontaneous non-secret ballots by a show of hands found to be the case at one extreme, to a written, but not detailed, secret ballot procedure at the other extreme. The procedures carried out by trade unions have on the whole been found to come within the latter category, e.g. in the British Steel Corporation at Rotherham it is the unions (*inter alia* the British Iron Steel and Kindred Trades Association) who organise the election of their representatives in the departmental committees, section councils and works council; or Lostock works or Castner-Kellner of ICI where the weekly staff are elected from various unions on the plant committees, but some establishments are also found to come within this latter category, e.g. the election of employees (other than shop stewards who sit by right) in the departmental committees at Cadbury Schweppes at the Bournville site; or the Pilkington Brothers fibreglass insulation division, which has separate site level consultative machinery from each of the different groups of employees, each of which elects two representatives. The most sophisticated company system encountered has been that which exists in Unilever (Blackfriars) where the full-time joint consultation manager's job consists *inter alia* of organising and supervising the elections for the departmental councils, committee of departmental councils, grade committees and the Blackfriars consultative council.
192. cf. the proposed statute for European companies, annexe II, art. 3(1).
193. As is the case in Belgium and in France as far as the first election list is concerned.
194. The system proposed by the statute for European companies, annexe II, art. 3(2)–(4), is that employees entitled to vote should prepare a separate list to that prepared by the union(s).
195. The proposed statute for European companies, annexe II, arts. 5(1) and

6(1)–(4) provide for proportional representation where more than one list of candidates is submitted. Such necessity would not arise under this writer's proposals since only one list (trade unions' or employees' as appropriate) will exist; cf. art. 7.
196. See note 190 ante, in particular the section on 'Bureau électoral'.
197. Proposed statute for European companies, annexe II, section II, art. 9.
198. cf. annexe II, art. 10(1) and art. 12 of the proposed statute for European companies which provides for a court of law to decide.
199. cf. annexe II, art. 11(4) of the proposed statute for European companies which provides for three members where less than 1,000 employees are employed in the establishment, five for up to 5,000 employees and seven for over that figure.
200. cf. annexe II, art. 13(1) of the proposed statute for European companies which provides for the appointment of a chairman, and art. 13(2)–(4) for his functions.
201. cf. ibid., art. 14.
202. cf. ibid., art. 17.
203. cf. this same distinction in France at p. 61 ante.
204. See note 190 ante.
205. e.g. art. 9(1) providing for publication within ten days of the formation of the SE in each establishment of the SE in which representatives are to be elected to the European works council; art. 9(2), fifteen days to contest the the composition of the electoral commission, art. 14(3), the electoral commission must publish within thirty days before the election date, the election notice; art. 15(2), any objections relating to the accuracy and completeness of the electoral roll must be lodged with the electoral commission within ten days of its display etc.
206. These must not be confused with the 'délégué du personnel'. On a number of occasions this writer has found that members of the comité d'entreprise have been referred to by employees in France as 'délégués du personnel'.
207. Loi du 9 janvier 1954 in France and loi du 16 janvier 1967, art. 2 amending art. 21 of loi du 20 septembre 1948 (Moniteur Belge, 27–28 septembre 1948) in Belgium.
208. See p. 196 post. Loi du 16 mai 1946. In Belgium similar conditions exist and the member of the 'conseil d'entreprise' ceases his function when his term of office expires, upon death of voluntary resignation, when he is no longer eligible to be a member, when he ceases to be a member of the company for whatever reason, when he no longer belongs to the union which has proposed him, or when he ceases to belong to the group of manual or clerical workers whom he represents unless the trade union which proposed him expresses the wish by registered letter to the employer that he should still represent his constituents, and finally when he has been dismissed for serious misconduct. (Loi du 16 janvier 1967, art. 2 amending art. 2(1–8) of loi du 20 septembre 1948.)

The above also applies to the third college (i.e. young workers) except that a trade union cannot express the wish that the member should continue to represent his constituents when he ceases to belong to the group of young persons which he represents.
209. Loi du 9 janvier 1954 modifying art. 12 of loi du 16 mai 1946 in France, and loi du 16 janvier 1967, art. 2 amending art, 21 of loi du 20 septembre 1948.
210. Art. 21 of loi du 20 septembre 1948 as amended by art. 2 of loi du 16 janvier 1967.
211. Loi du 18 mars 1950 amending art. 21 of loi du 20 septembre 1948.

Representative Establishment Councils   137

212. Loi du 9 janvier 1954 modifying art. 13 of loi du 16 mai 1946.
213. Art. 13-1 of loi du 16 mai 1946 as modified by loi 66-427, 28 juin 1966.
214. It is noted that in establishments of over 500 employees the 'représentants syndicaux' on the comité are given the same amount of remunerated time off in the exercise of their functions. Loi 66-427, 18 juin 1966, art. 14.
215. e.g. Pilkington Brothers, fibreglass insulation division, where the works consultative committee representatives are elected for two years.
216. e.g. ICI Mond division – consultation with staff.
217. e.g. Armstrong Patents, Eastgate Works, Beverley.
218. See also proposed statute for European companies, art. 107(1), proposing *four* years.
219. e.g. Armstrong Patents Ltd.
220. The proposed statute for European companies provides for similar provisions under art. 198(1).
221. Though in some cases it has been found that upon vacation of a seat an election was held to fill the vacant seat.
222. This is the practice in the other countries examined and this practice is also proposed by the statute for European companies, art. 108(2).
223. cf. proposal in the statute for European companies, art. 108(3).
224. i.e. the time spent by the actual member should count towards that spent by the deputy, and vice versa. It is interesting to note that the proposed statute for European companies does not provide any maximum time limit.
225. This procedure is the same for the trade union representative (délégué syndical) on the comité.
226. See p. 196 post. The Cour de Cassation did indicate '. . . les membres du comité d'entreprise bénéficient de mesures dérogatoires du droit commun à raison des fonctions par eux exercées, contre les congédiements dont ils pourraient être l'objet de la part de leur employeur' in Chambre Civile, Section Sociale, 3 juin 1948, JCP 1948, 11.4462.
227. Including trade union representatives and délégués du personnel.
228. Décret 59-99 du 7 janvier 1959, art. 1. The member who is being dismissed has no right of vote in this instance otherwise this would infringe the rules of natural justice in this respect, namely that a person cannot be judge in his own cause.
229. Ibid., art. 2. He may also, if he wishes, have a right to a hearing, Conseil d'Etat, 3 mars 1954, Droit Ouvrier 1954, p. 207.
230. Silence on the 'inspecteur's' part does not signify acceptance. *Express* acceptance or refusal must be given. (Tribunal de Bordeaux, 8 février 1951, Recueil Dalloz 1951, p. 393.)
231. Ibid., art. 3. The powers of the 'inspecteur du travail' to examine all cases of dismissal of members of the 'comités d'entreprise' are extensive. He examines '. . . la matérialité et le gravité des griefs allégués . . . ' This power has been confirmed by the Conseil d'Etat – see e.g. 12 novembre 1949, JCP 1950, 11.5909.
232. Ibid., art. 4.
233. Ibid., art. 5.
234. Ibid., art. 6. It must be noted that in the case of the dismissal of a 'délégué du personnel', where no 'comité d'entreprise' exists, dismissal or suspension is referred directly to the 'inspecteur du travail' within forty-eight hours of the event.
235. This identical protection is also given to the trade union representative on the comité d'entreprise.
236. Art. 22, al. 3, loi 66-427 du 18 juin 1966 and décret 66-677 du 21 septembre 1966, art. 4.

237. Cour de Cassation, Chambre Civile, Section Sociale, 2 juillet 1948, Jurisclasseur Périodique (Semaine Juridique) 1948. 11. 4624.
238. Cour de Cassation, Chambre Civile, Section Sociale, 23 octobre 1952, Droit Social 1953, p. 32. In this case three days elapsed between the actual dismissal and subsequent ratification; the court held that this practice was invalid.
239. Cour de Cassation, Chambre Civile, Section Sociale, 14 octobre 1954, Droit Social 1955, p. 38.
240. Of the contract of employment or outrageous conduct in the execution of his functions.
241. Thus the employer may 'en cas de faute grave prononcer la mise à pied immédiate de l'intéressé en attendant une décision définitive'. Ordonnance du 22 février 1945, art. 22, al. 1, as amended by loi 66–427 du 18 juin 1966.
242. See Lecourt, 'La mise à pied pour mesure disciplinaire et la jurisprudence française', Revue Française du Travail 1954, p. 25. See also Boitel, 'La mise à pied et les fonctions électives du délégué du personnel.' Droit Ouvrier 1955, p. 365.
243. In some cases of suspension the employee is not entitled to remuneration. If the suspension is wrongful the employee will be entitled to damages. (Suspension abusive.)
244. Cour de Cassation, Chambre Civile, Section Sociale, 21 mars 1952, JCP 1952, 11. 6971.
245. Loi du 20 septembre 1948, art. 21 as amended by loi du 16 janvier 1967, art. 2.
246. Conseil de Prud'hommes d'Appel, Liège, 7 avril 1962, Journal des Tribunaux 411; Conseil de Prud'hommes, Charleroi, 8 octobre 1968, Bulletin FIB 1970, p. 84; Conseil de Prud'hommes, Mons, 13 septembre 1969, Revue de Droit Social 1969, p. 336.
247. The 'commission paritaire' has to give its decision as to whether reasons of an economic or technical nature exist, within two calendar months of the employer's application (loi du 20 september 1948, art. 21 as amended by loi du 16 janvier 1967, art. 2, para. 2). The court cannot state whether these 'raisons' exist; the court may only deal with the case *after* the employer has consulted the 'commission paritaire' (Cour de Cassation, 23 février 1967, Revue de Droit Social 1967, p. 156). The same applies where the establishment has closed down (Conseil de Prud'hommes d'Appel, Mons, 8 février 1969, Revue de Droit Social 1970, p. 72. cf. however Conseil de Prud'hommes, 29 novembre 1965, Revue de Droit Social 1966, p. 167), though a trustee in bankruptcy may dismiss a 'conseil' member without consulting the 'commission paritaire' (arrêt 13 janvier 1971, Journal des Tribunaux du Travail 1971, p. 124).
248. It has also been found that dismissals which are referred to the 'commission paritaire' are mass dismissals by reason of redundancy where the whole or part of an establishment is to close down. A parliamentary debate on this aspect seems to confirm these findings. Mr Van den Daele in his report to the Chambre de Deputés (Rapport Complémentaire du 1 février 1950 – document Chambre, session 49/50, no. 204) said that dismissals '... pour raisons d'ordre économique ou technique ne valent que quand ils sont la conséquence de l'arrêt de *toute l'entreprise, d'une section* de celle ci ... ou de la mise hors service *d'un groupe spécial de personnel* bien déterminé' (stress added).
249. Document 50/195, p. 2.
250. The membre who is dismissed for 'faute grave' may also contest his dismissal

and the onus is on the employer to prove that serious misconduct has occurred.
251. i.e. the first step is the agreement of the comité d'entreprise; should there not be agreement then outsiders get involved, namely the 'inspecteur du travail' and the minister.
252. i.e. the first step is the 'commission paritaire's' unanimous agreement, failing that the 'conseil de prud'hommes' ' decision.
253. Faute grave in France and Belgium and 'raisons d'ordre économique ou technique' excepted.
254. Loi du 20 septembre 1948, art. 21 as amended by loi du 16 janvier 1967, art. 2, para. 3.
255. i.e. two years' service on the 'comité d'entreprise' or over. See p. 69 ante.
256. See p. 69 ante.
257. The Bruges court held '... il s'agit de listes de candidats *définitives* valable pour procéder aux opérations électorales, et non de listes qui subirent ensuite de modifications' (stress added). (RDS 1951, p. 146 (26 March 1951).) In this case the name of the plaintiff was inserted on the provisional list but was subsequently removed because of certain conduct unbecoming. The 'conseil de prud'hommes' in Anvers came to the same conclusion when the name of the candidate was inserted contrary to the limitation period. The court said, 'La protection légale a un caractère tout à fait exceptionnel et constitue une dérogation au droit commun. Un travailleur porté sur une liste de candidats présentée en dehors des délais prévus par la législation, ne peut en bénéficier.' (1 October 1951, RT 1951, p. 1238). In another case in the 'conseil de prud'hommes' of Charleroi the court stated that 'la loi n'a entendu protéger que les travailleurs qui ont été valablement portés sur une liste de candidats et qui réunissent les conditions d'éligibilité...' (RT 1951, p. 29). Such protection is also given to the délégué suppléant (see documents parlementaires, Chambre 1965–66 No. 264/1, p. 4. A member of the 'conseil' who resigns his post loses the protection given to him. (Conseil de Prud'hommes d'Appel, Namur, 12 août 1966, Revue de Droit Social 1966, p. 284; see also Conseil de Prud'hommes, Auvelais, 22 octobre 1965, Bulletin FIB 1966, p. 284). Similarly, if he resigns from the union which nominated him (Cour de Cassation, 30 avril 1969, Revue de Droit Social 1969, p. 259).
258. i.e. the Trade Union and the Labour Relations Act 1974, schedule 1, giving employees the right not to be unfairly dismissed, and the Employment Protection Act 1975, s.53 (actions short of dismissal) and ss.57–58 (time off work to carry out trade union duties and activities respectively).
259. An employee for example is protected from dismissal or discrimination for taking part in trade union activities either within or outside his working hours. Such protection does not necessarily cover the activities of a works council, despite the fact that its members could be trade unionists, since a works council's activities are not necessarily trade union ones.
260. Before agreement on dismissal is reached by the works council the rules of natural justice must be observed and a secret ballot held. A two-thirds majority vote of those voting should be required, thus giving greater protection to the member and avoiding the criticism made at p. 69 ante.
261. cf. art. 112 (1) of the proposed statute for European companies which only provides for gross misconduct such as would entitle the employer to terminate the employee's contract *without* notice. The present submissions go a great deal further.
262. See p. 69 ante.
263. In case of mass dismissals for redundancy then ss.99 and 100 of the

Employment Protection Act 1975 would be operative.
264. In that the court becomes involved and that should it find for the member, reinstatement would be difficult or impracticable at that stage (see p. 71 ante).
265. cf. proposed statute for European companies, art. 112(2).
266. See pp. 71 and 72 ante.
267. See the problems which have arisen in Belgium in this respect at p. 72 ante.
268. See p. 70 ante.
269. Cour de Cassation, Chambre Civile, Section Sociale, 9 juillet 1953, Droit Social 1954, p. 33.
270. See the decision in Tribunal Civil de St. Etienne, 2 juin 1951, Droit Ouvrier 1951, p. 421.
271. Cour de Cassation, Chambre Civile, Section Sociale, 27 novembre 1952, Droit Social 1953, p. 101.
272. Cour de Cassation, Chambre Civile, Section Sociale, 3 juin 1948, Droit Social 1948, p. 120.
273. Cour de Cassation, Chambre Civile, Section Sociale, 29 avril 1953, Droit Social 1953, p. 410
274. Though this has not been admitted by any of the employers interviewed.
275. The Tribunal de Valence went even further and said that such practices by the employer could do away with workers' organisations, and that that was clearly not the aim of the legislation (12 juillet 1955, Droit du Travail et de la Sécurité Sociale 1955, no. 8, p. 45). This writer feels that the first part of this court's suggestion is clearly farfetched since one cannot demolish a structure (namely a 'comité d'entreprise') laid down by Parliament merely because an outlet is available to the employer in the case of one or a few employees who serve on the 'comité'. That that was clearly not the intention of the legislation is in fact so.
276. See e.g. Cour de Cassation, Chambre Criminelle, 1 février 1957, JCP 1957, 11.6333.
277. This varies from 500 to 5,000 French francs and/or imprisonment of between six days to one year. These penalties are doubled for subsequent offences.
278. Art. 24 of loi du 18 juin 1966 talks of ' . . . entrave apportée *intentionnellement*, soit à la constitution d'un comité d'entreprise, soit à la libre désignation de ses membres, soit à son fonctionnement régulier, notamment par la méconnaissance des dispositions des articles et des textes réglementaires pris pour leur application' (stress added).
279. Although this is rather a delicate situation to which an employer will not own up, it is found in the sample examined that employers do not *intentionally* dismiss so as to disrupt the working of the 'comité'. Indeed some welcomed the 'comité' as an institution for consultation and therefore as an organ enhancing industrial relations, and since 1968 encouraged it in order to avoid the 'sections syndicales' which have since been instituted.
280. i.e. a wrongful dismissal does not necessarily show *intention* to disrupt or interfere with the constitution or functioning of the 'comité' (. . . entrave apportée intentionnellement . . . à la constitution d'un comité . . . à son fonctionnement régulier . . . à la libre désignation de ses membres . . .) or intention to paralyse the workings of the comité.
281. Cour de Cassation, Chambre Criminelle, 14 octobre 1954. Bulletin Criminel 1954, p. 511.
282. Reinstatement has the same meaning as it does in Britain, i.e. under the same terms and conditions of employment and in his previous position. cf. a similar provision under French law.
283. See Cour de Cassation, 29 octobre 1954. Pasicrisie belge 1955, 1, 178.

Application can even be verbal so long as proof of the thirty-day period is available: Conseil de Prud'hommes d'Appel, Mons, 16 janvier 1965, Revue de Droit Social 1965, p. 166. See also Conseil de Prud'hommes d'Appel, Mons, 20 février 1960, Revue de Droit Social 1961, p. 273.
284. Cour de Cassation, 3 mars 1967, Journal des Tribunaux 1967, p. 313.
285. Loi du 20 septembre 1948, art. 21 as amended by the loi du 16 janvier 1967, art. 2, paras. 5–8.
286. See p. 74 ante.
287. See p. 71 ante.
288. Loi du 20 septembre 1948, art. 32 as amended. 'Les chefs d'entreprise . . . qui ont mis obstacle à son (conseil) fonctionnement tel que celui-ci est prévu dans la présente loi, sont punis d'une amende de 100 F.B. multipliée par le nombre de travailleurs occupés dans l'entreprise, sans que cette amende puisse exceder 100,000 F.B.' (brackets added).
289. cf. the situation in France (see above, p. 74).
290. i.e. the Trade Union and Labour Relations Act 1974 as amended by the Employment Protection Act 1975 or the common law for breach of contract of employment.
291. With the possible exception of Belgium where a long-serving employee could get more compensation than the maximum in Britain.
292. cf. statute for European companies, art. 112(3).
293. Under ss. 73–76 Employment Protection Cat 1975 – up to a maximum of £11,760.
294. See p. 74 ante.
295. And not the rebuttal of the presumption as is the case in France – see p. 75 ante.
296. See the suggestion made in the case of France, p. 74.
297. See p. 73 ante.
298. Even though it is not a legal persona, it ought, as a trade union may, (TULRA 1974 52(c)) be sued in tort.
299. There is one exception in connection with the 'œuvres sociales' where décret du 2 novembre 1945 provides otherwise.
300. Loi du 16 mai, 1946, art. 16.
301. Ibid., art. 17.
302. It has been found on numerous occasions in practice that the employer has not been able to fulfil this provision because it has not been possible for action to be taken by the date of the following meeting. Invariably however a progress report on the matter is given. At one meeting attended, the employer agreed to set up a special insurance scheme. It took nine months to have this finalised, but progress on the scheme was given at subsequent meetings.
303. A sub-committee especially created (or sometimes a standing sub-committee) to bring into being or examine some schemes suggested by the comité d'entreprise.
304. Loi du 16 mai 1946, art. 18.
305. Ibid., art. 19.
306. Tribunal Civil de St Etienne, 13 juin 1953, Informateur du Chef d'Entreprise 1953, p. 903 and an appeal Cour de Cassation, Chambre Civile, Section Sociale, 4 mai 1956, JCP 1956, 11.9422.
307. Loi du 16 mai 1946, art. 20.
308. Loi du 20 septembre 1948, art. 22, para. 1. Arrêté royal du 18 février 1971, art. 59.
309. Some of the larger companies examined in France, Belgium and Luxembourg held at times as many as four meetings in one month when certain pressing

problems arose. As a general rule the smaller companies examined in these countries found it difficult to hold even one meeting for lack of discussion material and in France and Belgium instances were often found where the statutory requirements for monthly meetings were not fulfilled. In two instances in France, the 'comité' had only met three times and twice a year respectively. So as to respect the anonymity of these firms, names are not given.

310. Loi du 20 septembre 1948, art. 23. It is found in practice that most 'comités' in both France and Belgium meet during working hours. Of the sample examined 91 per cent did so. The remaining 9 per cent held their meetings at convenient times outside working hours and in both countries (though there exists no legal requirement in France) the time spent was paid as though it had been worked. In three instances (one in Belgium and two in France) it was found that overtime rates were paid, although in a report of the Belgian Senat on this very matter it was said that normal and *not* overtime rates are payable (see Documents Parlementaires Sénat 1947–8, No. 489, p. 25).

311. Loi du 20 septembre 1948 and arrêté du régent du 13 juin 1949 do not state how the 'conseils' are to reach their decisions. Hence Avis du Conseil d'Etat, 11 mai 1949, Moniteur Belge 1949, p. 7115. cf. also the rule of unanimity which exists in the 'commissions paritaires' (art. 11 of arrêts – loi du 9 juin 1945). Some 'conseil' rules do however provide for the majority rule. See J.P. Haesaert, 'Quelques aspects de la législation relative aux conseils d'entreprise', Revue du Travail 1952, p. 1226.

312. This writer attended a 'conseil' meeting in order to examine how this unanimity rule works in practice. At a preliminary interview all members of the 'conseils' (management, employees and manual workers) examined stated that they did not vote on any decision, but that the generally accepted practice was that the chairman (employer) would wait until some sort of agreement had been reached amongst the members. He would then express his opinion. If it was similar to the other opinions expressed then the decision would be taken. These statements were substantiated at that meeting. See also Horion, 'La représentation des travailleurs sur le plan de l'entreprise en droit Belge', p. 160, who comes to this same conclusion.

313. Loi du 20 septembre 1948, art. 22 as amended by loi du 15 jin 1953, art. 3 places an obligation upon the 'conseils d'entreprise' to have a constitution (règlement d'ordre intérieur) (see note 315 below for details). It is customary for the constitution to provide for the unanimity rule, even though the law is silent on this point. Thus for example in the constitution of the 'conseil d'entreprise' in the mines the unanimity rule of *all members present at the meeting* is provided for by art. 17. In the iron ore industry art. 14 of its constitution provides that the decisions of the 'conseil' '... sont normalement prises à l'unanimité des membres présents ...'. Though the constitution of the steel industry does not specifically provide for such unanimity, this writer is told that it is an accepted fact on all sides that it is the norm.

314. Or where the 'commission paritaire' fails, the constitution may be established by royal decree after consultation with the 'conseil national du travail'.

315. These are provided by para. 3 of loi du 20 septembre 1948, art. 22 as amended by loi du 15 juin 1953, art. 3 and consist of: (i) length of notice to be given by a member of the 'conseil' in connection with a matter to be referred to the 'conseil' for discussion; (ii) notice required before convening a meeting; (iii) agenda of the meeting mentioning all the matters to be

Representative Establishment Councils 143

discussed; (iv) role of the chairman and rules as to how he should be replaced; (v) role of the secretary and his replacement; (vi) conduct of the meeting; (vii) the taking of minutes and the way these should be communicated to all 'conseil' members; (viii) the manner in which all employees of the firm are to be informed of the 'conseil's' decision; (ix) the place where minutes of the meetings are kept and how and when these may be consulted by 'conseil' members; and (x) procedure for modifying the constitution. Prior to 1953, there was no legal obligation on a 'conseil' to have a constitution. Consequently very few had a written one and those that did were mainly in the nationalised industries (Professor P. Horion, in 'La représentation des travailleurs sur le plan de l'entreprise en droit Belge', p. 169, lists four in the mines, three in the iron ore industry and twelve in the steel industry out of ninety-seven establishments). Again very few provided their members with the minutes of the previous meeting (according to Professor Horion one in the mines, two in iron ore and sixteen in the steel industry out of 160 establishments) and the methods of informing employees was at times unsatisfactory, e.g. *viva voce* or by such means as 'the grape vine'.

316. Loi du 20 september 1948, art. 22, para. 5.
317. Inspectors (inspecteurs sociaux) may also attend meetings if requested to by the 'conseil' as a whole, or by the employer or employees. They attend solely in a consultative capacity (arrêté du régent, 13 juin 1949, art. 10 as amended by arrêté du régent 27 mars 1954, art. 3). cf. the powers of the inspecteurs du travail in France, see p. 77 ante with those of the inspecteurs sociaux (arrêté du régent, 11 janvier 1950, art. 3).
318. Loi du 20 septembre 1948, art. 23.
319. e.g. the works council which is at the top of a three-tier system of the Rotherham works of the British Steel Corporation meets every two months. The meetings are formal and planned in advance so that reviews of progress are given and discussed by various departments, minutes are taken and circulated, agendas are prepared, and the chairman observes the formal procedures of running meetings. Every six months (in May and November) a special meeting is held with the sole object of reviewing progress over the past six months (cf. French system). No constitution on the Belgium pattern exists, but then this is not required since the system in this works operates efficiently. The area councils which also meet approximately every two months are not as well organised as the works council. Their function is to deal with more than one department within the area but not the whole works. Departmental committees vary. Some do not meet at all, others meet monthly and others have degenerated and are only concerned with health and safety. Those that do meet hold formal meetings and minutes and an agenda are produced. The chair is normally taken by the departmental head and elections take place through the union structure (BISAKTA). The items discussed are varied and on occasion progress reports are made. It is found that this three-tier system is clumsy and there is a considerable overlap of functions between each of these (and a consequent waste of time). In ICI the monthly staff have a site staff committee which meets sometimes monthly but more usually every two months. The division staff conference meets every six months and the central staff conference at the top of this three-tier system once a year. The divisional standing committee prepares the agenda for the division staff conference. The weekly staff are represented on plant committees and one works committee. Before every works committee meeting the shop stewards meet alone. Meetings of plant committees tend to be formal, i.e. an agenda is prepared, matters arising from the minutes of the previous meeting are dealt with, matters on the

agenda discussed etc. In Unilever head office, departmental councils meet every month or month and a half and minutes are kept and circulated by the secretary who is appointed by the members. The departmental manager must attend six meetings of the council to report on progress, though he is not a member of the departmental council. The grade committees meet every two months and again a formal meeting structure is observed and minutes are circulated to all members of the committee. Not being an information channel, the grade committees do not circulate the minutes to all staff. The Blackfriars consultative council at the top of the tier, has fortnightly meetings. A formal procedure is observed and all minutes are circulated to all members of the council as well as to all employees by means of a news-sheet within forty-eight hours of the meeting. The joint consultation manager is responsible *inter alia* for circulating minutes of the various consultative bodies and for the provision of secretarial services to these bodies, and is the source of information to all employees. The system is considered as efficient and an excellent forum for being heard and as a source of information to all employees. In Pilkington's fibreglass insulation division the works consultative committee meets every three or four months, but as compared to Unilever for example the system is not as efficient. Minutes, though taken, are not always circulated and sometimes the agenda for the following meeting is not prepared. In Cadbury Schweppes the Bournville works council meets every fortnight and a formal meeting structure is observed, reports from management are given, and sales reports, production reports etc. are also discussed.

320. As is the case in Belgium — see p. 78 ante. cf. also art. 111 of the statute for European companies which lays the responsibility on the works council itself to draw up rules of procedure.
321. This need not be repeated and the reader is invited to consult note 315 above.
322. Problems of the kind found in the other countries examined will undoubtedly arise (see p. 77 and note 309 above), but it is submitted that these only arise because of inefficiency rather than lack of matters for discussion.
323. Although it *was* found that the unanimity rule works well in Belgium, cf. also art. 111(4) of the statute for European companies which talks of '... majority vote of the members present and represented'.
324. cf. art. 118(1) of the proposed statute for European companies.
325. cf. art. 111(3) of the proposed statute for European companies.
326. There exists no legislation on this aspect in the other countries examined but case law does exist in France (see p. 77 and note 306 above).
327. Interviews were held with some 200 individuals in British establishments of a varying nature. One of the questions asked was 'Do you think that a consultative body, such as a works council, has a role to play in your establishment?' Sixty-eight per cent considered that it did, 20 per cent considered that it had a limited use and the remainder were sceptical about, against, or indifferent to such organisations. The question which followed was 'If you feel that such a body has a role to play, what do you consider to be the most important aspect of that function?' Of the 68 per cent who replied in the affirmative, the consultation about various schemes etc. and welfare aspects were the ones which had been stressed. The individuals who thought that consultative bodies had a limited use nevertheless considered that within that limited use the consultation and welfare functions were their main aspects. This clearly shows that a substantial majority believe that the works councils' or similar consultative bodies' functions lie within the sphere of consultation about matters relating to the establishment and welfare within it. The employees interviewed were carefully selected from

the more intelligent. It is however interesting to note that many workers interviewed by this writer did not know what works councils were or what their functions consisted of. Others had heard of works councils but did not know what they did. The reason why *inter alia* these two questions were asked was to find out firstly if there was a consensus of opinion favouring works councils, and secondly, what functions these bodies should perform. If there exists a majority in favour and if there is a majority agreement as to their role then it is possible after proceeding with the comparison to make submissions for legislation so that an expansion of such bodies throughout British industry might take place.

328. In Reckitt and Colman Ltd for example the paternalistic aspect preceded the present situation. A similar development may be found in Armstrong Patents or in the Rotherham works of the British Steel Corporation when it was the United Steel Company. An expansion has taken place from the original welfare and other schemes run by the employer. Developments may also take place because of the unsatisfactory nature of the previous system, as was found in Unilever (Blackfriars) when the old system dating back to 1951 was replaced in 1972 by a new one. (See pp. 122 and 123 of 'Worker Participation in Britain', Financial Times Ltd, 1974.)
329. Loi du 28 juillet 1942, art. 9 al. 1.
330. Loi du 11 octobre 1946, art. 1, and loi du 15 mars 1955.
331. The syllabus for this certificate includes both theoretical and practical studies. This research shows that it is mainly women who fulfil this function. It is also found that the number of 'conseillères chef du travail' who are 'diplômés' is small. It is consequently the 'assistantes sociales' who, with the consent of the 'comité d'entreprise' exercise their functions. Décret du 2 novembre 1945, art. 14 (see also arrêté du 27 août 1945).
332. Décret du 2 november 1945, art. 16, al. 2.
333. This protection is similar to that of the 'délégués du personnel' and to members of the 'comité d'entreprise'. The intervention of the 'inspecteur du travail' is therefore necessary, not only in cases of dismissal, but also where the post becomes redundant. Décret du 2 novembre 1945, art. 13.
334. Décret du 9 novembre 1946, arts. 1 and 2(1)–(4).
335. Loi du 28 juillet 1942, art. 10.
336. Décret du 9 novembre 1946, art. 10, al. 1 and 2. The 'comité d'entreprise' must submit an annual report on the organisation, functioning and financial management of the 'services sociaux'.
337. Function (c) (see p. 82 above) has been found to be the predominant one, with functions (d) and (a) following closely as second and third. In three establishments visited it was found that because of female preponderance function (b) was the most important one. Function (e) was found to exist in only one of the establishments visited, namely Ets. Renault.
338. Members of 'comités', employees and workers interviewed and asked which of the functions they considered the 'conseillère' performed most in their establishments put these functions in a similar order to what the 'conseillères' put them in — see note 337 above.).
339. e.g. one of the items in the 'services sociaux' is item (e) (see p. 82 above). The 'œuvres sociales' for which the 'comité d'entreprise' is responsible are all for the benefit of employees or retired employees and *their families*. It is submitted that confusion may arise when a *family* is confronted with the 'conseillère' and a member of the 'comite' on any one given matter. In theory this should not happen since the 'comite' should liaise with the 'conseillère', but in practice it might well happen. More important however is the similarity of functions examined by the 'comités' in their role of

managing the 'œuvres sociales' with those of the 'conseillère' in her role of performing her functions and being kept an eye on by the 'comite'.

340. See annales parlementaires of 18 June 1948, p. 11, where it will be found that the amendment was moved by M. Heyman.

341. Generally speaking the 'services sociaux' are carried out in Belgium by the personnel department of the establishment. This is similar to the practice in Britain where the personnel officers carry out some of the functions entrusted to the 'conseillère' in France.

342. It is interesting that the proposed statute for European companies does not provide for any such system. Interviews held with officials in the labour and other sections of the European Commission in Brussels indicated that difficulties and problems would undoubtedly arise if a system such as the French one were introduced or suggested throughout the community.

343. By 'œuvres sociales' this writer means a *benevolent institution*, financed from *within the establishment* (i.e. by the employer, employees or both) with an element of (or the intention that it should have) *permanence* or continuity. The social security or other state schemes, bonuses (whether or not emanating from part of a collective agreement incorporated into an individual contract of employment) or other occasional benevolent acts by the employer or the work of charitable institutions do not come within the definition of 'œuvres sociales' as this writer understands these. Though any 'benevolent' acts or institutions deriving their source from the contract of employment are excluded from the term 'œuvres sociales' because the employer's obligations are strictly contractual and therefore not independent from that contract, it has been found in both France and Belgium that where such a benevolent scheme does emanate from the contract and that there is no institution to supervise or run that scheme, *and* the employees contribute towards it, then this could be classed as an 'œuvre social' and the 'committee' will be the competent body to *supervise* it. It may also be that a collective agreement provides for some benevolent institution to be set up, and specifically mentions the 'committee' to run it. Under these circumstances the benevolent institution will become an 'œuvre social' to be administered or supervised as the case may be by the 'committee'. In none of the countries' laws is the term 'œuvres sociales' defined, and the above definition has been promulgated from an examination and analysis of the *nature* of the various 'œuvres sociales' in the different countries under examination. A definition which supports this writer's findings may be found in the national agreement between the Employers' Federation and the CSCB (Confédération des Syndicats Chrétiens de Belgique), the FGTB (Fédération Générale du Travail de Belgique) and the CGSLB (Centrale Générale des Syndicats Libéraux de Belgique) of 16 July 1958 as amended on 29 March and 28 November 1962. Article 4(1) provides ' . . . il y a lieu d'entendre par "œuvres sociales" les advantages répondant aux critères suivants: avoir un caractère permanent; être octroyés dans l'entreprise; avoir pour objet de contribuer au bien-être des travailleurs de l'entreprise et/ou des membres de leur famille; ne pas résulter d'une disposition légal ou réglementaire; ne pas être fixés par le contrat de travail ou d'emploi'.

344. The 'œuvres sociales' for the benefit of employees or retired employees and their families may include any one or more of the following:

(i) Retirement pension schemes and social security schemes within the establishment.

(ii) Social matters relating to the improvement of welfare conditions, such as canteens, housing, colonies de vacances, clubs, gardening clubs and nurseries for children of working mothers.

(iii) Social matters relating to the use of spare time and to sport.

(iv) Educational or trade institutions which are attached to or dependent upon the establishment. These include apprenticeship centres and schools, centres for training and retraining, libraries, study groups, liberal and general study courses etc.

(v) Social services responsible for:

(a) The welfare of the worker within the establishment, facilitating to his adapting himself to the work and to collaborating with the works medical service.

(b) Co-ordinating and appraising social matters managed jointly by the 'comité d'entreprise' and the employer.

(vi) The medical service within the establishment. (See décret du 2 novembre 1945, art., 2(1)–(6).) (See also Spyropoulos, 'L'administration des œuvres sociales par le comité d'entreprise', 1961.)

345. Though the employer himself finances these.

346. 'Supervised' because it has been found that numerous 'comités d'entreprise' delegate their 'œuvres sociales' functions to either sub-committees or to individuals. This is provided for by art. 4 of the décret du 2 novembre 1945 which states 'La gestion des œuvres sociales . . . est assurée . . . par le comité d'entreprise lui-même ou par l'entremise d'une commission spéciale ou des personnes designées par lui ou d'organismes créés par lui et ayant reçu une délégation à cet effet . . . '

347. Paternalism by some employers, who instituted and administered welfare and assistance schemes for their employees, was evident prior to 1946. Ordonnance du 22 février 1945, art. 1, al. 1 as amended by loi du 16 mai 1946 substituted the 'comité d'entreprise' for the employer. For a scholarly work on the 'œuvres sociales' of the 'comités d'entreprise' see Renée Petit, 'La gestion des œuvres sociales par les comités d'entreprise' in Droit Social 1946; see also Poussière, 'Les comités d'entreprises et la gestion des œuvres sociales', Jurisclasseur Périodique 1946, vol. 1, and Rouast, 'Les comités d'entreprise et les œuvres dotées de la personalité morale', Droit Social 1952.

348. A comité d'entreprise (as well as a comité central d'entreprise, comité inter-entreprise and comité d'établissement) possesses legal personality (décret du 2 novembre 1945, art. 1, on 'comité d'entreprise' and art. 10 on 'comités inter-entreprise'. Nowhere in the Code du Travail has it been possible to find any statute giving the 'comité d'établissement' legal personality but the Cour de Cassation on 28 janvier 1954 (Droit Social 1954, p. 161) did state that this body is also endowed with legal personality. This being so, (i) it may acquire and own property necessary for its functioning (see décret du 2 novembre 1945, art. 1, al. 2) subject to certain formalities being fulfilled where gifts and legacies are left to it. These formalities being the 'préfet's' agreement after consulting the 'Directeur départemental du travail et de la main d'œuvre' and being authorised by the 'conseil d'état' (décret du 2 novembre 1945, art. 2, al. 3, and loi du 4 février 1901, art. 7); (ii) it may sue and be sued on all matters necessary for its functioning (décret du 2 novembre 1945, art. 1, al. 2; (iii) it can own the yearly contribution made by the employer for the purpose of financing the social institutions of the comité, (décret du 2 novembre 1945, art. 19); (iv) it is a separate legal entity from the establishment to which it belongs.

349. Art. 3, al. 1 of the décret du 2 novembre 1945 provides ' . . . assure . . . la gestion des œuvres sociales . . . ' For these see note 344 above.

350. Art. 3, al. 3 of the décret du 2 novembre 1945 states categorically 'Il contrôle la gestion . . . '

351. Art. 3, al. 3 of the décret du 2 novembre 1945. See also note 344 above at

352. Décret du 2 novembre 1945, art. 6, al. 1 and 3.
353. Ibid., art. 6, al. 4.
354. Ibid., art. 3, al. 1. See also note 344 above at (iv).
355. Ibid., art. 4 and see comment at note 346 above.
356. Under a law in 1901, which themselves are bodies possessing legal personality.
357. Loi du 7 mai 1917 as modified by the décret-loi du 20 mai 1955, al. 2.
358. Décret du 2 novembre 1945, art. 5, al. 1 and 2.
359. Ibid., art. 5, al. 3.
360. Thirty comités d'entreprise in the production sector were closely examined.
361. These include refreshment trolleys during breaks normally in the morning and afternoon, but also during breaks for shift workers.
362. These are mostly part-time services of a 'médecin du travail', though in some cases there is a full-time medical practitioner. A sick bay with qualified nurses was available at all times.
363. Sometimes with the aid of an 'assistante sociale', but usually by the comité detailing a fellow worker to keep an eye on the new recruit.
364. These were found to exist at enterprise level and not at establishment level.
365. Including mainly football, volley ball and rugby. But in three establishments the comité organised skiing parties in the French Alps, sailing, water skiing and in one (in Toulouse) even flying.
366. Mainly refresher courses and specialised courses for new products.
367. The type of material found in these libraries varied. In the libraries attached to training schools the material consisted mainly of manuals and technical books. In the libraries, in restrooms etc. the material consisted of thrillers, adventure stories, fiction and detective stories. In one library some classics were also found.
368. All these schemes are run through various insurance companies, though it was found that in two enterprises certain trusts were set up for these purposes.
369. In all seven enterprises loan schemes at favourable rates of interest were available.
370. See p. 83 ante.
371. i.e. the formulation or modification of works rules, organising dates of annual holidays, the taking over of functions of the comités de sécurité et d'hygiène, criteria for mass dismissals and re-engagements and the use of languages.
372. i.e. supervision orders, general matters of social order concerning the enterprise and the observance by the employer of safety and welfare legislation.
373. Loi du 20 septembre 1948, art. 15.
374. Accord National du 16 juillet 1958 as amended on 29 March and 28 November 1962.
375. See pp. 82 to 83 ante.
376. Loi du 20 septembre 1948 (Moniteur Belge des 27–28 septembre 1948), art. 15(h) provides 'Les conseils d'entreprise ont pour mission, dans le cadre des lois, conventions collectives ou décisions de commissions paritaires, applicable à l'entreprise: ... de gérer toutes les œuvres sociales institués par l'entreprise pour le bien-être du personnel à moins que celles-ci ne soient laissés à la gestion autonome des travailleurs ... ' (The hypothesis throughout this research is that the 'conseil' manages the 'œuvres sociales' and not the workers.) cf. the much more detailed provisions of the French law, e.g. décret du 2 novembre 1945, art. 2 (see also note 344 above); art. 3, al. 3 (see p. 83 and note 351 ante); and art. 5, al. 1 and 2 (see p. 84 and note

358 ante).
377. All the statute says is 'gérer'. cf. the detailed provisions in France, e.g. see p. 83 and décret du 2 novembre 1945, art. 6, al. 1 and 3 or art. 5, al. 1, 2 and 4.
378. See pp. 83 and 84 ante.
379. See note 376 above for these.
380. See note 343 above which gives the text of art. 4a of the national agreement.
381. Under the original 1958 National Agreement, complementary or private pension schemes, however financed, did not come within the competence of the 'conseils'.
382. The wording in the Accord National du 16 juillet 1958, art. 4(a) as amended by the agreement of 29 mars 1962 is as follows: 'Pour l'application des alinéas précédents, sont notamment à prendre en considération: les fonds et caisses d'entraide, les fonds de pension, les économats, les cantines et mess, les services de prêts et primes consentis par l'entreprise en vue de l'acquisition d'un logement, les activités récréatives et culturelles.' It will be noted that unlike France, group insurance schemes do not come within the province of the 'œuvres sociales' and therefore cannot be managed by the 'conseil d'entreprise'.
383. See note 343 ante.
384. See note 348 above.
385. The employer is compelled to make a yearly contribution for the financing of the social institutions of the comité (décret du 2 novembre 1945, art. 19(2)). The employer's yearly contribution must in no case be below the total sum spent on the social expenditure of the enterprise within the year in which such expenditure was the highest during the three preceding years of the 'œuvres sociales' being taken over by the 'comité' (loi du 2 août 1949, art. unique al. 1). Furthermore, the percentage between the contribution and the total sum paid in wages must not be below that of the year (among the three preceding years of the 'comité' being set up) when the employer made his highest contribution to the 'œuvres sociales'. The aim of this article is to prevent the employer from reducing the total contributions made by him to the 'œuvres sociales' at the time when these are taken over by the 'comité' (loi du 2 août 1949, art. unique al. 2.) The employer may however reduce his contribution if the total of wages has decreased or in cases where additional sums were paid by him for a temporary period of time or for a particular purchase (loi du 2 août) 1949, art. unique al. 1). An increase in contributions may be made by collective agreement. A 'convention collective susceptible d'extension' must of compulsion contain a clause relating to the financing of the 'œuvres sociales' run by the 'comité' (loi du 11 février 1950, art. 31g), e.g. a collective agreement examined provided that the employer had to contribute to the 'œuvres sociales' fund of the 'comité' at least 1 per cent of the total wage bill. There is nothing to prevent the employer from contributing greater sums than those stated above, this does not bind him for the future to continue paying at the same rate. He may subsequently decrease it to within the statutory or collective agreement limits. (Cour de Paris, 31 janvier 1956, ICE 1956, p. 312.) See also décret 7 novembre 1966 and circulaire ministériel 10 mars 1967 which provide for the 1 per cent rule. The 'comité' also has other financial sources. These are:
  (i) The moneys and property assigned to the now non-existent 'comité social d'entreprise' (created by loi du 4 octobre 1941) or other organisations that have since replaced it (by ordonnance du 27 juillet 1944). The transfer of these moneys and property had to be made during

the month following the formation of the 'comité d'entreprise'.

(ii) Sums previously given by the employer to the 'caisses de compensation d'allocations familiales', e.g. children's allowances and analogous funds for the organisations financed by these funds and which function within the establishment.

(iii) The compulsory reimbursement by the employer of the insurance premiums due to the 'comité d'entreprise' to cover his statutory duties.

(iv) The voluntary subscriptions of personnel within the establishment. The 'comité d'entreprise' fixes the amount.

(v) The sums or property having belonged to organisations called 'comités sociaux nationaux' or 'régionaux', which might have been attributed to them by an intervening decree in application of art. 29 of ordonnance of 27 July 1944.

(vi) The subsidies or grants made by trade unions or other bodies.

(vii) Gifts and legacies made by individuals.

(viii) The profits made out of social activities (dances, plays, dinners etc.) organised by the 'comité'.

(ix) The revenue from non-movable and movable property belonging to the 'comité' (décret du 2 novembre 1945, art. 19).

386. See décret du 2 novembre 1945, art. 4. In an important case the Cour de Cassation held that the comité is empowered to create new 'œuvres sociales' even though the employer objects (Cour de Cassation, Section Sociale, 4 janvier 1962, JCP 1962, 11.12594).
387. Namely no power of execution of its own decisions, only the power to suggest sums for 'œuvres sociales' and no power to institute or abolish 'œuvres sociales'. See p. 86 ante for an analysis.
388. See p. 84 ante.
389. Which can also emanate from a contract of employment or collective agreement which specifically places the management of these in the hands of the 'conseil d'entreprise'.
390. i.e. a non profit-making body for the welfare of employees, a benevolent society. This body has corporate personality.
391. See accord national du 16 juillet 1958 as amended by the agreement of 29 mars 1962, clause 4(b).
392. i.e. art. 15h of loi du 20 septembre 1948. See note 376 above for its provisions.
393. The statute says '. . . de gérer les œuvres sociales *instituées par l'entreprise* . . .' (stress added).
394. See *Appendix A* and p. 84 ante.
395. Accord national de 16 juillet 1958 as amended by the agreement of 29 mars 1962, clause 4(c).
396. See pp. 84 and 85 ante.
397. Thirty establishments of a similar nature and size as the French ones, and producing similar products, were examined.
398. e.g. the electricity supply industry consultation committees have executive powers in training only; the Boeke Trust committee in Cadbury Schweppes has executive powers in deciding what grants are to be made to outside organisations or workers and pensioners in need; the joint consultative committee in that same company also has management powers by organising conferences, study tours and series of lectures; the company schemes committee concerns itself with matters which are outside negotiated terms with the unions, e.g. when holidays are to be taken or the beginning and ending of the working day; the catering committee manages catering within the Bournville establishment. All these committees as well as others,

e.g. amenities committees, education and training committees, suggestions committee etc. report to the Bournville works council at the fortnightly meetings. Thus the Bournville works council and the standing committees jointly have limited decision-making powers: at Lostock works and Castner-Kellner works of Imperial Chemical Industries the works committee has decision-making powers over canteens, welfare of present employees (e.g. better restroom facilities, clean overalls), training, works amenities, safety matters (e.g. protection against chemical poisoning), holiday periods, car parking, welfare of retired employees, pensions, and at times the advertising and filling of weekly staff vacancies. The works consultative committee of Pilkington Brothers, fibreglass insulation division, through its sub-committees has decision-making powers over dances, factory outings, children's Christmas and other parties. The committee of departmental councils of Unilever Blackfriars deals with services, e.g. chiropody services, and additional benefits, e.g. maternity leave, and acts as a clearing house for the departmental councils by deciding what matters should go to the central council and what could be dealt with at departmental council level. At this latter level the decision-making powers lie mainly in welfare matters (e.g. canteens and catering, furnishing of offices etc.), social functions and training.

399. e.g. do the various standing committees of a particular works council themselves have decision-making or supervisory powers, or do decision-making or supervisory powers vest solely in the works council after the committee has reported or made recommendations? In some establishments examined it appears that these committees are powerless and can only recommend — the decision-making or supervisory element being vested entirely in the works council itself. In others the standing committee has decision-making or supervisory powers. The remainder were uncertain in what body the decision-making role was vested.

400. An attempt has been made to find out which were the most frequently exercised welfare matters in British enterprises. This would enable this writer to make a comparison with a similar study carried out in Belgium (see p. 89 ante) and France (see p. 84 ante). Because of (a) the under-development of some schemes, (b) the ill-definition of others and (c) a lack of generalisation in the sample examined, it has not been possible to go beyond the matter of canteens, car parks, social activities, sport, and welfare matters such as clean overalls, smoking room, shape of seats etc. There have not been found enough matters to make a comprehensive list and show how Britain compares with the other countries in this reference and to examine the popularity of each of the welfare matters.

401. See *Appendix A* post and p. 83 ante.
402. See *Appendix B* post and p. 87 ante.
403. *The submissions may be found in diagrammatic form at Appendix C post.*
404. See p. 80 et seq. ante.
405. See note 398 above.
406. See note 399 above.
407. This writer cannot agree with the statement made by Mr O.R. Wishlade in 'An overview of participation in British industry', p. 39, when he says, 'This of course is only to be expected, since by its very nature consultation can deal with areas less clearly defined than is necessary for negotiation. It does, however, illustrate one of the major difficulties which could be inherent in the introduction of legislation in this field.'
408. It has been found at some of the works council meetings attended that often difficulty had been experienced in distinguishing negotiation matters

from consultation matters and the remedy was found by making it a rule that at the request of shop stewards certain matters which they consider as negotiable would not be discussed. In one works council meeting, members themselves (as opposed to shop stewards) agreed to stop a particular discussion as they considered that it went into the realm of negotiation. By defining the areas of consultation more specifically this situation would not arise, or if it did, it would be reduced to a minimum.

409. Problems are envisaged with this type of scheme because it is found that the majority of establishments run their own training or retraining schemes and interviews held with some employers suggest that they would not wish these schemes to be run by other than themselves because they consider training as part of the production process, i.e. updating workers on recent developments in the industry. This is certainly a valid point, but there is no reason why employee participation (not management but participation in the management) may not take place. It will be noted that unlike the other countries examined no recommendation is made for a liaison between the medical services of the establishment and the works council. Interviews on both sides revealed that this would not be a practicable idea because of the system of industrial medicine in this country. Industrial medical practitioners interviewed agreed that they did not wish interference to take place by outside bodies, including works councils,
410. See p. 83 ante and *Appendix A*.
411. See p. 87 ante and *Appendix B*.
412. 130 works council members were intereviewed.
413. Namely 'controlling the management'.
414. See note 409 above.
415. cf. also the proposed statute for European companies, art. 123 (1) (b), (e), (f), (g), which deals with this matter and which states that any decision taken by the board of management in respect of matters (b), (e), (f), (g) without the consent of the European works council will be void (art. 123(2)). The withholding of consent for an unreasonable time would entitle the matter to be sent to arbitration (art. 123(3)).
416. See comment at p. 80 ante.
417. In the sense that it is obvious that on instituting a 'social or welfare matter' the works council will consider it of worthwhile permanence to institute it, otherwise it would be wasting its efforts. If it is found not to be successful, or there is no longer a requirement for it, then it would be abolished. This writer fails therefore to see the necessity for legislating on this element of permanence which exists in Belgium, since in practice it has been found that what has been described immediately above occurs.
418. See p. 85 ante.
419. Similar to the status of trade unions and comprising the five matters under s.2(1) of the Trade Union and Labour Relations Act 1974.
420. See note 348 and p. 83 ante.
421. See p. 86 ante.
422. See note 385 ante.
423. Unlike the Belgian situation, see p. 86 ante.
424. cf. the situation in Belgium at p. 88 ante.
425. See p. 85 ante and note 371.
426. See p. 87 ante.
427. 'Les conseils d'entreprise ont pour mission . . . (d) d'élaborer et de modifier . . . le réglement d'atelier ou le réglement d'ordre intérieur de l'entreprise . . . ' loi du 20 septembre 1948, art. 15(d). cf. also loi du 15 juin 1896 which originally imposed this duty upon the employer.

428. Where an establishment which qualifies to have a 'conseil' is newly formed, such a body is not set up immediately on the formation of the new establishment. This means that the employer drafts the works rules initially.
429. See also the debate which took place at the Conseil Paritaire Général on 27 May 1950 on this issue and where this procedure was unanimously agreed. The unions however seemed to have subsequently changed their mind and a Bill was introduced in Parliament to the effect that a third party should be appointed to settle the dispute rather than it being conciliated upon. Although this Bill was passed in the House of Representatives on 26 November 1953 it failed to gain support in the Senate and therefore was lost.
430. It may be argued that the situation could arise where the works council vetoes the whole of the works rules drafted by the employer. This should not be made possible otherwise it would vitiate the whole concept of works rules. It is only once the works rules are in existence that the process of the works council to approve or disapprove subsequent alterations becomes operative. Where a right of veto has been exercised conciliation should follow to allow a settlement.
431. Art. 15(g) of loi du 20 septembre 1948 states 'Les conseils d'entreprise ont pour mission . . . (g) de fixer les dates des vacances annuelles et d'établir, s'il y a lieu un roulement du personnel.'
432. Loi du 20 septembre 1948, art. 15(j) provides 'Les conseils d'entreprise ont pour mission . . . (j) selon les modalités et conditions à déterminer par arrêté royal, les conseils d'entreprise peuvent être habilités à remplir les fonctions attribuées aux comités de sécurité et d'hygiène, institués par arrêté du régent du 3 décembre 1946 et par l'arrêté du régent du 25 septembre 1947'.
433. According to the 1948 statute (see note 432 above), the 'conseils d'entreprise' may decide to take over the functions of the 'comité d'hygiène et de sécurité' (which is a body independent of the 'conseil d'entreprise') so long as the following conditions provided for by arrêté du régent du 13 juin 1949, art. 7, are fulfilled. These are that:
 (i) there must be agreement from the 'comité d'hygiène et de sécurité' to this effect;
 (ii) 60 per cent of the employees are represented in the 'conseil d'entreprise' by workers' organisations;
 (iii) persons already forming part of the 'comité d'hygiène et de sécurité' must remain on it, particularly the safety officer, foremen, medical practitioner, 'assistante sociale' and technicians in the enterprise;
 (iv) the Minister of Labour must approve the takeover.
The question has been asked as to whether a takeover which took place prior to arrêté royal du 21 mars 1958 (which considerably modified the old statutes on 'comité d'hygiène et de sécurité' by providing new provisions on conditions of elections and eligibility) remained valid after that date. Results of interviews held with government officials in Brussels show that the 'conseil d'entreprise' has to renew its decision in the light of the changes which have taken place. Interviews held with 'conseil' members and employees show that in practice this is not done and that the Ministry of Labour turns a blind eye to the few such situations which exist and which the trade unions accept.
434. See p. 83 ante and *Appendix A*.
435. As safety committees are outside the terms of this reference these are not discussed in detail in any of the countries under examination.
436. 'Sometimes' because there are cases where health and safety committees were not separate from the works councils, e.g. Armstrong Patents, Fenners.

437. e.g. (i) the advisory committees in the electricity supply industry have *inter alia* as a function the safety and health of employees in that industry; (ii) the British Steel Corporation nationalisation Act states: 'It shall be the duty of the Corporation . . . [to promote and encourage] . . . measures affecting the safety, health and welfare of persons employed by the corporation' (s.39 of the Iron and Steel Act 1949 as amended by s.31 of the Iron and Steel Act 1967), the functions are performed by the works council and the appropriate departmental committee where there is trade union representation (see e.g. the situation at Rotherham works); at the Lostock works of ICI the works committee covers *inter alia* safety, health and welfare and reports are prepared on accident rates, and accident prevention is discussed as one of the items on the agenda; in Pilkington Brothers' fibreglass insulation division, the works consultative committee deals with safety matters.
438. See this writer's comment in 'The Inspector', series IV, vol. 20, Sept./Oct. 1974, pp. 111, 112 and 113.
439. Where in prescribed cases there must be union representation on safety committees and safety representatives who are union members. See also Carby-Hall, 'The Health and Safety at Work Act 1974' in 'The Inspector', series IV, vol. 20, p. 112.
440. Art. 15 (e) and (i) of loi du 20 septembre 1948 as modified.
441. Arts. 3 and 5 of accord national du 16 juillet 1958 as amended.
442. Art. 15(e) of the statute states ' . . . des critères généraux à suivre en cas de licenciement et d'embauchage des travailleurs'.
443. The statute clearly states ' . . . ont pour mission dans le cadre des lois, conventions collectives ou décisions de commissions paritaires, applicables à l'entreprise . . . ' (art. 15 of loi du 20 septembre 1948 as amended).
444. The justification for art. 3 of the collective agreement states 'L'exercice de cette mission par le conseil d'entreprise ne restreint pas la responsabilité du chef d'entreprise d'assurer l'organisation et le fonctionnement de l'entreprise . . . '
445. Loi 66–427 du 18 juin 1966, art. 3(c), provides 'Il est obligatoirement informé et consulté sur les questions intéressant . . . les mesures de nature à affecter le volume ou la structure des effectifs . . . Le comité d'entreprise est obligatoirement saisi en temps utile des projets de compression d'effectifs; il emet un avis sur l'opération projetée et ses modalités d'application'.
446. See e.g. art. 28 of the convention collective des ouvriers dans les industries métallurgiques du Rhône of 24 December 1953 which states that the comité must be informed of all collective dismissals, and provides for certain guidelines to be followed.
447. Redundancies are *not always* a topic for consultation as was found in the Rotherham works of the British Steel Corporation where the works council does not take part in the decision to close down a factory. This is previously agreed by the employers and unions, and the works council is subsequently informed of the 'fait accompli'.
448. See e.g. collective agreement between Gallaher and ASTMS and APEX enumerating *inter alia* what topics consultation should include. Security of employment is one of them. The works committee at Castner-Kellner of ICI by discussing plant closures managed to avoid redundancies of *some* employees by transferring them to relief staff work. Consultation has therefore helped in redeploying workers who would otherwise have been made redundant. See also CBI's 'Responsibilities of the British public company', September 1973, where one of the topics for consultation covered by the

new structure in Cadbury Schweppes includes the contraction of the industry, i.e. redundancy. At Pilkington's fibreglass insulation division, certain policy topics including redundancy *were* never discussed in the consultative bodies, these being the prerogative of the employer. Now however it is found that redundancy and redeployment is discussed. It must however be made clear that 'redundancy' is primarily a negotiation topic with unions, and was found to be the case in *all* countries examined. Though of great importance, since this latter comes outside the realm of this reference it is not subject to analysis and discussion.

449. Mass dismissals for redundancy will always be a matter for negotiation, and provision is made by the Employment Protection Act 1975 ss. 99 and 100, in that the recognised unions and the Secretary of State must be notified. Negotiation with the unions also takes place in the case of smaller redundancies. Once this has been settled by negotiation, the works council should be given the prerogative of organising the criteria to be followed and where possible to try to fit suitable persons in other jobs (see e.g. the situation in Castner-Kellner in note 448 above).

450. It will avoid the kind of situation which has arisen with the freezer-fish bobbers in Hull, where the employer agreed with the GMWU that a number of bobbers will be made redundant on the principle of last in first out, and a dispute arose between the wet-fish and freezer-bobbers as to whether the freezer-bobbers were included. See Platten and Others v. Hull Fishing Vessel Owners Association Ltd., 22 December 1975, Industrial Tribunal unreported case no. 17921/75.

451. See p. 96 ante.

452. See p. 96 ante.

453. Art. 15(i) of loi du 20 septembre 1948 provides 'Les conseils d'entreprise ont pour mission . . . d'examiner toutes mesures propres à favoriser le développement de l'esprit de collaboration entre le chef d'entreprise et son personnel, notamment en employant la langue de la région pour les rapports internes de l'entreprise . . . '

454. Art. 5 of accord national du 16 juillet 1958 as amended provides 'Le conseil d'entreprise déterminera la langue à employer, pour son propre fonctionnement ainsi que, s'il y a lieu, les mesures d'ordre linguistique propres à favoriser les rapports entre la direction et le personnel.'

455. It was found in the Flemish-speaking part of Belgium that industrial relations were considerably enhanced where the language used for works councils proceedings was that spoken by the majority of workers in the establishment. It was also found that even where Flemish-speaking Belgians were in the minority in an establishment, measures were taken to use, where necessary, the Flemish language. In the Flemish part of the country it was also found that the dialogue not only in works councils, but between employer and employee is Flemish. In three establishments employing Italian and Greek labour it was found that these languages were used. A spokesman of the Fédération des Entreprises Belges told this writer that the parties in the national collective agreement envisaged and therefore included foreign languages where such labour was employed.

456. See p. 85 ante and note 372.

457. Art. 15(d) of loi du 20 septembre 1948 provides 'Les conseils d'entreprise ont pour mission . . . (d) . . . de veiller à la stricte application de la législation industrielle et sociale protectrice des travailleurs'.

458. The topics frequently brought up by the 'conseil' are such matters as cleanliness of toilets, food storage, factory cleanliness etc. all of which feature in various social and protective legislation.

459. In the Rotherham works of the British Steel Corporation an advisory committee of the works council exists on employees' national savings schemes, another one exists on rehabilitation of infirm or injured employees. At an information committee meeting at Armstrong Patents Ltd noise reduction and SAYE were discussed. Again at the Lostock works of ICI noise reduction was one of the discussion topics at a works committee meeting. At Reckitt & Colman, disciplinary procedures were the topic of discussion during one works council meeting. All these matters are dealt with either by statute, ministerial regulation or custom. At one meeting attended the appropriate paragraph of the Industrial Relations Code of Practice on 'disciplinary procedures' was politely pointed out to the employer.

460. Since there are enforcing authorities in three fields, e.g. the factory inspector will enforce the safety and health provisions under the Factories Act 1961, and the health and safety representatives or committee instituted under the Health and Safety at Work etc. Act 1974 will also play their part. The shops inspectorate will enforce the similar provisions under the Offices, Shops and Railway Premises Act 1963, the mines inspectorate under the Mines and Quarries Act etc. It is however found that the inspectorate, being pressed for time, is more anxious to enforce the safety and health provisions and seldom makes a conscious effort to look at the welfare provisions of the various legislation. Since this is a reality, the works council could fulfil a useful function in the welfare sphere of this legislation; this is not to say that it should not also have a peripheral functions of vigilance over health and safety matters.

461. i.e. any welfare regulations made by the minister under the Factories Act 1961, as for example the arrangements for preparing, heating or taking meals, supply and use of seats in work rooms, accommodation for clothing, supply of drinking water etc.

462. Art. 15(f) states '... de veiller à l'application de toute disposition générale intéressant l'entreprise ...'

463. Loi 66–427 du 18 juin 1966, art. 3(c), provides 'Il est obligatoirement informé et consulté sur les questions intéressant l'organisation ... et la marche générale de l'entreprise ...'

464. Art. 15(b) of loi du 20 septembre 1948 says 'Les conseils d'entreprise ont pour mission ... (b) de recevoir du chef d'entreprise, aux points de vue économique et financier: 1 au moins chaque trimestre des renseignements concernant la *productivité* ainsi que des informations d'ordre général, relatifs à la vie de l'entreprise; 2 périodiquement et au moins à la clôture de l'exercice social, des renseignements, rapports et documents susceptibles d'éclairer le conseil d'entreprise sur les *résultats d'exploitation* obtenu par l'entreprise ...' (stress added). Arrêté royal du 27 novembre 1973 provides for additional information to be given, e.g. expenses of employees (art. 10); scientific research (art. 12); grants from government (art. 13) etc.

465. Support for this writer's contention has also been found in the joint statement made during a meeting of the Conseil Central de l'Economie which was debating article 15(b) of loi du 20 septembre 1948 at the time when it was a Bill. The statement only refers to the 'reciprocal understanding' aspect. It stated 'Les représentants des employeurs et des travailleurs ont eu le souci, dans le domaine des renseignements d'ordre économique à fournir par le chef d'entreprise, d'assurer l'information la plus complète possible au travailleur et de donner ainsi satisfaction à son désir légitime de mieux connaître l'entreprise ...' See also the debate in the Belgian Senate 1947–48, Document 489, p. 15.

466. Article 15(a) of loi du 20 septembre 1948 provides 'Les conseils d'entreprise ont pour mission . . . (a) de donner leur avis et de formuler toutes suggestions ou objections qui pourraient modifier l'organisation du travail des conditions de travail et le rendement de l'entreprise'.
467. Loi 66–427 du 18 juin 1966, art. 3(a), states 'Dans l'ordre économique, le comité d'entreprise exerce, à titre consultatif, les attributions ci-après (a) il étudie les mesures envisagées par la direction et les suggestions émises par le personnel en vue d'améliorer la production et la productivité de l'entreprise et propose l'application de celles qu'il aura retenues'.
468. Employment Protection Act 1975 s.17. See also the provisions on disclosure of information in the repealed Industrial Relations Act 1971. See also the Industry Act 1975.
469. One of the aims in the Rotherham works of the British Steel Corporation is to communicate financial information (i.e. order books, customers etc.) and explain future management plans so as to ascertain employees' views. In Reckitt & Colman the company's financial position is given to the works council. In Cadbury Schweppes' Bournville site, detailed sales figures and a report on net losses and gains as well as future forecasts are given. In ICI Mond Division sales trends, investments and the economic situation of the company is given to the divisional council.
470. A great number of works councils do not receive any financial information and indeed it is the policy of some management that certain areas of finance must never be discussed with works councils, e.g. Pilkington's fibreglass insulation division.
471. cf. art. 121 of the statute for European companies.
472. See also discussion that has taken place in the Belgian Senate 1947–48, Document 489, p. 17 on arrêté du régent of 27 November 1950, Moniteur Belge, 2 December 1950. See also Annales parlementaires Sénat of 3 August 1948, p. 2004.
473. Arrêté royal of 27 November 1950 makes provisions to this effect. Art. 1 states 'Les renseignements concernant la productivité se rapportant: (a) à l'organisation du travail dans l'entreprise et aux moyens de la perfectionner; (b) au rendement des diverses catégories des travailleurs et aux possibilités de l'améliorer.'
474. Art. 1 2° of arrêté royal du 27 novembre 1950 provides 'les chefs d'entreprise sont tenus de communiquer au moins chaque trimestre aux conseils d'entreprise . . . les informations d'ordre général qui se rapportent: (a) à l'état de la production dans l'entreprise; (b) aux éléments globaux du coût de production, de fabrication ou d'exploitation, exprimés sous formes de pourcentages, ainsi qu'à leurs variations; (c) à la marche des affaires de l'entreprise; (d) à la situation du marché.
See also convention collective du 24 décembre 1970, art. 3.
475. Loi 66–427 du 18 juin 1966, art. 3, al. 3, provides: 'Au cours de chaque trimestre, le chef d'entreprise communique au comité d'entreprise des informations sur l'exécution des programmes de production, l'évolution générale des commandes et sur la situation de l'emploi dans l'entreprise. Il informe le comité des mesures envisagées en ce qui concerne l'amélioration, le renouvellement ou la transformation de l'équipement ou des méthodes de production et d'exploitation . . . Il rend compte, en la motivant, de la suite donnée aux avis et vœux émis par le comité.'
476. e.g. in Gallaher Ltd company business results, new products and new technology is one of the subjects of information and consultation given to works councils, another is the improvement of productivity and how to increase efficiency; in Fenners, Reckitt and Colman and Armstrong Patents

the company performance is given to the respective works councils as well as previous statistics on competitors, organisation etc. A number of engineering firms, such as David Brown Gears, inform their works councils (and sometimes all employees as in Dunlop) of the current trading position; the British Steel Corporation for example has as one of its aims the giving of information on manufacturing cost trends, general profitability of the firm, production etc. It was reported that production per man was another matter given to the works council for information; in Cadbury Schweppes a sales report is given to the works council once a month, but it is understood that this is not recorded in the minutes so as to allow a free exchange of ideas (cf. the Belgian situation). Production estimates are also given and problems relating to production are discussed. A production report is also debated and it is reported that from the reduction of production might follow the reduction of a link shift, for example. The works council's job would then be to consider the implications, and perhaps involve the unions if redundancies were to follow; at Pilkington Brothers' fibreglass insulation division, information is given at each meeting about sales, profitability and production costs.

477. Arrêté royal du 27 novembre 1950, art. 2, provides 'Les renseignements susceptibles d'éclairer le conseil d'entreprise, sur les résultats d'exploitation, à fournir périodiquement et au moins à la clôture de l'exercice, doivent comporter notamment: (a) les éléments globaux de la situation active et passive de l'entreprise; (b) les résultats d'exploitation; (c) un exposé sur la marche et sur le rendement de l'entreprise; (d) un exposé relatif à l'influence, sur les résultats de l'entreprise, des variations des éléments globaux du coût de la production, de la fabrication ou de l'exploitation; (e) une comparaison des résultats obtenus au cours de la période ou de l'exercice et de ceux obtenus au cours des deux périodes ou exercices précédents; (f) un exposé expliquant les différences que ferait ressortir cette comparaison.
478. See p. 101 ante.
479. Art. 3, arrêté royal du 27 novembre 1950.
480. Why was there less profit made in the course of one quarter? what made production slump? why were there less orders? the financial situation of the international market, were some of the variations which were answered.
481. Arrêté royal du 27 novembre 1950, art. 5(a)(b).
482. Ibid., art. 6.
483. Loi du 20 septembre 1948, art. 15(b).
484. Loi 66–427, 18 juin 1966, art. 3, al. 4–7.
485. e.g. in Cadbury Schweppes the financial situation and how the company performed is given yearly. This information is sporadic and given at short intervals as previously outlined, but it is found that detailed annual reports with supporting documents are very seldom given.
486. e.g. the works council of British Steel Corporation, Rotherham works, holds half-yearly meetings where detailed documents are issued which deal with exports, production forecasts for the following six-monthly period, stocks, outputs etc., and sometimes it is found that comparable figures for previous periods are given (cf. the situation in Belgium).
487. The chartered accountant must be chosen from a panel of chartered accountants inscribed in the rolls within the jurisdiction of the appropriate court of the area in which the establishment is situated. Where such a roll is non-existent in the area the chartered accountant is chosen from a panel appointed by the Minister of Labour, the 'Garde des Sceaux' and the Minister of Justice upon recommendation of the 'Procureur-Général' (décret 60–606 du 24 juin 1960, art. 3).
488. cf. art. 120(2) of the proposed statute for European companies proposing

rights to certain information.
489. Art. 121 of the proposed statute for European companies proposes contrary provisions, i.e. that the European works council should receive the same communications and documents as the shareholders.
490. cf. art. 126(2) of the proposed statute for European companies which proposes to deal with the procedure for consultation and especially that the board of management must give its *reasons* for disregarding the European works council's opinion.
491. Loi du 20 septembre 1048, art. 15(a), provides 'les conseils d'entreprise ont pour mission ... (c) de donner des avis et de formuler toutes suggestions ou objections sur toutes mesures qui pourraient modifier l'organisation du travail, les conditions de travail, et le rendement de l'entreprise ...'
492. Accord national du 16 juillet 1958 as amended. Art. 2 which deals with enterprises having numerous branches and how matters common to all 'conseils' (e.g. reorganisation, closure of some branches, transfer of production from one branch to another) are to be dealt with.
493. i.e. those enumerated in note 491 above.
494. Art. 15c of loi du 20 septembre 1948 provides 'les conseils d'entreprise ont pour mission ... (c) de donner des avis ou rapports contenant des différents points de vue exprimés en leur sein, sur toute question d'ordre économique relevant de leur compétence, telle que celle-ci définie au présent article et qui leur a été préalablement soumise, soit par le conseil professionnel intéressé, soit par le conseil central de l'économie ...'
495. i.e. '... sur toute question économique *relevant de leur compétence* ...' and '... et qui leur a été préalablement soumise ...' (stress added) (extracts from art. 15c of loi du 20 septembre 1948).
496. This must be distinguished from the power of the 'conseil' given to it by art. 3 of the national agreement to determine the general criteria to be followed in cases of *mass dismissals* and *mass re-engagements*, See p. 96 ante.
497. This word has been found to be limitative in that it only applies to the opinion of the conseil in relation to 'workers'. See parliamentary debates in Doc. Parl. Senat No. 489, session 1947–1948, p. 19, where an amendment was moved to add the word 'personnel de maîtrise' to that of 'travailleurs'. The amendement was not carried because it was considered that the specialised role of the 'personnel de maîtrise' does not allow for similar rules to those for 'workers'.
498. e.g. experience, family ties and obligations, age, local connections, connections in the establishment such as brother, wife, close friend etc. ... have been found to exist in these criteria.
499. e.g. art. 2 of ordonnance du 22 février 1945 as amended by loi 66–427 du 18 juin 1966 provides 'Le comité d'entreprise coopère avec la direction à l'amélioration des conditions collectives d'emploi et de travail ainsi que les conditions de vie du personnel au sein de l'entreprise; il est obligatoirement saisi pour avis des règlements qui s'y rapportent'. In art. 3(c) as amended by the 1966 law may be found the following provision: 'Il est obligatoirement informé et consulté sur les questions intéressant l'organisation, la gestion et la marche générale de l'entreprise, et notamment sur les mesures de nature a affecter le volume ou la structure des effectifs, la durée du travail ou les conditions d'emploi et du travail du personnel. Il peut formuler ses vœux sur ces divers points.' The loi du 27 décembre 1973 (arts. 1–5) places a duty on the employer to consult the 'comité' on all changes which take place in the organisation of work etc.
500. Thus the 'convention collective des ouvriers dans les industries métallurgiques du Rhône' of 24 December 1953, art. 20, provides that the

'comité d'entreprise' must be consulted on all vacancies for manual workers which occur within the establishment. Art. 28 of that same collective agreement provides that the comité must be informed of all collective dismissals.
501. Art. 54(h), loi du 29 avril 1946 – see Code du Travail, livre II, p. 208.
502. Cour de Cassation, Chambre Civile, Section Sociale, 20 juillet 1953, Droit Social 1953, p. 599.
503. Décret 60–606 du 24 juin 1960, art. 3.
504. Loi 66–427 du 18 juin 1966, art. 3.
505. Ibid., art. 2, al. 3 and 4.
506. These are establishment representatives in the local social security offices.
507. Décret du 8 juin 1946, art. 4. See also loi du 3 octobre 1946, art. 4, which provides that in certain cirumstances the 'comité' has limited management powers in the 'caisses primaires' on matters relating to accidents at work only.
508. See p. 107 ante.
509. e.g. craft training, operative training, youth services, non-supervisory staff training, to be found in David Brown Industries and the Rotherham works of the British Steel Corporation. Arrangements for holiday pay, training and certification of drivers of mobile equipment (Rotherham works). Aspects of working life (Bournville site of Cadbury Schweppes, Fenners, Reckitt and Colman, ICI Mond Division), and conditions of work and communications system (ICI Mond Division) job-gradings, pay differentials between grades, overtime rates, principles to be followed for overtime (grade committees of Unilever Blackfriars).
510. The local social security offices which have been consulted think this to be an unacceptable suggestion.
511. cf. the Belgian situation at p. 106 ante.
512. As a result of this writer's talks in Brussels with one of the draftsmen of the proposed statute for European companies, it was interesting to note that the European Commission has found that the European countries' wishes were that some of these matters for consultation be specifically provided for in the proposed statute. See now arts. 124(1) and 125(1)(a)–(d).
513. Problems found to exist in some establishments where a sub-committee was instituted by the 'comité' were libraries, retirement problems, social clubs, crèches for working mothers' children, training and regrading of trades.
514. Loi du 16 mai 1946, art. 15 bis, amending ordonnance du 22 février 1945.
515. Loi 66–427 du 18 juin 1966 and loi du 16 mai 1946 amending ordonnance du 22 février 1945, art. 4.
516. Art. 8, arrêté du régent du 13 juin 1949 and art. 17, du 20 septembre 1948.
517. Thus in British Steel Corporation, Rotherham works, the section councils or departmental committees have committees each with a special function. The administrative committees concern themselves with welfare services to existing and retired employees, and hospitalisation and recreational services. The advisory committees on the other hand advise mainly on training of crafts, youth, and non-supervisory staff, as well as catering, the rehabilitation of employees who suffered industrial or other injuries and such services as car parking, transportation, playing fields etc. On the Bournville site of Cadbury Schweppes the works council has set up a number of standing committees. These consist *inter alia* of the joint consultative committee which is the liaison committee of the works council and has *inter alia* an educational function organising courses on relevant topics such as industrial relations, labour law, visits and conferences. The Boeke Trust Committee is a welfare committee for Cadbury pensioners and other workers. The Schemes

Committee deals with various company schemes such as bonuses. Other committees deal with suggestions, catering, training, safety and recreational activities. In Pilkington Brothers' fibreglass insulation division at company level the Maintenance Trades Council (a consultative body) formed a working party to examine problems which occur in retirement and to recommend ways in which these problems may be mitigated.

518. cf. art. 111(5) of the proposed statute for European companies which provides for delegation of certain tasks to committees.
519. cf. art. 117 of the proposed statute for European companies.
520. Art. 22, loi du février 1945.
521. Art. 16, loi du 16 avril 1946.
522. Art. 13, décret du 2 novembre 1945.
523. Art. 9, décret du 27 novembre 1952 and art. 17, décret du 2 novembre 1945.
524. Such functions as ensuring, participating or controlling the management of certain 'œuvres sociales' have been distinguished, analysed and critically examined. Other functions also analysed and examined critically are the consultative functions, the receipt of information on certain matters, supervisory functions etc. All of these have proved invaluable towards creating a bond between employer and employed.
525. Another (though not officially admitted) is the proposals made for a European works council of the European company, other reasons may be found in projet de loi 1689, chambre des députés of 26 April 1973, pp. 3–5. 'Les objectifs de la participation des travailleurs aux décisions dans l'entreprise', where the ethnic, social, political and economic reasons are considered.
526. Loi du 6 mai 1974 – Mémorial Journal Officiel du Grand Duché de Luxembourg recueil de législation A – no. 35, 10 mai 1974 – and règlement grand-ducal du 27 septembre 1974 – Mémorial Journal Officiel du Grand Duché de Luxembourg A, no. 69, 27 septembre 1974.
527. The other reasons are harmonisation of the laws of the member states and finding an answer to the divergencies which exist between the member states.
528. See also 'Worker participation in Britain', part IV, 'Pattern of future development', pp. 135–6 where Professor J.C. Wood states, 'It follows . . . that progress is unlikely in the near future through legislation.'
529. Such as worker directors, supervisory board etc. Consider the Bullock proposals (January 1977).
530. In the sense that the institution of the works council is not as generalised as it might be.
531. i.e. without, as has already been stated, upsetting the functioning of the existing works councils.
532. M. Monterclard of the Laboratoire de sociologie industrielle d'Aix-en-Provence in 'La dynamique des comités d'entreprise', Paris CNRS 1963, p. 43, said ' . . . cette dynamique ne comporte d'ailleurs aucun secret. Elle n'est ni mécanisme aveugle ni fonctionnalisme automatique et désincarné. Elle n'est ni le pur résultat de l'institution, ni le pur effet des "luttes ouvrières" car elle ne peut être isolée d'aucun des problèmes posés par le développement industriel'.
533. By accord national of 16 July 1958 since modified and completed by those of 29 March and 28 November 1962, or collective agreement of 4 December 1970 on the matters of consultation and information which has been made mandatory by arrêté du 22 janvier 1971 (see Moniteur Belge, 19 février 1971) and that of 30 June 1971 concerning facilities and time off to be given to 'conseil' members in order that they should carry out their duties.

534. e.g. by the Convention Collective des Ouvriers dans les Industries Métallurgiques du Rhône, 24 December 1953, art. 20, which enlarges the powers of the 'comité d'entreprise' by providing that it must be consulted on all vacancies for manual workers which occur in the establishment, or of art. 28 which provides that the 'conseil' must be informed on all collective dismissals.
535. e.g. art. 15e of loi du 20 septembre 1948 providing for the general criteria to be followed by the 'conseil' in cases of mass dismissals are made more precise by art. 3 of the 'accord national' which talks of the criteria to be followed in such cases.
536. e.g. art. 4 of the 'accord national' defines the term 'œuvres sociales' because the loi du 2 septembre 1948 in no way provides for a definition of that expression.
537. This, it must be observed, is an accepted principle in all countries examined.
538. See 'Perspectives', p. 25.

3 EMPLOYEE REPRESENTATION

The first limb[1] of the fifth compulsory requirement that has, under loi du 11 février 1950, to be agreed in a French 'convention collective susceptible d'extension'[2] is the matter relating to the 'délégués du personnel'.[3] A 'délégué du personnel' is an elected worker who represents his fellow workers in an establishment in order to inform the employer of the individual rights of the worker, which have not been met by this former, and which relate to wages, the trade classifications of the Code du Travail, protective legislation, hygiene and social security.[4] His other functions include the investigation of complaints, the accompaniment of the 'inspecteur du travail'[5] during his visits to the appropriate part of the establishment and the making of suggestions in relation to the legal requirements which must be met by the employer. His functions,[6] it will be readily noticed, though not identical, are not dissimilar to one important aspect of those of the British shop steward's,[7] namely the representation of his constituents in dealings with management, and his involvement to regulate workers' pay and working conditions. In Luxembourg the equivalent is the 'délégation ouvrière' and the separate 'délégation d'employés'.[8] It must be noted that the functions of these representatives are not identical to those of their French and British counterparts, since they overspill into the domain of works councils in Britain, 'comités d'entreprise' in France and 'conseils d'entreprise' in Belgium.[9] The reason for the width of functions of the Luxembourg 'délégués' is that Luxembourg has not, until recently,[10] had an equivalent to the works council etc. before the institution of the 'comités mixtes'.

It is proposed to consider this aspect under the following headings: (a) historical; (b) current law; (i) number of délégués, (ii) the method of their election, (iii) their term of office, (iv) their rights, and (v) their functions. A consideration of the comparative aspects under French, Luxembourg and British law will simultaneously take place within these headings. Belgium does not possess such an institution, it has 'délégués syndicaux' who, since they are mainly concerned with trade union functions, come outside the terms of this reference.

(A) HISTORICAL PERSPECTIVES

The concept of the institution of a 'délégué du personnel' agreed to by the 'confédération générale de production française' in the Accord Matignon[11] has not in practice brought about any serious problems. Some minor problems did, however, occur and these will be examined below. As a result of the Accord Matignon the loi du 24 juin 1936[12] made it compulsory for a 'convention collective susceptible d'extension' to contain clauses relating to 'délégués du personnel'. This compulsion only applied, however, to establishments in which ten or more persons were employed.[13] Where less than ten persons were employed, and in the 'établissements artisanaux'[14] there was no requirement for collective agreements to contain provisions on 'délégués du personnel'.

The legislative provisions under the 1936 law relating to 'délégués du personnel' have brought about some minor difficulties. One of these was that it appeared that home workers employed by definition *outside* the establishment were not eligible to take part in the election of 'délégués' du personnel', nor themselves entitled to be delegates. Though the legislature did seem so to indicate this writer has found at least one collective agreement of the time providing that outworkers should participate in the election of delegates.[15] Furthermore, it was suggested by Renée Petit[16] that it was desirable that the parties to a collective agreement should be encouraged to agree that such outworkers should participate in the election of delegates. 'Délégués du personnel' are after all the representatives of the personnel within the establishment, and not the representatives of *some* of the personnel. It is submitted therefore that a clause in a 'convention collective susceptible d'extension' that provides for a 'délégué du personnel' to be elected from among a certain category only, as for example, full-time or trade union members, could not have been in accordance with the legislative intention of the 1936 law. That law was silent as to the conditions to be satisfied in order to qualify to become a member of the electorate.[17] Some help may, however, be obtained from the Accord Matignon which seems more informed and more detailed than the legislative provisions themselves. It stated ' . . . seront électeurs tous les ouvriers et ouvrières âgés de 18 ans, à condition d'avoir eu au moins trois mois de présence à l'établissement au moment de l'élection et de ne pas avoir été privés de leurs droits civiques. Sont éligibles les électeurs définis ci-dessus, de nationalité française, âgés d'au moins 25 ans, travaillant dans l'établissement, sans interruption depuis un an, sous réserve que cette durée de présence devra être abaissée si elle réduit à moins de cinq le nombre des éligibles'.[18]

Another problem created by the 1936 legislative provisions related to the constitution of the electoral college. The question has been asked as to whether the 'délégués du personnel' should be elected by the whole of the personnel within an establishment, thus forming one electoral college, or whether each workshop or section within such establishment should elect its own delegate thus forming numerous electoral colleges. Both the 1936 law and the parliamentary debates of the time were silent on this subject. This research seems to show that the latter (i.e. numerous electoral colleges within an establishment) is the better view. Apart from the provisions of certain 'conventions collectives susceptibles d'extension' of the period, to be examined below, Professor M. Brèthe de la Gressaye[19] was of the opinion that a system of election of delegates on a workshop basis is preferable to a system based on delegates representing the whole factory. This has the advantage of allowing each specialist part of the establishment in question to be represented by a competent delegate. Judging from the materials available at the time his opinion did not seem to have been contested. This suggestion seems to the present writer extremely reasonable not only in the case of big establishments, but also in the smaller ones since even in the late 1930s industrial specialisation, sophistication and complexity were apparent. One collective agreement of the time[20] provided for a number of delegates to be elected from each of the workshops within the establishment, another[21] provided that each 'délégué du personnel' and his deputy were to represent workers from a particular section, or part of a section, according to the importance of the establishment.[22] In circumstances where collective agreements provided for homeworkers to take part in the election of delegates, they also seem to have provided for different delegates to be elected from those already elected from within the establishment itself, since the interest of each of the groups varies. In one collective agreement examined, home workers had a right to elect their own delegates on the basis of two delegates to ten home workers or a fraction of ten.[23]

The provisions of the 1936 law brought about one further problem: this was whether Algerian workers employed in an enterprise situated in France qualified for election as 'délégués du personnel'. This problem arose because, although of French nationality, Algerian workers did not enjoy the same civic rights as Frenchmen. Once again the 1936 law was silent on this point. Some light was derived from the Accord Matignon which stated ' . . . les salariés ne peuvent être électeurs qu'à la condition *de ne pas avoir été privés de leurs droits civiques* . . . '. It has been suggested[24] that Algerian workers had not in fact been deprived of their civic rights; theirs were simply civic rights that were peculiar to their status. Research carried out by this writer[25] supports this contention, and certainly Algerians now qualify for the office of 'délégué du personnel'.

One final problem arose out of the 1936 law. This law did not provide for the method of election of a delegate. The Parliamentary reports of the time, however, did suggest that voting was to be by secret ballot.[26] The president of the Conseil d'Etat stated that the electoral procedure would be the same as that which already existed for miners' delegates.[27] These had already been fixed by the then Code du Travail.[28] The somewhat complicated rules were as follows. A majority plurinominal poll[29] was to be held; envelopes of a uniform type had to be used; the person(s) nominated for election had to be isolated; there was to be a prohibition by the person(s) nominated to be simultaneously canvassed at polling stations during the poll by more than two persons. These rules enhanced the principle of a secret ballot.

The 1936 law which made it necessary for the 'convention collective susceptible d'extension' to contain clauses relating to the 'délégué du personnel' was clearly inadequate. The difficulties, though of a relatively minor nature, are apparent from the above examination, where help had to be sought either from parliamentary debates or from actual collective agreements.

Whereas the Accord Matignon (resulting in the 1936 law) brought about the institution of the 'délégué', the origins of British shop stewards do not emanate either from a comparable agreement or from legislation. Indeed even today no legislation governs the status of the shop steward in Britain. It must be emphatically stated that the French 'délégué' is not the exact equivalent of the British shop steward.[30] The functions of the shop steward have a duality of groupings, whereas those of the 'délégué' have a single grouping.[31] It is the 'délégué syndical' who exercises most of the union functions of the shop steward.[32] The term 'shop steward' was first used, it is submitted, by the Amalgamated Society of Engineers[33] who gave their district committees powers to appoint shop stewards. Their functions were of a representative nature and related almost exclusively to recruitment, the maintenance of union membership, and keeping the members informed of the observance of union rules. It was not until the period of the First World War[34] and after[35] that the status of the shop steward increased in importance. A great number of manual unions subsequently gave extended recognition to this institution but there was a sharp decline both in numbers and in activities during the depression of the 1930s. At the time when the French 'délégué' was receiving recognition the office of the shop steward in Britain was declining. It will, however, be recalled that complete parity did not and does not exist between these two offices.[36] During the Second World War the office of shop steward revived, mainly because of its recognition by both the unions and employers.[37] Since then it has increased in importance.[38] The history of white-collar unions has experienced a similar background to that of manual unions. With the growth of white-collar unions there has been a growth of white-collar representatives. In the early stages of development the role of these representatives consisted mainly in the collecting of union dues and the recruiting of membership. Later their functions were extended to negotiation,[39] grievance procedures and consultation. It can therefore be said that there has been in Britain a parallelism between the growth of manual unions and that of white-collar unions in the representatives' functions.

When comparing the historical aspects it seems clear that the office of the 'délégué' was created overnight;[40] that of the shop steward, on the other hand, has evolved as a result of the needs to meet the different circumstances. What is said above about the difference in functions between the two offices must, however, be considered at all times.

A fundamental distinction is discernible in that the office of the 'délégué du personnel' is a statutory one[41] and mandatory in a French 'convention collective susceptible d'extension'. In Britain the office of shop steward has never been statutory and there is neither compulsion nor it seems a desire[42] to include their functions etc. in collective agreements.[43] It is significant that even in their origins the functions of the 'délégué' were not identical to those of the second grouping of the shop stewards.[44] The 'délégué' had had from the beginning defined functions,[45] whereas the shop steward had not: his grew with the requirements of the times. So that whereas the French 'délégué' knew and had his rights and obligations positively defined as early as 1936, those of the shop steward were of a negative nature and grew from the trade union representative aspect of his functions.[46] The first grouping of his functions therefore generated the second.[47] When one goes further and examines historically the second grouping of the shop steward's functions with those of the 'délégué', it seems clear that from the earliest of times they were not identical. They were, however, similar. For example, the accompaniment of the inspecteur du travail, which is one of the 'délégué's' functions, has no equivalent in Britain. There is no requirement that the shop steward must accompany the factory inspector.[48] On the other hand, the shop steward has similar functions to the 'délégué' in that he represents his constituents in matters of wages, job description, protective legislation, hygiene and social security, the investigation of grievances, and the employer's respect for legal requirements.[49]

In Luxembourg, the situation is found to be of lesser complexity. Although 'délégués ouvriers' existed before 1958[50] on a non-statutory basis the institution was put on a statutory basis only in[51] industrial, commercial or artisanal establishments employing fifteen or more workers. It has been impossible to trace the historical development of this institution since there is no known publication on this aspect. Interviews held with the older workers seem to indicate that the functions of the 'délégués ouvriers' did not differ greatly from the statutory ones which exist today. Some of these are therefore comparable to those of the representatives in Britain and France. It is found that the reason why the 'délégué's' functions (to be examined below) are so wide was to compensate for the lack of an institution which would take up with the employer matters of a collective nature.[52] Such institutions have existed from early times in Britain, France and Belgium. It may therefore be said that a historical accident has necessitated the breadth of the Luxembourg 'délégué's' functions.

This research shows that the three historical difficulties which had arisen under the 1936 French law[53] have no historical equivalent in Britain or Luxembourg.

(B) THE CURRENT LAW

As was the case in France under the 1936 law so under loi du 11 février 1950, clauses relating to 'délégués du personnel' must compulsorily be included in a 'convention collective susceptible d'extension'. It will readily be noticed that whereas the 1936 law did not regulate the institution of the 'délégué' to any significant extent,[54] the 1950 law now regulates almost every aspect in some detail. Thus the role of the collective agreement *per se* in modern French law is necessarily reduced since actual collective agreements merely refer to the legislative requirements.[55] *Two* matters are, however, not legislated upon in any detail, thus allowing a free hand to the parties to a collective agreement. These are firstly, the procedure to be followed in the election of 'délégués', and secondly, an extension to the field of application of the law.

It is proposed to consider the legislation that regulates the institution of a 'délégué' and at the same time and where applicable to consider the two matters (see above) that have not been so regulated.

Section i. Number of representatives

The loi du 16 avril 1946 enacts that in all industrial, commercial and agricultural establishments, in all ministries, in the professions, societies, trade unions and associations, whatever be their constitution or object, where ten or more persons are habitually employed, there must be a 'délégué du personnel'.[56] Similarly in Luxembourg a 'délégation des ouvriers' must compulsorily be instituted in all industrial, commercial, artisanal and nationalised concerns as well as in government offices where fifteen or more workers are employed.[57] A 'délégation d'employés' must also be formed where the enterprise employs twelve or more employees.[58] It becomes clear therefore from the start that both white-collar and blue-collar workers are included in France and Luxembourg. In Britain, on the other hand, the position is not so cut and dried. Before one may even consider the number of shop stewards in any establishment it is submitted that two prior conditions must be met. The first is that the employer should recognise the union. This is so because the basis in Britain is in theory[59] different from that in France. In France and Luxembourg the 'délégué' is not a union representative, in Britain he is. In practice, of course, this research shows that recognition[60] is not a great obstacle in Britain, especially in the blue-collar unions.[61] The result therefore in practice is that shop stewards, although they emanate from a different source are as 'répandus' as 'délégués' in France and Luxembourg. The second is the employer's acceptance of the individual steward from among employees put forward by the union.[62]

It has further been found that whereas in France *all* establishments employing ten or more persons and in Luxembourg fifteen or more workers or twelve or more employees must by law have and do have a 'délégué', in Britain that is not so. There are numerous areas in which no shop steward will be found, either because of recognition problems or because there exists little or no union organisation in that trade.[63]

The French 1946 law also regulates the number of delegates and relates their numbers to those of the employees in the establishment.[64] Where less than ten employees are employed in the establishment, there is no legal requirement for a 'délégué'. Where, however, there are eleven or more employees, there is a legal requirement for one or more 'délégués titulaires' and one or more 'délégués suppléants'[65] to be elected.[66]

It is clear that French law makes highly detailed provisions as to the number of 'délégués' that has to be appointed. It will also be noted that 'délégués suppléants' feature as an important aspect of French law. The same is found to be the case in Luxembourg law where there could be up to twenty 'délégués ouvriers'.[67]

When one looks for an equivalent in Britain, one may well search in vain. Firstly, there is no legislation, and never has been, which regulates the number of stewards to the number of employees. This research shows that no suggestion has ever been made either by trade unions or by employers to bring about such legislation in Britain. An examination of collective agreements themselves shows that in very few cases is this subject touched upon. In those few cases where the ratio of shop stewards to that of membership is considered, the provisions are very fluid and general. One of these agreements, which epitomises the general situation in this area, states ' . . . The number of shop stewards will be determined in the factory by agreement with the union concerned; due regard being given to the specific needs of the situation'.[68] Only one collective agreement examined was more specific than the rest and did provide for the ratio of shop stewards to members. It stated 'Any change in the number of shop stewards will be agreed between the union and management. With the labour force at its current level (approx. 20) there will be no more than two shop stewards . . . '.[69] The Donovan Report[70] considered this aspect *indirectly* and seemed to indicate that this ratio depended upon the circumstances of each case.[71]

Whereas 'délégués suppléants' form an important office in the French and Luxembourg system of industrial relations, such an office does not exist in Britain. No collective agreement examined provides, no legal requirement exists, and no union rules stipulate, for such an office. When a shop steward is not available to perform his duties, as for example if he is away sick, on a course, or on holiday etc., he has no deputy and therefore his functions cannot be effectively fulfilled. It is submitted that this is an area in which the French and Luxembourg systems are more precise and developed, and that therefore an equivalent in the British system would be advantageous.

It was stated above[72] that under the law of 1950 the role of the collective agreement in France in this field is limited since most collective agreements adopt the legislative requirements as to the number of 'délégués'. The legislation does, however, leave certain matters open thus allowing the parties to a collective agreement a free hand. One of the matters mentioned above is that relating to the extension of the field of application of the law so that collective agreements sometimes contain additional provisions in order to give employees more favourable conditions. In a number of collective agreements examined, it is apparent that the field of application of the law concerning the number of 'délégués' in relation to the number of employees in the firm has been extended. In one collective agreement,[73] it was found that where six to ten employees are employed in textile establishments there has to be elected one 'délégué titulaire' and one 'suppléant', *if two employees at least express this wish*. Furthermore, in textile establishments where less than six persons are employed, the employee(s) are enabled to be assisted by a trade union respresentative *if they so request*. In another[74] a 'délégué de production'[75] is elected by the technicians who form part of a production team for the duration of a film. This additional 'délégué' is in existence at the same time as the official 'délégués' of the establishment elected by the permanent personnel. In another collective agreement examined[76] there was to be a delegate in *all* establishments where more than *five* persons are employed. In Luxembourg however it was found that the legal requirements were strictly observed in this sphere though it was admitted that collective agreements could provide for more favourable conditions. Due to the fact (explained above) that there is no hard and fast rule as to the ratio of employees to shop stewards in Britain, there cannot consequently be, as there are in France, additional provisions which give employees more favourable conditions than those imposed by legislation. All that can be said at this stage is that the possibility of equally advantageous collective agreement provisions to those that exist in France could also exist in Britain if the parties so wished. This research shows that whereas problems of communication have arisen in Britain because the shop steward membership was too large[77] this did not happen in France firstly because of the statutory minimum and maximum requirements, and secondly because the 'délégué' had a 'suppléant' in all firms examined. Conversely it was found in at least one instance in Britain that a large number of stewards in proportion to the membership created co-ordination problems and thus had a detrimental effect on industrial relations.[78] This situation could not occur in France or in Luxembourg because of the maximum and minimum legal requirements.[79] Of the sample studied the 'délégué' and the 'suppléant' in France and Luxembourg have an average of some fifteen and fourteen constituents respectively, whereas in Britain a steward has an average of some forty-three[80] Why therefore could Britain not have a more representative system by reducing the number of constituents?

Section ii. Mode of election of the representative

The French 1950 law stipulates for the mode of election of delegates, but as in the case of the 'number of delegates'[81] leaves it to collective agreements to provide for the details to be followed in these elections.[82] The legal provisions treat the election procedure of the 'délégué' in a comprehensive manner. 'Délégués' must be elected by the workers and employees on the one part, technicians, and foremen of the different categories, on the other, and engineers and management on the third,[83] upon lists prepared by the most representative trade union organisations within each establishment for each category of personnel.[84] Thus French law provides for *three electoral colleges*.[85] The law does, however, give some freedom on this matter. It provides that the *number* and *composition* of these electoral colleges may be modified by collective agreement[86] between organisations representing workers and organisations representing employers. Nor does the law state in any categorical terms the distribution of persons in each of the categories. Thus the distribution of persons and of seats in the different categories in the electoral colleges are agreed upon by the management and the interested trade unions. Should agreement between the parties fail, the 'inspecteur du travail' will decide upon the distribution.[87] It is evident therefore that the legislature has given the parties a free hand in two important matters[88] relating to the electoral procedure. This research shows that advantage of this liberalism has been taken in very few cases in France. On the electoral procedure, for example, only five collective agreements of the sample show any departure from the legislative requirements.[89] Similarly with the number of electoral colleges, the parties to a collective agreement mostly[90] respect the legislative provisions.

In Luxembourg candidates from each of the electoral colleges[91] are put forward by a prescribed number of electors within the college.[92] There is here an important distinction between the French and British systems. In France the most representative trade unions initially prepare the list of candidates, in Britain shop stewards are elected or appointed through the union membership. The Luxembourg unions therefore take no part in nominating candidates for the election.

An examination of British union rule books[93] and collective agreements[94] shows that, apart from mentioning the fact that shop stewards will be elected, there exists no 'constitution' or 'procedure' on the method of conducting these elections. In some instances it has been found that shop stewards are elected by custom established within the firm.[95] The method of election of shop stewards in Britain is fluid, disorganised and in certain instances haphazard, whereas the opposite is true in France and Luxembourg. The reason for this is that there exists no legislation on shop stewards in Britain, as there exists in the other two countries under examination. Furthermore, and since it is not a compulsory requirement in a collective agreement, nothing on election procedure can be found in British collective agreements etc. nearing the detail which exists in French ones.[96]

This research indicates that since the shop steward is a union official, it is bound to be the case that the source of the election procedure and facilities emanates mainly from union rule books, and to a very much lesser extent from collective agreements. In France it is the exact opposite; the legal requirements of a 'convention collective susceptible d'extension' in regulating this aspect state that clauses must be included in collective agreements to deal with elections of the 'délégué' and his 'suppléant'. Since the 'délégué' is not a union official but a representative of all his constituents it is the collective agreement (and the legislative requirements) which provide the source of the election procedure and election facilities.[97] This is even more true of Luxembourg, except that it has been found that the election process there relies much more heavily on the statutory requirement.

Though legislative provisions in France state that there should be three electoral colleges, thus laying a guideline, it does allow the parties variations (see above). In France, these variations are rare (see above) but they do exist.[98] In Britain, no legislative provisions exist, therefore the parties are not influenced by already laid-down guidelines. Not being so influenced, the sample examined shows that it is the practice to have only one electoral college. In Luxembourg, France and Britain the evidence shows that the area of a constituency is determined firstly by the firm's work structure and secondly by the work patterns of the labour force.[99]

French law allows for variations to take account of local needs in the distribution of persons in the electoral colleges as agreed between employers and unions (see above). Of the sample examined in France when compared with that examined in Britain it was found that distribution of personnel within the constituency was determined in both countries by the firm's work arrangements.[100] This was also found to be the case in Luxembourg.

A difference exists, however, between the position in France and in Britain where agreement between unions and management on the distribution of persons and seats in electoral colleges (see above) cannot be reached. In France the Inspecteur du Travail decides upon this issue, in Britain the inspectorate has no such powers and indeed it was found that in those few establishments where such arrangements exist, unions are sensitive in guarding their prerogative to determine

174 Worker Participation in Europe

these areas of influence. Of the British sample studied only three establishments had arrangements with unions to determine jointly the area of the constituency, and the distribution of persons within that constituency.[101] Where a disagreement in the field occurs in Britain the ultimate sanction if agreement cannot be reached would be industrial action. It is submitted that the French system which allows for an appeal is a good one, and although it is not suggested that the British inspectorate be given this additional duty, perhaps use (since their functions are *totally* different from those of the French inspector), so far not ever made, could be made of the ACAS in this respect. It must be stressed, however, that the distribution of persons and seats in electoral colleges in Britain are of more interest to the unions than to management, since the shop steward is the person who is elected or appointed by the union and who represents the union to his constituents, who are *stricto sensu* themselves union members. In France, on the other hand, the 'délégué' represents all persons in his constituency whether union members or not, therefore the employer is bound to have a greater interest in the composition of the constituency etc. The union merely acts in a consultative capacity. This nuance in balance between the two countries must therefore be carefully noted. But, having said that, it is submitted that in both countries, though divergences are apparent in this sphere, there are advantages in joint agreement between unions and management in that there would be an acknowledgement that rights and obligations exist between the parties in connection with the procedure used to determine the distribution of persons and seats in electoral colleges. Joint agreement raises the status of the 'délégué' or the shop steward, gives credence to the constituency in all its aspects and strengthens collective bargaining. A strange system has been found to exist in Luxembourg, which is quite unlike the British or French patterns. If objection to the electoral lists, or any dispute arises on these, it is the employer who, after hearing all the parties, decides on the issue.

In France and electors consist of all employees (male and female) of French nationality (till 1973 only) over sixteen years old who have worked for at least six consecutive months in the establishment and who have not been convicted for contravening the electoral code.[102] Similar provisions to the above exist in Luxembourg in the case of 'délégués ouvriers', with the only difference that electors never had to be of Luxembourg nationality.[103] As for the 'délégués d'employés' there exist no statutory requirements. In France where an employee has been convicted for having committed a serious crime[104] he is deprived of his right to vote during his term of sentence.[105] An employee sentenced to less than three months' imprisonment without a remission of sentence (*sursis*), or to less than six months with a remission may vote, unless he committed certain prescribed offences.[106] It appears that where an employee is suspended he is not *per se* barred from taking part in elections.[107] Though national service has the effect of suspending the contract of employment, reinstated employees after completing their national service retain both in France and in Luxembourg the benefit of their previous service.[108]

Important differences exist between France and Luxembourg, and Britain in this sphere. Whereas in France and Luxembourg those entitled to vote are *all* persons in the constituency who qualify under the respective statutory provisions, in Britain only trade union members in the constituency may do so.[109] Again in France and to some extent in Luxembourg, there are strict legislative provisions as to who may vote, no such legislation or rules (at least directly) exist in Britain; indirectly *some* of those rules found in France and Luxembourg could have a similar effect under British law.[110] It may be said therefore that French law spells out the disqualifications in a way in which legislation in this country does not. Any disqualifications in Britain rest on the union rules themselves, and this research shows that no rules have been found which disqualify a person from voting because he has not been in the establishment long enough, because he is not of British nationality, or because he has contravened the electoral code. This latter would in any case be inapplicable in Britain since there is not one laid by statute. Nor has any rule book examined shown a disqualification for contravening such a code imposed by the union rules. Some rule books mention disciplinary action upon union members, but in none has it been found that a suspended member is not entitled to vote in the election of his shop steward. In practice, however, the situation *may* (though it is not certain) be different.[111]

The conditions as to eligibility for 'délégués' in both France and Luxembourg are more rigorous than those for electors. In France to be eligible a person must be over twenty-one, and had until recently to be of French nationality or possess a pass of 'résident privilégié'.[112] He must be able to read and write and to have worked in the establishment for at least twelve consecutive months.[113] The close relatives of directors[114] are not eligible for election.[115] Employees expelled from their trade union[116] are not eligible to become 'délégués'.[117]

The 'inspecteur du travail' is empowered, after consultation with the most representative trade unions, to substitute the statutory qualifying period of service in both the case of the eligibility for election of a 'délégué' as well as for the elector. Such substitution can only take place when the effective number of employees is reduced to less than a quarter.[118] The rules which exist in France on the age and service qualifications also exist in Luxembourg and foreign workers are eligible to become 'délégués ouvriers'. Close relatives of the employers and directors are not eligible to stand as candidates. In the case of young worker representatives, the age limit is a minimum of eighteen and a maximum of twenty-one.[119]

In some rule books of British unions it has been found that certain qualifications are necessary for election or appointment to shop steward.[120] These vary from union to union, some of them not providing for any qualification.[121] What is obvious is that no general rule is laid by legislation or the TUC as to the shop steward's qualifications as is the case in France and Luxembourg. It is submitted that it would be desirable for general rules, which are binding on unions and their members, employers and employees, to be drawn up either by the legislature or the TUC, which would bring uniformity and order to both the qualifications necessary for election to shop steward as well as those necessary to be an elector. Uniform rules would make for certainty and order in this sphere, both of which at the moment do not exist.[122] Of the sample examined this research shows that in Britain 89 per cent of the members are *unaware* of what election arrangements exist in their union, what the necessary qualifications are for electors and what they are for candidates to become shop stewards. Seven per cent thought that some *sort of arrangement* existed but did not know the details and the remainder had an *accurate* knowledge of these arrangements or qualifications. In France, on the other hand, some 78 per cent of the sample were well versed in the election arrangements and the qualifications necessary to be a voter and to become a 'délégué', 19 per cent had a vague knowledge and only 3 per cent had no knowledge or were disinterested. In Luxembourg the respective figures were 83, 15 and 2 per cent.

Detailed and complex rules relating to the conduct of the election of a French 'délégué' are laid down by legislation. The election takes place by secret ballot and there are separate votes for the 'délégués titulaires' and for the 'délégués suppléants'[123] in each of the categories within the electoral colleges.[124] Any contested matters relating to the election[125] are within the competence of the judge of the 'canton' where the establishment is situated and he has to deal with the matter urgently.[126]

The rules regarding the conduct of elections in Luxembourg, though regulated by statute, are not considered to be as detailed as the French ones. All that legislation provides is for a secret ballot to be held, for a relative majority in the case of 'délégués d'employés' and by proportional representation in the case of 'délégués ouvriers'. Where however there is no list of candidates in the case of the latter, then the relative majority rule operates. It is interesting to note that statute empowers the Minister of Labour to appoint 'délégués' where no candidates stand for election.[127]

Although there is no legislation in Britain comparable to that which exists in France and Luxembourg on the *conduct of the elections*, it has been possible to find union rule books which talk of such procedure.[128] In none, however, can it be said that there exists the wealth of detail which appears under the French requirements;[129] and nowhere has it been found that contested matters relating to the elections of shop stewards are referable on appeal to a court of law,[130] as they automatically are in France. In a number of unions interviewed it was found that any irregularities would be the subject of internal union discipline,[131] and in any case most unions interviewed preferred to have a fluid arrangement regarding elections so that if the rules of the unions did not provide for a procedure etc. one would be made up. Unlike France and Luxembourg where it is determined by law (and sometimes collective agreements), the method of election in Britain is determined unilaterally by the unions.

It will be noted that ballots in France and Luxembourg have to be secret. Although most unions in Britain hold secret ballots in elections of shop stewards, this research shows that some unions prefer to elect them by a show of hands.[132] One other difference is evident. In France and Luxembourg *all* members of the electoral college have a right of vote whereas in Britain only trade union members in the electoral college may do so.

One important problem arises in Britain which cannot arise in Luxembourg or France: this is where there is multi-union membership in one constituency. It has been found in the course of this research that this can cause such problems as minorities not having a fair say, interunion conflict of policies and even discontent affecting good industrial relations.[133] The only solution offered is either to have smaller constituencies representing each of the trade unions (which could be impracticable mainly because of fragmentation of collective bargaining), or to adopt a system whereby the interests and policy of the constituency, and not the union, would be the operative one. This would involve changing the concept upon which the present system is based, but at least it would remedy the existing difficulties. These difficulties do not and cannot occur in either Luxembourg or France. It appears to this writer that the French and Luxembourg peoples have formulated the ideal solution in this field, and perhaps we in this country have a lesson to learn from these countries.

What conclusions may be drawn from the election process? There is little doubt that in all countries studied the employer has a particular interest in *who* is elected, be he shop steward or 'délégué'. From discussions held with various employers it is clear that they are concerned as to who the potential steward or 'délégué' will be, since it is he who will play an important role in determining the future of industrial relations within the establishment. The very fact that most employers give facilities and encourage elections[134] confirms this point.

Granted that the employer has 'an interest' in the institution of shop steward or 'délégué' since they have certain influence in industrial relations in the firm, one other question was asked of employers: 'Do you consider that the institution of shop steward or "délégué" is an essential one, disregarding your interest in this institution in relation to its good industrial relations' role?' It was interesting to note that the great majority of employers[135] genuinely believed that this institution was essential to their establishment, and that it was not the pressure put upon the employer [in Britain by trade unions and in France and Luxembourg by statute] that merely made them accept the institution. It was, however, detected that the French and Luxembourg employer accepted this fact more readily than the British employer. It is submitted that the reason for this is that the French have since 1936[136] had to include clauses on 'délégués' in their 'conventions collectives susceptible d'extension' and that being compulsory it has been accepted, similarly with the Luxembourg employers; whereas in Britain, there is no legal compulsion but trade union pressure.

It becomes evident (from what has been said above) that unions in Britain are particularly weak in the field of 'elections of shop stewards' compared with France and other European Community countries. This weakness manifests itself in the following spheres: (i) election or appointment of shop steward procedures in rule books; (ii) methods of informing the various constituencies of this procedure; (iii) qualifications of potential shop steward; (iv) the nomination procedure; (v) secret ballots; (vi) determination of a constituency; (vii) length of office. It is not proposed to lay down a specimen draft of proposals on each of these weaknesses, but it is proposed to put forward ideas based primarily on French or other European experience examined above which could remedy the present omissions. It must be stated *ab initio* that these ideas are not a transposition of foreign laws, this would be alien to British industrial relations and would not work; the ideas are based on an adaptation taken from European systems.

Before examining these ideas, it is necessary to consider what methods could be used to encourage their observance. It is suggested that the weaknesses under items (i) to (vii) above can be remedied in a variety of ways. Either (a) there be some statutory provisions on each of them which would make it compulsory to observe the norms laid down; or (b) recommend to the TUC to draw up guidelines to be sent to its affiliated unions advising them to draw up procedures etc. on elections of shop stewards; or (c) leave it to individual unions and employers to draw up their own procedures; or (d) strong encouragement from the Department of Employment for a voluntary settlement of these matters perhaps based on (or part of) a code of practice; or (e) make it a legislative requirement for a compulsory clause in all collective agreements which should include items (i) to (vii) above.

In this writer's opinion, suggestions (a) and (d) are the only realistic ones with a strong preference for (a). Human nature being what it is, suggestion (b) is, in this writer's opinion, unworkable. Unions it would seem would only pay lip service to TUC advice in this case, and nothing concrete would be achieved.[137] It is suggested that (c) is equally unworkable. If TUC encouragement had little effect, it is obvious by parity of reasoning that the initiative would not come from the unions themselves, or from individual employers. Nor is (e) above workable in Britain. Firstly, because a collective agreement is presumed unenforceable in law unless the parties wish it to be otherwise.[138] Secondly, even if parties are enabled to have this part of a collective agreement alone binding in law[139] they would not do so anyway because of the reasons given in (b) and (c) immediately above. For legislation to make this part of a collective agreement binding irrespective of the 1974 Trade Union and Labour Relations Act provisions that presume unenforceability would be a negation of, and make a nonsense of, the philosophy behind the 1974 Act. This would mean, in effect, the adoption of the French or Luxembourg system which considers collective agreements as enforceable in law and which could not work in Britain.

Two viable alternatives are (d) above or (a) above. In the case of the former, it seems the vogue today to have codes of practice. Is there any reason why such a code could not be drawn laying down guidelines on items (i) to (vii) above and encouraging employers and unions to observe it? It should not be binding in law (as the Code of Industrial Relations Practice is not) but it should be used in evidence in industrial tribunals and courts of law. This would go some way towards giving in particular the trade unions (and to a lesser extent the employers) an incentive and the requisite knowledge and guidelines to plan their own arrangements. Unions and employers are very conscious of the Code of Industrial Relations Practice and *generally* observe it; could it therefore not be said that the same would apply to a code (or part of a code) on the election of shop stewards? This would have the advantage of making these arrangements of a quasi-voluntary nature.

In the latter case, weaknesses (i) to (vii) above would be remedied in no uncertain terms by legislation which would lay down the minimum norms to be observed. These norms would not become part of all collective agreements but would stand on their own as a separate piece of legislation. In this writer's view, it is the best and perhaps the only effective way in which to remedy the present unsatisfactory situation in Britain. Nor could it be argued that legislation would be an impracticable means of remedying the situation, because the law cannot deal with every contingency at workshop level. The law should merely lay down the basic rules which could be adapted to different situations that might arise. This is, in fact, what is happening in Luxembourg and France, except that in the case of the latter country it is not legislation *per se* but legislation which provides for a compulsory clause within a collective agreement. There, the minimum norms are laid down (as was examined above) and the parties involved are able to adapt these to suit their particular circumstances (as was shown above).

Having looked at the alternative methods that could be used to encourage their observance by trade unions and others, ideas must be put forward as a possible basis which could help remedy the weaknesses already mentioned.[140]

A requirement should be made[141] on the procedure of electing (or appointing) a shop steward. This could be short but concise as well as general in application, thus allowing for the maximum amount of adaptation. A provision should exist stating that all union rule books must provide a procedure for electing or appointing a shop steward. Alternatively, the onus could be put on both the employer and the recognised union (or other unions) to draft such procedure. Details of the procedure should be left to the parties as is the case under French law.[142] Nothing more need be said in this respect except that the election or appointing procedure should be democratic. If by election, it must be by all entitled to vote, and the ballot must be secret. If it is by appointment, then the employer must also be consulted by the union, and an appointing board should be constituted to discuss and interview competing candidates. On the board employer's representatives should also sit. This writer has, in consequence of his research, no illusions as to the attitude of some unions who would wish to have the sole prerogative of appointment or election. It is submitted that this is shortsighted and undemocratic, particularly since, as was shown above, the employer has an interest in who is elected or appointed as shop steward.

It has already been noted[143] that in Britain white-collar union representation in the private sector is not so widespread as in the blue-collar unions. It is submitted that the above suggestion would *indirectly* help remedy this situation by making reluctant employers at least aware of an existing procedure. Such requirement as described above should prove flexible enough to allow unions (preferably with the consultation of employers) the maximum amount of freedom in how they plan their procedures.

The second weakness which manifests itself in Britain is the method of informing the constituencies of this procedure. By having a laid-down procedure in the union rule book as described above, this will *a priori* considerably remedy this weakness. The constituents will in theory[144] be able to consult the rule book for the procedure. This writer's investigations show that the great majority of constituents in France and Luxembourg are informed of the election procedure; this emanating from the legal requirements. Furthermore, the putting into practice of this procedure will automatically give constituents practical knowledge of the procedure, since prior to the election taking place they will be briefed on it, and then exercise it themselves. It appears to this writer that this second weakness will automatically remedy itself as soon as the first one is decided.

Then come the qualifications of potential shop stewards. This aspect, we have already seen, is treated in a tertiary manner in Britain, but is highly regulated in Luxembourg and France.[145] It is not suggested that it should be as rigid in Britain. It is submitted however that, as in Luxembourg and France, the conditions for eligibility should be more rigorous than those for electors. The first requirement should be that such an office should attract an *experienced person*. It will be recalled that there is a minimum age limit in Luxembourg and France.[145] This writer does not believe that this limit (i.e. twenty-one years old) is beneficial, and would prefer to make this qualification wider in scope and leave the decision to the proposers and voters.[146] Obviously, the second requirement should be that the shop steward should have a certain amount of education. Illiteracy has not usually been a problem in Britain[147] but it had at one time been in France, hence the provision that a 'délégué' should be able to read and write.[148] Such a specific requirement in Britain would be an insult to a potential candidate. Thirdly, it is not necessary to spell out the amount of service in the establishment in order to qualify as a shop steward, the first requirement (i.e. experience) should take care of that aspect. This fluid system would have the added advantage of not empowering some other body to change the minimum requirement in exceptional cases, which could be (as it has proved to be in France)[148] a cumbersome procedure. Finally, two further requirements would be advisable. An expelled, suspended, or ineligible union member should not be deemed to qualify as a shop steward and a potential shop steward who is closely related to a director of the establishment should also be ineligible.[149]

The fourth 'weakness' in Britain manifests itself in the nomination procedure. It has already been shown how the nomination procedure comes about under French law.[150] This system clearly cannot be adapted to Britain; nor can the Luxembourg system. Since shop stewards are, unlike the 'délégué' in Luxembourg and France, union representatives it is not proposed that constituents be enabled to change a candidate proposed by the union, after the proposal has taken place. However, this cannot remain so since other persons are also involved, namely the constituents and management. It is submitted that a procedure exists whereby the union(s) concerned, *before* nominating a candidate for election (or appointment), may consult with both the interested parties. It is true that where an election is held the constituents will vote for the person they prefer, therefore it may be argued that the constituents need not be consulted at the nomination stage, but management would then have no say in the matter. Moreover, neither management nor the constituents will have a say where the union *appoints* a person.[151] This writer submits that the nomination procedure should consist of (a) nomination by the union, upon (b) consultation with the constituents and (c) management. The union should still have the power to nominate but with approval from the parties concerned.[152]

It is a principle of any democratic system that a person holding the office of shop steward should be elected, and not appointed. It has been shown above that this aspect along with the others is not regulated in union rule books in Britain, and that great divergences exist in practice. Some unions appoint their stewards, others elect them by a show of hands, and others elect them by secret ballot. In a few instances one of these methods is provided for in the rule book, in others it is customary; there is therefore no consistency as things stand at present. In France,[153] Luxembourg and other European democracies this aspect is highly regulated. It is submitted that the union practice of appointing a shop steward should cease, that elections by a show of hands should also cease and that the only realistic method is by secret ballot. This would put some organisation in the present disorganised state, and would, furthermore, be democratic and fair.[154] Any contested election matters should go to an industrial tribunal, from where there would lie an appeal in the usual manner to the higher courts.[155]

It has been stated[156] that three electoral colleges are provided for under French law, but that there exists freedom to vary the number.[157] In Luxembourg there can only be two electoral colleges. This seems a complicated arrangement and one from which Britain would derive no advantage. It is suggested that only one electoral college is necessary consisting of the constituency of the shop steward. Such constituency should be determined by the union(s) and employer jointly. It is not possible to be more precise on constituencies, since a great deal will depend on the internal organisation of the establishment and conditions of the industry.

Finally some certainty and uniformity is ncessary in Britain in connection with the steward's term of office. In France it is of one year's duration and cannot be tacitly renewed. In Luxembourg it is of four years' duration for the 'délégués ouvriers' and of three years' duration for the 'délégué d'employés' and can be renewed for an indefinite period. In Britain it is not clear what the duration is,[158] and it appears that there can be tacit renewal especially where there are no competing candidates. It is submitted that the shop steward's period of office in Britain be set for one year at a time, but that there be allowed a tacit renewal of the office from year to year until other candidates are nominated or present themselves[159] when an election by secret ballot must be held.

Section iii. Term of office

The French 'délégué' is elected for *one* year, but he may be re-elected from year to year. In Luxembourg the 'délégué ouvrier' is elected for four years and the 'délégué d'employes' for three. The question has been asked whether in France 'délégués', and in Britain shop stewards, automatically lose their status if no election is held at the end of the year. Such a question has not been asked in Luxembourg since there can be an indefinite renewal. It would appear that in France there cannot be a tacit renewal and that, therefore, the 'délégué' cease to retain his office at the end of the period.[160] Upon his death, resignation, termination of his employment contract, or upon the loss of conditions of eligibility, the 'délégué's' office (as well as the shop steward's) comes to an end. The trade union control over the 'délégué' it originally nominated[161] is evident, since it may propose the revocation of his office subject to a majority secret ballot of the electoral college to which he belongs.[162] Where the 'délégué titulaire's' office ceases (see above) he is automatically replaced by the 'délégué suppléant'. This latter becomes the 'délégué titulaire' until the expiration of time of the person he replaces.[163]

From the sample interviewed, it appears that the majority (though by no means all) of shop stewards in Britain (like the 'délégué' in France) hold their office for a year at a time[164] but most are re-elected.[165] Unlike France, but like Luxembourg, the sample studied indicates that there can be a tacit renewal at the expiry of the shop steward's period of office until the next election, especially if there are no competing candidates and where the collective agreement so provides.[166] Where, however, there are competing candidates then an election is usually held.[167] It is evident that the French unions have a certain amount of say in the office of the 'délégué' since they *usually* are the original proposers, and since they are also enabled to propose his revocation subject to the vote of the constituency personnel. In Britain, however, the shop steward being a union official and controlled by the union, the latter is in a stronger position to suggest revocation of his mandate than French trade unions are with the 'délégué'.

Whereas in France, like in Luxembourg, the 'délégué titulaire', on ceasing his functions, is automatically replaced by the 'délégué suppléant', and that therefore there is no need to hold an election until the 'délégué titulaire's' period of office expires, in Britain since there are no acting shop stewards, on the steward's cessation of office there is no one to automatically replace him.[168] It is submitted that it would be advantageous to create throughout industry in Britain the office of acting, deputy or assistant steward; this would remedy the situation described above and, furthermore, such person would be the shop steward's 'right-hand man'.

Section iv. Rights and facilities

In France management must allow each 'délégué' a maximum of fifteen hours a month with a possible increase in exceptional circumstances[169] to enable him to carry out his duties. This time is remunerated as though it had been worked. There is however a proviso that it must not seriously affect the terms of his employment contract.[170] A number of difficulties have occurred as a result of this provision. Firstly, it has been asked whether the time allowed was to be devoted to the 'délégué's' work *within* the establishment, or whether it would be legitimate to incorporate within that time any *external* activity. The Cour de Cassation held that delegates were entitled to perform *external* activities in the course of their duties,[171] subject to one condition, that these activities are exclusively pertinent to the duties and functions of delegates.[172] A second difficulty which arose was whether a 'délégué' has a right to fifteen hours a month irrespective of whether he accomplishes his functions in a lesser time. It seems clear from the wording of the article that fifteen hours is the *maximum* amount of time to be allowed, and that it does not give an absolute right; it only gives a right to 'le temps nécessaire à l'exercice de leurs fonctions'. It should be remembered that a 'délégué' is also an employee and that an interruption of the contract of employment is not authorised for a longer period than the law requires.

It is found in Luxembourg that the practice varies since it is not regulated by legislation but that on average 'délégués ouvriers' spend some fifteen hours a month on their work, and that 'délégués d'employés' spend considerably less, namely seven hours. However the 'délégations ouvrières' are invariably allowed by the employer to meet during working hours once a week as a body. It is in the course of these meetings that workers' wishes or problems are raised. The 'délégations d'employés' may also meet but before they are entitled to do so, there must be over fifty employees employed.

A comparison with the shop steward in Britain shows a broad similarity, but there exist considerable differences of detail. Shop stewards perform two functions — industrial relations functions[173] and trade union functions[174] — whereas 'délégués' usually[175] perform only one. Since a realistic comparison can only relate to the industrial relations functions, it is upon these that this research is principally concerned.

In France there is a statutory requirement for leave from his job to be given to a 'délégué' in order to perform his functions. In Britain, until recently, (and Luxembourg) no such statutory requirement existed and therefore it could have been argued that in theory the shop steward had no such right which would allow him to perform his industrial relations functions.[176] In practice, however, this research indicates that employees (i.e. shop stewards) in both the white- and blue-collar unions are given time off to carry out their industrial relations functions.[177] This aspect is mainly regulated in Britain by procedure agreements,[178] whereas in France it is regulated by law.

The statutory requirement in France lays down the maximum number of hours allowed to the 'délégué'; no such statutory rights exist in Britain. In practice however this research shows that a great majority of shop stewards are given adequate time to perform their industrial relations functions.[179] In Luxembourg, France and Britain permission must first be sought however.

Though a specific time allowance is given in France there is the proviso that a 'délégué's' duties must not seriously affect the terms of his employment contract. It is submitted that this indicates in some instances a restriction on the rights of the 'délégué' in cases where the terms of his employment contract would be seriously jeopardised. It has been found in a few instances that restrictions in such circumstances have been imposed in France and that meetings between *'délégués' and their constituents* during working hours have been disallowed.[180] This situation has also been found in Britain, but to a much larger extent. This research shows that most British establishments do not allow for regular meetings between stewards and their constituents during working hours.[181] It has been found that this is not always the fault of British management, because either the stewards themselves or the individual constituents prefer for tactical or other reasons to have these meetings *outside* working hours. This feeling on the part of 'délégués' and constituents does not seem to prevail in France, and certainly not in Luxembourg. It is submitted that the reason lies within the 'conceptual idea' which motivates the three systems. In France and Luxembourg, the 'délégué' represents his constituents and therefore any meetings which he may have, being of an industrial relations nature (and limited to such), are part of the work of the establishment seen as a whole. In Britain on the other hand, only one of the shop steward's functions is industrial relations, *and* he is also (and is seen mainly as) the union representative, thus union matters could inevitably crop up at such meetings. Since this latter is likely to happen in Britain, management feels that this is not an appropriate topic for discussion during working hours, and similarly shop stewards and constituents in many instances prefer to discuss union matters outside working hours. One other matter has been discovered in the course of this research. In France and Luxembourg meetings held at the workplace during working hours are concerned with all aspects of industrial relations problems — the sample examined showed such varied matters as safety, redundancies, social security, complaints, dismissals, working conditions, terms of employment, interpretation of agreements etc. as being the subjects of discussion. In Britain however it is found that such meetings as are allowed during working hours at the workplace are a great deal more limited. The sample examined showed that a majority of meetings are often held for the sole purpose of communicating to constituents certain information or the results of joint negotiations that have already taken place. In Britain it has been found however that meetings other than with constituents, e.g. to conclude with management and unions shop floor agreements, or to discuss a particular problem,[182] i.e. to do with industrial relations, are more prolific.

It will be recalled that the time off allowed to the 'délégué' in France and Luxembourg is always remunerated. This research reveals that problems have arisen and are arising in both Luxembourg and France in connection with, in particular, payment by results and overtime work. It is found that employers in almost all cases examined either calculate the average of previous months earned by the 'délégué' or the average earned by colleagues of the 'délégué'. In the detailed investigation which was carried out, nowhere has it been found that the 'délégué' is out of pocket.[183] This comparative aspect in Britain however shows that shop stewards are often out of pocket as a result of their shop steward activities,[184] and that British management, like French management, is generally[185] not prepared to accommodate the steward for loss of earnings. It is suggested that the reasons for this phenomenon are as follows: first, the 'délégué' is only concerned with industrial relations functions which are of benefit to the employer; the latter will therefore be more willing to remunerate than the British employer who regards the shop steward as a union official, also having union functions. It is evident that British management is aware of the steward's industrial relations functions and therefore considers it of benefit to such management,[186] but it has been made abundantly clear to the writer in the course of this research that management sees the shop steward as primarily *the* union representative.[187] Secondly, there is in Luxembourg and France a statutory requirement that the 'délégué' must be remunerated while performing his legally authorised functions as a 'délégué'. Until recently (i.e. S.57(4) E.P.A.) no such statutory compulsion was imposed on British management. Thirdly, the French and Luxembourg employer has long accepted this phenomenon as being part of the industrial relations system, whereas his British counterpart has not yet done so for the reasons advanced above.

Having examined the position in relation to leave from the shop steward's and 'délégué's' job and his remuneration for time spent on his functions, submissions for improvement in the present position in Britain (taking into consideration the Luxembourg and French situation) must be made.

It was stated above that in Britain there was until recently no statutory requirement for leave to be given to stewards to enable them to perform their *industrial relations* functions but that in practice no problem arose since such leave was normally granted. It is suggested that such arrangement was not satisfactory since it did not give the steward any guarantee of leave to enable him to fulfil his *industrial relations* functions.[188] The original submission that a shop steward should be given a statutory right for leave to perform *inter alia* his industrial relations functions is no longer necessary since he has now been given one. So as to avoid the situation whereby the steward would have the automatic right to take this leave when he pleases, which could prove detrimental to the establishment, this right should be curtailed by two requirements.[188a] Firstly, that prior permission should be asked from management and secondly, that management should not refuse permission unless the granting of such permission would cause serious loss to the establishment. Furthermore, the time allowed off should entitle the steward not only to devote this time *within* the establishment, but also to any *external activities* (as was decided by the Cour de Cassation in France) which are in connection with his industrial relations duties. The giving of such statutory rights cannot but enhance industrial relations within the establishment.

In contrast to leave being given to enable the steward to fulfil his *industrial relations* functions, it was stated above that less happy is the situation where the steward and his constituents are able to meet during working hours. The problems that such a statutory right would, if it were granted, bring about are innumerable; it is therefore not suggested that such a right be given. Instead, it is thought that the French and Luxembourg experience could work well in Britain. Such a statutory right should be given *subject* to the proviso that the establishment will not be in danger of making a loss, i.e. subject to agreement between management and the shop steward as to the most convenient time in which to hold the meeting. This sort of arrangement, it is suggested, can only improve industrial relations within the firm and would be particularly useful during periods of tension or upon the imminence of industrial action.[189]

Though such a right exists in Luxembourg, nowhere in French law is there any right for the 'délégués' of the different constituencies to meet and discuss mutual problems. In practice however it was found that these meetings occur to a lesser or greater extent on an informal basis. In Britain, inter shop steward meetings during working hours are not encouraged and are therefore infrequent.[190] Though such meetings can in many instances be beneficial, their value is limited, and therefore it is not felt necessary to give any such statutory right to shop stewards.

A statutory maximum time allowance of fifteen hours a month is given to the 'délégué' in France. No such right is given to the shop steward in Britain. It seems to this writer that there is a good case for a monthly statutory number of hours to be allowed to the steward. It could be argued that such right would not be conducive to flexibility. It is difficult to see how such an argument can be sustained, since there can be flexibility within the maximum statutory period. This is clearly demonstrated by the position in France examined above. Should the steward have the statutory right to leave his place of work whenever he feels like it? Clearly the answer must be 'No'. A proviso must exist to the effect that prior permission should be obtained.

Finally, loss of earnings was considered earlier and it was shown that time off in France and Luxembourg was remunerated as though it had been worked. An equivalent examination as to the British position revealed that the majority of shop stewards lose a certain amount of their wages as a result of their functions. It is not fair that a shop steward should lose part of his wages when one aspect of his work (i.e. industrial relations functions), is benefiting the employer.[191] It is therefore submitted that, like in France and Luxembourg, legislation should give the shop steward a right to his full wages[192] when he is performing his industrial relations functions, since he is benefiting the employer.[193] It is not suggested however that he be given a statutory right to being remunerated for time off on trade union functions, but perhaps advice should be given to the employer that should he extend his generosity to making such payment, it would help improve relations between the union and the establishment and thus aid industrial relations. The union itself should normally be responsible to pay the balance of the shop steward's loss when he is performing his trade union functions.[194]

Management must in France and Luxembourg provide the 'délégué' with a room to enable him to carry out his duties and to hold meetings. Of the sample examined in France 98 per cent of establishments which had collective agreements provided this facility on a *permanent* basis, 2 per cent provided it on a *temporary* basis. The 'délégué' is authorised to display notices giving the necessary information which his duties require him to give.[195] Such notices may be displayed upon notice boards provided for trade union notices, and upon doors at the entrances of work places.[196] The law therefore considers that information to workmen by their 'délégué' is indispensable, yet the law expects a happy balance to be struck by the 'délégué' between on the one hand his function of keeping employees informed, and on the other the maintenance of discipline within the establishment; so that the 'délégué' cannot proceed at will to display on notice boards any notices he wishes. Notices must relate to professional matters only, so that as was found in France, where a 'délégué' regularly displays notices inviting personnel to cease work,[197] or where notices contain defamatory allegations against the employer,[198] the courts held that the 'délégué' acted *ultra vires*. On the other hand, the employer is liable if he obstructs the display of notices, unless those be of a detrimental character to the establishment.[199] The law is silent in France and Luxembourg as to whether information may be transmitted to workmen other than through notices, as for example verbally, during meetings. This is no doubt a matter for the 'réglements internes'[200] to settle, and often the rules provide for such meetings, so long as certain limits are observed. Nor does the law make any provisions relating to the way in which employees are to consult the 'délégué'. Again, it is presumed that the 'règlements d'atelier'[201] will deal with the method and time to be allotted for consultation. 'Délégués' in France must be received by the management collectively at least once a month, but they may in case of urgency and upon their request be received more often. 'Délégués' may also be received by the management upon request either individually, or by workshop, trade or service, depending on the matter to be dealt with. Furthermore the 'délégué' may upon his request be assisted by trade union representatives. It is stressed however that he is not compelled to be, since officially he is independent of trade unions. The intervention by a trade union representative cannot be extended to cases other than those expressly stated by law or collective agreements.[202] Since the 'délégué du personnel' is often also the trade union representative, he must be careful to distinguish the two offices since his powers and prerogatives are different according to the functions which he exercises. In all cases the 'délégués suppléants' may also attend these meetings.[203] Two days before a meeting with management (unless exceptional circumstances arise) the 'délégué' must submit a written note indicating in outline the object of his requests. A copy of that note is written in a special register kept by the employer, in which must also be mentioned within a maximum of six days the reply to that request. This register must be kept available on one working day a fortnight and after working hours to employees who wish to consult it. It must also be made available to the 'inspecteur du travail'.[204]

This research shows that specific, stringent and well-regulated legal requirements exist in France in the sphere of facilities afforded to the 'délégué'. It is found that in practice the establishments examined indicated in varying degrees of practicality, i.e. depending upon their size and internal structure, observance of the legal requirements, but two other matters are evident. Firstly, it is found that, without exception, those establishments subject to a 'convention collective susceptible d'extension' all had detailed *clauses* relating to facilities; secondly, it is found that there is a *great awareness* by establishments of the legal requirements relating to facilities. These observations apply to both manual and non-manual workers within an establishment. The same may be said to be the position in Luxembourg.

An equivalent examination in Britain indicates that facilities offered varied from establishment to establishment; they also varied according to the internal industrial relations structure of the establishment. In general it may be said that facilities in Britain are not as extended, and management is not as aware of *what* facilities should be given to shop stewards, as is the case in France and Luxembourg.

This research also shows that office accommodation on a permanent basis for the shop steward is a rare luxury. Of the sample examined only 3 per cent of the establishments provided permanent accommodation for the manual shop steward, and only 1½ per cent for the non-manual shop steward. The convenor or senior shop steward did significantly better, but again, by French standards, he is poorly provided for. It is found that of the sample only 30 per cent of manual senior stewards and 19 per cent of non-manual senior stewards were given this facility.[205] Two phenomena however manifest themselves in Britain (which have little or no equivalent in France). Firstly, stewards (especially senior stewards) are often allowed accommodation for a specific occasion, e.g. to hold a meeting or to do certain industrial relations work. Of the establishments examined, it was found that 88 per cent of establishments allowed this facility to either stewards or senior stewards. Although in a very small minority in France it was found that *temporary* accommodation was given to the 'délégué' (see above), no case has been found there where borrowing of a room for a specific occasion has occurred. The position in Luxembourg in this sphere is similar to Britain though Luxembourg statute does provide that premises be put at the disposal of 'délégués'. Secondly, it is found that employers are more ready to provide a room for meetings at which industrial relations topics within the firm are discussed (i.e. communication of information, redundancies etc.).[206] Of the establishments examined 92 per cent of manual stewards and 89 per cent of non-manual stewards were granted this facility.

Unlike 'office accommodation' which is a rarity, it has been found that British establishments are generous with the provision of notice-board facilities. Of the establishments examined, 95 per cent afforded the use of notice boards to manual shop stewards and 85 per cent to white-collar shop stewards. These high percentages could appear misleading for whereas in France and Luxembourg notice boards and doors are used exclusively by the 'délégué', in Britain it has been found that their use is not exclusive to the shop steward. In many instances a part of a notice board is allocated to the shop steward, in others notice-board facilities are available on special request from management. It may therefore be said that whereas in Luxembourg and France the 'délégué' is given a specific right to a notice board, no such right exists in Britain. It may also be concluded that whereas the law in France recognises by implication that the passing of information to constituents is essential to good industrial relations, no such legal recognition[207] is given in Britain. This comparison shows further that in France there has been some litigation (see above) on the contents of notices to be displayed and on the rights of management and the 'délégué' in this respect. In Britain and Luxembourg no such litigation seems to have taken place.[208]

The frequency and procedure of meetings is clearly laid down in Luxembourg and France (see above) by statute. In Britain no such statutory requirement exists, and this research indicates that very few establishments (2 per cent) have prearranged meetings (as in France) between shop stewards and management. Although meetings are held regularly they do not therefore occur on set days. Nor has it been found that in any establishment in Britain there exists a register of requests etc. (see above) to be consulted by employees. Furthermore, although the Luxembourg and French 'délégué' has a statutory right of access to the employer (see above) no such right exists in Britain, though it has been found that in only 5 per cent of cases has management refused a shop steward's request to discuss problems. Finally, in France there is a legislative requirement for the 'délégué' to request assistance from a trade union official (see above). No such statutory requirement exists in Britain (or Luxembourg) but of the establishments interviewed it was shown that the majority of employers were willing to discuss any matter with both the shop steward and the local union official.[209]

It will be noted that the law in France is silent on the ancillaries to the provision of an office, i.e. filing cabinets, telephone, secretarial help and duplicating facilities. This does not mean that these are not provided. It has been found that very few complaints have been directed by 'délégués' towards the use of these facilities.[210] The Luxembourg statute talks of ' . . . le matériel de bureau . . . ' only. In Britain however the great majority of both manual and white-collar shop stewards (97 per cent of establishments examined) have access to external and internal telephones.[211] The low percentage in Britain of office accommodation given to shop stewards (see above) has a corollary in that, of the establishments and shop stewards interviewed, it was found that the provision of storage facilities was poor (some 48 per cent of manual shop stewards and 43 per cent of white-collar stewards) while typing and duplicating facilities, though better, could be improved (68 per cent of the manual stewards and 75 per cent of the white-collar stewards).

As a result of the above examination, it is evident that in this field too Britain is lagging well behind France, Luxembourg and other of its European partners.[212] The following suggestions, some of which are based on and adapted from a combination of the French and Luxembourg systems, are therefore proposed in order to improve the present and inadequate situation which exists in Britain. It is submitted that the main premise should be that if the steward is expected to carry out his duties competently — i.e. to communicate with and have adequate contact with his constituents, management, and the union — then he must be given adequate facilities to achieve this. This will in turn contribute towards a good industrial relations system and be of benefit to the employer.

Legislation (as being the only realistic way to achieve the aim) should provide for the following which are considered the most important facilities to be given to shop stewards.

It has already been noted that the provision of office accommodation in a great majority of establishments is either poor or non-existent. It is therefore suggested that legislation should make provision for such accommodation to be given to shop stewards. It is readily recognised that this will be a great imposition on the smaller establishment which perhaps is already short of accommodation for its own needs. To deal with this contingency legislation should place limits by exempting for the time being the smaller establishments (those with under 100 full-time employees) from such a requirement. In France, all establishments subject to a 'convention collective susceptible d'extension', whether large or small, are compelled to provide accommodation. The French employer has long accepted this and does not seem to find that any hardship results from it, indeed he sees the sense of it in that it is of advantage to him. Might it therefore not be said that the same could result in Britain?

In those establishments which are exempt from providing permanent accommodation, legislation should state that the use of occasional accommodation should be given (as is the case in Luxembourg). It has already been noted that this is prevalent in a majority of British establishments. Such legislation should therefore not impose hardship on the smaller firms. The occasional accommodation should be provided only for meetings of an industrial relations nature (and not trade union meetings). Shop-floor agreements should provide for such details as what type of meetings will be held, i.e. with constituents or with other shop stewards or convenors; when they are to be held, i.e. during working hours or outside working hours; and what temporary accommodation shall be provided. Legislation should not involve itself with such details which could be a burden on the establishment because anyway there will be a variation according to the processes, the works rules, overtime, management attitudes etc.

It was stated above that ' . . . British establishments are generous with the provision of notice-board facilities'. A warning was however given that the high percentages are misleading and reasons for these were given. It is therefore suggested that legislation should (as is the case in France but unlike Luxembourg) give a right to the shop steward to have a notice board for his own exclusive use. This will do away with the present practices (described above) which cause practical difficulties and problems. The type of notice to be affixed to the notice board should not lie within the realm of legislation, this being a detail to be agreed between the shop steward and the employer. Legislation should however provide that 'derogatory' or 'inflammatory' notices should not appear. This would take into account the problems which have arisen in France (and described above). Alternatively, neither should the employer be entitled to remove notices.

A system which would considerably enhance industrial relations within an establishment and which would help alleviate the mistrust which so often exists between employees and employers, would be to hold regular meetings at set intervals (weekly, monthly or quarterly) between the shop steward and management. This would enable management to 'feel the pulse' of the employees, and vice versa. This research showed that only 2 per cent (see above) hold such regular meetings. It is therefore submitted that legislation should be passed to impose such requirement on the parties concerned. Furthermore, it should, as is the case in France, give a right to the shop steward's constituents individually, or collectively with other shop stewards and their constituents, to ask for a meeting with management to discuss any imminent or existing difficulties.

Some order is also necessary in connection with the agenda for these meetings and records. It has been found that these aspects represent a weakness in Britain. It is therefore considered that legislation would remedy this weakness by providing that an agenda be sent to the employer in time for him to prepare the points to be discussed at the meeting. Similarly, proper records of meetings should be kept and a register of grievances should be instituted to show what action has been taken by the establishment, or if no action can be taken, the reasons why this cannot be done. Such a register should be available at set times for inspection by all employees. This may sound an imposition on an already overburdened employer, but it seems that in the long run some good will be done to industrial relations where these are already strained or frayed.

Finally, it is submitted that legislation is the only effective way to remedy the problems which are currently arising in Britain (as shown above) in connection with physical facilities which relate to filing cabinets, the use of telephones and typing and duplicating facilities. Obviously, the indiscriminate imposition of such duties would impose hardship on the smaller employer. It is therefore suggested that initially only establishments employing over 100 full-time employees should be bound by the legislative requirements. The legislation should provide that the employer must adequately furnish the accommodation with one or more filing cabinets, a telephone for internal and external use and typing and duplicating facilities during a certain number of days a month. Legislation could not be more specific, as these facilities will have to vary according to the internal structure of the establishment. General legislation of the kind outlined would have the added advantage of providing a sense of *awareness*. Nor would legislation of this kind provide enormous hardship for the larger employer.[213] It would only result in giving more facilities and thus improving industrial relations.

Section v. Representatives' dismissal procedure

The 'délégué' has in France and Luxembourg been sheltered from any reprisal by his employer. Under the French 1946 law he cannot be dismissed without the prior consent of the 'comité d'entreprise'. This applies not only to the dismissal of a 'délégué', but also to that of a 'délégué suppléant'.[214] A check therefore is instantly discernible under French law on the employer against arbitrary dismissal of a 'délégué'. Where the 'comité d'entreprise' and the employer disagree, dismissal will depend upon the decision of the 'inspecteur du travail' in charge of the particular establishment, but the employer has always got the power to suspend a 'délégué' where a serious breach (faute grave) has occurred until a final decision has been reached by either the 'comité d'entreprise' or the 'inspecteur du travail'. Where no 'comité d'entreprise' exists in an establishment the matter is submitted directly to the inspector.[215] A further check is thus placed to safeguard the 'délégué' where the employer and the 'comité' do not agree to the dismissal and in cases where no 'comité' exists. Dismissal takes place only on the date on which the 'comité d'entreprise' or the 'inspecteur' agreed to it.[216] An ordinance in 1959[217] states that the above procedure applies to the dismissal of former 'délégués' during a period of six months from the date of expiration of their office, and for candidates presented by trade unions during the first cycle of an election, from the date of publication of the list of candidates and thereafter for a period of three months.

The French experience shows that a number of difficulties have arisen in connection with the dismissal of 'délégués'. These must now be examined before considering the position in Luxembourg and that regarding shop stewards in Britain.

Firstly, the article relating to the dismissal of a 'délégué du personnel' states that 'en cas de désaccord, le licenciement ne peut intervenir que sur la decision de l'inspecteur du travail dont dépend l'établissement'; a parallel article is contained in ordonnance du 22 février 1945 relating to the dismissal of members of the 'comité d'éntreprise'. This article states 'En cas de désaccord, le licenciement ne peut intervenir que sur la décision *conforme* (which agrees with) de l'inspecteur du travail . . . dont dépend l'établissement'. It has therefore been asked whether the method of dismissal was the same for the 'délégués du personnel' as for the members of the 'comité d'entreprise'. Whereas ordonnance du 22 février 1945 carries the word *conforme* within its definition, the law of 16 April 1946 makes no mention of the word. It was therefore argued that the dismissal of a 'délégué' was not subordinated to an agreement by the 'inspecteur du travail'. The Cour de Cassation, however, held that the omission of the word 'conforme' in the 1946 law was of little significance, and that the consent of the 'inspecteur du travail' remained indisputable where the 'comité d'entreprise' did not agree with the employer.[218]

In the second place, some discussion has taken place as to whether the legal guarantees against the dismissal of 'délégués' are available when the dismissal is of a collective nature. In other words do the rules provided by ordonnance du 24 mai 1945, which relates to the collective dismissal of employees,[219] eliminate the provisions of the 1946 law relating to 'délégués'?[220] According to one decision[221] the special measures relating to the 'délégués' must merge with the general provisions applicable to all employees, and the Cour de Cassation[222] held that the law makes no distinction – whether it concerns 'délégués' or members of the 'comité d'entreprise' – in cases of mass dismissals. Thus, the special protection of 'délégués' no longer applies when it concerns mass dismissals.

It is submitted that this decision by the Cour de Cassation is prejudicial to the 'délégué', since an opportunity is given to the employer to dismiss a troublesome 'délégué' under the pretext of mass dismissal. Furthermore, it seems illogical that so much protection (see art. 16) should be given to the 'délégué' against individual dismissal, yet when it comes to mass dismissals the 'délégué' ranks along with other employees.[223] It would appear that the additional protection given to the 'ex-délégué' who completed his term of office, or to the unsuccessful trade union nominee (see above) would, by parity of reasoning, also disappear. In this latter case, it would appear however that the former 'delegue' has a civil law remedy for wrongful dismissal ('rupture abusive') (see in particular Cour de Cassation, Ch. Civ., Sect. Soc., 16 Feb. 1956, ICE 1956, p. 512). It is however suggested that it would be an impossible task for the former 'délégué' to prove his case.

Art. 16 (above) states that where the 'comité d'entreprise' and the employer disagree on the dismissal of a 'délégué', the case must be referred to the 'inspecteur du travail' who will decide upon the issue. If an arbitrary decision resulting in a refusal to dismiss is made by the inspecteur, the employer has three remedies open to him. Firstly, he may appeal to the Minister of Labour against the decision of the 'inspecteur du travail'. The right of appeal in this instance forms an interesting exception since the appeal lies from the 'inspecteur' direct to the minister, who will examine both the form and contents of the case, thus bypassing the 'inspecteur divisionnaire' and the 'directeur départemental du travail'.[224]

In the *second* instance, the employer may have recourse to the *tribunal administratif* of the place where the dismissal took place.[225] This administrative jurisdiction is of a limited nature as it confines itself to an examination, according to the 'dossier', as to the accuracy or inaccuracy of the facts upon which the inspector has based his decision. The tribunal is not competent to pronounce, having stated the facts, as to whether the inspector's decision is right or wrong, nor can it decide upon the seriousness of the 'délégué's' alleged wrongdoing.[226] On the other hand the fact that the case is pending in the tribunal administratif will neither delay nor affect in any other way the decision of another court in an action for damages for wrongful dismissal brought by the 'délégué'.[227] Conversely, the inspector's decision will not be tainted by irregularity if he has not taken into account the summing up and comments given upon the facts by the tribunal administratif.[228]

In the *third* instance, the employer may have recourse to the civil courts which are competent to deal with matters relating to the contract of employment, in this instance to discharge the contract of employment of the 'délégué'.[229] This solution is however very controversial.[230]

Dismissed 'délégués' may, on their part, appeal to the minister and to the tribunal administratif (as above) if they contest the inspector's approving a dismissal, but such appeal cannot be made without the prior consent of the inspector himself. They are also enabled to bring a civil action for wrongful dismissal, even though the dismissal was consented to by the 'comité d'entreprise' or the inspecteur du travail.

It becomes clear firstly that a well-established procedure is laid down by legislation in France before a 'délégué' may be dismissed and secondly that the 'délégué' is afforded special protection not given to other employees. Neither does a legislative procedure exist in Britain to specifically protect the shop steward nor is he afforded any greater protection than the ordinary employee.[231]

Whereas in France (and Luxembourg where a similar protection is given[232]) a system of checks exists (see above) before dismissal takes place, there is no equivalent system in Britain, so that a dismissed shop steward can only complain to an industrial tribunal *after* the event. Even the former 'délégués' are protected for a limited period (six months) and candidates who are not elected as 'délégués', but are merely nominated (in Luxembourg) by their union (in France), enjoy such protection (three months). In Britain such generous protection is non-existent in the case of shop stewards.

The system of checks which exists in France has not only been provided for by legislation, but it has been reinforced by case law.[233] No case law is known to this writer giving special protection to the shop steward in Britain.

As is the case in France on mass dismissals where it would appear that no protection is given to the 'délégué', so it is in Luxembourg (it is thought) and in Britain where the equivalent situation would also provide no safeguard.

One further check exists by statute in France in the case where the employer and the inspecteur disagree on the dismissal and where this latter refuses to dismiss. This is that various appeals are open to the employer (see above). There also exists since 1970 an appeal in Luxembourg.[234] Again the 'délégué' is safeguarded pending the result of the appeal. No such statutory safeguard may be found in the case of the shop steward.

Though no legislation in Britain gives additional safeguards to the shop steward against dismissal (see above), this research attempted to find out whether any establishments had some procedure or other agreement which would safeguard the steward. It has not been possible to find a single such procedure agreement.

As a result of these findings[235] it is proposed to suggest a course of action which would give shop stewards additional protection to that they have at present. This writer firmly believes that because of the nature of the shop steward's job he is more vulnerable than other employees, and because of that it therefore becomes necessary for him to have additional protection.[236] The proposals made below are based mainly on the French experience which works well in practice but, as is the case with previous suggestions made, these are adapted to meet the British requirements.

Leaving it merely for voluntary procedure agreements to regulate this aspect is unworkable. There are a number of reasons why this is so. It is submitted that the main reason is that there will not be one uniform procedure which would regulate this aspect. There will be as many procedures as there are procedure agreements which would result in making this protection farcical. Then there is a danger, if it were merely a TUC recommendation that all unions be asked to conclude such agreements, that some might and some might not conclude procedure agreements, and some might even find difficulty in doing so because of an employer's unwillingness, which would inevitably be a contributing factor towards creating poor industrial relations within the stablishment. There is a further problem in that considerable delays will occur between the TUC recommendation and the conclusion of the collective agreement.

The only realistic remedy seems to be legislation. The present law is applicable to *all workers* who take part in trade union activities and who are dismissed and for that reason are deemed to have been unfairly dismissed.[237] It may therefore be said that this legislation is adequate to cater for the needs of the shop steward. This argument cannot be accepted since it does not necessarily cover any unpalatable act to the employer and committed by the shop steward in connection with some *industrial relations aspects* of his functions.[238] Nor can this argument be accepted because, by not giving additional protection to the shop steward, the present legislation enables the employer (despite the reinstatement provisions) to get rid of the shop steward by paying him compensation. This is a cheap way to get rid of a troublesome shop steward.[239] One last reason why this argument cannot be accepted is that there are no 'checks' as there are under the Luxembourg and French systems, *before* the dismissal actually takes place. In Britain, the only check on the employer dismissing is ultimately the industrial tribunal, which comes *after* the event has occurred. In other words there is a need in this country for a prophylactic rather than for a reparative function.

It is bearing in mind all these matters that the submissions below are made. Legislation should therefore provide a right for additional protection to be given to shop stewards against both dismissal and actions falling short of dismissal as is the case in France and Luxembourg. Such protection should specifically provide for all their industrial relations functions. This right should be expressed in more positive terms than those which exist under sch. 1 para. 6(4) of the 1974 Trade Union and Labour Relations Act, in that it should include specifically all the shop steward's *industrial relations functions*. The right would be 'in more positive terms' if the shop steward's functions in each of his trade union (as at present) and industrial relations ones were (in fact) spelt out individually.

This right should not stop there. There should be, as there are in Luxembourg and France, 'checks' on the employer *before* he is enabled to dismiss. The situation which exists in France for these 'checks' is not appropriate to Britain,[240] and therefore an alternative system will have to be devised. Besides, the French system is cumbersome and complicated and therefore a simpler one is required.

Some collective agreements examined provide what this writer calls the 'embryonic stage' of a dismissal procedure for shop stewards[241] in that the management may bring before the union any matters which concern the failure of the shop steward to carry out his responsibilities as a shop steward.[242] For the reasons given in the previous note (i.e. 242) though this first step in the procedure ought to be kept, it ought also to be expanded to cover not only failure of a shop steward to carry out his responsibilities as a shop steward, but also abuse of power as a shop steward as well as serious breaches of his contract of employment as an employee. It is submitted therefore that the first step in such procedure should be that management brings up the matter (in the suggested expanded form) with the trade union concerned. Displeasure by the management should therefore concern itself with contract of employment breaches, shop steward duties (including his individual relations duties) and excess of shop steward duties and militancy, and any other matters pertinent to the shop steward as a person. It is important that the unions concerned be the first to be notified of the employer's displeasure since the shop steward is a union official. It will be readily noticed that this is not so and need not be so in France since the 'délégué' is not a union official, nor can it be so in Luxembourg where the union has officially nothing to do with the 'délégué'. The submission therefore cannot be compared to the French system in this respect, mainly because the systems of industrial relations in the two countries are different. Assuming that the 'offence' within the expanded sphere suggested is of considerable magnitude, and the employer wishes to dismiss the shop steward, and the union agrees, then dismissal should take place. The shop steward will of course have the right to bring a *separate* action for unfair dismissal in the industrial tribunal if he wishes to do so. On the other hand a reprimand or other recommended action may take place where management and union agree. This submission already brings in one procedure which is tailored towards the special needs of dismissing shop stewards. One which it is suggested covers not only his employee functions but also his trade union functions, his industrial relations functions and all other matters upon which no protection exists at the moment. There is the further advantage that it is a domestic procedure, determined by the persons most directly concerned, namely the employers and trade unions.

What would happen however where the union and the employer disagree? Where this happens, it is submitted that a second stage be provided. Because of the deadlock between employer and union(s) it is essential to have a domestic appeal tribunal set up which mainly consists of *independent* members. The proposed composition should be:

an independent chairman with a casting vote, two independent members with one vote each and a representative of employers and unions respectively with no vote. These latter will put their points of view forward where necessary and will generally act in an advisory capacity after the hearing by the shop steward and any witnesses has taken place. The decision of this domestic appeal tribunal should be final and the parties should be bound by it, whether it be a decision recommending dismissal of the shop steward or whether it be a recommendation to put him on probation, or to reprimand him. Again, the shop steward would have a right to bring an action for unfair dismissal in the industrial tribunal if he wished to do so.

The three advantages of the proposed system are firstly that there would exist a *specialised dismissal etc. procedure* expressly tailored for the shop steward. Any dismissal (or other action) of a shop steward would then be regarded by the parties and his constituents as just. In the second instance, the domestic tribunals will have jurisdiction on, and the shop steward will have protection relating to, the *totality* of his functions as a shop steward. Thirdly, the tribunal and the appeal tribunal will be *domestic tribunals* which could either recommend the dismissal of the shop steward as a shop steward *simpliciter* or the dismissal of the shop steward as both a shop steward and an employee. From these tribunals the shop steward will always have the right to bring an action in the industrial tribunal if he still feels, despite the decision of the domestic tribunals, that he has been unfairly dismissed.

This system seems a great deal simpler than the French system examined above. It also has the advantage of being of a domestic nature, which the French system is not.

One further matter must be considered, i.e. what happens in the case of mass dismissals. It is submitted that, as is the case in France with the 'délégué', the shop steward should rank equal with the other employees. Although this has been criticised by this writer in the case of France as not giving the 'délégué' the security of tenure of his office,[243] it is nevertheless fair and just. However, unlike the case in France, if it is suspected that the employer is dismissing a shop steward under the guise of mass dismissal, or if the employer is not strictly observing the rules of precedent in the mass dismissal procedure, or for any other reason which shows that the shop steward is being discriminated against, then the domestic tribunal procedure outlined above should be put into operation, but this time by either the steward himself or his union.

In France and in Luxembourg where a serious breach (faute grave) in the contract of employment has occurred, the employer is enabled to immediately suspend (mise à pied immédiate) the 'délégué', while awaiting for a final decision to dismiss.[244]

The question that has often been asked in France is, whether the suspension of a 'délégué' leaves in 'suspended animation' not only the contract of employment but also the office of 'délégué'. If the answer were in the affirmative, the employer would be able to refuse the suspended 'délégué' access to the establishment premises thus making it impossible for him to exercise his function as a 'délégué'. The question has been discussed at length both for and against the proposition.[245] The Cour de Cassation,[246] however, has put an end to the discussion and authoritatively held that the suspension of a 'délégué' because of a breach, considered by the employer to be serious enough to merit dismissal, deprives the 'délégué' both of his privileges under his contract of employment, as well as *his right to carry out his functions of 'délégué' within the establishment.*[247] The Cour de Cassation has, however, laid down certain defined limits beyond which an employer is unable to go. In the first instance, the breach of contract, the tort or the crime committed by the 'délégué' must be of a serious nature (faute grave); in the second instance, the employer must act *bona fide* when suspending a 'délégué', especially as his suspension is of some consequence since it temporarily deprives the personnel of its representative. A suspension cannot therefore be made by the employer unless (a) he acts *bona fide* and (b) *there exists a 'faute grave'.* Does the fact that because the employer has acted *bona fide* mitigate, or on the contrary does it reinforce, the requirement of the 'faute grave'?[248] In itself the suspension is a fetter upon the functions of a 'délégué', but the employer accepts liability if he has not meant intentional harm to the 'délégué'.[249] In the third instance, suspension is merely a temporary phenomenon and cannot subsist after the decision of the 'comité d'entreprise' has been taken (or the inspecteur du travail as the case may be) relating to dismissal. Thus the employer cannot appeal to a court after the decision of the 'comité d'entreprise', while at the same time keeping the 'délégué' 'suspended' until the court decision. Suspension will therefore end with the decision of the comité (or the inspector) and either dismissal will be authorised by the 'comité' whereupon the 'délégué' will cease to belong to the establishment, or dismissal will be refused, whereupon his contract of employment will subsist and his functions as a 'délégué' will be resumed.[250]

According to case law,[251] the employer who wishes to *dismiss* a 'délégué' has a choice of either following the special procedure given in art. 16 of the law of 16 April 1946, or to bring an action in the 'conseil des prud'hommes' asking for the *termination of the contract of employment* from which will automatically follow the cessation of the employee's functions as 'délégué'. The period of suspension will therefore last until the end of the court hearing, which normally will be longer than that of the procedure laid down under art. 16.

In Britain the situation on suspension is not as succinct as it is in France, and there are no statutory provisions (or case law) specifically concerned with the *suspension of a shop steward*. The employer who wishes to suspend a shop steward will therefore have to base his case on the law which applies to employees generally.[252] This situation is unsatisfactory for three reasons. First, because no additional protection is given to the shop steward in the exercise of his functions; second, because the present legislation[253] which protects the ordinary employee did not until recently even protect him against discrimination falling short of dismissal,[254] therefore the shop steward also had no protection; and third because by his not having any special protection, his constituents are deprived, albeit temporarily, of their representative.

It is this writer's view that for the reasons given the shop steward should enjoy some additional protection against suspension, not enjoyed by other employees. It is not suggested however that he should have complete immunity. Perhaps the system which now operates in France and Luxembourg in that the employer can only suspend a 'délégué' when he has committed a 'faute grave' is fair, and the procedural suggestions which follow on the suspension of a shop steward are motivated by that system. At present no comparable system exists in Britain.

Legislation should therefore be enacted to provide that before an employer be enabled to suspend a shop steward, the shop steward should have committed a serious breach of his contract of employment.[255] He should also be protected against suspension for performance of his trade union functions. In the case of this latter it is thought that the provisions of the Employment Protection Act 1975 are sufficient protection in this respect.[256] The shop steward therefore needs protection from suspension in two spheres, namely as an employee representative and as a trade union representative. The result of a suspension of the shop steward should, as in the case in France, lead to a deprivation of his rights to carry out his functions as a shop steward within the establishment. Thus he would be suspended both as an employee and as a shop steward. This is considered as fair since it would be inequitable for him to be allowed to retain his shop steward's functions. In France one of the conditions laid down by the Cour de Cassation is that the employer should have acted *bona fide* when suspending a 'délégué'. This is not considered as of any importance since it would be very difficult to prove or disprove the subjective state of mind of the employer at the time of suspension. Because one of the reasons for having a procedure on suspension is that the constituents should not be deprived of their representative for an undue length of time, speed must be of the essence. It is therefore suggested that priority be given over all other cases of suspension or dismissal to the shop steward's case. So as not to have too cumbersome a system it is submitted that the procedure on suspension of a shop steward be the same as that suggested for the dismissal of a shop steward.[257] If the domestic tribunal finds that the cause of suspension is fair and should lead to dismissal, then the functions of the shop steward both as union representative and employee representative should cease forthwith, but if it finds that the suspension was unjustified then there should be an immediate reinstatement with no loss of benefits, whether or not there is an appeal by the employer.[258] This procedure should remedy the three objections raised above.[259]

The only effective way of achieving such procedure is through legislation. Reliance on collective agreements cannot be and is not effective. Of the sample of procedure agreements examined not one dealt with the suspension of a shop steward, though some dealt with the matter indirectly.[260]

Section vi. Sanctions

The outcome of the three topics treated from the critical discussion of the French art. 16 of the law of 16 April 1946[261] leads to an examination of the sanctions available for the non-observance by the employer of the terms of art. 16 and of other regulations. The sanctions are either civil or criminal.

By virtue of art. 18 of the 1946 law[262] the employer is criminally liable where he has wrongfully dismissed a 'délégué', as he would 'porter atteinte, soit à la libre désignation des délégués du personnel, soit à l'exercice régulier de leurs fonctions'.[263] The penalty is either 15,000 to 150,000 francs fine and imprisonment from six days to one year, or one of these penalities only. Thus the employer who contravenes art. 14 of the 1946 law by not meeting 'délégués' would be liable for obstructing the exercise of their functions.[264] Similarly the refusal by the employer to allow the 'délégué' to leave his place of work in the establishment to carry out his functions,[265] or the insisting by the employer of a joint (instead of separate) meeting with the 'comité',[266] or the censorship by the employer of all notices,[267] or where the employer refused the 'suppléants' access to meetings,[268] or the refusal to reinstate a wrongfully dismissed 'délégué'[269] or where the 'délégué' was summarily dismissed with no good reason[270] have all constituted 'atteinte, soit à la libre désignation ... soit à l'exercice régulier ...'

Originally it was necessary to show that the employer *intended* to obstruct a 'délégué's' duty by dismissing him, but subsequently the Cour de Cassation has held that it is no longer necessary to show intent, so long as a *material obstacle* is proved to have affected the 'délégué's' activities.[271] In this last instance there is a presumption of culpability and the onus is on the employer to show that no material obstacle was placed by him.[272] The wrongful dismissal of a 'délégué' also gives this latter a civil right of action for damages for wrongful dismissal.[273] The employer, having wrongfully dismissed the 'délégué', is not able to cover up the irregularity by a subsequent ratification,[274] but the Cour de Cassation has been equitable and has held that the irregularity that tainted the dismissal could be purged if the employer acted promptly in applying the procedure laid down in art. 16 before the 'délégué's' effective departure.[275]

Substantial differences exist in Luxembourg and Britain. The employer who dismisses a shop steward unfairly suffers no additional penalty, since a shop steward has the same rights against dismissal as any employee.[276] Unlike the French system no criminal penalties exist in Britain and Luxembourg for the unfair dismissal of a shop steward or 'délégué ouvrier' or 'délégué d'employés' respectively. This research shows however that whereas indirect sanctions exist in Britain,[277] no similar sanctions have been found in France or Luxembourg. It must however be pointed out that these sanctions only exist in a few instances.[278] It may therefore be said that indirect pressure on the British employer is of greater significance in most instances[279] than it is in France.[280] Perhaps the greatest difference detected through this research between the system of the two countries as a result of interviews and discussions held with both employers and 'délégués' is the psychological one. In France and to some extent in Luxembourg, it has been found that the reliance upon the legal sanctions gives both sides of industry a psychological responsiblity[281] which has not been found in Britain. Some similarities do however exist between the three countries. The wrongfully dismissed 'délégué' in France and Luxembourg, like the wrongfully dismissed shop steward, may bring a civil action for damages for wrongful dismissal at common law.[282] In Britain (but not in France) the shop steward (being an employee) has yet another civil action in that he may apply for compensation etc. for unfair dismissal under the Trade Union and Labour Relations Act 1974, as amended by the Employment Protection Act 1975. Although the philosophy of the system in the two countries is different the onus of proof lies on the employer.[283]

Clearly, there is no system in Britain of sanctions for non-observance by the employer of the protective measures granted to shop stewards, since there are no such protective measures. The only system which exists is sanctions for unfair dismissal of the employee (equally applicable to the shop steward) relating to the exercise of union activities.[284] The other sanction is the indirect sanction[285] referred to above. This writer did say above that a procedure must be set up to deal with the dismissal or suspension of shop stewards, and submissions have already been made.[286] It is no use having a procedure if there is no effective way of enforcing it. The following submissions should therefore complement the suggested procedure. These are made by considering particularly the French system and by tailoring it to British needs. The indirect sanctions[287] which exist at present should be done away with and replaced by more positive measures. The existing remedies of reinstatement, re-engagement or compensation under the Trade Union and Labour Relations Act and Employment Protection Act cannot always be effective since they are not specifically tailored for the shop steward.

Legislation therefore seems the only effective way to deal with this aspect. These legislative sanctions should deal with both a breach by the employer of the *procedure* already outlined, as well as the actual *unfair* expulsion from the establishment. Automatic criminal sanctions on *unfair expulsion*, as is the case in France, are not appropriate to this country (there should therefore be no system of fines or imprisonment). The tribunal which has found for the shop steward should be given the power to automatically reinstate him.[288] The employer will therefore be *compelled* to reinstate and there would be no alternative. Compensation, which could be a cheap way of getting rid of a shop steward, will therefore not be open to him. This seems the most effective way to deal with this situation since it gives the shop steward greater safeguards than it does to other employees.[289] Should the employer refuse to reinstate the steward, then application should be made by the tribunal for a court order. Breach of that would amount to contempt of court and the employer would then be criminally liable. Where it is found by the tribunal that the dismissal of the shop steward was fair, but that the procedure was not, then the fairness of the dismissal should not be affected. In order to deter employers for not observing the *procedure* (but not the unfair expulsion) a maximum fine should be imposed, the amount to be at the discretion of the tribunal.

Section vii. Functions

The functions of a 'délégué du personnel' in France are threefold:[290] (a) to represent the employees vis-à-vis the employer; (b) to act as auxiliary to the inspecteur du travail; (c) to collaborate with the 'comité d'entreprise' (or to replace it).

(a) Representation of employees

The most important duty of a 'délégué' is to inform the employer of all individual and collective requests and grievances made by the employees he represents.[291] It is pointed out that a 'délégué' is able to intervene not only on behalf of one employee, but also on behalf of a collectivity of employees. Originally only individual requests could be made by the 'délégué', leaving collective requests in the hands of trade unions. The distinction has however been abandoned by art. 2 of the 1946 law.[292] This article enumerates a list of matters[293] which may be brought up by the 'délégué'. Does this in fact mean that the list is exhaustive? A restrictive doctrine has sometimes been upheld, but it seems that the 'délégués' are able to deal with *all* matters relating to the employment etc.[294] It would also appear that the 'délégué' is compelled to inform the employer of all requests made to him by the employees, even though he finds them to be ill-founded. But, as is the case in Britain and Luxembourg with shop stewards and 'délégués' respectively, the French 'délégué' may only deal with requests of employees who belong to his electoral college. As he is elected to represent a specific category of employees he therefore cannot deal with the interests of employees in other electoral colleges.[295] Art. 2 has however one proviso; this states 'qui n'auraient pas été directement satisfaites'.[296] This phrase it is submitted must not be taken at its face value to mean that before a 'délégué' may make a request etc. to the employer, the employee(s) making the request must first ask it of the employer himself and fail. The law wants to enforce a direct contractual relationship between the employer and his employees, and this phrase merely confirms this; it does not wish to imply that all requests must precede the intervention of the 'délégué'. The law wants to avoid giving the 'délégué' a monopoly over the representation of employees, and it is suggested that this is reinforced by the last clause in art. 2 which states that employees may if they so wish make their requests *direct* to the employer.[297] In Luxembourg, the 'délégués ouvriers' have a similar function of representing workers and safeguarding their interests by receiving requests, complaints, suggestions, observations etc. from the workers and passing these on to the employer. They also have the function of conciliating upon problems which arise between employer and employees.[298] Similarly the 'délégué d'employés' safeguards and defends the rights of employees.

(b) Auxiliary to the inspecteur du travail

Art. 2 states that the French 'délégué' must 'saisir l'inspection du travail'.[299] The continuous presence of the 'délégués' at the place of work allows them to exercise a constant control, whereas the control of the inspector of labour is sporadic and over long and intermittent periods of time. In order to stress the official character of their functions as auxiliaries to the inspecteur, the inspecteur must be accompanied by the 'délégués' when he visits the factory to inspect or investigate a complaint. This research shows that the fact that the 'délégué' is to deal with all complaints relating to breach of regulations with his constituency does not entitle him to carry out an *investigation* himself. He may only inform the inspecteur of the complaint, and must notify the employer.[300] The same has been found to be the case in Luxembourg where the 'délégué ouvrier' *contributes* to the prevention of accidents and industrial diseases by being 'a watchdog'.[301]

(c) Collaboration with the 'comité d'entreprise'

The 'délégués' are principally the liaison agents between the employees and the 'comité'. Their function is therefore to communicate to the 'comité' the suggestions and observations made by the personnel on all matters which the 'comité' is competent to deal with.[302] 'Délégués' also take part with members of the 'comité' in choosing employees' representatives on the 'comité d'hygiéne et de sécurité',[303] and take part in the constitution of inter-enterprise committees which are responsible for the organisation of works medical services.[304] It is evident that 'délégués' as collaborators of the 'comité d'entreprise' have a wider role to play than merely intermediaries between employees and the employer. Case law has had a tendency to enlarge the role of the 'délégué' and the Cour de Cassation held that he can participate in local collective bargaining and that the employer has to pay his wages for the time spent on the preparation of the agreement.[305] The relationship of the 'délégués' with the 'comité d'entreprise' are facilitated by the simultaneous exercise of numerous functions (*cumul*) of the 'délégué' and of the members of the 'comité d'entreprise'. The solution has however been criticised as there are numerous practical inconveniences.[306] It has been found that the 'délégué' is often also an elected member of the 'comité d'entreprise'.

Collective agreements examined seem to follow closely and do not depart extensively from the legal provisions relating to the functions of 'délégués'. Certain collective agreements however make small changes or stress certain items more than others.[307] In Luxembourg, there being no 'comité mixte' until 1974, it has not yet been possible to assess the collaboration with it of the 'délégué'; trends however show that co-operation is taking place and that a rapprochement is inevitable.

The shop steward in Britain, unlike the French and Luxembourg 'délégué', has two distinct areas within his set of functions. Described loosely, the first area consists of his trade union functions, the second consists of his functions as a representative of his workmates.[308] As a result of interviews with 100 shop stewards from various branches of industry and an examination of most union rule books and most shop steward handbooks, this research shows that in Britain the emphasis on shop steward functions is, particularly in the first area[309] and even the second area (i.e. representation of workers),[310] union orientated. In France and Luxembourg it is not.[311] When comparing the functions of the 'délégué' with those of the shop steward, the only cases which are comparable to the French and Luxembourg systems are those which fall within the second area of the shop steward's functions (i.e. industrial relations functions and representation of his workmates). Those in the first area (i.e. trade union functions) are therefore outside the scope of this research. Even the second area of the shop steward's functions is of necessity[312] union orientated, and this must at all times be borne in mind. In France and Luxembourg, though the functions are similar, they are not union orientated, but orientated through the law towards all the workmen in the 'délégué's' constituency.[313]

It is proposed to divide the comparison under the same three headings which appear above.[314]

(i) Representative functions. As is the case in France and Luxembourg, it is found that the most important[315] duty of a shop steward is to represent his constituents and to inform the employer of their individual or collective requests and grievances, i.e. communication.[316] In so doing prior discussions with his constituents (and often other stewards) take

place.[317] The survey carried out shows that 49 per cent of his time is spent on this aspect of his functions.[318] Both the steward and the 'délégué' are disseminators of information and gatherers of views. One of the questions asked of employees about shop stewards and 'délégués' was 'Did his role as a communicator aid him in obtaining the confidence of his members?' In all three countries the overwhelming majority answered in the affirmative. A few did however indicate that either the shop steward or 'délégué' sometimes was not interested enough to keep the constituents informed of developments in the establishment, or that in particular the individual requests and grievances were not passed on to management.

The following question was then asked of management, 'Do you consider that the shop steward or "délégué" represents clearly the views of his constituents?' Again an overwhelming majority answered in the affirmative. A small minority of employers in France and Britain did however feel that the representatives either voiced their own opinions, especially where militants were concerned, or were unable to contact their constituents on a regular basis.[319] This research shows that the problems which have arisen in France between individual and collective representation[320] have never arisen in Britain, entirely, it is submitted, because of the fact that shop stewards are union officials and therefore have a dual role, whereas 'délégués' are not union officials. The problem consequently arose in France on the distinction between collective (union-orientated) and individual (representation) requests.

The list of functions which the 'délégué' is competent to fulfil appears in the actual law in France,[321] and the question as to whether these are exhaustive has already been answered.[322] No equivalent legal provisions on the functions of shop stewards exist in Britain and the only valid comparison which may be made is through an examination mainly of the shop steward handbooks, and to a much lesser extent rule books and industry-wide or establishment collective agreements. It is found that functions vary in both content[323] and number[324] from handbook to handbook, but as a result of extensive interviews[325] it is concluded that, as is the case in Luxembourg and France, in practice the functions are not necessarily limited to the list in the particular handbook etc. and that therefore these are not exhaustive.[326]

Of the industry agreements examined very few[327] go beyond the shop steward's function of dealing with individual and collective grievances after the initial procedure (i.e. usually complaint to the foreman) has been exhausted. Also to be borne in mind is the emphasis that is placed on the shop steward's or 'délégué's' functions in different industries. It is found for example that the functions in mobile industries[328] are different from those in static industries.[329] In no country is it possible for industry-wide agreements, which cover numerous establishments, to deal with every aspect of the representative's functions, nor is it possible for those functions which are enumerated to apply to every establishment. Having said that, however, British industry-wide agreements tend to be a great deal more silent on shop stewards' functions than do French industry agreements, solely because, it is suggested the French law requires that functions should be mentioned in all collective agreements. Would a similar enactment in Britain not remedy the present omission?[330] The TUC did suggest that '... industry-wide procedures and substantive agreements are an *unsatisfactory guide* to the actual functions of shop stewards' (stress added).

The judgement of the British shop steward, at least as far as the texts are concerned, is relied upon a great deal more than that of the French 'délégué'. Although he knows that a grievance, request etc. be ill-founded or frivolous, nevertheless according to the texts the 'délégué' has to report it to the employer.[331] This is a strange phenomenon and an investigation had to be made. It was found, after interviews with both employers and 'délégués', that in practice ill-founded claims are not reported. The 'délégué' must make sure that a *prima facie* case exists *before* taking any action upon it. It is submitted that the reason why it was considered that 'délégués' were to report everything is that in the early days, when 'délégués' had little or no experience, *all* matters had to be passed on to management, and it was left to management's discretion whether or not to take action on the request. Now that there exists greater sophistication and a greater degree of education on the part of the 'délégué', he is allowed to use his judgement in every case. Only a few British texts talk of the exercise of this judgement[332] by shop stewards, but this research[333] shows that it is always exercised in practice.

Though a few handbooks state specifically or by implication that individual and collective grievances or problems are to be brought in the first instance to the employer's attention by a shop steward,[334] most require the member to discuss the matter first with the foreman,[335] before the steward gets involved. This procedure was found generally to work also in practice but numerous exceptions were detected, especially among the better organised industries where shop stewards are in a strong position, e.g. engineering. There, it was found that the early stages of a grievance procedure were bypassed and members reported to the shop steward in the first instance, who in turn reported to the foreman; in some cases however even the foreman was ignored and the steward went straight to the works manager or even to the higher echelons of management.[336] This in practice was found to be true in France as well, and there now seems to be an increasing number of employees consulting the 'délégué' in the first instance. It has already been stated[337] that in France the *law* wishes to enforce a direct contractual relationship between the employer and employee, and in practice the research shows that the 'délégué' seldom intervenes at the first stage of a grievance.[338] It may therefore be said that the intention behind the provisions of art. 2 of the French law is generally achieved. In Britain the same arises, but there is no equivalent statutory provision enforcing a direct contractual relationship between employer and employee. This conclusion is reached in Britain as a result of the grievance procedures that have evolved through either custom (to a much lesser extent), and collective bargaining (to a larger extent). In none of the countries (and for different reasons) does the 'délégué' or shop steward have a monopoly over representation.

There is of course one other problem in Britain which does not arise in Luxembourg or France. In these countries it has been stressed that the 'délégué' represents *all* his constituents, while in Britain the shop steward represents only his trade union members. Where there is not a 100 per cent union shop or closed shop, this will mean that there will be employees who cannot have the benefit of representation and in these circumstances they have to act on their own. In France and Luxembourg this cannot arise since the concept of the 'délégué' is not based on union membership but on being an employee of the firm. It may therefore be said that the employee is generally better protected in France and Luxembourg than he is in Britain, if he is not a trade union member. If he is a union member, on the other hand, the employee is better protected in Britain because he has the power of his union behind him (via the shop steward), which the French and Luxembourg 'délégué' does not *officially* have.

(ii) An auxiliary to the factory inspector. The 'délégué' in France has a statutory duty to be a watchdog on all matters of safety and health. In Britain no legal duty is imposed on the shop steward as such[339] but union shop steward handbooks[340] stress this as one of the shop steward's functions.[341] It may therefore be said that a great similarity exists in this aspect between the shop steward in Britain and the 'délégué' in Luxembourg and France — the only difference being that

the sources for their respective responsibilities are different. Two other matters are of importance in this comparison. Firstly, it is found that the British shop steward is better guided and given greater detail on not only the avoidance of industrial accidents[342] but also the procedure for accident reporting[343] than the French and Luxembourg 'délégué' is. This latter merely relies on his legal powers which tend to be very general.[344] Secondly, British trade unions have for some time *claimed* that safety control is to be in the hands of the unions.[345] In France, this is not so; the unions do not so far claim control over safety matters though they are interested in this aspect.

(iii) Collaboration with the works council. The liaison functions of the 'délégué' in France between his constituents and the 'comité d'entreprise' has already been noted.[346] Similarly the shop steward is the liaison between his constituents and the works committee.[347] It must however be stressed that whereas in France this has always been the case,[348] in Britain the development has come[349] and in some instances is still coming about[350] gradually. Having said that the liaison functions of the respective representatives are similar, this similarity ends there, because whereas in Britain a rapprochement between negotiation and consultation has already taken place[351] or is in the process of taking place,[352] a similar rapprochement cannot be said to be coming about in France.[353] This is mainly due to the structure of the law on industrial relations in France.[354] This research shows that the 'comité d'entreprise' is almost, though not entirely,[355] a consultative body, and the 'délégué' is the 'porte parole' of his constituents on this body. To be carefully noted however is the fact that the 'délégué', like the shop steward, does take part in the formation of plant agreements,[356] and some of his time is spent on these.[357] It is found that the British shop steward spends more time than his counterparts in France on both taking part in the formation of plant agreements (i.e. 4·8 per cent) and the time spent in order to achieve this (i.e. 6 per cent). It becomes evident therefore, that if we are to accept that one of the functions of the 'délégué' is to take part in *local* collective bargaining at the 'comité d'entreprise' level, he obviously exercises influence *beyond* his own constituency. The comparison shows that the same applies but to a much greater extent in Britain where shop stewards take part in joint negotiating committees.

The distinction which arises in Britain between the functions of white-collar and blue-collar representatives[358] does not arise in Luxembourg or France. In these countries, the law on representation applies to all, whether white- or blue-collar workers, whether in the private or public sectors.[359] It is submitted that the system which operates in France and Luxembourg on this aspect is a great deal more straightforward, and less complex. Would it not be right to suggest that the British system could do with an equivalent simplification?

Section viii. Comparative conclusions and submissions on the representative's functions

The inevitable and perhaps the most important conclusion to be drawn is that in France and Luxembourg the 'délégué's' functions are defined by the law.[360] It will be recalled however that the definition is not exhaustive.[361] French collective agreements examined show that very few depart from the provisions established by the law;[362] this means therefore that the legislative provisions are wide enough to encompass most of the requirements of the parties to a collective agreement.[363] In Britain on the other hand it has already been pointed out that no legal (and therefore guiding) provisions exist[364] and the best source is the shop steward's handbook[365] (if any), and to a *much* lesser extent, national or establishment collective agreements[366] and union rule books.[367] The now defunct CIR found that '... steward's functions are rarely defined with much clarity and precision'.[368] The independent findings of this research support the statement without reservation. It therefore becomes necessary to suggest a possible solution to this problem. The starting point, for the only realistic solution, must be legislation which would lay down certain functions defined in *generic terms* which must appear in every collective agreement, whether industry-wide or shop-floor. These should be enacted in general terms, yet cover all the basic functions of a shop steward discussed above, i.e. communication, consultation, individual and collective grievance procedures, watchdog on health and safety etc.[369] So far, this would be equivalent to the position in France (not Luxembourg since there are no legal provisions for incorporating 'délégué' functions in collective agreements) and Britain might well learn to its advantage from the French experience which shows that since the legislative provisions are wide *enough* to deal with most of the parties' requirement, French collective agreements examined do not depart significantly from the legislative provisions themselves (see above). Legislation on this aspect would have the added advantage of making negotiators, as well as employees, shop stewards, management and trade unionists generally, *aware*, and *more certain*, of the shop stewards' industrial relations functions. It is this uncertainty which exists in the present, that this submission is intended to combat.

Once legislation exists on this matter, it will then become the duty of the parties to a collective agreement (whether local, regional or national) to have a clause in that agreement defining the shop steward's industrial relations functions. It is here that the legal provisions, which should be of a basic and general nature, will have to be adapted to the requirements of the industry, region or plant concerned; so that establishment or plant agreements should define the shop steward's functions in a more amplified manner than they do now.[370] It is in that type of agreement that an amplified definition will be of most benefit; it is also at this level where a more complete definition of functions to suit the individual contingencies of the establishment may be given. As far as industry agreements are concerned a more general definition should be given on shop steward functions (as given at p. 215), but adapted to meet the needs of the industry. Such agreements will provide the lead for plant agreements on shop steward functions to be concluded. Once the legislative *generic* functions are present as a guide, it will be easier for the parties to the collective agreement to direct their minds to what is required and adapt these to their individual industry. This is where Britain would depart from the French experience, because in France it is only 'conventions collectives susceptibles d'extension' which have a compulsory requirement on 'délégués'. The 'conventions collectives ordinaires' do not have this compulsory clause. It is found however that even this latter type of collective agreement in numerous cases contains clauses on *inter alia* the functions of 'délégués'. This shows the way in which legislation can help towards creating 'awareness'.

Awareness and more certainty have been mentioned as an advantage of having legislation on this matter. A secondary result of this awareness would manifest itself in the very areas which were found in this research to be totally or near-devoid of provisions on shop steward industrial relations functions, namely union rule books,[371] the production of shop steward handbooks where these do not exist,[372] and a more detailed reference in industry agreements. In the case of the first area such legislation would help *standardise* the functions of the shop steward. At the moment, the union rule books (when they do mention the shop steward) attribute to him varying functions. With the growing importance of the office of shop steward surely there is now a need to have greater standardisation of his functions in the union rule book.[373] In the case of the second area, such legislation would encourage those unions which do not produce shop steward handbooks[374] to do so. It is after all in such a handbook where every aspect and detail of his functions should appear, and in the case of the third area, the legislation would encourage the parties to an industry agreement to deal with functions of the steward in a more comprehensive way. The Donovan Report[375] did find that most shop steward handbooks refer the steward to the industry-wide agreement in force in the particular industry, but it also found that these latter are rarely comprehensive, and say nothing about the functions the steward is competent to deal with.[376] In other words, there is a lack of liaison between the industry-wide agreement and the shop steward's handbook. The submission above would in this writer's opinion remedy this lack of liaison.

'Awareness', through the proposed legislation and its subsequent effects,[377] will manifest itself in a different light, and a further result would come about. Since unions and employers will be made more aware of the shop steward's function, firstly through legislation and secondly by putting this legislation into practice by the conclusion of industry and shop-floor agreements, and by their being mentioned in union rule books etc., the unions will be able to provide more precise advice than at present on *inter alia* the functions of shop stewards in regard to their members, thus generating awareness even further afield.

The *conflict of functions* features eminently in any conclusion which is reached on the functions of a shop steward in Britain. From all the sources examined there is no doubt that the shop steward's functions present a conflict between his union functions and his representative functions.[378] Of the shop steward's handbooks (these being the main source enumerating his functions), union rules and collective agreements examined, this conflict does not expressly make itself apparent, though it does impliedly, and from this writer's interviews there is no doubt that at one time or another most shop stewards are during their careers faced with problems of allegiance and loyalty — either to their union or to their constituents. Indeed one handbook recognises this and specifically states so,[379] though it does not provide a remedy. This problem does not arise in France or Luxembourg, for two reasons. Firstly, because the 'délégué' is not a union representative but a representative of the employees in his constituency, therefore there is no doubt where his loyalties lie. Secondly, because even though the 'délégué' be a trade union member (as he often is), the union does not dictate to him a course of action, nor is he bound by the policy of the union. So long as the British industrial relations system remains as at present, there is no solution

218 Worker Participation in Europe

to this problem, and the steward and others involved, e.g. employees, have no alternative but to accept it.[380]

Notes

1. The second limb deals with 'comités d'entreprise'.
2. Code du Travail, livre 1, art. 31g (5).
3. The 'délégué du personnel' are, like members of the 'comité d'entreprise', employee representatives. Their role is however different from that of the 'comité' members. The 'délégués' are *in principle* only required to solve problems of an individual nature, whereas the 'comités d'entreprise' concern themselves with those of a general nature. It is found however that often the 'délégué' is also a union official, but his union functions are separate from those of the 'délégué' functions.
4. Individual workers may however represent themselves and present their complaints directly to the employer without recourse to the 'délégué', see supra.
5. i.e. the employment inspector; he also has powers on contract of employment matters. Research carried out shows that it is not customary for a shop steward to accompany the factory inspector in Britain.
6. To be discussed in greater detail below.
7. The other aspect of the shop steward's dual role is the representative function of his union, communications between members and the union he represents and often the collection of union subscriptions.
8. Created by the 'texte co-ordonné' du 20 novembre 1962. See Mémorial Journal Officiel du Grand Duché de Luxembourg — Recueil de Législation No. 65, 6 décembre 1962.
9. Art. 3 of arrêté grand-ducal of 20 november 1962 provides for the following functions which in the other countries examined are clearly works council, comité or conseil functions. These are '(1) à donner son avis sur l'élaboration ou la modification du réglement de service ou du réglement d'atelier de l'entreprise et de surveiller strictement l'exécution de ce règlement, (2) de collaborer à l'établissement et à l'exécution du régime de l'apprentissage, (3) à participer à la gestion de toutes les institutions créés par le patron en vue de l'amélioration de la situation, des ouvriers et de leurs familles.'
10. See loi du 6 mai 1974 which provides for the setting up of 'comités mixtes'. Mémorial Journal Officiel du Grand Duché de Luxembourg, A. No. 35, 10 mai 1974. See also réglement grand ducal du 24 septembre 1974 on elections of these representatives in Memorial A. No. 69, 27 septembre 1974 and the various 'Projets de Lois' (White papers) in the Chambre des Députés No. 1689 (20.4.73); 1689(1) (11.7.72); 1689(2); 1689(3) (3.8.73); and 1689(6) (22.1.74). See also 'Colloque sur la participation des travailleurs aux décisions dans l'entreprise', Oslo 20—30, aout 1974 — R. Schintgen.
11. This was an agreement entered into at 15.15 hours on 7 and 8 June 1936 at the Hôtel Matignon in Paris comprising representatives of the Conféderation Générale de Production Française representing the employers and the CGT representing employees. The employers' respresentatives consisted of Messrs. Duchemin, Richemond, Dalbouse and Lambert-Ribot; those of the trade union were Messrs. Jouhaux, who at the time was general secretary of the CGT, Belin, Franchon, Semat, Cordier and Milon. The chairman was Léon Blum. One of the numerous matters discussed was the

'délégués du personnel'. Other matters dealt with terms and conditions of employment, wages, trade union rights etc.
12. See Code du Travail, livre 1, art. 31 v.c.al.2.
13. This was the formula adopted by the Accord Matignon.
14. Artisans, who normally employed less than ten persons.
15. See 'Convention collective concernant la couture dans les départements de la Seine et Seine et Oise', of 18 November 1936. See also p. 165 post and note 20 below.
16. In her doctoral thesis 'Les conventions collectives de travail', Bibliothèque de la Faculté de Droit, Université de Paris 1937, particularly pp. 18–19.
17. Nor did loi du 24 Juin 1936 provide as to the eligibility of delegates, and as to their quota in relation to the number of members in the establishment.
18. See Petit, 'Notions historiques et commentaire théorique et pratique de la loi du 24 juin 1936', p. 119.
19. In 'La Gazette des Prud'hommes', 15 November 1936.
20. See 'Convention Nationale de l'Imprimerie' of 17 September 1936, clause 3 (2).
21. See 'Convention collective des employés-techniciens de l'industrie chimique de la région parisienne' of 30 January 1937, clause 5.
22. The collective agreement in 21 above stipulated '. . . chaque titulaire et chaque suppléant représentent un groupe de services, un service, une fraction de service, ou un groupe de collaborateurs de même catégorie, suivant l'importance de l'établissement'.
23. See 'Convention collective concernant la couture dans les départements de la Seine et Seine et Oise', 18 November 1936 and in particular clause 6 of the collective agreement in Journal Officiel of 13 July 1937, p. 7933, which provided 'les ouvriers et ouvrières à domicile ont droit à leur délégation ouvrière sur la base de deux délégués par dix ou fraction de dix'.
24. Petit, 'Notions historiques et commentaire théorique et pratique de la loi du 24 juin 1936'. Doctoral thesis in Bibliothèque de la Faculté de Droit, Université de Paris, p. 120.
25. Talks with representatives of an Algerian syndicate, members of the CGT – Paris.
26. Journal Officiel of 18 June 1936, p. 519, reporting the debate held in Senate on 17 June 1936.
27. M. Leon Blum in the debate referred to in 26 above, said '. . . en ce qui concerne le mode d'élection des délégués du personnel, nous sommes disposés . . . à reprendre des dispositions déjà inscrites dans le Code du Travail, en ce qui concerne l'élection des délégués mineurs. Il prévoit l'élection au scrutin secret et il applique même un ensemble de garanties tres analogues à celles que la loi a organisées quand il s'agit des élections politiques'.
28. Code du Travail, livre II, titre III, section III, clause 134 et seq.
29. i.e. scrutin de liste – votes are counted for each candidate, even if he is included in a list, and vote-splitting and isolated candidatures were also permitted.
30. See p. 163 ante and p. 210 post. The term 'shop steward' is used here in its generic sense to denote an unpaid representative recognised by his union at the place of work. 'Fathers' or 'mothers' of a 'chapel' in the print unions; 'staff representatives' in the clerical and administrative union; 'works representatives' in the Iron and Steel and Kindred Trades Association. No such terminological differences exist in France or Luxembourg. The trade union representatives are all termed 'délégués syndicaux'.
31. The term 'grouping' is preferred to that of 'nature' because the shop

220 Worker Participation in Europe

steward or the 'délégué du personnel' each have numerous functions within each of their groupings.
32. See p. 210 post for a brief discussion of the délégué syndical's functions, and a comparison with those of the shop steward.
33. See rules of Amalgamated Society of Engineers (1878), established in 1851 with 5,000 members – Webb, *History of Trade Unionism*, p. 492; Wigham, *Trade Unions*, p. 45 and CIR report no. 17, 'Facilities afforded to shop stewards' (May 1971), p.4.
34. Because employers encouraged shop steward representation to ensure that their establishment ran smoothly under the emergency regulations.
35. There were two reasons for this. Firstly, because unofficial leaders (especially in the Clyde shipyards) rebelled against the wartime restrictions on unions in order to ensure industrial peace. Secondly, because of the enormity of the problems created by wartime changes. See also various 'Shop steward and works committee agreements' from 1917 to 1919, where clearly the engineering employers recognised shop stewards as a key factor in grievance procedures.
36. See pp. 163 and 166 above.
37. The main factors for such increase in shop steward numbers being firstly changes in production methods, and secondly demand leading to increased productivity and the consequent increase in joint production committees which, because of their personal involvement, considerably increased stewards' numbers.
38. The number of stewards in Britain has been put at roughly 200,000, but there is no means of checking this figure. The 1960s and 1970s have been marked by the emergence in some industries, such as transport and the docks, of unofficial joint shop stewards' committees who attempted to establish unofficial and unconstitutional strikes. See *Midland Cold Storage Ltd v. Turner, Steer, Watkins and others (1972), ICR 230* as one of numerous examples. Another example may be found more locally in the Hull docks, under the unofficial steward Mr Cunningham. Though they must be borne in mind, it is not with these that this research is concerned.
39. This is particularly applicable to white-collar unionism in the *private* sector where, despite rapid growth recently, national level negotiations are weak. Negotiations in the private sector therefore occur usually at establishment level. See e.g. drydocking agreement between West Riding and Humberside Engineering and Shipbuilding Employers' Association and the ASBSB and SW. One noteworthy exception however may be found in the engineering industry. See e.g. collective consolidated agreement between Engineering Employers' Federation and Confederation of Shipbuilding and Engineering Unions dated 8 August 1974 – 15 May 1975 – 18 August 1972 etc., in Engineering Employers' Federation handbook of national agreements. In the public sector, where white-collar unionism first developed (and which consequently is stronger, e.g. nationalised industries, education, government) there are a great number of national collective agreements which determine terms and conditions of employment, thus leaving less scope to the representative to negotiate at establishment level.
40. As a result of the Accord Matignon – see above. It has been impossible to assess how far back the délégué has exercised his functions unofficially.
41. Loi du 24 juin 1936.
42. Of the numerous national or industry-wide collective agreements examined in Britain very few ever mention shop stewards.
43. Shop stewards of course are mostly the originators and invariably parties

Employee Representation 221

to shop-floor agreements. Of the sample examined 93·3 per cent of shop-floor agreements were originated by shop stewards, and in all cases they have been signatories. Consider also note 42 above for industry-wide collective agreements.
44. Namely representation of his constituents in matters of wages and conditions of employment, i.e. industrial relations functions.
45. i.e. informing employer of individual rights of workers relating to wages, job description, safety legislation, hygiene, social security; the investigation of complaints; the accompanying of the factory inspector; the making of suggestions to the employer about legal requirements – see pp. 163 ante and pp. 208 et seq post.
46. i.e. the shop steward's second grouping of functions evolved purely from his trade union functions. This also occurred more recently in the case of the white-collar unions. See p. 167 above.
47. It is not possible to state any definite time or date when the second grouping evolved; that depends on a number of factors, such as upon the evolution of the office, the strength of the union, its recognition by the employer, facilities etc.
48. Of the sample interviewed, a majority (52 per cent) agreed that factory inspectors do ask shop stewards' opinions etc. on safety and health matters.
49. It is not possible to assess historically the weighting of this part of a shop steward's function (i.e. the second grouping), but it is possible to say that this writer has found that 36 per cent of a shop steward's work in 1975 is spent in discussions with his constituents, and 18 per cent in taking up constituents' grievances. cf. these percentages with McCarthy, 'The role of shop stewards in British industrial relations', Research Paper I, Royal Commission on Trade Unions and Employers' Associations, HMSO 1966, p. 10. An increase in the shop steward's second grouping of functions is apparent in nine years. It must be borne in mind however that such a high percentage in his second group of functions is only apparent in latter years, since historically the second grouping of functions grew out of the first, and therefore were non-existent initially.
50. Since 1958 'arrêté grand ducal du 30 octobre 1958' put the 'délégations ouvrières' on a statutory basis. This law was expanded by 'arrêté grand ducal du 21 novembre 1958' which provided for the election procedure of these representatives.
51. By a texte co-ordonné of 20 novembre 1962 representation was extended to the public sector.
52. i.e. there not being, until 1974, 'comités mixtes' which essentially deal with collective problems. It will be recalled that works councils in Britain have existed since the second decade of the century and that 'conseils d'entreprises' in Belgium and 'comités d'entreprise' in France have been put on a statutory basis after the Second World War.
53. Namely homeworkers, see p. 164; constitution of the electoral college, see p. 164; and Algerian workers, see p. 165.
54. See in particular p. 164. It is apparent that the 1936 law, apart from stating that collective agreements had to contain a clause which related to 'délégués du personnel' where more than ten workers were employed, neither fixed nor regulated and status of the 'délégué'. The parties to a collective agreement had complete freedom in connection with all matters concerning a 'délégué du personnel'.
55. See e.g. convention collective de l'imprimerie de labeur.
56. Loi du 16 avril 1946, art. I, alinéa 1. The 1950 law refers to the 1946 law in this respect. It is readily noticeable that the 1936 law did not provide

222 *Worker Participation in Europe*

       in such detail the establishments in which 'délégués' should be elected.
57. Texte co-ordonné du 20 novembre 1962 – Memorial Journal Officiel du Grand Duché de Luxembourg No. 65, 6 decembre 1962, art. 1 (amending arrêté of 30 October 1958).
58. Loi du 20 avril 1962, art. 24. Mémorial Journal Officiel du Grand Duché de Luxembourg, A. No. 19, 21 avril 1962.
59. 'In theory' because in Britain the recognition hurdle has first to be overcome.
60. As far as a shop steward's representation is concerned. The union recognition problems, i.e. cases, such as Stratford v. Lindley, CIR reports, as for example the Parsons dispute, or ACAS reports, e.g. the London Docks and Cowley disputes, lie outside the sphere of this research.
61. In two establishments examined tacit recognition was given to a union for shop steward representation purposes. Membership was so small as to be insignificant. In another establishment, membership was so scattered that the union was not conducive to recognition, though the employer was not averse to recognising the union. Nevertheless a shop steward was appointed. This research indicates that the position in white-collar unions is more complex. In the public sector, apart from one isolated case, there was no problem with union recognition and consequently with the appointment of stewards, but in the private sector, despite the fact that blue-collar unions are represented by shop stewards, the white-collar ones are not always so represented.
62. This research shows that once the proper procedure for appointment had taken place it is very seldom that an employer refuses to recognise an individual as a shop steward. Only three cases have come to light where objection towards an individual had been raised. In two cases, the person was a communist and a 'known agitator'; in the third, a rather unusual case, the person selected had a rare disease only known to the employer which could have impaired his functions as a shop steward. This is not to say however that collective agreements do not contain a 'precautionary provision' enabling the employer to object to a particular individual. See e.g. 'An agreement setting out the role and functions of shop stewards, and domestic procedure for settlement of grievances' (anonymous agreement obtained from ACAS 1975) which contains the following provision on p. 2, chapter 1 (d): 'The Division shall have the right to raise, with the Trade Union concerned, any objection which it may have to the election of any particular individual or individuals. Such objections shall receive consideration by the Union.'
63. See note 61. This is found especially in connection with white-collar workers in the private sector.
64. Loi du 16 avril 1946, art. 4.
65. The 'délégué titulaire' is the actual 'délégué', the 'suppléant' is his deputy or acting delegate who takes over from the 'titulaire' normally when this latter is unable to function either through illness, absence, delegation, suspension, dismissal etc.
66. Where there are from eleven to twenty-five employees employed in an establishment, only one 'délégué titulaire' and one 'délégué suppléant' need be elected. Where there are twenty-six to fifty employees a minimum of two 'délégués' and two 'suppléants' must be elected, where 51 to 100 employees are employed there must be three 'délégués' and three 'suppléants'; where there are 101 to 250 employees there must be five 'délégués' and five 'suppléants'; where there are 251 to 500 employees there must be seven of each, and from 501 to 1,000 employees there must be nine 'délégués' and nine 'suppléants', and an additional one

'délégué' and one 'suppléant' for every 500 additional employees.
67. Texte co-ordonné du 20 novembre 1962, art. 2, provides for the 'délégation ouvrière', art. 24 for the 'délégation d'employés' and art. 6 provides for special representation of young workers in the 'délégations ouvrières'. The details in tabulated form are as follows:

Délégations ouvrières

Number of workers	Délégues ouvriers Titulaires	Suppléants
15 to 25	1	1
26 to 50	2	2
51 to 100	3	3
101 to 150	4	4
151 to 200	5	5
+ 200 and any part of 100	+ 1 (max: 15)	− 1 (max: 15)
+ 300 and any part of 500	+ 1 (max: 20)	− 1 (max: 20)

Délégations d'employés

Number of employees	Délégues employés Titulaires	Suppléants
12 to 50	3	2
+ 50 and any part of 100	+ 1	+ 1

Young Workers

Number of young workers	Representation of young workers in 'délégations ouvrières' Titulaires	Suppléants
5 to 25	1	1
26 to 50	2	2
51 to 100	3	3
+ 100	4	4

68 See e.g. clause 1 (b) of the 'Agreement setting out the role and functions of Shop Stewards and Domestic Procedure for settlement of grievances', ACAS, 1975. See also the 'Model Procedure Agreement between local management and trade unions' prepared by the ACAS, 1975, p. 5, section C — Trade Union Recognition 1 (1.1) which states 'The Management and Trade Unions will jointly establish an appropriate number of constituencies for each division and the representation of these constituencies by Shop Stewards'. Nowhere will be found in this agreement the ratio of shop stewards to the number of employees in either the constituency or each of its divisions. The collective agreement between an electric motor manufacturer in the southwest of England and unions of 1974, p. 7, section 4, clause 19, states 'Each Union shall arrange for the election amongst its members in the plant of a shop steward or shop stewards, and shall notify the companies of the name or names of such steward(s) in writing'. Again it will be noted that no mention is made of this ratio. The collective agreement between the Engineering Employers' Federation and the Association of Professional, Executive, Clerical and Computer Staff, the Association of Clerical, Technical and Supervisory Staff and the Managerial, Administrative, Technical and Supervisory Association dated 12 September 1973, para. 21, states '(i) Staff representatives may be elected in accordance with rules of their union from among members of the Union employed in the establishment

in occupations covered by this agreement'. The agreement goes on to state that constituencies will be determined by domestic agreement but that where such agreement cannot be reached the question will be discussed in procedure following the principle that '... generally the number of staff representatives should be determined having regard to the size of the establishment, the number of union members, and the nature of the constituencies covered...'.
69. See collective agreement entitled 'Procedures covering Contracts of employment, Discipline, Grievances and Trade Union facilities' between an engineering company (door division) and the AUEW, 1974—5, clause 3.
70. i.e. Royal Commission on Trade Unions and Employers' Associations, 1965—8, Cmnd. 3623.
71. Ibid., para. 34 '... In a company possessing two or more factories it is normal for managers in each factory to deal separately with representatives of groups of their own workers...' or para. 166 '... Within the limits of union rules it (i.e. factory agreement) can set out the steward's constituencies and the method of their election...'
72. See p. 168 ante.
73. Convention collective du textile.
74. Convention collective des techniciens de la production cinématographique.
75. A production delegate elected from technicians connected with the production of a film.
76. Convention collective nationale des industries de la conserve.
77. As e.g. at David Brown Tractors in Meltham, Yorkshire, where the ratio on the assembly line is one shop steward to eighty-three constituents, or at the BLMC works in Cowley where the ratio is one to seventy-one. A high rate has also been found in the coal mines (average of sixty-seven (11) and on the railways (average of sixty-eight).
78. As e.g. in Fords of Dagenham where admittedly the large number of shop stewards was explained by the numerous unions represented therein and the overlapping of certain constituencies.
79. See note 66 for detailes. It is surprising to note in Report No. 17 of the CIR on 'Facilities afforded to shop stewards', May 1971, Cmnd. 4668, p. 30 that '... it is not possible to suggest guidelines on the ratio of members to a steward'. The writer cannot accept this statement. It is submitted that a system which operates through legislation could provide for Britain the basis of a guideline.
80. cf. W.E.J. McCarthy, 'The role of shop stewards in British industrial relations', Research Paper I for Royal Commission on Trade Unions and Employers' Associations, p. 38, where in 1966 he found that '... the average steward has about 50 constituents'. Since then there seem to have been an increase in the ratio of constituents per shop steward, e.g. Pedler, 'Shop stewards as leaders', *IRJ No. 4, 1973—4*, p. 55, states that he found that 'the average representative had a constituency of 71...' Consider also Glegg, 'The system of Industrial Relations in Britain', p. 14.
81. See pp. 169—171 ante.
82. See Savatier, 'Les accords collectifs relatifs à l'organisation des élections des représentants du personnel.' Droit Social 1961, p. 608.
83. Loi du 18 juin 1966 as modified by loi du 29 décembre 1972.
84. Each electoral college must consist of members nominated who *belong* to that college. So that, where an office manager not belonging to that college was nominated by workers for the purpose of representing them and was eventually elected, such election was held null and void by the Cour de Cassation, Ch. Civ., 6 mai 1949, Jurisclasseur Périodique (Semaine

Employee Representation 225

Juridique) 1949 vol. II, p. 5019. Representativity of the union must be within the establishment concerned. Cour de Cassation, Ch. Civile., 29 mars 1962, Recueil Dalloz 100.
85. A division of the electoral college into *four groups* had at one time been proposed. The proposal was rejected because it was considered more democratic to have a greater number of persons in each college.
86. It was held that the 'agreement' may be either an *express* or a *tacit* agreement. See Cour de Cassation, Chambre Civile, Section Sociale, 15 juin 1961, Recueil Dalloz 1961, 533. Cour de Cassation, Chambre Civile, 9 janvier 1948, Jurisclasseur Périodique (Semaine Juridique) 1948 vol. II, p. 4381. See also 1 avril 1954, Bulletin des Arrêts de la Cour de Cassation 1954, vol. II, no. 142, p. 102.
87. Loi du 16 avril 1946, art. 5, al. 1 and 2.
88. Namely (1) the number and composition of each of the elctoral colleges, and (2) the distribution of personnel and seats in each of these.
89. In the convention collectives de la conserve, de la manutention ferroviaire, du textile, des transports routiers and des banques, there exist very detailed procedural provisions.
90. The exceptions are few, see e.g. the convention collective du textile, which provides for *four* electoral colleges composed each of (a) workers (b) employees (c) technicians (d) foremen, engineers and management. See also the convention collective nationale des transports routiers which provides for two electoral colleges (which conformed with the old legislative provistions (i.e. under loi du 16 avril 1946, art. 5)), which could be united into one when the number of electors of the second college is below a stated number.
91. i.e. 'ouvriers' (which also includes the young workers) and 'employés'.
92. Texte co-ordonné du 20 novembre 1962, art. 8.
93. e.g. rule II of the TGWU rule book merely states: 'Shop stewards shall be elected wherever possible by the membership in organised factories, garages, depots, wharves and on building jobs etc.' See also TGWU shop stewards' handbook, p. 5.
94. See e.g. electric motor manufacturers and the AUEW, TGWU, G & MWU, and the EET and PTU collective agreement sect. 4, p. 7, in particular clauses 19 and 22.
95. i.e. the election of multi-union shop stewards as exemplified in the Dagenham plant of Fords. See e.g. the Court of Inquiry report into industrial relations at Fords 1963, Cmnd. 1999, particularly p. 51. See also a similar enquiry in 1957, Cmnd. 131, particularly p. 26. This practice was found in only a very *small* minority of cases and discussions entered into by this writer with unions clearly show that unions do not approve of this practice.
96. Recognising the 'fluidity' of the present arrangements on the election of shop stewards in Britain, the TUC in 'Good industrial relations – a guide for negotiators' recommends that 'unions should ensure that their rule books and shop stewards' handbooks or other appropriate publications: (a) state clearly the *method of election* or appointment of shop stewards . . . ' (p. 21, para. 61) (stress added).
97. Subject to the limited union involvement discussed above in nominating potential candidates and agreeing to the distribution of seats etc.
98. See in particular note 90.
99. i.e. production areas, assembly line workers, shift systems, distribution of various skills etc.
100. Thus in Hull Breweries the shift work arrangements determined the

personnel in the constituency, and in Ets. Renault again work arrangements on the production line determined the constituency.
101. See also the parallel findings of the CIR on joint credentials in its Report No. 17, 'Facilities afforded to Shop Stewards', Cmnd. 4668, para. 131, p. 28.
102. Décret orginaque of 2 février 1952, arts. 15 and 16 as amended by loi du 30 mars 1955 (on the code électoral), arts. 15 and 16 and loi du 22 juin 1972.
103. Art. 7 of texte co-ordonné du 20 novembre 1962.
104. e.g. treason, rape, murder etc. . . . 'pour indignité nationale'.
105. Loi du 16 avril 1946, art. 6, al. 1 and 2.
106. Usually connected with contravention of the electoral code. See note 104 above.
107. See Cour de Cassation, Ch. Civ., 9 juillet 1953, recueil Dalloz 1953, J. 614 Jurisclasseur Périodique (Semaine Juridique) vol. IV, p. 130.
108. See Cour de Cassation, Ch. Civ., 12 février 1954, Dr. Soc. 1954, p. 291, where it was held that despite the fact that employment law states that national service discharges the contract of service, the court treated it as merely suspending the contract of service. Luxembourg statute specifically provides for such contingency. Art. 7, al. 3, texte co-ordonné du 20 novembre 1962.
109. Where however a closed shop or a 100 per cent union shop is in operation then all employees being union members are entitled to vote.
110. (a) Under the now repealed Trade Union Act Amendment Act 1876, s. 9, a person between sixteen and twenty-one could not be a member of a trade union *unless the union rules provided to the contrary*. If they did, such a person could not be a member of the committee of management, trustee or treasurer of a union. (b) The 1876 Act *implied* that a person under sixteen may not be a trade union member. (c) A person convicted of a criminal offence is not eligible to join a union, *if its rules specifically forbid membership*. Faramus v. Film Artistes' Association [1963] 1 All ER 636 (H.L.). See also Carby-Hall, *Principles of Industrial Law*, pp. 440 and 442.
111. cf. *Goad v. AUEW* [1972] ICR 429.
112. Instituted by ordonnance of 2 février 1945 [art. 9, décret du 5 juin 1946]. Loi du 27 juin 1972 has taken away the French nationality requirement.
113. It was held that the suspension of an employment contract, e.g. through illness (Cour de Cassation, Ch. Civ., 21 mars 1952, Bulletin IV No. 244, p. 178) does not render a person ineligible (Cour de Cassation, Ch. Civ., 27 mars 1952, Dr. Soc. 1952, p. 401).
114. Chefs d'entreprise.
115. These are ascendants and descendants, brothers, sisters and relationships of the same degree. Loi du 16 avril 1946, art. 7, al. I.
116. See ordonnances of 27 juillet and 26 septembre 1944.
117. Loi du 16 avril 1946, art. 7, al. 2.
118. Loi du 16 avril 1946, art. 8. It must be noted that the inspector's powers are subject to stringent administrative controls and must be based upon valid motives and reasoning. The inspector cannot therefore contend that the *unstable* number of workers calls for a substitution of these conditions – Conseil d'Etat 20 May 1952, Droit Social 1952, p. 604. In other cases however a substitution for legal requirements may be made – Conseil d'Etat 19 décembre 1952, s. 1953 III 38, Dr. Soc., p. 600.
119. Texte co-ordonné du 20 novembre 1962, art. 8.
120. See e.g. rule 11 (p. 27 of the rules of the National Society of Operative Printers and Assistants, 1962) which lays down that fathers of chapels are

Employee Representation 227

eligible for election to this office from '... any member working in the firm for one month...' See also AEU rule book (1965) rule 13–21 (p. 50) where '... 12 months' adult membership' is *normally* required.
121. See e.g. rule 4 of the rules of the Transport and General Workers' Union (1971) and rule 21 of the National Union of Public Employees (1973) which treats of shop stewards but where no quaifications are mentioned.
122. cf. the findings of CIR report No. 17 on 'Facilities afforded to shop stewards', Cmnd. 4668 May 1971, para. 129 (i) (ii) (iii). The TUC in its 'Good industrial relations — a guide for negotiators' takes this up at p. 21 para. 61(a) but dismisses it in two and a half lines. Surely what is required is a detailed guide for unions to follow.
123. See note 65 ante.
124. Each elector votes for a group of candidates (scrutin de liste) in two cycles (a deux tours). For the first election, each list is made out by the most representative trade unions. Should the number of persons voting be below half that of the total number of listed electors, the election will be followed within a fortnight by a second election, and in this latter case, the electors have a right to vote for lists other than those prepared by the trade unions. (See Circulaire travail 47/48 du 5 juillet 1948). It is permitted to cross off names from one list and to substitute them with names from another list (within the scrutin de liste). This is known as 'panachage' (see Cour de Cassation, Ch. Civ., Sect. Soc., 23 mars 1950, Bulletin des Arrêts de la Cour de Cassation IV No. 277, p. 190). If two candidates have the same number of votes the vacancy is filled by the older candidate, otherwise the law of 7 July 1947 applies the majority rule. [Loi du 7 juillet 1947, art. 9.] This research shows that the reason why the most representative trade unions prepare the list for the first election is that the law is anxious to preserve trade union freedom by ensuring that unions have some say within the establishment. It is not because the union necessarily ought to nominate its own members, although this invariably occurs.
125. Recourse to the cantonal court may only be had where (1) the contested matter relates to the electorate and is made within *three* days of the publication of the electoral list and (2) where it relates to the irregularity of the election. In this latter case the appeal must be made within *fifteen days* following the election date. The judge must give his verdict within ten days, and no fees or any procedural form are required except that the interested parties must be given *three days'* notice of the trial date. There is an appeal against the cantonal judge's decision to the Cour de Cassation. In these circumstances the appeal must be lodged within *ten days* after notification to the 'greffe de la justice de paix' and it must be notified by a 'huissier' within ten days of the judgement. (See décret organique du 22 février 1852 modified by the laws of 30 novembre 1875 and 6 février and 31 mars 1941.) It is the Cour de Cassation that has adopted the above solution relating to appeals being made, heard and decided, within strict time limits, because the law of 1946 is silent on this matter. The court thus adopted the law of 1852 relating to ordinary elections. (See Cour de Cassation, Ch. Civ., 27 mars 1952, Bulletin 1952 vol. IV. no. 269, p. 197).
126. Loi du 7 décembre 1952, art. 9, al. 10. See also décret 58–1284 of 22 décembre 1958, art. 10(4).
127. Texte co-ordonné du 20 novembre 1962, art. 8 (for 'délégues ouvriers') and art. 24 (for 'délégues d'employés').
128. The rules of the National Society of Operative Printers and Assistants, rule 6–11 (p. 27), gives a most tertiary treatment to election procedure.

It states 'Fathers of Chapels are to be elected every three months and any member working in the firm for one month shall be eligible for office.' Similarly with rule 11−4 paras. 2 and 3 (p. 28) of the TGWU rules (1971) which leaves election procedure to a minimum. The most comprehensive election procedure was that found in the Executive Council statement of the National Union of Public Employees entitled 'Provisions for Union Stewards', 14 June 1970. (See also NUPE Rule Book (1973) rule 21−1 (p. 33)).

129. One of the most detailed procedures appears in the AEU rule book (1965), rule 13−21, which talks of district committees authorising the appointment of shop stewards, the twelve-month qualification period, discretionary exemption of this qualification, approval by the district committee of the steward before resuming his functions etc. It will readily be noted that these general points bear no comparison with the detailed provisions which exist under French law.

In its evidence to the CIR (unpublished) the Engineering Employers' Federation stated the trade unions were not required to show that proper elections of the shop steward took place and pointed out the impartial and detailed provisions which existed *inter alia* in France. The CBI in its evidence (unpublished) to the CIR also considered that a more formal shop steward election procedure was required, and that it should be strictly adhered to.

130. It will be recalled however that Lord Denning (in another context − i.e. wrongful expulsion from a union) did say (in *Lee v. Showmen's Guild* of GB (1952) I AII ER, p. 1181) '. . . If parties should seek, by agreement, to take the law out of the hands of the courts and into the hands of a private individual, without any recourse at all to the courts in case of error of law, then the agreement is to that extent contrary to public policy and void.' Lynskey, J. in *Baker v. Jones (1954) 2 AII ER 553, p. 558* made a similar comment. '. . . The parties can, of course, make a tribunal . . . a final arbiter on questions of fact. They can leave questions of law to the decision of the tribunal, but they cannot make it the final arbiter on questions of law.' By parity of reasoning could it not be said that *inter alia* these dicta would be applicable in Britain to contested matters relating to the election of shop stewards?

Furthermore, the court in Britain will intervene where the tribunal has failed to observe the rules of the union, or where the rules of natural justice have been violated. See *inter alia Annamunthodo v. Oilfields Workers' Trade Union (1961) A.C. 945* and *Taylor v. National Union of Seamen (1967) I AII ER 767*. See also Carby-Hall, *Principles of Industrial Law*, pp. 448 et seq.

131. This was said in the course of interviews with union officials but it has not been possible to find either in rule books or in practice any provision for disciplinary action concerning shop steward election irregularities.

132. See e.g. rule of TGWU (1971), rule 11−4 (p. 28) where 'a show of hands' is one of the options.

See also the opinion of W.E.J. McCarthy, in Research Paper 1, 'The role of shop stewards in British industrial relations', p. 6 para. 8, where he states that '*most* stewards are elected by a "show of hands" in the work place . . . ' (stress added). This writer cannot agree with the findings of McCarthy on this point.

133. Officials of the National Association of Stevedores and Dockers in the docks have told this writer 'that because of *inter alia* TGWU shop stewards their members have not at all times been properly represented'. A union

official brought this problem out most clearly in the Court of Inquiry held to enquire into the industrial relations system of the Dagenham plant of Fords (1963) (Cmnd. 1999, p. 51). '... Each geographical area in the factory has to elect a shop steward and that shop steward may well be representing three, four or five unions. In many cases there may well be 70 per cent of my members with a shop steward of another union of only 10 per cent. You cannot do much to that shop steward if he calls the 70 per cent out, he is not one of your union and no other union wants to know anything because not many of their people are involved...'

134. See p. 184 et seq below for attitudes on facilities in the various countries.
135. Ninety-two per cent of a sample of ninety-eight employers.
136. See p. 164 ante.
137. Experience has shown that this is unworkable. It will be recalled that in December 1969 the TUC did suggest through a circular to its affiliated unions two proposals: (a) that they should provide in their rule books or elsewhere a procedure for electing shop stewards or (b) a procedure for appointing them. Although these do exist in *some* rule books, from the union rule books and other documents examined it is more the exception than the rule. It is true that the TUC did not provide sample guidelines with its circular as suggested by this writer in (b), but had it done so, it is submitted that that would have made little or no difference.
138. Trade Union and Labour Relations Act 1974, s.18.
139. Ibid., s.18(1) (a) (b).
140. i.e. (i) to (vii), p. 178.
141. By whichever method (a) to (e) chosen above, but this writer would prefer to see method (a) used as being the most effective and immediate one.
142. See pp. 172 et seq.
143. See note 61.
144. 'In theory' because it is not certain that constituents will have the diligence to read the union rule book. This research shows that 'in practice' very few union members are well acquainted with the union rules; by parity of reasoning therefore it could be said that any electoral procedure that is laid down may not be read by constituents. Perhaps a surer way to remedy this deficiency is to publish the procedure on the notice board at the works during the election period.
145. See pp. 175 et seq.
146. M.J. Pedler in 'Shop stewards as leaders', IRJ no. 4 1973–4, p. 47, shows that the average age of representatives is thirty-seven.
147. M.J. Pedler at ibid. p. 48 shows that 'there is no difference in school leaving age, if anything the average member is slightly better qualified on leaving school, 35 per cent claiming qualifications of some kind compared with 20 per cent of representatives'. However, representatives seem to be interested in further education courses a great deal more than their members.
148. See p. 175 ante.
149. cf. the French and Luxembourg situation, pp. 176 et seq.
150. See p. 176 et seq and note 123 illustrating that the trade union nominees may be changed by the electorate in certain circumstances.
151. It is suggested below that *appointment* by the union should cease and that a democratic secret ballot be held.
152. This research shows that cases have occurred in Britain where shop stewards have been removed from office through a vote of no confidence by the constituents, or through continuous pressure being put upon shop stewards by constituents, or by reporting a shop steward to his union whereupon he would be suspended. There would be a decrease of those situations occurring

if prior consultations took place.
153. See p. 171 et seq. above.
154. Pedler asks in 'Shop stewards as leaders', IRJ no. 4 1973–4, p. 49 '... do most representatives really stand for re-election in any meaningful sense?' The answer is left open. By parity with re-election, the same may be said of elections, though most shop stewards and constituents feel that the method is a democratic one.
155. cf. the French system, p. 176.
156. See p. 172.
157. See note 89.
158. See (below) pp. 183 et seq.
159. This research shows that some 12 per cent only of shop stewards are opposed in any re-election, it therefore appears that re-elections will not in the majority of cases happen too often. There is the added advantage in a tacit renewal of office in that the formality, expense and time factor of a re-election will be dispensed with.
160. See Cour de Cassation, Chambre Civile, Section Sociale, 19 janvier 1961, Bulletin no. 86, p. 67. Cour de Cassation, Ch. Civ., 24 février 1955, Bulletin 1955 vol. IV 176, p. 130, Droit Social 1955, p. 429. It must be noted that in a previous decision the Cour Supérieure d'Arbitrage held that where the employer, trade unions and the personnel of the enterprise agree, there could be a tacit renewal of office. (14 décembre 1954, Droit Social 1955, p. 282). This latter decision has therefore been reversed. It is submitted that the latter decision is the writer's preferred one. It is illogical to go through the motions of an election when all the parties are agreed on renewing the 'délégué's' period of office.
161. See p. 172.
162. Loi du 16 Avril 1946, art. 10, al. 1 and 2.
163. Ibid., art. 11.
164. Some rule books state so categorically, but most do not, e.g. GMWU rule book and steward's handbook. The shop stewards' manual of the AEU stated '... your fellow members put their trust in you to represent them for the next *twelve months* in all matters connected with their employment'. See also model procedure agreement (ACAS) p. 5, para. 1–2, which states 'All shop stewards will be elected annually in accordance with the rules of their unions'. The NUPE stewards' handbook says: 'Stewards will hold office for one year; they will be eligible for re-election' (p. 34). Some 70 per cent of shop stewards stand for re-election annually — see Pedler, 'Shop stewards as leaders', IRJ no. 4 1973–4, p. 49, who seems to have come to the same conclusive percentage. But note the TGWU rule book which states 'Special elections will be held on the requisition of the membership concerned or at defined periods but in any case elections shall take place at least once every two years' (p. 28).
165. See H.A. Clegg, A.J. Killick and R. Adams, *Trade Union Officers* (Blackwell) who, in 1959, seem to come to the same conclusion. They state, p. 163, 'Regular re-election appears to be the general practice, for 81 per cent of our sample stated that they were subject to it.' M.J. Pedler, in 'Shop stewards as leaders', IRJ no. 4 1974–4 gives an even higher percentage, p. 49, '... 86 per cent say they are subject to regular re-election...'.
166. Camerlynck, 'La prorogation conventionelle du mandat de délégué', JCP 1959, 1. 1525.
167. But see note 154.
168. The fact that senior stewards or conveners exist is not overlooked. These offices cannot be compared to a 'délégué titulaire'. If it were so,

then one would have to accept that shop stewards are not equivalent (used in a loose sense) to 'délégués'. A senior steward has no equivalent in France or Luxembourg, despite the fact that some of his functions could be identical.
169. Important meetings with the employer of both a 'délégué' and 'suppléant' constitute an exceptional circumstance – Cour de Cassation, Ch. Civ., Sect. Soc., 9 juin 1971, Liaison Sociale no. 3784, but the putting up of a Christmas tree does not, Cour de Cass., Ch. Civ., Sect. 300, 22 Civil 1964. In industrial concerns décret du 16 mai 1974 no. 74481 allows for an additional ten hours every six months where under 100 employees are employed, with one hour per six months more for every 100 workers subsequently.
170. Loi du 16 avril 1946, art. 13, al. 1 and 2.
171. Cour de Cassation, Ch. Civ., Sect. Soc., 4 décembre 1952 Jurisclasseur Périodique (Semaine Juridique) 1954 II 7903. Prior to this decision it must be noted that the Minister of Labour was of the opinion that external activities did not qualify as being within a 'délégué's' duties. (See Circulaire Ministérielle 8 janvier 1948.)
172. The attendance of a 'délégué' before the Conseil de Prud'hommes in order to support an employee was held not to be one of his functions (see Cour de Cassation, Ch. Civ., Sect. Soc., 1 août 1950. Informateur du chef d'entreprise 1951, p. 215). Nor is the attendance of trade union meetings considered as such. (See Cour de Cassation, Ch. Civ., Sect. Soc., 14 décembre 1951, Gazette du Palais 1952, I. 228 and cf. Cour de Cassation, Chambre Criminelle, 2 mars 1961, Recueil Dalloz 1961, 476, where there was no justification since it was not in the course of his duties, as the matters did not relate to his constituents. The attendance of trade union meetings in relation to collective agreements which concern his constituents could be one of his functions (Cour de Cassation, Chambre Civile, Section Sociale, 18 avril 1963, Droit Social 1963, 421).
173. i.e. representation of his constituents and relationship between management and employees. This function mainly concerns the employer.
174. i.e. representing the trade union vis-à-vis his constituents and the employer. This function is of direct interest to the union.
175. Because in France sometimes he is also the trade union representative.
176. It will be recalled that his trade union functions are not the subject of discussion in this research, and therefore are disregarded in the discussions on leave from a shop steward's job. The Trade Union and Labour Relations Act 1974 and formerly the Industrial Relations Act 1971 did not give a shop steward the right to perform his *industrial relations* functions, it merely made it unfair to dismiss an employee for *inter alia* taking or proposing to take part at any appropriate time in independent (or formerly, in registered) trade union activities. Since writing the above the Employment Protection Act 1975 has been passed and ss.57 and 58 now allow time off with pay for carrying out trade union duties and activities, including industrial relations activities.
177. Of the sample interviewed (350 shop stewards) it was found that 90 per cent of them were granted leave by their firms to carry out their industrial relations activities. Some 3 per cent found it impossible to obtain any leave during working hours and 7 per cent were able to do so but with considerable difficulty. It must be pointed out that the 7 per cent and 3 per cent of the sample consisted of stewards working in small firms.
    In the white-collar unions the trend is similar but it was found that a greater proportion (95 per cent) were allowed time off. The two reasons for

this phenomenon seem to be that industrial relations business is carried out in many instances at the same time as other business, and therefore an informal approach seems to manifest itself, and that the taking of time off is usually easier in this category of employees.
178. See e.g. sect. C, para. 3 of a procedure agreement of 10 March 1973, obtained from ACAS which states:
'3.1 A shop steward wishing to leave his/her normal work,
   (i) to investigate any problem on behalf of a member in his/her constituency;
   (ii) to contact a Union Official;
   (iii) to visit another department on Union business shall first obtain permission from his/her supervisor.
3.2 On entering another department in his/her constituency to represent employees, he/she will obtain the permission of the supervisor of the department he/she is visiting.
3.3 Such permissions shall not unreasonably be withheld.
3.4 Reasonable facilities will be provided for Stewards to report back to their members, generally outside normal working hours.'
179. It has also been found that, generally, adequate time is given during working hours for shop stewards to contact their full-time union official, to meet other shop stewards and to meet the senior steward or convenor.
180. In most instances because the manufacturing process would be disrupted, and there would consequently be loss of production.
181. Of the sample examined only 12 per cent allowed regular constituency meetings to take place during working hours and on the premises. To be noted in particular is the case of *Ravyts v. Post Office [1971] ICR 174* where the NIRC held that despite the s.5 rights given by the Industrial Relations Act 1971, management had to approve any activities conducted on establishment premises. The Court of Appeal case of *Post Office v. Crouch [1973] ICR 366 (CA)* may however have cast certain doubts on this former case.
182. See e.g. Hull Fishing Industry Association minutes of meeting on the 'Redundancy situation – labour landing fish cargoes' of 23 May and 9 June 1975.
183. It must be stressed that although 'délégués' are not out of pocket, their wages do suffer in that they do not receive the full amount they could have earned had they actually worked their overtime etc. What they do receive is the *average* earnings which is below their maximum potential.
184. This was so in the case of 94 per cent of the sample examined in the blue-collar unions' shop stewards. In the white-collar unions however the sample examined showed that none of the shop stewards was out of pocket. The reason given was mainly because, being monthly paid, it was difficult for the employer to assess what time had been spent by the steward in performing his representative functions. The other reason found was that it is more conducive in staff situations to take time off unofficially.
185. Isolated cases have been found in this research where management has been prepared to compensate the steward for his representative functions in cases where management itself has called the meeting and in cases where overtime pay was granted to stewards (and others) for attending such meetings outside working hours.
186. Hence the situations described in note 185 above coming about.
187. This being the main reason advanced by management for not remunerating the steward especially when he is exercising trade union functions during working or overtime hours.
188. It will be recalled that time off is sometimes regulated in Britain by 'procedure

agreements'. What would happen in the smaller firm where no such procedure agreement exists? In these latter circumstances the steward could have no such facilities.
188a. See s.57(2) Employment Protection Act 1975, referring to the proposed code of practice to be drawn up by ACAS.
189. Although it was stated above that the shop steward's trade union functions are *ultra vires* the terms of this research, it might be worth making the submission that management should allow the steward time off for his trade union functions as well, as he might well find it beneficial in the long run to allow leave for these purposes. This submission is now covered by s.58 of the Employment Protection Act 1975, which came into effect since completing this research.
190. A distinction must be drawn between 'inter shop stewards' meetings' and 'joint shop stewards' meetings'. These latter meetings occur frequently during working hours.
191. It may even be said that his trade union functions are of benefit to the employer in that he maintains some sort of relations and liaison between the union and the employer.
192. Though the steward be now given a statutory right to his full wages (by S.57(4) E.P.A.), the problems experienced in Luxembourg and France when 'délégués' are on payment by results and overtime (discussed above) will not be surmounted.
193. As Marsh points out in 'Shop steward organisation in the engineering industry', BJIR June 1963, many stewards are paid out-of-pocket expenses by management though 'no provision is made to recompense stewards for working time lost in the performance of their duties' in the engineering procedure.
194. A number of unions already compensate their shop stewards for loss of earnings as a result of their trade union functions, e.g. the engineering unions. In some cases a fund is set up by the union constituents for this purpose.
195. This right cannot be restricted by collective agreement (Cour de Paris, 30 mars 1962, JCP 1962, II. 12738).
196. Loi du 16 avril 1946, art. 13, al. 3 and 4 in France, texte co-ordonné du 20 novembre 1962 in Luxembourg.
197. Cour de Cassation, Ch. Civ., Sect. Soc., 5 avril 1954. Informateur du chef d'entreprise 1954, p. 694.
198. Tribunal correctionnel. Le Harve, 23 juin 1952, Dr. Soc. 1952, p. 538.
199. Cour de Cassation, Ch. Civ., Sect. Soc., 5 avril 1954, Dr. Soc. 1954, p. 408.
200. Works rules.
201. Shop-floor rules (usually concluded through shop-floor agreements). In Luxembourg the 'délégué' may receive workers' complaints, problems etc. outside working hours.
202. i.e. (i) 'Délégués du personnel' may be assisted by a trade union representative during meetings with the employer. Loi du 16 avril 1946, art. 14.
 (ii) Certain collective agreements provide for the trade union members (of signatory trade unions) to attend meetings with employers, in cases other than those prescribed by law — see e.g. Convention Colléction des Contreplaqués, art. 7.
 (iii) The most representative trade unions within the establishment may send a representative to meetings of the comité d'entreprise for *consultative purposes* only. Ordonnance du 22 février 1945, art. 5.
 (iv) In nationalised industries (or in some compagnies d'économie mixte) the trade unions choose the workers' representatives who take part in and manage the conseil d'administration.
 (v) In the case of miners the trade unions must be notified of all

applications for posts that have not been filled in Statut du Mineur, art. 6.
- (vi) In ordinary establishments trade unions do not appoint the members of the 'comité d'entreprise' or the 'délégués du personnel', but they provide the list of candidates for the electors. Loi du 16 avril 1946, art. 9, al. 3.
203. Loi du 16 avril 1946, art. 14, al. 1–3.
204. Ibid., art. 15, al. 1–3.
205. cf. also the percentages given in IRRR no. 56, May 1973, p. 7, which show a somewhat higher percentage.
206. e.g. the frequent provision of accommodation provided by the Hull Fishing Industry Association to discuss the redundancy situation in the labour landing fish cargoes – from May to September 1975.
207. Though it seems common sense, and also seems accepted by the great majority of establishments interviewed, that the keeping of constituents informed is an essential ingredient in the recipe for good industrial relations.
208. Although in a number of cases in the field of 'inducing breaches of contract' as an economic tort or under the short-lived Industrial Relations Act 1971 ss. 96–98 as an unfair industrial practice, notices affixed within the establishment have been a contributory factor to materially bringing about 'the inducement'.
209. It was discovered 'en passant' that in some smaller firms management bypassed the shop steward and dealt directly with the full-time union official. Such practice, it is submitted, can only cause a breakdown in the communication and negotiation structure and can only have detrimental results on industrial relations. In general however it was found that management prefers to deal directly with the shop steward because he understands the particular problems within the establishment better than the union official does. S.4 of the Contracts of Employment Act 1972 and the Code of Industrial Relations Practice on grievance procedures are of relevance.
210. In two French establishments the 'délégués' complained that they were not allocated a permanent secretary, and that they therefore had to do secretarial work themselves thus wasting their time when they could have been doing something more profitable. A 'délégué' in another firm complained that filing cabinets did not lock and that therefore the privacy of certain documents could be at risk, while another felt that the employer was slow in providing him with office furniture.
211. But it must be stressed that in 92 per cent of these the shop steward did not have the telephone exclusively for himself, and frequently complaints have been heard about the element of privacy when making telephone calls of a confidential nature.
212. The survey was carried out before the part of the Employment Protection Act 1975, giving *limited* union facilities, became operative.
213. It has already been seen above that 97 per cent of shop stewards have access to internal and external telephones and that typing and duplicating facilities are reasonable (68 per cent and 75 per cent for manual and white-collar workers respectively). The only poor facilities found in this respect were storage facilities (48 per cent and 43 per cent for manual and white-collar workers respectively). Surely no great imposition will be made upon any employer to provide a filing cabinet for his shop stewards.
214. See Verdier, 'Du contrat au statut du droit individuel aux libertés publiques', JCP 1971, 2422: Cour de Cassation, Ch. Criminelle, 10 novembre 1953. Jurisclasseur Périodique (Semaine Juridique) 1953, 4. 178. See also Cour de Cassation, Chambre Civile, Section Sociale, 4 décembre 1968, Recueil

Dalloz 69.276 — dismissal can only take place by a majority secret ballot of the 'comité'. Cour de Cassation, Ch. Civ., Sect. Soc., 2 juillet 1969, Droit Social 1969, p. 588.
215. Loi du 16 avril 1946, art. 16, al. 1–3.
216. Cour de Cassation, Ch. Civ., 24 avril 1953, Annales de Justice de Paix 53, p. 342.
217. Ordonnance 59–81, 7 janvier 1959.
218. Cour de Cassation, Ch. Civ., Sect. Soc., 15 mai 1952, JCP (Semaine Juridique) 1954, II. 7903.
219. The rules provided by ordonnance du 24 mai 1945 which relate to collective dismissals may stem either from works rules or collective agreements. These are briefly as follows:
   (i) The order of dismissal must be fixed by an *internal regulation*, which regulation is compulsorily preceded by an opinion given by the comité d'entreprise or by the délégués du personnel (if any). The provisions of the regulation must therefore consider such factors as family responsibilities, seniority in the establishment, effectiveness, and professional or trade qualifications. Any breach of such regulation renders the employer criminally (fine) and civilly ('rupture abusive') liable.
   (ii) Internal regulations are operative only when there exists no provision of collective dismissals in the collective agreements. Such a provision is not compulsory for conventions collectives ordinaires but it is so for conventions collectives susceptibles d'extension (art. 31g Code du Trav., livre I.). Here the employer will be civilly liable ('rupture abusive').
220. See p. 196 ante.
221. Cour de Chambery, 27 janvier 1955, JCP Semaine Juridique 1955, IV. 78.
222. Rather hesitantly in Ch. Civ., Sect. Soc., 9 mai 1953, Droit Social 1953, p. 411, but affirmed in more positive terms in Cour de Cassation, Ch. Civ., Sect. Soc., 19 January 1956, Droit Soc. 1956, p. 352. Consider also Cour de Cassation, Ch. Criminelle, 3 janvier, 1965, Informateur du chef d'entreprise 1965, p. 416, where the court awarded penal sanctions when special rules protecting employees (see note 219 above) were not observed during a mass dismissal in which 'délégués' were included. It must be noted that the sanctions awarded were for breach of regulations relating to employees generally and not to 'délégués' in particular.
223. But see Droit Social 1962, p. 566, where the opposite was held in this case. Is this case the exception?
224. The reason for this phenomenon is that initially the Minister of Labour had refused to pronounce on such matters, but the 'conseil d'état' reminded the Minister that the inspector's decision 'reste soumise, à défaut de dispositions contraires de la loi et conformément aux principes généraux du droit public, un contrôle hiérarchique'. His negative attitude has thus been censured, and he alone was made competent to hear such appeals. The 'conseil d'état' has furthermore stated that despite the ordinary procedure, appeals lie to the immediate superior in the hierarchy, i.e. the 'directeur départemental du travail'; in this instance, the law having specifically given the power of decision to a named agent (the inspecteur), only the highest official in the hierarchy, and not the direct superior, is qualified to hear the appeal. It is submitted that this argument is difficult to follow as this would mean that when, in French law, a named individual is given the power of decision in a particular case, an appeal will never lie to his immediate superior, whereas where a regulation specifically gives a right of appeal to

the immediate superior then an appeal would lie. It is against the principle of any legal system, even the French one, that a specific right of appeal to the immediate superior should lie only in cases where the law specifically so states.
225. This recourse to the tribunal administratif has only been available since 1 January 1954. Prior to that date, the conseil d'état was the only competent body to hear such appeals. The decree of 30 September 1953 reformed the administrative court system, hence this change.
226. Conseil d'Etat 29 July 1953, Recueil Lebon, p. 432. Conseil d'Etat 20 octobre 1954, Recueil Lebon, p. 545. Conseil d'Etat 12 novembre 1959 JCP (Semaine Juridique) 1950 II. 5909.
227. Cour de Cassation, Ch. Civ., Sect. Soc., 18 décembre 1952, Bull. Vol. IV, para. 930, p. 667.
228. Conseil d'Etat 20 octobre 1954, Recueil Lebon, p. 545.
229. This appeal originates from case law of the Cour de Cassation, namely Arrêt Artus Cour de Cassation, Ch. Civ., Sect. Soc., 21 février 1952, Droit Soc. 1952, p. 325.
230. See the comments made by President of the Court Patin, in Cour de Cassation, Ch. Criminelle, 24 mars 1955, Droit Soc. 1956, p. 30. The court has to await the decision of the minister before deciding the case. Cour de Cassation, Ch. Civ., Sect. Soc., 5 mai 1970, Droit Social 1970, p. 517. See also Droit Social 1972, p. 584.
231. The now repealed Industrial Relations Act 1971 s. 5(1)(c) did, it is true protect as between *any worker* and his employer, a worker by giving him the right *inter alia* where he was a *registered* trade union member at any appropriate time to take part in the activities of a trade union and the right to seek appointment or election as an official. It was an unfair industrial practice under s. 5(2)(b) and the corresponding s. 24(4) to *inter alia* dismiss a worker for exercising his rights. The Trade Union and Labour Relations Act 1974 sch. 1 para. 6(4)(b) gives protection against dismissal (and not anything short of dismissal) to the worker who *inter alia* had taken or proposed to take part at any appropriate time in the activities of an independent trade union. The Employment Protection Act 1975 now provides for protection for the employee for actions by the employer short of dismissal. Thus under past and present British legislation the shop steward has no more protection than his fellow workers. In any event the protection given to all workers is in connection with trade union activities. The shop steward also performs industrial relations activities and for these (if in some circumstances by their exercise he displeases the employer) he is also given protection but only for the ordinary right open to all employees to bring an action for unfair dismissal (reparative right (see p. 200 post)).
232. Both 'délégués' and their 'suppléant' in Luxembourg are protected against dismissal during their period of office. They can only be dismissed by the consent of the 'délégation' of which they form part. Unsuccessful candidates are also protected for a period of three months from the date of presentation of their candidature, and the past 'délégué' has special protection for six months. In case of serious misconduct (faute grave) the employer may suspend the 'délégué' while awaiting the decision of the 'conseil des prud'hommes'. (Arrêté grand-ducal du 20 novembre 1962, art. 9.) Under loi du 27 juin 1970 the 'délégué' dismissed for serious misconduct may within eight days of dismissal appeal to the president of the 'juridiction du travail' asking him that the 'délégué' should be allowed to receive his wages until the case has been heard.
233. See the first difficulty experienced in France and discussed on p. 196 and

Employee Representation 237

note 218 above.
234. See note 232 above.
235. i.e. that (a) no legislation and (b) no procedural agreement give any protection against dismissal to a shop steward in Britain.
236. There have been cases which have come to this writer's attention where shop stewards have either been dismissed or otherwise penalised by the employer because of their activities, but no legal action was taken because it was either difficult or impossible to prove the employer's motive.
237. Trade Union and Labour Relations Act 1974, sch. 1 para. 6(4). See also Carby-Hall, *Labour Relations and the Law*, pp. V. 7 et seq.
238. e.g. attitudes of shop steward in connection with matters arising daily within the establishment, attitudes on safety at work, attitudes on conditions of work of his constituents etc.
239. Assuming the industrial tribunal does not, despite the Employment Protection Act provisions, recommend re-engagement of reinstatement which it could quite easily not do as it might not be practicable under the circumstances. Alternatively the employer might show that it is not practicable for him to reinstate etc. and thus escape paying the additional award under the Employment Protection Act 1975.
240. Because (a) although there are works councils in Britain which are equivalent to the 'comité d'entreprise', they do not have the same role in this sphere and it is not proposed to suggest that they do; (b) the inspector's functions in Britain are not the same as those of the French inspector, and (c) the various appeal systems that exist in France result either from historical accidents (e.g. appeal to the Minister of Labour) or are restrictive (e.g. tribunal administratif) or non-specialised (e.g. the ordinary courts). In other words, the system is cumbersome and complicated, which could result in ineffectiveness.
241. See procedure agreement between electric motor manufacturers and the AUEFW, TGWU, G & MWU, EET and PTU, p. 8, clause 31, which states: 'If, in the opinion of management a shop steward at any time fails to carry out in a proper manner the functions and responsiblities that are normally carried out by shop stewards, the management shall have the right to bring the matter before the union concerned for discussion. While such discussions are proceeding, the position of the shop steward shall be maintained.' See also the procedure agreement with this company and these unions relating to non-managerial staff employees in connection with representatives, p. 5, clause 28, which makes similar provisions to the above. See also ACAS document entitled 'An agreement setting out the role and functions of shop stewards and domestic procedure for settlement of grievances', p. 4, para. 0, where again similar provision to the above may be found.
242. It will be noted that the existing procedures that do exist, as in note 241 above, only talk of failing 'to carry out in a proper manner the functions and responsiblities . . . [of a] shop steward'. The clause is vague for two reasons, firstly because it does not seem to deal with the shop steward as an employee but only as a shop steward. What would happen if the steward committed serious theft in the course of his employment? *Prima facie* this clause would not take care of such a situation, since it only restricts the matter to failing to carry out his shop steward responsiblities. Secondly, this clause is also restrictive because it does not seem to deal with the situation where for example the shop steward is a militant with subversive aims. These matters do not relate to the functions of a shop steward and therefore by implication do not come within the procedure agreement terms

outlined above.
243. See p. 197 ante.
244. Loi du 16 avril 1946, art. 16. Droit du Travail et de la Sécurité Sociale 1954, no. 2, p. 7. Thus an immediate suspension by the employer was held to be valid when a 'délégué' summoned workers to the cloakroom to transmit to them a report on a *trade union* meeting. (Cour de Cassation, Ch. Civ., Sect. Soc., 30 juin 1955, Recueil Dalloz 1956, Sommaire 77.)
245. See and cf. decision of Tribunal de Montluçon, 12 juin 1952, Drt. Soc. 1952, p. 681 with that of Tribunal de Bordeaux, 16 juin 1953, JCP 1953 vol. 11, p. 7960.
246. Cour de Cassation, Ch. Crim., 24 mars 1955, Droit Soc. 1956, p. 27. See particularly the president's (M. Patin's) comments. See also on appeal Poitiers, 8 décembre 1955, JCP 1956 vol. II, p. 9443 and in particular note by Brèthe de la Gressaye.
247. The president of the Cour de Cassation said in his judgement '. . . la mise à pied d'un délégué du personnel décidée par l'employeur sous sa responsabilité, et à raison d'une faute jugée par lui assez grave pour provoquer un licenciement, prive le travailleur aussi bien des avantages de son contrat de travail que de tout droit de s'immiscer dans le fonctionnement de l'entreprise au titre de délégué ouvrier'.
248. Sic Brèthe de la Gressaye.
249. See Cour de Poitiers, 8 décembre 1955, Droit du Travail et de la Sécurité Sociale 1956, no. 9, p. 39. See also Cour de Cassation, Ch. Crim., 24 mars 1955, Droit Social 1956, where it was held that the employer was mistaken as to the nature of the 'faute grave' (it was in fact a 'faute légère') but he had *reasonable* belief that it was serious enought to suspend the 'délégué'.
250. See Cour de Cassation, Ch. Crim., 24 février 1955, Gazette du Palais 1955 vol. I, p. 304, for this reasoning.
251. e.g. Cour de Cassation, Ch. Civile., Sect. Sociale, 4 août 1952; Droit Ouvrier 1952, p. 488; ICE 1956, p. 601; Cour de Cassation, Ch. Civ., Sect. Soc., 20 mars 1956.
252. The employer has no common law right to supend an employee without pay. (*Hanley v. Pease and Partners (1915) IKB 698*.) etc. . .
253. i.e. the Trade Union and Labour Relations Act 1974.
254. Under the Industrial Relations Act 1971 the employer had to be careful not to *suspend* an employee in such circumstances as would have amounted to discrimination or penalisation under s. 5. The Trade Union and Labour Relations Act 1974, sch. 1, para. 6(3) no longer affords this protection to the employee. Though employees are protected against dismissal on grounds of union activity, the 1974 Act did *not* protect the employee against discrimination falling short of dismissal on such grounds or against the preventing or deterring of a worker from taking part in such activities. Under the 1974 Act it therefore appeared that the employee who exercised trade union functions could legally be discriminated against, e.g. suspended.

The Employment Protection Act 1975 has now rectified this situation. The employee has a right not to have action taken against him by his employer for the purpose of *preventing* or *deterring* him from, or *penalising* him for, *inter alia* taking part at any appropriate time in union activities (see Carby-Hall, *Labour Relations and the Law*, p. V.10), but despite these provisions it is felt that this is not adequate protection for the shop steward.

The Trade Union and Labour Relations Act 1974 states that a dismissal by way of lockout will not be regarded as an unfair dismissal if the employee is offered re-engagement as from the date of resumption of work (sch. 1, para. 7(I)). A lockout in contemplation or furtherance of a trade dispute

constitutes in fact a *suspension* of the contract of employment. The effect of sch. I, para. 7(I) as far as unfair dismissal is concerned is that suspension does not constitute dismissal where the employee is offered re-employment (identical provisions existed under the Industrial Relations Act 1971, s. 25(I)). At common law the effect of suspension was stated to operate as a *dismissal* with an intention, at the end of the period of suspension, that the employee will be re-employed should he wish to apply to be reinstated. (See Lord Goddard in *Marshall v. English Electric*.) At common law during the period of suspension the mutual obligations of employer and employee are thought to be 'frozen'.
255. What constitutes a serious breach or serious industrial misconduct is hard to define, but generally the standard to be applied is that of a fundamental breach of the contract of employment which entitles the employer to dismiss summarily. The employer would still be enabled in these circumstances to dismiss summarily, but it would always be advisable for him to suspend pending investigation.
256. See note 254 above.
257. See pp. 201 et seq ante, which bases this dismissal in the first instance on domestic tribunals.
258. As is the case in France, see p. 203 ante.
259. See p. 204 ante.
260. i.e. either (1) indirect obliquely as in a procedure agreement dated 10 August 1973. Page 5 (section 'C' — trade union recognition para. 2.2) provides 'In the event of an established union representative performing his/her duties in a manner prejudicial to the mutual interests of the management or the members, the management reserve the right to withdraw recognition of credentials. The sequence of events would be as follows: (i) warn the representative; (ii) inform and consult the district official; (iii) withdraw recognition.' In another such agreement, i.e. electric motor manufacturers dated 23 October 1974, p. 8 para. 31, states: 'If, in the opinion of management, a shop steward at any time fails to carry out in a proper manner the functions and responsibilities that are normally carried out by shop stewards, the management shall have the right to bring the matter before the union concerned for discussion. While such discussions are proceeding, the position of the shop steward shall be maintained,' or (2) indirect involutio as e.g. in 'Points of procedure', *Personnel Management*, August 1972, pp. 24 and 25, where procedures on *inter alia* precautionary suspension have no direct relevance to the shop steward *per se* but involve him either as far as it applies to other employees or as it applies to himself as an employee.
261. i.e. (i) difficulties that have arisen which relate to the dismissal of 'délégués'; (ii) the remedies available to the employer and 'délégué'; (iii) suspension of a 'délégué'.
262. As amended by ord. 59—81 du 7 janvier 1959.
263. The full text reads 'Quiconque aura porté ou tenté de porter atteinte, soit à la libre désignation des délégués du personnel, soit à l'exercice régulier de leurs fonctions, notamment par la meconnaissance des dispositions de l'article 16 ci-dessus et des textes reglementaires pris pour son application, sera puni d'une amende . . . ' (see Code du Travail 35, 1968). See also Larguiers' 'Délit d'entrave aux fonctions de représentant du personnel', Droit Social 1967, pp. 550 et seq.
264. See Cour de Chambéry, 1 juillet 1948, Drt. Soc. 1948, p. 347.
265. Cour de Cassation, Chambre Criminelle, 17 novembre 1966, Recueil Dalloz 1967, p. 201; See also Cour de Cassation, Chambre Criminelle, 24 janvier

1962, Droit Ouvrier 1962, p. 90.
266. Cour de Cassation, Chambre Criminelle, 12 mars 1970, Droit Social 1970, p. 378.
267. Cour de Cassation, Chambre Criminelle, 8 mai 1968, Recueil Dalloz 1968, p. 563. Consider also the case note by Verdier.
268. Cour de Cassation, Chambre Criminelle, 16 juin 1970, Recueil Dalloz 1970, p. 652.
269. Cour de Cassation, Chambre Criminelle, 3 juillet 1968, Recueil Dalloz 1969, p. 597.
270. Cour de Cassation, Chambre Criminelle, 25 février 1959, Recueil Dalloz 1959, p. 241.
271. See Cour de Cassation, Ch. Crim., 1 février 1951, Recueil Dalloz 1951, p. 186; see also Cour de Cassation, Ch. Crim., JCP 18 novembre 1953 vol. IV, p. 178 and 5 mars 1953, vol. IV, p. 7903.
272. Cour d'Aix 8 novembre 1955, JCP 1956 vol. IV, p. 82.
273. Cour de Cassation, Ch. Civ., Sect. Soc., 27 mars 1952, Bulletin vol. IV no. 273, p. 201; Cour de Cassation, Chambre Civile, Section Sociale, 27 mai 1970, Recueil Dallow 1970, p. 742.
274. Cour de Cassation, Ch. Civ., Sect. Soc., 23 octobre 1952, ICE 1953, p. 28.
275. Cour de Cassation, Ch. Civ., Sect. Soc., 19 janvier 1956, Drt. Soc. 1956, p. 352.
276. See discussion supra, and Trade Union and Labour Relations Act 1974, sch. 1, para. 6(4), and the Employment Protection Act 1975.
277. In the TGWU's rules (1971) rule 11–4 para. 5 states '... immediate enquiry shall be undertaken by the appropriate trade group or district committee into every case of dismissal of a shop steward with a view to preventing victimisation, either open or concealed'. This same provision has existed in these rules prior to 1971. See e.g. TGWU rule book (1968) rule 11–4 para. 2. See also NUPE appendix 6 advance letter (ASC) 2/71 issued by the Department of Health and Social Security which states 'No recognised steward shall be dismissed or otherwise penalised in any way whatsoever for carrying out his functions as a steward in accordance with the provision of this agreement'.
278. The majority of union rule books do not contain similar indirect sanctions as exist in the TGWU rules (see e.g. rule book of Merchant Navy and Airline Officers' Association (1973); National Union of Seamen (1972); NATSOPA (1962); NUPE (1973); AUEW etc.) but interviews with union officials clearly indicate that it is an *unwritten* rule that pressure, through an investigation, court of enquiry or industrial action, will always be put upon the employer who dismisses a shop steward.
279. 'Most' because in some instances these are written (see note 277 above), in others they are unwritten (see note 278 above).
280. This is evident since the 'délégué' not being a union official, union pressure cannot normally be put upon the employer.
281. The employer knows the exact nature of his liability, and the 'délégué' feels psychologically secure in the protection that is given to him by law.
282. How inadequate this sanction is in Britain has already been pointed out elsewhere by this writer. See *Studies in Labour Law*, Carby-Hall (ed.), 'Three termination aspects of modern employment.'
283. In France the onus of proof lies on the employer to show that no material obstacle was placed by him (see supra); in Britain the onus of proof for unfair dismissal also lies squarely on the employer (Trade Union and Labour Relations Act 1974, sch. 1, para. 6(8)). See also comment in Carby-Hall, *Labour Relations and the Law*, p. V.13.

284. Under sch. 1, para. 6(4) of the Trade Union and Labour Relations Act 1974.
285. See also notes 277 and 278 above.
286. See pp. 200 et seq ante.
287. See note 277.
288. Even though the domestic appeal tribunal recommends a certain period of probation or a reprimand. See p. 202 ante.
289. This, and other research (see *Studies in Labour Law*, Carby-Hall (ed.), 'Three termination aspects of modern employment', p. 205 et seq) shows that re-engagement and reinstatement orders by industrial tribunals are not as prolific as are awards for compensation. In numerous cases the employer who has been ordered to reinstate or re-engage prefers to pay that little extra in compensation to get rid of a 'troublesome' employee, rather than reinstate or re-engage him.
290. The full text of a 'délégué's' functions will be found in arts. 2 and 3 of loi du 16 avril 1946.
291. Loi du 16 avril 1946, art. 2, al. 1. The survey carried out for this research shows that 62 per cent of his time in fulfilling his functions as 'délégué' is spent on this particular aspect, 19 per cent on negotiations (see also note 357 post dealing purely with plant bargaining), 10 per cent on acting as an auxiliary to the inspecteur du travail, and 9 per cent in correspondence etc.
292. See note 290 above where the term 'réclamations . . . collectives' will be found.
293. See reference in note 290 where a full list will be found.
294. Looked at critically, the legal formula seems comprehensive enough and covers any situation that could arise; it can therefore hardly be called limitative. Cf. the décrèt-loi of 12 novembre 1938 relating to the functions of 'délégués' in mines which did not distinguish between the nature of the topics which could be dealt with by 'délégués'. By parity of reasoning there is nothing to indicate that the legislator of the 1946 law wished the 'délégué' to be restricted in this sphere. This research shows, from interviews held with 280 délégués, that in practice there is no restriction, and that any topic may be brought up.
295. The composition of the 'electoral college' has already been discussed. This research indicates that in a few cases and because of the composition of electoral colleges shop stewards in Britain and 'délégués' in France have found it difficult to cater for the different interests of their members. This was found particularly in the engineering industry in both countries where disparate groups exist within the representative's constituency. The conclusion to be drawn is that individual establishments and local union representatives should agree on constituencies having the same job definition, class of work etc.
296. See reference to text in note 290 above. ieology.
297. See also the opinions of Brun et Galland on this matter in *Droit du Travail*, Edn. Sirey 1958, p. 847.
298. The texte co-ordonné du 20 novembre 1962, art. 3, provides 'La délégation principale à pour mission de sauvegarder et de défendre, dans le domaine social, les droits et les intérêts des ouvriers; ses attributions consistent notamment . . . 3° à recevoir les réclamations des ouvriers et à aplanir par voie de conciliation, les difficultés surgies entre patrons et ouvriers . . .'
299. See reference in note 290 above where the full text will be found.
300. The 'delegues' interviewed unanimously agree that they do not and have never carried out investigations where accidents etc. occurred. They are reporters rather than investigators. This is also true of Britain and of Luxembourg.

301. The texte co-ordonné du 20 novembre 1962, art. 3, provides '... 6° à *contribuer* à la prévention des accidents du travail et des maladies professionnelles conformément aux dispositions légales et règlementaires y relatives...' (stress added).
302. For the matters which the 'comité d'entreprise' is competent to deal with see ordonnance du 22 février 1943. See also art. 3 of loi du 16 avril 1946. The functions include social services, medical services, safety committees, consultative functions in specified matters such as works rules, mass dismissals etc., and judicial functions. These are all discussed supra.
303. See décret du 1 août 1947, art. 4.
304. See décret du 16 novembre 1946, art. 6.
305. See Cour de Cassation, Ch. Civ., Sect. Soc., 3 janvier 1957, p. 98.
306. These have been discussed in 'Enquête du Droit Social 1951', Droit Social 1952, p. 14 et seq and concern mainly job definitions.
307. In the convention collective des établissements de santé privés, for example, may be found a clause stating that the opinion of the 'délégué du personnel' must be sought on matters relating to the order of departure for holidays of employees. Similar provisions exist in the convention collective du textile des établissements hospitaliers. In the convention du textile the 'délégué's' opinion must be sought on matters relating to the period of holidays of employees and in the convention collective des établissements hospitaliers d'assistance privée it will be found that the 'délégué's' opinion has to be sought on the procedure to be followed in collective dismissals.
308. The term 'loosely' is used here because even his second area of functions has some connection with the trade union of which he is a member e.g. negotiating shop-floor agreements, seeing to the observance of safety legislation etc. (all of which will be examined below).
309. See *inter alia*:
    (i) Boilermakers, Shipwrights, Blacksmiths and Structural Workers Shop Steward manual, pp. 2, 5, 6, 7; The Procedural Guide, pp. 8 and 9; the rule book rules 30 and 47. See also Clegg, *A System of Industrial Relations in Great Britain*, pp. 16–18.
    (ii) Union of Shop, Distributive and Allied Workers' shop stewards' handbook pp. 2, 3, 4, 18, 19 and 22.
    (iii) Printing and Kindred Trades' Federation chapel officers' companion, pp. 4, 5 and 10.
    (iv) General and Municipal Workers' Union shop stewards' handbook, pp. 7, 10, 11, 13 and rule 41.
    (v) Amalgamated Union of Engineering Workers' shop stewards' manual, p. 11. The Engineers' rule book stresses the union-orientated duties of shop stewards, rule 13 clause 21, clause 3 and clause 5.
    (vi) National Union of Public Employees (health service ancillary staff), pp. 7 and 11. See also statement of The Executive Council of NUPE on 14 June 1970 at (3) and (7) and the NUPE rule book 1971 edn. (2) and (3).
    (vii) The Transport and General Workers' Union shop stewards' handbook, pp. 4, 5, 6 and 76.
310. Thus all shop stewards interviewed have told this writer, and this is substantiated by *all* the shop steward handbooks and some union rule books, that the second area of a steward's functions, namely his industrial relations functions and representation of his constituents' functions, emanate from his position as a union official. In other words it is the union which lays down the second area of his functions. An examination of the shop steward handbooks etc. clearly supports this view. See *inter alia*:
    (i) Transport and General Workers' Union shop stewards' handbook,

pp. 4, 17, 18, 29, 37, 81, 82 and 83.
    (ii) General and Municipal Workers shop stewards' handbook, pp. 12 and 17.
    (iii) Printing and Kindred Trades Federation chapel officers' companion, p. 6.
    (iv) The Amalgamated Society of Boilermakers, Shipwrights, Blacksmiths and Structural Workers shop stewards' manual, pp. 7, 12, 13, 16, 17 and 18.
    (v) Union of Shop, Distributive and Allied Workers handbook for union shop stewards, pp. 3, 8, 13 and 14.
    (vi) National Union of Public Employees handbook for union stewards representing local government service, pp. 12 and 15.
    (vii) Amalgamated Union of Engineering Workers shop stewards' manual on wage rates and conditions of employment of workers, pp. 14 and 18.
    (viii) National Society of Operative Printers and Assistants rule, p. 26 and rule 7(8).

311. The reason for this is that the French and Luembourg industrial relations system is totally different to that of Britain. The unions (syndicats) are not mainly based on the category of employment or trade, but on either political or religious affiliations. Thus the Catholics will join a Catholic union, the Communists a Communist one, and so on. This also explains why there are fewer unions in continental countries than in Britain.

312. Since the shop steward is a *union* official it cannot be otherwise. See note 310 above.

313. See pp. 171 et seq ante.

314. Namely representative functions, auxiliary to the factory inspector, collaboration with the works committee (see pp. 208–210 above). These, it will be noted, are all industrial relations or representation functions (i.e. what has been termed as the second area of the shop steward's functions). As has already been explained, his trade union functions (i.e. the first area) lie outside the scope of this research and are therefore *not* considered.

315. There is no doubt that that is his most important industrial relations function, but it is not considered that it is his most important overall function. Union rule books and stewards' handbooks stress a great deal more his trade union functions and all other functions revolve, it is suggested, around the union functions. From a time point of view, however, there is no doubt that he spends comparatively little time on trade union functions. This research shows that only 10 per cent is spent on trade union duties. The stressing of his trade union functions to this magnitude is therefore of psychological importance.

316. It is found in this research that whereas in Britain the *attitudes of management* within the establishment influences the functions of the shop steward as a communicator and negotiator, by either inhibiting or increasing his activities, e.g. in BP Chemicals and Reckitt & Colman, where it was found that management's policy is to strengthen procedural agreements (increasing), contrasted with some insurance companies examined, where white-collar representatives were not recognised (decreasing the shop stewards' activities), in France and Luxembourg the attitude of management seems such that it increases the 'délégué's' activities as a communicator. It is submitted that the reason for this phenomenon is twofold, firstly that the 'délégué' not being the trade union representative does not generate hostility in the mind of some employers, and secondly the employer has grown accustomed to the concept of the 'délégué' since the law demands it. These two features do not exist in Britain, hence the varying attitudes of management towards the shop steward.

317. Changes in technology as, for example, containerisation or certain modern industrial processes have made the representative in both countries emerge as a key figure as a communicator (and as a negotiator). Similarly substantive agreements enhance the representative's role. It was found that payment by results gave more scope for negotiation than payment on time rates.

318. See note 291 ante and cf. the higher percentage (i.e. 62 per cent) in France. cf. Research Paper 1 for the Royal Commission on Trade Unions and Employers' Associations, 'The role of shop stewards in British industrial relations', by W.E.J. McCarthy HMSO 1966, who equally finds that this aspect is of importance. His research shows however that only 32 per cent of a shop steward's time is spent in discussions with his members and other stewards etc. The discrepancy is explained by the fact (i) that a great deal more discussion takes place now than it did ten years ago — stewards are certainly 'talkers rather than writers' (see McCarthy, p. 10), and (ii) by the fact that this writer included the *reporting* of *requests* and *grievances* by the shop steward to management consequent on discussions with members. Its importance is evident from an examination of *all* shop stewards' handbooks and other documents. See for example, (i) The TGWU shop stewards' handbook at pp. 17, 30 and 39. (ii) The AUEW shop stewards' manual, p. 14. (iii) The GMWU shop stewards' handbook, pp. 10 and 13. (iv) The Amalgamated Society of Boilermakers, Shipwrights, Blacksmiths and Structural Workers shop stewards' manual, pp. 7—9 and 10. (v) The USDAW union shop stewards' handbook, p. 18, 19, 20, 21 and 27. (vi) The Printing and Kindred Trades Federation's chapel officers' companion, pp. 7, 8 and 9. (vii) The NUPE union stewards' handbook, pp. 15—17, 22 and 23. See also the similar wording of Circular NM 191 of the National Joint Council (local government service) of 24 January 1969, para. 2(b)(ii) and Appendix to Advance Letter (ASC) 2/71 issued by the Department of Health and Social Security.

319. In some cases, and because of the type of industry involved, the views of the members were not always easy to obtain. This was found in particular in SNCF and British Rail, and the road haulage workers in Britain and France.

320. See p. 208 ante.

321. See note 290 above.

322. See p. 208 ante.

323. See General and Municipal Workers' Union shop stewards' handbook, pp. 10, 11, 13, 15, 17 and 18. The Amalgamated Union of Engineering Workers shop stewards' manual, pp. 14, 16—17, 18, 21, 22 and 23. The Transport and General Workers' Union shop stewards' handbook, pp. 9, 12, 17, 18, 19, 23, 28, 30, 40, 41, 44, 46, 54, 63 and 74. The Union of Shop, Distributive and Allied Workers shop stewards' handbook, pp. 8, 13, 17 and 20.

    The Amalgamated Society of Boilermakers, Shipwrights, Blacksmiths and Structural Workers shop stewards' manual, pp. 6, 8, 9, 10, 11 and 12—18. The National Union of Public Employees stewards' handbook, pp. 12—15 and 21. See also 'Facilities afforded to shop stewards', CIR Report No. 17, p. 15 para. 70, which unfortunately deals with functions far too briefly and in very general terms.

324. Note 323 above refers to the variety of functions enumerated in handbooks, rule books and collective agreements, and gives an indication of the number of functions given to shop stewards in each of these.

325. Some 100 shop stewards have been interviewed.

326. In any case it is found in this research that since stewards' handbooks deal

with functions in such general terms any matter in the 'generic term' could be comprised within the functions themselves.
327. As for example in the 'Principles and procedures of productivity bargaining' in the chemical industry, where the stewards' function is to take part in local productivity negotiations. See also 'Agreement setting out the role and functions of shop stewards', p. 5 para. 2(a) (ii)–(v).
328. e.g. railways, road haulage, building etc. industries.
329. e.g. engineering, agriculture, textile industries.
330. It is recognised that it is easier to define and enumerate a shop steward's function in the public sector where, because of standardisation of the industry agreements and central pay negotiations the functions of the steward do not vary immensely from establishment to establishment, than it is to enumerate or define them in the private sector where a diversity of technology products, industrial relations systems, working conditions, management policy etc. exists. Even in this latter case, there should be no objection or difficulty in enumerating, as is the case in France, the *basic* functions such as representation, communication and individual and collective grievances. This research shows that this is happening in some industries and it is even possible to go beyond the *basic* functions suggested above. In the 'code of good practice' directed to shop stewards in the electrical contracting industry, mention is made of consultations in cases of redundancy as well as his other functions of grievance handling, communication and enforcement of the National Joint Industrial Board regulations. See also submissions made at pp. 215 et seq post.
331. See p. 208 ante.
332. See e.g. AUEW shop stewards' manual which states '*Justifiable* grievances should be taken up with the management in accordance with the grievance procedure operative in your works' (p. 14) (stress added). Some handbooks do not use such direct language but the intention is clearly that such judgement should be exercised in all cases. The NUPE local government service union stewards' handbook talking of grievances says, 'This calls for the exercise of careful *judgement*: you have to decide if the member has a genuine grievance . . . ' (p. 15) (stress added). The USDAW handbook for union ship stewards states, 'Does a case exist and is it one that you should pursue? . . . If, however, you think there is a *justifiable* case, you must then *consider* whether you, as shop steward should take it up and who in the management structure you should see' (p. 20) (stress added). The GMWU advises the steward to ' . . . investigate the case thoroughly and check the facts. Talk to witnesses, find out names, dates, and times' (p. 13). The TGWU shop stewards' handbook advises the steward to assess the evidence. 'Has the member a case, and if so, how much of one? . . . If you feel you cannot judge the issue because you have not yet sufficient information tell the member so and explain how you are to get it' (pp. 32 and 33). Other handbooks do not even show this intention, but the innuendo is clear. (See e.g. the 'procedural guide' of the ASBSB and SW shop stewards' manual, pp. 8 and 9.)
333. Interviews with some 100 shop stewards unanimously conclude that their judgement is exercised in all grievances etc. brought up by the membership. In some cases it was found that management encouraged employees to consult the shop steward first. This confirms the findings of Scott, Mumford, McGivering and Kirkby in *Coal and Conflict – A study of Industrial Relations at Collieries* (1963). They say, referring to a manager, 'He felt that the men were often anxious to ascertain if they had a case before taking an issue further. In this sense such a procedure was valuable as it

prevented men wasting their time bringing up matters which had arisen through misunderstandings.' The shop steward was therefore considered by this manager as a man of judgement, and as a filter in the grievance procedure.
334. See e.g. TGWU shop stewards' handbook, pp. 3 et seq. See also the AUEW shop stewards' manual which clearly lays down that 'first the members must raise the matter themselves with their own foreman ... If they are not satisfied they report the matter to their Shop Steward who goes with them to the foreman again ... ' (p. 14). The NUPE union stewards' handbook makes similar provisions: 'Make sure that the member has raised the grievance with his immediate superior' (p. 15).
335. See e.g. the Boilermakers' Union shop stewards' manual which states '(1) A member or members wishing to raise any problem or grievance in which they are directly concerned shall in the first instance discuss same with their foreman' (p. 8). This is very emphatic and clearly lays down that an approach to the employer must first be made. The GMWU shop stewards' handbook provides 'If the procedure requires an individual to raise a grievance firstly with his or her immediate supervisor, make sure that this has been done' (p. 13). The USDAW union shop stewards' handbook says, ' ... you must then consider whether you, as shop steward, should take it up and who in the management structure you should see. It is here that a Disputes Procedure can give you a clear answer' (p. 20). Compared to the Boilermakers' Union the GMWU and the USDAW are not as emphatic in their approach. The Atomic Energy Authority handbook on rules and agreements states, 'An employee ... wishing to raise any matter with which he is directly concerned should in the first instance discuss it with the foreman. If settlement is not reached the employee may again approach the foreman accompanied by the appropriate shop steward' (p. 28, para. 51).
336. For a comparable situation in the coal industry see W. H. Scott, Enid Mumford, I.C. McGivering and J.M. Kirkby, *Coal and Conflict – A study of Industrial Relations at Collieries* (1963), p. 119.
337. See p. 208 ante.
338. Some ninety-eight 'délégués' and employees from different industries out of 130 interviewed indicate that where a grievance occurs the employee will first go, or is sent by the 'délégué', to the contre-maître (foreman) before the 'délégué' himself gets involved.
339. There is of course a legal duty on employees to take reasonable care for the safety of themselves and others, but no specific duty on the shop steward, e.g. Health and Safety at Work etc. Act 1974, s. 7. Similarly under s. 143(1)(2) of the Factories Act 1961 the employee has a duty not to wilfully interfere with or misuse any appliance securing his or others' health, safety and welfare. Here again, however, no such duty lies specifically on the shop steward.
340. It is surprising to find that union *rule* books do not mention this aspect. Similarly it is interesting that none of the collective agreements examined deals with this matter.
341. The AUEW shop stewards' manual states that every accident, however slight, should be reported and entered in the accident book. Mention is also made of the consequences, i.e. social security benefits (see p. 18). The chapel officers' companion of the Printing and Kindred Trades Federation again gives *detailed* guidance (p. 12) based on the factory accident prevention code, and procedure (p. 11). The TGWU shop stewards' handbook being very conscious of safety (pp. 28–9) devotes numerous pages on the actual legislation, and even includes a short reading list (pp. 46–53). Lengthy

Employee Representation 247

advice is given as to what action should be taken when members suffer accidents at work or contract industrial diseases (pp. 54–7). Procedures for claiming industrial injuries benefit and compensation are given in some detail (pp. 58–65) and even rates (pp. 65–8) and prescribed diseases are provided (pp. 69–75).

342. For examples of this prophylactic element see the GMWU's shop stewards' handbook which talks *inter alia* of consultations by employers with 'worker representatives' on all matters relating to safety. Joint safety committees are mentioned, and written statements to employees by the employers on their general policy on safety and health is provided for. (These are based on the Health and Safety at Work Act 1974). The shop steward is advised to equip himself with copies of the safety procedures, DE pamphlets on the relevant processes, the dealing with anxieties by members of the union etc. (p. 17). A similar *detailed* procedure is given in the AUEW shop stewards' manual (p. 18), and the Amalgamated Society of Boilermakers, Shipwrights, Blacksmiths and Structural Workers' shop stewards' manual (pp. 11 and 12). The Union of Shop, Distributive and Allied Workers shop stewards' handbook entitles the relevant paragraph 'Prevention better than cure', and talks of 'legally enforceable standards of safety, health . . . ', of posters, and of the duty of the shop steward 'from time to time to make sure the regulations are being carried out'. A reporting procedure through the works safety committee is also mentioned, as are the physical requirements, e.g. first-aid boxes with all the requisites, and a qualified person in charge (pp. 13 and 14). The TGWU shop stewards' handbook goes into great detail on the prophylactic element by ensuring that the shop steward is familiar with the main provisions of the Factories Act 1961 and the OSRPA 1963, by asking him to be a watchdog and to see that these regulations are enforced, and to see that the factory inspector is brought in in appropriate circumstances (pp. 46–53).

343. See e.g. GMWU shop stewards' handbook which states that all accidents, even the most trivial, must be reported, the first-aid department must be notified and the accident entered in the accident book. Witnesses and written statements should also feature, and medical certificates should be provided. Application to the local social security office for industrial injury benefit should where appropriate be made. A *detailed* list of the entry on the 'blue claim form' is also given (p. 17). See also the Amalgamated Society of Boilermakers, Shipwrights, Blacksmiths and Structural Workers shop stewards' manual (p. 12). An elaborate list exists in the Union of Shop, Distributive and Allied Workers shop stewards' handbook on the procedure for accident reporting, e.g. reporting *all* accidents, accident book, application forms for legal assistance, injury benefit forms etc. (pp. 14 and 15). Again in the TGWU shop stewards' handbook a very detailed list of 'Do's and Don'ts' exists in connection with accidents and industrial diseases (pp. 54–75).

344 The prophylactic element discussed above and in note 342 may be found in a few words ' . . . du code du travail et des autres lois et règlements concernant la protéction ouvrière, l'hygiène, la sécurité . . . ' (loi du 16 avril 1946, para. 2) and 'Les délégués du personnel auront pour mission de veiller à l'application des prescriptions législatives et règlementaires concernant la sécurité et de proposer toutes mesures utiles en cas d'accidents ou de maladies professionnelles graves' (loi du 16 avril 1946, para. 3). The procedure aspect is clearly discernible in the last twelve words.

What we are concerned with here are the sources of the respective representatives' functions on safety etc., *NOT* the actual laws on safety, as for example the Factories Act in Britain, nor the statutes on 'hygiène et sécurité des travailleurs' namely décret 23 août 1947; décret 15 octobre 1962; décret 8 janvier 1965; décret 15 mars 1967 etc.

345. See e.g. the Employment Protection Act 1975 and previously the consultative document on employment protection and the Employment Protection Bill 1975 clause 103 proposing to amend s. 2(5) of the Health and Safety at Work Act 1974 which permits the election of safety representatives other than those appointed for the purpose by a recognised trade union. See criticism by this writer in 'The Inspector', series IV, vol. 20, nos. 9–10, October 1974, pp. 111–12. Some union handbooks make it quite clear that they wish their shop stewards to take part in safety committees or be the safety representatives. The GMWU shop stewards' handbook advises 'You should ensure that yourself or other GMW shop stewards are included in those committees . . . ' (p. 17). The TGWU shop stewards' handbook is even more emphatic: 'Union policy is for safety *control* to be in the hands of shop stewards' (p. 29).

346. See p. 209 ante.

347. Even where works committees are elected from among the workers, regardless of union membership, the shop steward is either elected on it or is a committee member, e.g. railway's local departmental committees. At one time joint consultation and negotiation were distinct. The trend today is that consultation and negotiation are often, though not always (see part 2), one single process. Clegg, in *The System of Industrial Relations in Great Britain*, put it this way: 'With the decline of joint consultation there has begun to develop a new view that consultation and negotiation are part of a single process of involvement of workers and their representatives in decisions affecting their working lives, and that both should be handled by a single committee in which managers meet shop stewards' (p. 192). Thus joint consultative committees *generally* operate where the unions or where shop stewards are either non-existent or weak. The shop stewards' manual of the AUEW clearly shows the intention that 'joint consultation and negotiation' functions are part of this 'single process', when it states 'A works committee may be set up in each establishment consisting of not more than seven representatives of the Management and not more than seven shop stewards, who should be representatives of the various classes of workpeople employed in the establishment' (Appendix A – Procedure Manual Workers II 3(b), p. 32). See also W.E.J. McCarthy in 'The role of shop stewards in British industrial relations' paras. 57–63 and in particular para. 58. At para. 60 McCarthy quotes Derber who found that where JPCs continued to play a significant part in labour relations in well-organised firms they operated in such a way that 'in practice there was little difference from the negotiation process'. See also Wigham, *Trade Unions* (1969), pp. 100–1, who expresses a similar view. See also note 352 post.

348. Since it came about by ordonnance du 22 février 1945.

349. The Whitley Committee in its proposals for the post First World War reconstruction of industrial relations recommended that the functions of the *joint industrial councils* should include (a) the settlement of pay and conditions of employment, and (b) the better utilisation of the practical knowledge and experience of the workpeople, improvements in processes, machinery and organisation and appropriate questions relating to management and the examination of industrial experiments, with special reference to co-operation in carrying new ideas into effect and *full consideration of the workpeople's point of view* in relation to them. The Whitley recommendation considered it equally important to

enlist the activity and support of employers and employed in the districts and in individual establishments (see the Interim Report on Joint Standing Industrial Councils, Cmnd. 8606, 1917, pp. 4 and 5). The Whitley Committee principles gradually underwent changes and by the end of the Second World War two systems of workshop representation were widely recognised, one through shop stewards, for collective bargaining, the other through elections whereby all employees whether union members or not could vote, for consultation purposes. (See H.A. Clegg, *The System of Industrial Relations in Britain*, p. 191.) Joint consultation declined at the expense of the new view that consultation and negotiation are part and parcel of the same process (see note 347 above). Note also what the Industrial Relations Handbook said in 1961: 'While matters discussed by joint consultative committees . . . are, in general, quite different from those dealt with by negotiating machinery, *the two sets of subject matter may, of course, be closely related*' (p. 126) (emphasis added).

350. Note what is said in note 347 above about joint consultative committees generally operating where unionisation is weak or non-existent. See also Clegg, op. cit., pp. 252–4 and his observations on an electricity generating station and the oil distribution plant on pp. 254 and 255. See also Derber, who concluded that one of the main determinants of the importance of the joint consultative committee within an establishment was the strength of union organisation, and that the most active of these consultative committees occurred in establishments where unions had no members. (M. Derber, *Labour-Management Relations at the Plant Level under Industry Wide Agreements*, University of Illinois (1955), p. 79.)
351. See note 347 above.
352. See note 350 above. CIR Report No. 17 (May 1971) shows the attitude of management towards consultation, and the reservations on this by the unions (p. 16, paras. 76–8). An interesting exception may be found in some non-federated firms which do not recognise trade unions. Here a direct comparison with the French system may be made.

Kodak Ltd is one of the firms which operates committees for *manual* workers. According to the Royal Commission on Trade Unions and Employers' Associations minutes of evidence, the system which operates in Kodak is as follows: there exists a committee of seven internal representatives elected by all employees of the firm (some 12,000) whose function is for consultative purposes. In its written evidence Kodak said that they cannot envisage the working of the organisation ' . . . without the existence of representatives of employees, who can be consulted on matters affecting employees, or with whom negotiations can be carried out' (see minutes of evidence, p. 2896). Safeguards for employees were therefore provided by this independent committee (see Q. 10966). Wages in Kodak are settled on the basis of what other national companies of similar standing to Kodak and generally accepted as good employers paid their employees (see minutes of evidence, p. 2897).
253. Mainly because ordonnance du 22 février 1945 sets out the functions and powers of the 'comité' and 'délégué'. There is a rigidity therefore which does not exist in Britain, and this rigidity in theory obstructs the development of such rapprochement. Before such rapprochement is enabled to take place it is submitted that the law will have to be altered.
254. See note 311 ante.
355. 'Almost entirely' because in practice a great deal of plant collective bargaining takes place, in connection with the matters upon which the 'comité' is competent to deal. Consultation and negotiation have in some

instances been found to become fused into one, e.g. at Ets. Renault. The 'Petit Guide Pratique' of the CFDT stresses this (p. 185) '... et de leur permettre de jouer un rôle dans l'amélioration de leurs propres conditions collectives de travail...' In the same breath the 'guide' admits its consultative role: '... et seront consultés sur les questions intéressant la marche générale de l'entreprise' (p. 185).

356. See e.g. the extended role of the 'délégué' approved by the Cour de Cassation, Ch. Civ., Sect. Soc., 3 janvier 1957, p. 98. The sample interviewed for this research shows that the 'délégués' sometimes take part in plant collective bargaining, but a much higher proportion of British shop stewards said that they took part in plant collective bargaining. (This proportion also includes senior shop stewards or conveners.)

357. Of the sample examined from various industries (manufacturing, processing, electricity, railways, shipbuilding), an average of 8 per cent of the 'délégué's' time is spent on plant bargaining. In Britain however it was found that the steward spends 25 per cent of his time on local negotiations (this includes senior stewards and conveners). Note also the figures given in McCarthy, 'The role of shop stewards in British industrial relations', p. 10. It is also found that the *industrial relations system* within the particular industry influences a great deal the steward's bargaining potential. Engineering industry-wide agreements allow for considerable shop-floor collective bargaining, whereas in the public sector there is less scope for shop-floor bargaining since all important matters are dealt with at industry level. Situations of change within an industry, e.g. method of wage payment, procedural agreements etc., tend to extend the negotiating potential of the representative; this has been found in *inter alia* Ets. Renault in France as well as in *inter alia* Fords of Dagenham. It is found that the nature of substantive or procedural agreements determines the functions of the representative, whether he be a shop steward or a 'délégué'. Thus in France where the functions of the 'délégué' are formalised (i.e. are enumerated by law) it is found that 'délégué' involvement is generally greater than is it in Britain where it is found that procedures varied from one industry to another, thus affecting to a greater or smaller degree shop steward participation. In Britain more than France it is found that representatives negotiate over all issues concerning employment, i.e. discipline, conditions of work, wages, piecework earnings, overtime, hours of work, redundancies, dismissals and suspensions, distribution of jobs etc. (See in particular the social survey carried on by the Government entitled 'Workplace industrial relations' (1968), pp. 29—30 and 79—80. See also Donovan Report, Cmnd. 3623, para. 99, where the proportion of time spent in each of his functions, based on McCarthy and Parker's 'Shop stewards and workshop relations', Research Paper No. 10, is given.) It is significant that the power of the constituents of the 'délégué' as well as of the shop steward as a body seems in certain cases only to override that of the unions and of the employers, e.g. where negotiations take place which relate to the particular constituency these are governed by the *will* of no one else but the constituency itself, and no industry agreement between unions and employers can affect these. The combination of 'délégué' and 'comité d'entreprise' in France constitute this 'workforce power', imposing the will of the unit over everything else — this is the very *raison d'être* of the French system. It is found that in Britain the same thing happens. It is the work-group as an entity which decides the course of action. After all, before unionisation in the docks was it not the 'ganger' who negotiated terms and conditions of employment? Similarly the father of a chapel

existed before unionisation in the printing industry.
358. Most of what has been said of blue-collar representatives' functions apply equally to white-collar representatives, *but* there exist differences, in that in white-collar unions committee systems of representation exist, see e.g. the Draftsmen's and Allied Technicians' Association (DATA) where an office committee of three members is elected annually from among the office members and where a corresponding member is also appointed. The committee carries out all office representation and negotiates with management. It is also the watchdog on the observance of existing collective agreements. The corresponding member's functions are more union orientated. Furthermore, in the white-collar public sector it is found that functions are well defined, while in the private sector this is not always the case.
359. Art. 1 of the French loi du 16 avril 1946 makes it clear that the law on 'délégués' applies also to 'les professions libérales', 'les offices ministériels', 'les sociétés civiles' et 'les associations quels que soit leur forme et leur objet'. Similarly in Luxembourg arrêté grand ducal du 20 novembre 1962, art. 1, provides 'Dans toutes les entreprises industrielles, commerciales et artisanales, ainsi que dans les établissements publics et d'utilité publique . . . '
360. See note 290 above and pp. 208 et seq ante.
361. See p. 208 ante.
362. See p. 210 ante and note 307 above.
363. It is pointed out here that the collective agreements examined were all national or industry-wide. Inevitably, their provisions will be as general as those provided for by the legislature. Some local or plant agreements examined showed, however, an adaptation of the industry-wide agreement to accommodate the requirements of the particular establishment.
364 See p. 211 ante.
365 See notes 323 and 324 above.
366 See p. 211 ante and note 327 above. See also note 330 and in particular the 'Code of Good Practice' of the electrical industry. See also the Joint Industry Board (JIB) for the Electrical Contracting Industry (1970 edn.), National Worker Rules and Industrial Determinations for the Electrical Contracting Industry, p. 32, sect. III – 3(b).
367. See e.g. Electrical Electronic Telecommunication and Plumbing Union rule book (1973), pp. 79–80.
368. In 'Facilities afforded to shop stewards', Report No. 17 (May 1971), Cmnd. 4668, p. 10, para. 43. See also, 'What is said about the TUC's feelings', p. 34.
369. It will be noted that the shop steward's trade union functions are not included in this suggestion. The reason has already been given at p. 210 ante. Legislation will also have to deal with this aspect.
370. At present, of the establishment agreements examined, a number are silent on the question of functions, e.g. drydocking agreement, or boilermakers working in confined space agreement of the West Riding and Humberside Engineering and Shipbuilding (employers) and the ASBSB and SW; some make passing allusion to these when referring to other matters, as for example in the Brewers' Association of Scotland agreement with the TGWU (Sept. 1970) where the shop steward is only mentioned in connection with stage 1 on the 'Procedure for Appeals and Resolving Disputes' (paras. 6.07–6.09). Various intereviews conducted by this writer also showed that many establishments relied on 'practice and custom' as to what the industrial relations functions of the shop steward actually are.

252 *Worker Participation in Europe*

371. e.g. rules of Furniture, Timber and Allied Trades Union, NUS, ASTMS etc.
372. e.g. Merchant Navy and Airline Officers' Association, National Union of Seamen, Furniture, Timber and Allied Trades Union, National Graphical Association, ASTMS etc.
373. It is of course recognised that in certain industries it would be difficult to standardise the shop steward's functions, particularly in coal and engineering.
374. Examples appear in note 372 above.
375. Cmnd. 3623 (June 1968).
376. Ibid., paras. 100 and 101.
377. These effects being the exposition of functions in industry or shop-floor agreements, as well as the secondary results discussed above (i.e. rule books and handbooks).
378. See pp. 208 et seq ante.
379. The USDAW shop stewards' handbook states, 'As a workplace representative you are likely to have a wide range of duties and responsibilities, some of which may at times appear to create a conflict of loyalties' (p. 2). M.J. Pedler, in 'Shop stewards as leaders', IRJ No. 4 1973—4, p. 53, states, 'Inevitably . . . this complex of responsibilities and loyalties results in conflict which conventional training at present neglects. The union representative's rule set — those people holding offices within the organisation directly related to the representative role — have differing role expectations of him and the way in which he ought to behave. The breaking of procedures is an obvious case where the membership expect him to do his best for them, but . . . the union expect him to follow procedure.'
380. See also the Donovan Report suggestions on the contents of union rule books, paras. 654 and 698. Surprisingly enough no recommendation is made for the *functions* of a shop steward to be set out in union rules.

APPENDIX A

FUNCTIONS OF THE COMITE D'ENTREPRISE IN FRANCE IN DIAGRAMATIC FORM

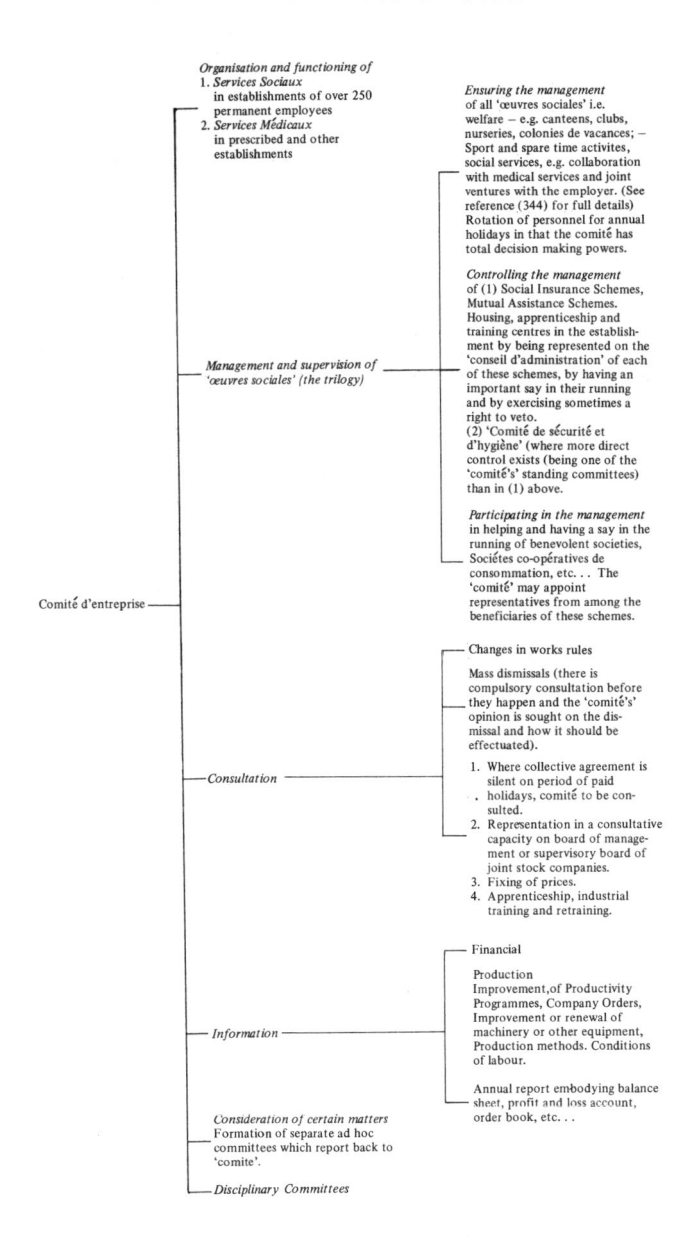

Comité d'entreprise
- Management and supervision of 'œuvres sociales' (the trilogy)
  - *Organisation and functioning of*
    1. *Services Sociaux* in establishments of over 250 permanent employees
    2. *Services Médicaux* in prescribed and other establishments
  - *Ensuring the management* of all 'œuvres sociales' i.e. welfare — e.g. canteens, clubs, nurseries, colonies de vacances; — Sport and spare time activites, social services, e.g. collaboration with medical services and joint ventures with the employer. (See reference (344) for full details) Rotation of personnel for annual holidays in that the comité has total decision making powers.
  - *Controlling the management* of (1) Social Insurance Schemes, Mutual Assistance Schemes. Housing, apprenticeship and training centres in the establishment by being represented on the 'conseil d'administration' of each of these schemes, by having an important say in their running and by exercising sometimes a right to veto.
    (2) 'Comité de sécurité et d'hygiène' (where more direct control exists (being one of the 'comité's' standing committees) than in (1) above.
  - *Participating in the management* in helping and having a say in the running of benevolent societies, Sociétes co-opératives de consommation, etc... The 'comité' may appoint representatives from among the beneficiaries of these schemes.

- Consultation
  - Changes in works rules
  - Mass dismissals (there is compulsory consultation before they happen and the 'comité's' opinion is sought on the dismissal and how it should be effectuated).
  - 1. Where collective agreement is silent on period of paid holidays, comité to be consulted.
  - 2. Representation in a consultative capacity on board of management or supervisory board of joint stock companies.
  - 3. Fixing of prices.
  - 4. Apprenticeship, industrial training and retraining.

- Information
  - Financial
  - Production Improvement, of Productivity Programmes, Company Orders, Improvement or renewal of machinery or other equipment, Production methods. Conditions of labour.
  - Annual report embodying balance sheet, profit and loss account, order book, etc...

- Consideration of certain matters
  - Formation of separate ad hoc committees which report back to 'comite'.
- Disciplinary Committees

APPENDIX B
FUNCTIONS OF THE CONSEIL D'ENTREPRISE IN BELGIUM IN DIAGRAMATIC FORM

Note:* This writer would have thought that the specified 'œuvres sociales' (i) to (iii) and items (2) and (5) under 'Ensuring the Management' would have featured more appropriately under the heading 'Controlling the Management' which does not exist in Belgium. It is inserted under this heading because Belgian law regards these as part of the 'conseil's' decision making powers. The statute says 'ont pour mission' de gérer, de fixer, d'examiner, d'élaborer, de remplir, etc... Since by 'Ensuring the Management' this writer means total decision making, he has no option but to put it under this heading. There thus appears to be an inconsistency of fact which is not so from a purely legislative aspect.

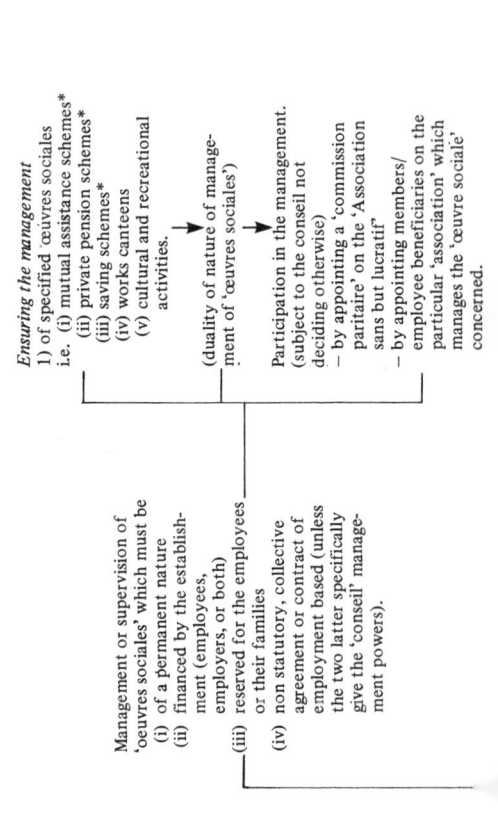

Ensuring the management

1) of specified 'œuvres sociales
   i.e. (i) mutual assistance schemes*
   (ii) private pension schemes*
   (iii) saving schemes*
   (iv) works canteens
   (v) cultural and recreational activities.

(duality of nature of management of 'œuvres sociales')

Participation in the management. (subject to the conseil not deciding otherwise)
– by appointing a 'commission paritaire' on the 'Association sans but lucratif'
– by appointing members/ employee beneficiaries on the particular 'association' which manages the 'œuvre sociale' concerned.

Management or supervision of 'œuvres sociales' which must be
(i) of a permanent nature
(ii) financed by the establishment (employees, employers, or both)
(iii) reserved for the employees or their families
(iv) non statutory, collective agreement or contract of employment based (unless the two latter specifically give the 'conseil' management powers).

Conseil d'Entreprise

- *Information*
  - Financial
    - Budget and profits, financial situation, wages, loans, etc... (Increase of this information by the Arrêté royale du 27 novembre 1973)
  - Production
    - (a) Work Organisation
    - (b) Its improvement
    - (c) Production of units of workers
    - (d) Improvement of this production
    - Verbal information on state of production, cost of production, company order book, competition (foreign and home).
  - Trading position of company.
    - The provision yearly of a balance sheet, profit and loss account, comparative performance of the enterprise and explanation of changes made in the enterprise.

- *Consultation*
  - Organisation of work. Conditions of work and matters relating to production.
  - Opinions and reports on all economic matters submitted to the conseil by the 'Conseil central de l'économie' or the relevant 'conseil professionnel'.
  - On all matters relating to the general criteria to be followed for mass recruitments.

- *Consideration on certain matters*
  - Through a sub-committee of the conseil itself (and not a separate committee as in France).

APPENDIX C
FUNCTIONS OF PROPOSED WORKS COUNCIL IN BRITAIN IN DIAGRAMATIC FORM

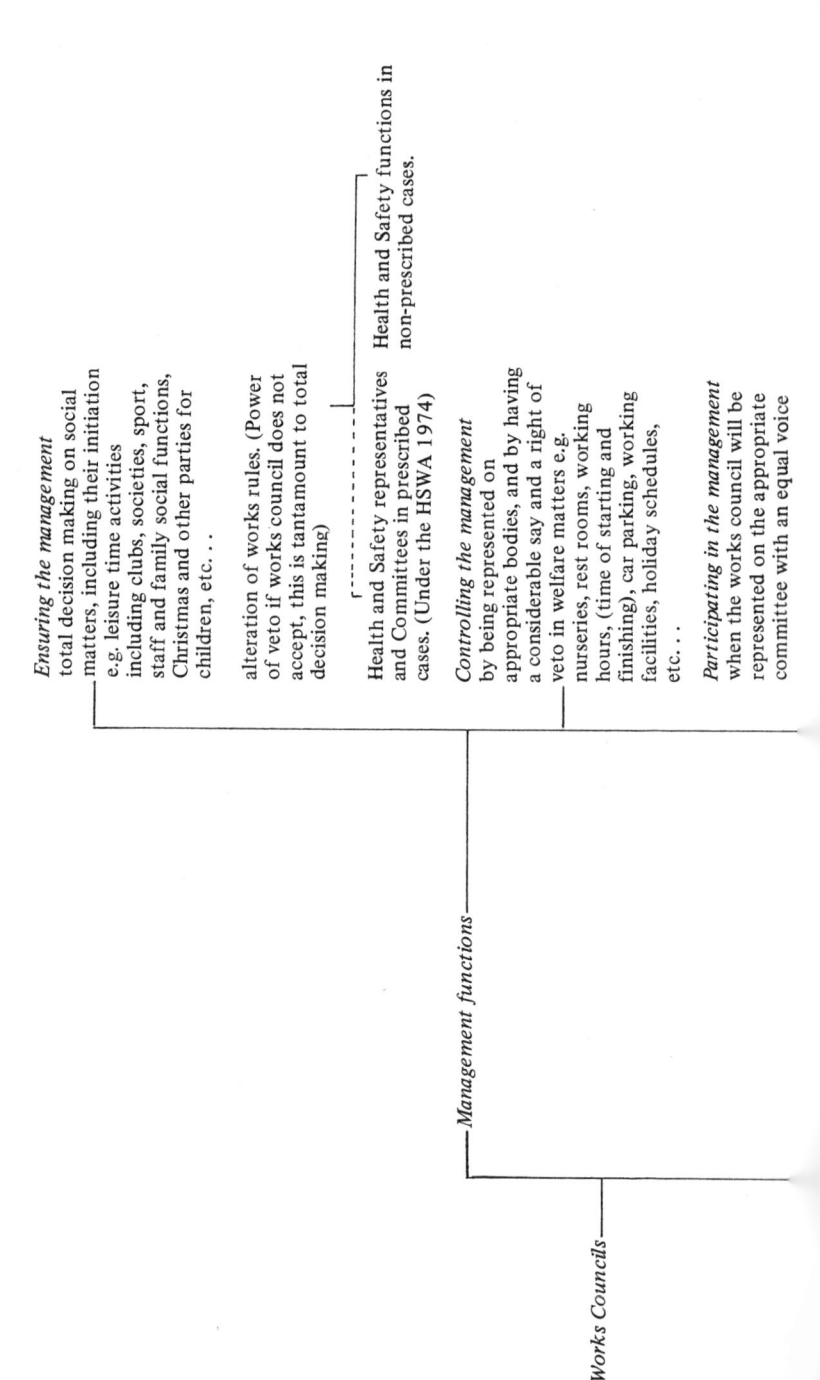

Works Councils — Management functions

- *Ensuring the management* total decision making on social matters, including their initiation e.g. leisure time activities including clubs, societies, sport, staff and family social functions, Christmas and other parties for children, etc...

  alteration of works rules. (Power of veto if works council does not accept, this is tantamount to total decision making)

  Health and Safety representatives and Committees in prescribed cases. (Under the HSWA 1974)

  Health and Safety functions in non-prescribed cases.

- *Controlling the management* by being represented on appropriate bodies, and by having a considerable say and a right of veto in welfare matters e.g. nurseries, rest rooms, working hours, (time of starting and finishing), car parking, working facilities, holiday schedules, etc...

- *Participating in the management* when the works council will be represented on the appropriate committee with an equal voice

- *Consultative functions* ─┬─ with employers, insurance companies, etc... in welfare schemes, e.g. sickness insurance, pension schemes, social security schemes, saving schemes, loan schemes, industrial training schemes, etc...
  └─ Mass dismissals ─┬─ Negotiation through recognised unions, informing Secretary of State EPA 1975.
                      └─ Determination of general rules to be followed in mass dismissals. (After being informed prior to negotiation having taken place)

- *Supervisory functions* ─┬─ Same as consultative functions in Belgium and France, except in the case of this latter the exclusion of items 2 and 4.
                           ├─ Welfare legislation and to a lesser extent protective and social legislation.
                           └─ Extra legislative matters such as collective agreement provisions.

- *Receipt of Information* ─┬─ Financial
                            ├─ Production (See matters under the same heading in Belgium and France).
                            └─ *Simplified* version of annual report to shareholders.

- *Consideration of certain matters* ─── Through the institution of sub-committees.

TABLE OF EMPLOYERS

Below is a list of employers in the four countries under examination from whom employees, shop stewards, délégués du personnel, délégués ouvriers or délégués d'employés, or from whom some of the members of works consultative councils, comités d'entreprise or conseils d'entreprise have been drawn. Some of these employers have contributed by answering the questions addressed to them and which will be found in the text.

Britain

Redifon Telecommunications Ltd.
Mintex Ltd.
Brooks Motors Ltd.
Jackson's Foodmarkets.
Selles Ltd.
British Steel Corp. (Scunthorpe works).
Smith and Nephew Ltd.
Osprey (Plastics) Ltd.
David Brown Industries (Gears) Ltd.
David Brown Foundries Ltd.
Skelton A.C. & Sons Ltd.
Ready Mixed Concrete Ltd.
Armstrong Patents Ltd.
Dale Farm Foods.
Reckitt and Colman Ltd.
Allied Breweries.
Geo. Houlton & Sons Ltd.
British Steel Corporation (Rotherham works).
I.C.I. (Saltend).
Silverline Caravans Co. Ltd.
Hoover Ltd.
Associated Portland Cement Ltd.
J.H. Fenner & Co. Ltd.
Horsley-Smith & Co. Ltd.
Humberside Hydrolics Ltd.
J.R. Rix & Sons Ltd.
Northern Radiators.

Hawker Siddeley Aviation Ltd.
Keighley Paper Mills Ltd.
Dunlop Ltd.
G.K.N. Sankey Ltd.
Metal Box Co.
Imperial Typewriters.
Ford Motor Company (Dagenham).

Note: For the following companies the research made by Alexander, Orwell, Wishlade in 'Worker Participation in Britain' (Financial Times) was relied upon.

Unilever.
Pilkington Brothers.
Mobil Oil.
Imperial Chemical Industries.
Gallaher.
Esso Petroleum.
Cadbury Schweppes.
John Lewis Partnership.
Scott Bader Commonwealth.

Belgium

Hainaut — Sambre.
Amelinckx n.v.
Manufacture Cables Electriques et Caoutchouc s.a.
Société Belge des bétons S.A.
Picamol n.v.
Forges de Clabecq S.A.
Papeteries de Belgique S.A.
Raffinerie Tirlemontoise S.A.
Chocolaterie Callebaut n.v.
Tabacofina n.v.
Siemens s.a.
Francois et fils S.A.
Usines à tubes de la Meuse S.A.
Brasserier Artois S.A.
Usines Emile Henricot S.A.
CBR Cimenteries S.A.
BASF Antwerpen n.v.
D'Ieteren Frères S.A.
Forges de Thy — Marcinelle et Monceau S.A.

Petrofina S.A.
Electrogaz S.A.
I.B.M. Belgium S.A.
Eternit n.v.
Bouteilleries Belges Réunies S.A.
De Coene & Cie S.A.
Intermills S.A.
General Biscuit Co. n.v.
Agfa — Gevaert S.A.
Fabricom S.A.
Compagnie d'Entreprises C.F.E. S.A.

Note: I am indebted to the following Belgian federations who have had discussions with me and answered questions.
Fédération de l'Industrie Textile Belge.
Fédération Pétrolière Belge.
Union des Producteurs Belges de Chaux, Calcaires, Dolomie et Produits Connexes.
Fédération Belgo-Luxembourgeoise des Industries du Tabac.
Fédération des Industries Chimiques de Belgique.
Comité de la Sidérurgie Belge.
Confédération Nationale de la Construction.
Fédération des Industries Céramiques de Belgique et du Luxembourg.

France
B.S.N. Gervais Danone.
Pechiney Aluminium.
Perrier S.A.
Régie des usines Renault.
Générale Sucrière.
Agache Willot.
Rhône-Poulenc S.A.
Ferodo S.A. Française.
Elf-ERAP.
Citroën S.A.
Saint Gobin Industries.
Pernod Ricard.
Creusot —Loire.
Manufactures Française des Pneus Michelin.
Dollfus Mieg.
Saint-Gobain-Pont-à-Mousson.

Usinor.
Gaz de France.
Solmer.
Charbonnages de France (Noeux les Mines).
Compagnie des Compteurs.
Antar — Petroles.
Thompson — Brandt.
Tréfimétaux.
Cellulose du Pin.
Le Printemps.
Ciments Lafarge.
Sommer Alibert.
Schneider S.A.
Hauts Fourneaux de la Chiers.

Luxembourg

Hoffman — Schwall S.a.r.l.
Soludee S.A. (Societe Luxembourgeoise d'Entreprises et de Constructions).
Villeroy et Boch — Usines Céramiques.
S.A. Métallurgique et Minière de Rodange — Athus.
Bay State Abrasives S.A.
Luxembourg Industries S.A.
S.A. des Ciments Luxembourgeois.
Fan International S.a.r.l. Dudelange — Bettembourg.
S.A. des anciens établissements Paul Wurth.
Brasserie De Diekirch S.A.
Luxmold S.A.
Monsanto Cie S.A. (Monsanto Luxembourg S.A.).
Commercial Hydraulics.
Eurofloor S.A.
Arbed S.A. — Aciéries Réunies de Burbach — Eich — Dudelange.
Manufacture de tabacs et cigarettes, Heintz. Van Landewyck.
C. Diederich — Colas.
Entreprise de Construction Eustache. Giorgetti et fils.
Société électrique de l'Our S.A.
Luxwire S.A.
Fonderie et Ateliers de Mersch S.A.
S.A. des Chaux de Contern.
Etablissements Félix Cloos S.a.r.l.
Dupont de Nemours (Luxembourg) S.A.

Lutex S.A.
Soutirages Luxembourgeois S.A.

INDEX

absence 125n; authorised 132n
accidents 209, 166n, 247n
accommodation, office, for shop
    stewards 191-2, 193, 194
Accord Matignon 164, 165, 166,
    219n, 220n
Accord National 87, 88, 122n, 148n,
    150n, 154n, 159n, 161n, 162n,
    in relation to Oeuvre Sociale
    (qv) 85
Accords d'Etablissement ou de
    Salariés 28n
accountant, reports of the 103
action, disciplinary 175
administrative disputes procedure
    (French) 61-2
agenda, the 195
agreement, collective, the 27-8n,
    29n, 38, 48, 98, 107, 114n, 115n,
    119n, 120n, 124n, 125n, 149-
    50n, 154n, 155n, 168, 170, 171,
    172, 177, 179, 184, 190, 200-
    01, 205, 210, 215, 216, 219n,
    223-4n, 225n, 233n, 235n, 251n;
    industry 217, 250n; interpret-
    ations of 187; planning of 31n;
    procedural 117-8n, 237n; shop
    floor 217, 221n; voluntary 112,
    199-200
agriculture 113-44n; compulsory
    formation of Comité d'Entreprise
    (qv) in 124n
allegiance, of shop stewards 217
annual general report, the 103
annual report, the, detailed 158n
appeal, pre-election (qv) 134n; in
    cases of dismissal (qv) 197; right of
    of 126n
appointments boards 181
apprenticeship 89, 147n; general
    problems of 108; schools,
    provision of (French) 83
arbitration 65
area councils 128n, 143n
'assistante social diplomée' 81
associate committees 109
autonomy, types of, in Belgium 37-
    8

balance sheet, compulsory production
    of (in Belgium) 102
ballot, secret, the 51, 61, 62, 63,
    65, 68, 118-19n, 166, 177, 178,
    180, 182, 183, 235n; as opposed
    to show of hands (qv) 177
Betriebsrat 16; see also works
    councils
board of directors, report of the
    103; see also management
Boeke Trust 127n, 150n, 160n;
    schemes committee of 161n
bonus schemes 18
British Institute of Management 21
Bullock Committee of Inquiry on
    Industrial Democracy 1975-6
    12, 15, 27n, 30n, 42, 108, 161n
bureaux electoraux 65; see also
    electoral college, the

Caisse Centrale de Activités Sociales
    36
Caisse d'Action Sociale 36
caisse de compensation d'allocations
    familiales 150n
canvassing 166; see also vote, the;
    electoral college, the
case law 16, 69, 203-4, 209; in
    dismissal (qv) procedures 72, 75;
    in reinforcement of legislation
    (qv) in respect of dismissal (qv)
    199; regarding suspension (qv)
    204
Centrale Générale des Syndicats
    Libéraux de Belgique 116n, 119n,
    146n
Chambre des Députés 30n, 138n
chapel, father of 228n, 250-1n
Chef d'Entreprise; see Informateur
    de Chef d'Entreprise
Cie de Transport Intercommunal
    Bruxelles 19
City Company Law Committee, the,
    opposition by 21
clerical staff, representation of 115n
closed shop, the 213
closure, factory 108

263

Code du Travail 163, 166, 218n, 219n, 239n, 147n
code, electoral, contravention of 175
co-determination 41
Code of Industrial Relations Practice 121n, 156n
collaboration, between trade unions (*qv*) and management (*qv*) 43, 110, 112
collective bargaining 31n, 32n, 41, 43, 44, 106, 112, 121n, 123n, 174, 213, 214, 249n, 250n; fragmentation of 177; role of consultation (*qv*) in 45; role to be played by future (British) legislation (*qv*) in 54; statutory backing to 20; structure of 25
collectivity 208, 210, 211
college, electoral, the 49–51; differences between French and Belgian 49, 50, 51; distribution of personnel in 61; trade unions' (*qv*) role in 51
comfort at work 122n
Comité [Central] d'Entreprises 15, 19, 26n, 35, 39, 47–8, 58, 70, 71, 82, 83, 85, 96–7, 107, 113n, 114n, 115n, 119n, 131n, 137n, 139n, 140n, 142n, 145n, 147n, 148n, 157n, 160n, 162n, 196, 197, 198, 203, 209–10, 214, 218n, 221n, 237n, 242n, 249n; abolition of 123n; agenda for 77; as relating to dismissal (*qv*) 76; committees of 109; comparison of function of with Conseil d'Entreprise (*qv*) 81; conditions relating to elections (*qv*) 60–1; consultative functions of 108; contribution by management (*qv*) to 149–50n; corporate personality of 86; dismissal (*qv*) of members from 68–70, 74–5; frequency of meetings of 77; funds provided for 86–7; length of time members hold office 65; management of 83–4; meetings of 77; obligations of management (*qv*) to members of 77; power of 94–5; over Œuvres Sociales (*qv*) 85; practical nature of in the public sector (*qv*) 36; 'supervision' in 98; time served by members of 65–6; voting (*qv*) in 77

Comité de Gestion 113n, 115n
comité d'Etablissement 131n, 132n
Comité de Securité et d'Hygiène 36, 95, 148n, 153, 209
Comité d'Organisation 77
Comité inter-entreprises 131n
Comité Mixte 15, 26n, 29n, 38, 40, 51, 110, 119n, 218n, 221n; composition of 51; law on 81
Commission of Experts, report of 121n
Commission Paritaire d'Industrie 28n, 38, 78, 96, 116n, 138n, 139n, 142n, 154n; concerned in dismissal (*qv*) 70–1
Committee for Industrial Relations 215, 222n, 227, 228n, 249n
committee, the negotiating, rule of unanimity (*qv*) of 73
common law 11, 35, 141n, 238n, 239n; action in against dismissal (*qv*) 72, 207; *see also* législation du droit commun
communication 43, 160n, 210–22, 215; lack of 195, 171
Companies Acts 32n; Danish 33n
companies, decision-making structure of 14; conferences of 127n; organisation of 30n; schemes committees of 125n; transport 122n
company law 20; draft fifth directive on 24; reform of 22; *see also* Sudrean Commission
compensation 141n
complaints 187, 221n, 246n
conciliation 65
Confédération des Syndicats Chrétiens 22, 33n, 116n, 119n, 146n
Confédération Générale de Production Française 164, 218n
Confederation of British Industry 21, 31–2n, 40, 43, 120n, 121n
Conseil Central de l'Economie 107, 156n
Conseil Consultative Paritaire 77
Conseil d'Administration 19, 28n, 29n, 30n, 88, 108, 114n, 115n
Conseil d'Entreprise 22, 26n, 36, 37–8, 40, 49, 62, 71, 72, 78, 85, 87, 96, 97, 100–1, 114n, 116n, 117n, 119n, 126n, 134n, 135n, 136n, 142n, 148n, 153n,

Index

155n, 156n, 157n, 159n, 161n, 162n, 221n; agenda for 78; autonomy in 87; as relating to dismissal (*qv*) 76; comparison of functions against Comité d'Entreprise (*qv*) 81; consultative functions of 108; constitutional affairs of 142–3n; dismissal (*qv*) of member of 75; election (*qv*) for 62; exclusion of participation by the courts by 88; expiry of each term of 67; frequency of meetings of 77–8; most important function of 85; necessity of showing initiative by 106; power of 95; role of management (*qv*) in 78; rotation of staff for holidays by (*qv*) 95; subdivision of 109; supervisory duties of 98
Conseil de Prud'Hommes d'Appel 62, 71, 117n, 125n, 134n, 138n, 139n, 141n, 204, 231n
Conseil de Surveillance 19, 108
Conseil d'Etablissement 15
Conseil d'Etat 30n, 35, 236n; electoral procedure of 166
Conseil de Travailleurs, as replacement of Conseil d'Entreprise (*qv*) 22
Conseil National de la Résistance 15
Conseil National du Travail 115n
Conseil Paritaire Général 153n
Conseil Professionel 38, 107
constituency, determination of 178
constitution, legal requirement for in Conseil d'Entreprise (*qv*) 78
consultation 55, 97, 99, 105–6, 107, 108, 112, 119n, 121n, 122n, 127n, 128n, 129n, 130n, 132n, 144n, 160n, 162n, 214, 215, 248n, 249n; functions of 99; joint 248n; lack of specific provisions for (in France) 107; powers of 90; procedures for 159n; system of 90
consultative committee, the 55
containerisation 244n
contract, the 122n, 150n; breach of 141n, 201, 203; termination of 139n, 204
Contracts of Employment Act 32n, 234n
contre-maître; *see* foreman
control bodies 33n

convenor, the 118n, 191
Convention Collective des Ouvriers dans les Industries Metallurgiques du Rhône 162n
Convention Collective du Textile 224n
Convention Collective Nationale des Industries de la Conserve 224n
Convention Collective Ordinaire 28n, 216
Convention Collective Susceptible d'Extension 163, 164, 165, 166, 168, 178, 216, 191, 194
co-operation, between management (*qv*) and employees 108, 110, 112
Correspondents d'Entreprise des Caisses Primaires 108
co-surveillance 19
Cour de Cassation 132n, 133n, 137n, 138n, 139n, 140n, 141n, 147n, 150n, 185, 188, 197, 203, 205, 206, 209, 225n, 226n, 227n, 230n, 231n, 233n, 234–5n, 236n, 238n, 240n, 242n, 250n
Cour de Chambéry 235n
Cour Supérieur d'Arbitrage 230n
court of enquiry 240n
crèche, the 122n, 132n
custom 48, 213

deadlock 20; casting vote (*qv*) for avoidance of 21
defamation 80
Délégations Syndicales du Personel 36, 60–1, 166, 220n
democratisation, increasing recognition of 17
departmental committee, the 126n, 127n, 128n, 144n, 160n
deputy representative, lack of, in Great Britain 56–7
Directeur Départemental du Travail et de la Main d'Œuvre 48, 77, 131n, 197–8
directors, difficulty presented by 14
discipline 250n
discrimination 139n; against representatives by management (*qv*) 72; against shop stewards 204
dismissal 68–70, 72, 73, 74, 75–6, 96, 97, 132n, 138n, 139n, 140n, 145n, 148n, 159n, 162n, 187,

266 Index

196–205, 206, 207, 208, 229n, 235–8n, 240n, 250n; conditions for 201; economic or technical reasons for 70, 71; unfair 197, 239; without notification to the Comité d'Entreprise (*qv*) 69
disputes, industrial, role of shop stewards in 251n
divisional consultative committees, the 126n
doctor, factory 109
domestic appeal tribunal 201; constituents of 202, 205
Donovan Report; *see* Royal Commission on Trade Unions and Employers' Associations
'dossier' as used in cases of dismissal (*qv*) 198
Draft National Agreement on the Establishment of Works Councils 120n
duality, in nature of management (*qv*) 90

earnings, loss of, by shop stewards in conducting union business 189
election, the 52, 53, 62, 65, 119n, 132n, 133n, 143n, 153n, 164, 172, 182; conduct of 177, 178; eligibility for 58–9, 60, 153n, 171–83, 219n, 248n; nomination of employee candidates for 51; procedure for 31n, 134–35n; use of proportional representation (*qv*) in 34n
election process, the, conclusions to be drawn from 178, 181
Electoral Code, the 58
electoral college, the 48–9, 62, 125n, 126n, 130n, 131n, 136n, 165, 172, 173, 174, 176, 177, 183, 208, 241n; future British 56; principles of division of 57–8; recommended nature of (in Britain) 183; *see also* works councils
Electoral Commission, the 136n
electoral committee, the 63, 64–5, 66
electoral system (in Britain) 62–3
employee director, the, non-executive, introduction of 21
employee, the, collective representation of 16; emancipation of 14–16

Employers' Federation 146n
employer, the; *see* management
employment 30n, 187; conditions of 116n, 122n, 123n, 140n; continuity of 132n; contract of 132n; security of 97
Employment Appeal Tribunal 114n
Employment Protection Act 13, 27n, 30n, 121n, 139n, 140n, 141n, 155n, 157n, 204, 207, 231n, 233n, 234n, 236n, 237n, 238n, 240n, 248n
Employment Protection Bill 248n
enterprise council, the 120n
European Commission on European Works Councils 25
European Economic Community 13, 14, 17, 24, 41, 75–6, 130n, 133n, 146n, 178; draft legislation (*qv*) of, on works councils (*qv*) 16; green paper by 15; harmonisation of legislation (*qv*) by constituent countries of 18, 33n, 45
European Economic Commission, proposed statute for the European Company; *see* Statute for the European Company, proposed
European Works Council 34n, 57, 64, 110, 111; draft proposals of 56
extra-legislative matters 98

Factories Act 156n, 246n, 247n
factory inspector, auxiliary to 213–14; *see also* Inspecteur du Travail
faute grave 74, 138n, 139n, 196, 203, 204, 238n; in relation to dismissal (*qv*) from electoral committees (*qv*) 69
faute légère 238n
faute lourde; *see* misconduct, gross
Fédération des Entreprises Belges 13, 33n
Fédération Générale du Travail de Belgique 22, 31n, 116n, 119n, 146n
fifth directive 26n
final list, the 72
finance, 28n, 120n
Finance Act 32n
financial reports, nature of 103
flexibility, in consultative structure (in Britain) 54
foremen, representation of 115n,

246n
'fringe' benefits 122n

generalisation 12
General Trade Union Council for Advice 38
grade committee system, the 128n, 130n
grievance 246n; investigation of 168; procedures 215, 234n, 245n; register of 195
group councils 127n

health 127n, 143n, 154n, 156n, 213, 215
Health and Safety at Work Act 27n, 32n, 95, 96, 123n, 154n, 156n, 246n, 247n, 248n
holiday pay 160n
holidays 148n
homeworkers; *see* outworkers
house purchase, loans for 89, 91; for French workers 83, 85
hygiene 163, 167, 221n, 247n

illness 125n, 132n
imprisonment, French workers' rights on 174–5
incentive schemes 18
individual representation 25
industrial action 189, 240n
industrial agreements 211
Industrial Democracy Bill, possible introduction of 30n
industrial democracy, extension of 27n
industrial diseases 247n, prevention of 209
Industrial Injuries Benefit 247n
industrial relations 16, 17–18, 32n, 54, 97, 178, 179, 186, 187, 188, 191, 215, 216, 226n, 231n, 232n; discontent affecting good 177; French law on 214; functions of 185, 189
Industrial Relations Act 236n, 238n, 239n; repeal of 114n, 121n, 157n
Industry Act 27n
information committee, the 119n
information, financial 99, 100; provision of 104–5
industrial tribunals 180, 183, 241; action in for dismissal (*qv*) 201; appeals to 65

Informateur de Chef d'Entreprise 132n, 226n
'In Place of Strife' 30n
Inspecteur Divisionnaire 197
Inspecteur du Travail 77, 82, 137n, 139n, 145n, 163, 167, 173, 175, 191, 196, 197, 198, 203, 209, 218; permission of, as required for dismissal (*qv*) of member of Comité d'Entreprise (*qv*) 68–70; role of 61
Inspecteur Général de la Production Industrielle 77
Inspecteur Social 135n
Institute of Directors, opposition by 21
integration, between trade union (*qv*) and management (*qv*) 43
inter-enterprise committee, the 209
Interim Report on Joint Standing Industrial Councils 249n
International Institute of Labour Studies 33n
investment 30n, 120n
Irish Congress of Trade Unions 120n
Iron and Steel Act 154n

job description 167, 221n, 250n; evaluation 108; gradings 160n
joint advisory councils 129n
joint consultation, in public sector (*qv*) 46
joint consultative committees 121n, 127n, 129n, 144n, 160n
joint consultative schemes 117–19n
joint industrial councils 248n
joint local committees 129n
Joint National Council 129n
joint working party 123n
juge de paix 61, 62, 134n; *see also* Conseil de Prud'Hommes d'Appel
jurisdiction, administrative 198

lay-off, temporary 132n
leave, paid, for shop stewards to undertake industrial relations (*qv*) functions 186, 188, 231n, 232n
Left, the, attitude of, towards worker participation 22
legislation 13, 16, 17, 18, 19, 20, 25–6, 35, 36, 39, 46–7, 49–50, 54–5, 59–71, 72, 75–6, 79, 80,

268   *Index*

84–5, 90, 94, 97, 98, 100, 102, 112, 164, 165–6, 167, 168, 169, 170–1, 177, 180, 196, 197, 199, 200, 207, 208, 214, 215–17, 221n, 235n; British need of 27n, 28n, 29n, 30n, 32n, 54, 56, 60, 94, 109, 110, 114n, 130n, 148n, 156n, 173, 176, 186, 193, 195, 199; British objections to 111–12; British, provision by, for membership ratios 56; company, differences of between various European countries 14, 77; compulsory 22; contingency 194; convergent aspect of 47, 53, 54, 56, 58, 62, 63, 72, 81, 90, 100, 109, 110; divergent aspect of 53, 54, 58, 62, 81; harmonisation of 26; proposed 217; protective 163; reform of 16; requirements regarding collective agreement (qv) 168; role of in providing working base for British works council (qv) 108; social 98; welfare 98; *see also* case law; common law
législation du droit commun 35
leisure activities 85, 89
liaison 152n, 214; lack of 217
libraries 84, 89, 148n
loan schemes 92, 148n
local advisory committees 129n
lockout 238n
loyalty, of shop stewards 217

management 30n, 32n, 34n, 43, 44, 48, 49–50, 74–5, 76, 90, 91–4, 96, 98, 99, 109, 113n, 118n, 121n, 122n, 123n, 125n, 126n, 127n, 128n, 132n, 139n, 152n, 168, 172, 174, 182, 184–5, 186, 187, 189, 190, 194, 195, 196, 201–2, 239n, 243n, 245n, 246n; acceptance of individual shop steward by 169; as benefited by industrial relations functions 189; attitude of, towards consultation (qv) 249n; legal requirements of 163; moral obligation for (British) to provide paid leave (qv) to shop stewards 188; obligations of toward Conseil d'Entreprise (qv) 100–1; procedure of in cases of dismissal (qv) 74;

refusal of to recognise shop stewards 222n; representation of 115n; role of in maintaining good industrial relations (qv) 178; sanctions against 80, 205–8; two-tier structure of 34n; view of shop steward by 187, 243n, 246n
Médecin du Travail 148n
meetings, times of 192
militancy 211, 237n
Mines and Quarries Act 156n
minorities 177
misconduct 70, 73, 76, 129n; gross 139n
mise à pied immédiate; *see* suspension
mistrust, between management (qv) and employees 194–5
mobile industries, function of shop stewards in 212
motif grave 75
mutual agreement, as against collective bargaining (qv) 122n
mutual assistance scheme, the 85, 89

Naamloze Vennootschap 26n
National Collective Agreement, the (Belgian) 96, 97, 106
Nationalisation Act, 51
National Joint Advisory Council for England and Wales 129n
natural wastage 125n
negotiating committees 100
negotiation 41, 44, 90, 97, 127–8n, 129n, 130n, 151–2n, 214, 248n, 249n, 250n
nomination (of shop stewards), procedure for 178, 182, 183; *see also* election, the
non-prescribed establishments 95
notice-board facilities 192, 194

Oeuvre Sociale 81, 82, 83, 85, 86, 88, 94, 141n, 146–7, 194n, 150n, 161n, 162n; duality of 89; funds provided for 86–7; management of 83–4, 85; participation in management in by Conseil d'Entreprise (qv) 87; popularity of 84–5; power of Comité d'Entreprise (qv) over 85
offices committee, the 118n
Offices, Shops and Railway Premises Act 156n
opinion, expression of 99

Index 269

outworkers 164, 165
overtime pay, rates for 160n
participation 28n, 32n, 110; procedures necessary for 31n
pay differentials 160n
pay, regulation of 163
penalties 140n
pension schemes 89, 91; private 85
personnel, committees of, function of 38
personnel director, the 117n; as nominal employer at works council (*qv*) meetings 52
piecework earnings 250n
plant agreements, formation of 214
plant committee 128n, 143n
practice, codes of 179–80
premises, provision of (in France) 83
private sector, the 19, 23, 36, 38, 39, 43, 119n, 181, 220n; privilege in 144n; share participation schemes (*qv*) in 28n
production committee 118n
production, technical unit of 36, 37, 38, 39, 46, 116–17n, 119n
productivity 123n; improvement in 99, 157; methods of improving 106; reports on 101–3
profit and loss account, the 103; compulsory production of (in Belgium) 102
profit participation schemes 18, 24, 25; *see also* share participation schemes
profit sharing; *see* share participation schemes
proportional representation (in Luxembourg) 51, 130n; *see also* Comité Mixte
public sector 19, 28n, 38, 39; white-collar 251n

recruitment, collective 107
redundancy 73, 97, 121n, 139–40n, 155n, 187, 250n
Régie Autonome des Transports Parisiens 115n
Registrar of Trade Unions and Employees' Associations, abolition of 114n
règlements d'atelier 190
règlements internes 190
rehabilitation 160n

reinstatement, of workers after dismissal (*qv*) 96, 140n, 159n
répendus 169
representation 210; comparable systems of 67; differences of, between the French and British forms of 167–8
representative, the, blue-collar 214, 215; dismissal (*qv*) procedure for 196–205; functions of 208–13, 215–18; mode of election (*qv*) of 171–83; numbers of 169–71; office of, length of term of 183–4; rights and facilities of 184–96; white-collar 167, 214, 215
résident privilégié 131n, 175
Right, the, attitude of toward worker participation 22
Royal Commission on Trade Unions and Employers' Associations 44, 121n, 122n, 123n, 170, 217, 224n, 244n, 249n, 250n, 252n
Royal Decree (in Belgium) 38
rule books, union 216, 226n, 227n, 228n, 230n, 242n, 243, 244n, 245n, 246n, 247n, 248n, 251n, 252n
rules, internal 98
rupture abusive; *see* dismissal, unfair

safety 127n, 143n, 148n, 154n, 156n, 187, 213, 214, 215, 221n, 246n, 247n
sanctions, criminal 207
saving schemes 18, 85, 89, 91, 92
savings, on increased productivity (*qv*) 123n
section councils 128n, 160n
share participation schemes 18, 24, 25
shift workers 148n
shop-floor, role of workers of, in communication system 43
show of hands 63, 135n, 182, 183; as opposed to secret ballot (*qv*) 177
Societas Europea 46
Société Anonyme 19, 26n, 28n, 29n; structure of 33n
sport 148n; *see also* leisure activities
staff committee, the 128n
static industries, functions of shop steward in 212
status 131n

270 *Index*

Statut du Mineur 234n
Statute for the European Company, proposed 14, 24, 26n, 45, 47, 63, 65, 75, 123n, 133n, 135–6n, 137n, 139, 140n, 144n, 146n, 152n, 157n, 158–9n, 160n, 161n
statute law, 16
Stock Exchange, the, opposition by 21
supervision orders 148n
supervisory boards 30–1n, 33n, 34n, 99, 161n
Sudreau Commission, report of 19, 40
susceptible extension 28n
suspension 138n, 203, 204, 238n, 239n, 250n; non-effect of, on rights of Comité d'Entreprise (*qv*) member 70

takeover, of companies 108; effect of on individuality of employees 15
tea break, the 148n
technology, changes in 244n
tenure (in Britain) 66
texte co-ordonné 221n, 223n, 226n, 241n, 242n
three-tier structure, the 24, 57
time and motion study 101
trade committee, the 118n
Trade Union Act Amendment Act 226n
Trade Union and Labour Relations Act 179, 200, 207, 229n, 231n, 236n, 238n, 240n, 241n
Trade Union Council for Advice (in Belgium) 38, 117n
trade union, the 23–4, 34n, 43, 129n, 174; blue-collar 115n, 162n, 169, 181, 222n, 231n, 251n; Belgian and British, differing approaches by in realising aims 23; British, role of in future British legislation (*qv*) 54–5; disagreement of with management (*qv*) over dismissal (*qv*) 201–2; expulsion of members from 73–4; French, agreement of with electoral college (*qv*) 172; French exclusive right of to nominate candidates to electoral college (*qv*) 62; functions of 185, 210; in conflict with work works councils (*qv*) 43; organisation of 30n; organisation, strength of 249n; parallelism of blue-collar with white-collar 167; recommended role of in works council (*qv*) 51, 63; role of in Comité d'Entreprise (*qv*) 113n; status of 152n; rules of 175, 213, 216, 217; theoretical role of in Comité Mixte (*qv*) 51; uncooperativeness with management (*qv*) by 44; white-collar 167, 169, 181, 193, 220n, 222n, 231n, 243n, 251n
Trade Union and Labour Relations Act 27n, 30n, 114n, 139n, 141n, 152n
Trades Union Congress 27n, 31n, 33n, 40, 43, 121n, 176, 199, 200, 229; General Council of, attitude of towards two-tier system (*qv*) 20 1; Joint National Council of 129n, 244n; Steel Committee of 20
training 30n, 89, 92, 147n, 152n, 160n; general problems of 108
Tribunal Administratif 198
Tribunal de Première Instance 62
Tribunal de Valence 140n
Tribunal du Travail 125n
two-tier system 20, 21, 23, 24, 57, 119n

unanimity 73, 144n; indisputable nature of in British works council (*qv*) 79–80; rule of (in Belgium) 78
Unité Technique d'Exploitation; *see* production, technical unit of

veto, power of 23, 92, 93, 95; right of, by Comité d'Entreprise (*qv*) 83
vote, the 63, 180, 202, 227n, 249n; casting 117n; differences in 175

wages 167, 221n, 250n; negotiation of 32n, 116n, 122n, 149–50n
welfare 90, 91, 92, 94, 148n, 156n; in Oeuvre Sociale (*qv*) 146–7n
West Germany, councils of confidence in 15
Whitley Committee 248–9n
work, conditions of 32n, 106, 163, 187, 250n; hours of 250n;

Index 271

organisation of 106
worker control (in Britain) 23, 24–5
worker directors 23, 120n, 161n
worker, the Algerian, rights of 165–6; emancipation of 17; ratio of shop stewards to 125–6n, 170, 171; representation of 210
works canteens 85, 89, 127n, 132
Works Constitutions Law 16, 120n
works council, the 16, 17, 22, 24, 25, 27n, 34n, 38–9, 43, 51, 52, 54, 57, 58, 59, 62, 63–5, 66–8, 72–3, 74, 75–6, 77, 78, 79, 80, 90, 91, 96, 97, 98, 99, 100, 101, 102, 104, 105, 108, 110, 111, 112, 119n, 123n, 128n, 132n, 143n, 151n, 152n, 153n, 155n, 156n, 158n; agreement on dismissal (qv) by 139n; associate committees of 109; collaboration of 214–15; consultation at level of by proposed Conservative Party measures 21; election to, 62; exploration of 111; Irish 120n; lack of British legislation (qv) for 56, 60, 63, 73–4, 79, 110, 111, 119n; organisation of 126n; recommended nature of (in Britain) 79; research on requirement for 144–5n; standing committees of 151n; varying decision-making role of 83
Works Council Bill 40
works medical services 209

van Zeeland 37